PARTITIONS

EDITED BY ARIE M. DUBNOV
AND LAURA ROBSON

# PARTITIONS

*A Transnational History of Twentieth-Century Territorial Separatism*

STANFORD UNIVERSITY PRESS
STANFORD, CALIFORNIA

Stanford University Press

Stanford, California

©2019 by the Board of Trustees of the Leland Stanford Junior University.
All rights reserved.

This book has been partially underwritten by the Peter Stansky Publication Fund
in British History. For more information on the fund, please see www.sup.org/stanskyfund.

Printed in the United States of America on acid-free, archival-quality paper

Library of Congress Cataloging-in-Publication Data

Names: Dubnov, Arie, editor. | Robson, Laura, editor.

Title: Partitions : a transnational history of twentieth-century territorial separatism /
edited by Arie M. Dubnov and Laura Robson.

Description: Stanford, California : Stanford University Press, 2019. |
Includes bibliographical references and index.

Identifiers: LCCN 2018035357 (print) | LCCN 2018036465 (ebook) |
ISBN 9781503607682 (e-book) | ISBN 9781503606982 (cloth : alk. paper) |
ISBN 9781503607675 (pbk. : alk. paper)

Subjects: LCSH: Partition, Territorial—History—20th century. | Palestine—
History—Partition, 1947. | Ireland—History—Partition, 1921. | India—
History—Partition, 1947. | Great Britain—Colonies—History—20th century. |
Decolonization—History—20th century.

Classification: LCC KZ4028 (ebook) | LCC KZ4028 .P37 2018 (print) |
DDC 341.4/2—dc23

LC record available at https://lccn.loc.gov/2018035357

Typeset by Newgen in 10.75/15 Adobe Caslon

Cover design by Christian Fuenfhausen

Cover art by Piotr Debowski, Shutterstock

# CONTENTS

# ACKNOWLEDGMENTS

This collection has been a long time in the making, and we owe debts to the many institutions and people who helped along the way. Some of the chapters were first prepared for the workshop "Partitions: Towards A Transnational History of Twentieth Century Territorial Separatism," which took place at Stanford University's Humanities Center, April 18–19, 2013. Others grew out of conversations that began at the International Seminars on Decolonization, sponsored by the National History Center, the American Historical Association, and the John W. Kluge Center of the Library of Congress. We are grateful to Aron Rodrigue, Amir Eshel, and Kristen Alff, each of whose help was crucial to kicking off the project, and to Dane Kennedy for his commentary and camaraderie. At Stanford University Press, Margo Irvin deserves an additional note of appreciation for her generous support and sedulous work, from initial review through production to the final product. We also thank our institutional homes, the Departments of History at George Washington University and Portland State University, for their support throughout this process.

Above all, we extend our sincere gratitude to the civic-minded contributors to this volume, for their perseverance throughout the prolonged process of turning abstract ideas into an actual book and for their long-term commitment to the joint project. The subject matter we have chosen to investigate—which demands not only familiarity with a large number of archival depositories but also linguistic skills and regional expertise beyond the abilities of a single individual—necessitates a group effort. But more crucially, it requires scholars willing to step outside their comfort zones to engage in an unusual transnational inquiry and work together toward a common vision. We are delighted to have the opportunity to thank all of them for making this project such an intellectually rewarding journey.

MAPS

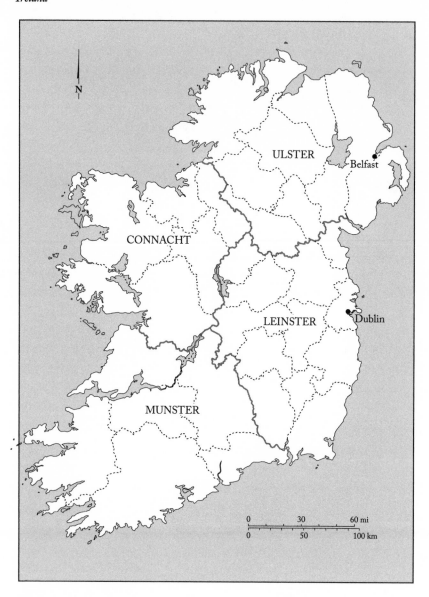

Map 1a    Ireland before 1921

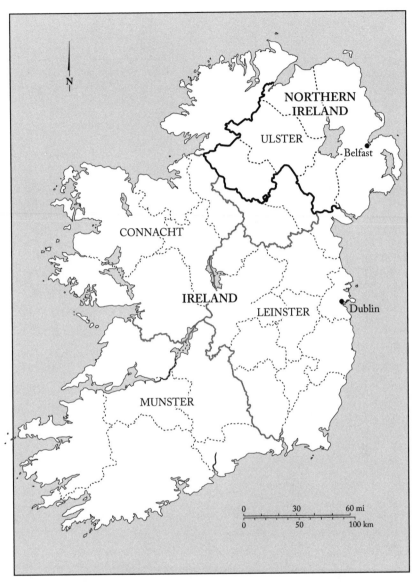

Map 1b    The Free Irish State and Northern Ireland and the 1925 Irish Boundary Commission Line

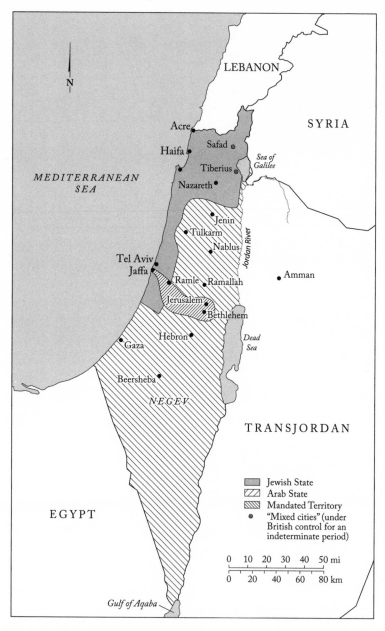

Map 2a   Royal Commission Partition Plan, 1937

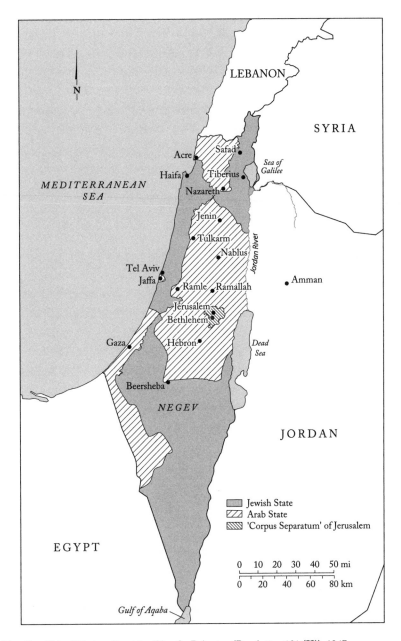

Map 2b   United Nations Partition Plan for Palestine (Resolution 181 (II)), 1947

*India*

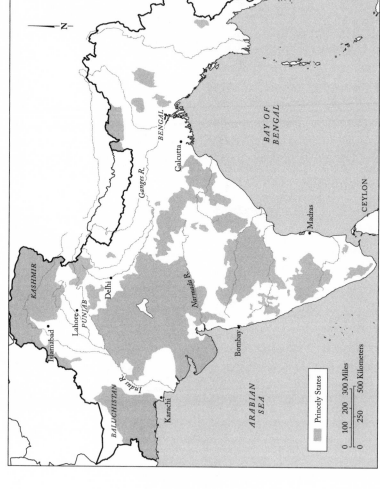

Map 3a  The British Raj, 1919–1947

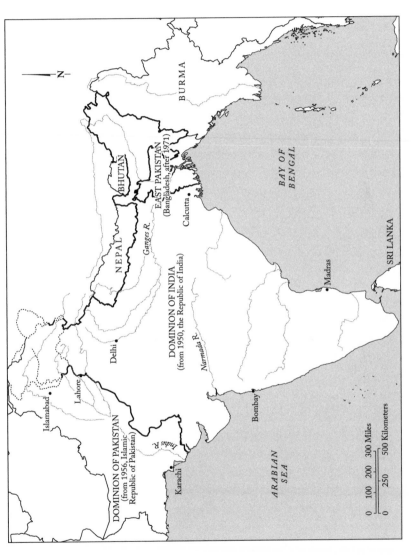

Map 3b   The Partition of India and Pakistan, 1947

# PARTITIONS

# DRAWING THE LINE, WRITING BEYOND IT
*Toward a Transnational History of Partitions*
Arie M. Dubnov and Laura Robson

## THE MODERNITY OF PARTITION

Partition is having a moment. In the past twenty years, the idea of physically dividing territories along ethno-religious lines as a solution to communal strife has suddenly reemerged, conveniently divorced from its disastrously violent history, as a fashionable technique of "conflict resolution." From the former Yugoslavia to Syria, from Israel/Palestine to Sudan, varying forms of internationally organized, ethnically based redivisions of territory have repeatedly been proposed—and in some cases implemented—as useful tools for solving intractable ethnic conflicts.[1] Such contemporary discussions depict partition as a logical and even inevitable, if regrettable, answer to widely divergent but equally difficult problems of ethnic strife across the globe. But it was not always so. Far from representing a natural solution to ethnic discord, the concept is no more than a hundred years old.

The idea of partition as an answer to ethnic, national, and sectarian conflict emerged for the first time out of the new conversations surrounding ethnicity, nationhood, and citizenship during and immediately after the First World War, against a backdrop of European imperial politics. The wartime collapse of the old central European and Ottoman empires and the emergence of new notions of the nation-state highlighted an essential paradox: the rise of new anticolonial nationalisms and a formidable discourse of national sovereignty at precisely the same moment that the power, authority, and ambition of the British and French empires were reaching their zenith. Facing this difficulty, the political and diplomatic leadership of the old "Great Powers" began envisioning a new global order comprising self-consciously modern, sovereign, more-or-less ethnically homogenous states under the continued economic authority of the old imperial players.[2] The multiple treaties of the immediate post–World War I era (encompassing Versailles, Sèvres, and Lausanne; the many minorities treaties with Eastern Europe; and the League of Nations "mandate" agreements under which much of the Middle East would be governed for the next three decades) collectively articulated a new "internationalist" vision that bore the imprint of both nationalist discourse and imperial ambition, with the unspoken intention of containing the former and extending the latter.[3]

These agreements promoted a new political language of ethnic separatism as a central aspect of national self-determination, while protecting and disguising continuities and even expansions of French and, especially, British imperial power.[4] The partition of Ireland in the early 1920s thus emerged alongside discussions of mass population resettlement in Iraq and Syria; brutal population exchanges between Bulgaria and Greece and between Greece and Turkey; and new borders and categories of "minority" and "majority" in Poland, Romania, and other former Habsburg and Russian imperial territories. All these contributed to an imperially sponsored remaking of the global order that embraced a number of ways to align national populations with political borders (always under external supervision): population transfer, mass deportation, forcible denationalization, and partition, all legitimized by a political narrative of self-determination for national populations and protections for newly designated "minorities."[5]

Partition, then, belonged firmly within the imperial realm; it was less a vehicle for national liberation than a novel, sophisticated *dīvide et imperā* tactic that sought to co-opt the new global tilt toward the ethnic nation-state. As such, the meaning of partition necessarily shifted after a second world war and the concomitant collapse of British imperial rule. Schemes originally conceived as part of a new type of imperial governance in the guise of internationalism seemed, after 1945, to offer quick and efficient exit strategies that also held out the tantalizing possibility of continued postcolonial influence for Britain. Following the Second World War, two further partitions were proposed and partially enacted in the decolonizing territories of India-Pakistan and Palestine-Israel, accompanied by a level of violence and dislocation unprecedented in either place (though perhaps matched by the brutality of the almost simultaneous mass population expulsions in Eastern Europe). By midcentury, the political "solution" of partition had arrived with a vengeance.

This volume examines the three earliest and most prominent instances of partition—Ireland, India, and Palestine—in tandem. Our goal is to understand why and how this "moment of partition" occurred—that is, why partition emerged as a proposed solution for perceived or real communal and ethno-national conflict across these disparate geographical and political spaces at this particular historical moment. Making use of the transnational framework of the British Empire, the central originary space for the idea of partition, this volume seeks to go beyond side-by-side comparisons to find concrete connections among the three cases: the mutual influences, shared personnel, economic justifications, material interests, and political networks that propelled the idea of partition forward, resulted in the violent creation of (theoretically) ethnically specific postcolonial political spaces, and set the stage for subsequent partitions in other places like Germany, Korea, and Vietnam. Such a juxtaposition of cases allows us to understand partition as a transnational rather than a local phenomenon, a consequence of decolonization and the global upheavals of the interwar era, rather than as an expression of permanently incompatible ethnic or religious identities in benighted areas of the world.[6] In other words, this volume seeks to move the scholarship beyond "area studies" as well as the nationalist frameworks that served in the first instance to promote partition as a natural phenomenon and have buttressed its political formulations ever since.

## THE IRELAND-PALESTINE-INDIA TRIANGULAR: A CHRONOLOGY

First, we must clarify our terms. Partition, in its modern sense, does not mean simply a redivision or new allocation of territory.[7] Though a number of pre–twentieth-century instances of carving up territory—for instance, the oft-cited dissolution of the Polish-Lithuanian Commonwealth via its forcible division into three separate territories in the late eighteenth century—have been commonly designated as partitions, they did not constitute partition in our terms: that is, they did not devolve real political authority onto local populations newly defined as national. This is what differentiates the many earlier imperial divisions of territory for administrative purposes from the modern partitions of the twentieth century: Ireland, India, Korea, Vietnam, and Germany. As sociologist Robert Schaeffer has put it, "The simultaneous devolution and division of power is what distinguishes partition . . . from the division of other countries in previous times."[8] Political scientist Brendon O'Leary, in demarcating partition from other, related phenomena such as secession, decolonization, and political or military disengagement, offers a further specification of intent: "The ostensible purpose of a political partition, its formal justification, is that it will regulate, that is reduce or resolve a national, ethnic or communal conflict."[9] Indeed, one notable aspect of the rhetoric of partition is its frequent naturalization through a language of biology and science—for instance, the much-repeated medical metaphor depicting partition as a "surgery" intended to cure the "sickness" of ethnic violence.[10]

By this definition, post–World War I Ireland represented the first instance of partition in its modern sense. The Irish partition arose from both a local and an international context: the long-standing set of domestic demands for new forms of national representation and the immediate circumstances of war, both featuring a backdrop of increased violence. From the 1880s, a vast majority of Ireland's electorate had favored some form of what had come to be called "Home Rule"—Irish self-government within the administrative framework of the United Kingdom and the British Empire. The quest for such autonomy, of course, was complicated not only by the reluctance of Whitehall to allow for Irish sovereignty but also by continued resistance from the long-standing Protestant settler community centered in Ulster and other parts of Northern Ireland and backed by English political and economic interests.[11] After decades of negotiation, the Home Rule Bill—the third legislative attempt to secure

Irish autonomy—passed in the House of Commons in 1914, only to be suspended as a consequence of war in Europe.

World War I created new conditions for Irish nationalism in the form of heightened demands from the British center for resources and men, alongside intensified international political rhetoric about the rights of small nations and the question of self-determination. Two years into the war, the Irish Republican Brotherhood staged a military takeover in Dublin—the "Easter Rising" of 1916—and declared the establishment of an Irish Republic, a move that brought a vigorous and violent response from the metropole.[12] Two subsequent attempts to implement the 1914 act in a way that would exclude the Protestant-dominated Ulster counties failed. In the immediate aftermath of the war, the pro-independence Sinn Féin party won a majority in the 1918 general election and declared a separate parliament. The nationalists' increased use of guerrilla tactics, met by increasingly brutal "counter-insurgency" methods, not only aroused controversy in Britain but also exposed internal divisions within Sinn Féin and among supporters of republicanism. In the words of one historian, this "declaration of war on behalf of the legitimate government of a 'virtually established' republic" entailed a new kind of struggle—not for some measure of Home Rule to which the British government might accede, but "a struggle for 'freedom' that would be total."[13]

The subsequent multilateral conflict among revolutionary republicans, Ulster Unionists, and the British Army was thus a consequence as much as a cause of the wartime violence.[14] Events unfolded rapidly: in December 1920, the Government of Ireland Act created separate Northern and Southern Irelands by setting up two devolved parliaments: one in Belfast for the six northeastern counties and another in Dublin, linked by a "Council of Ireland." Initially, nationalists ignored it, and the violence continued. Militarily, however, the conflict was notably asymmetrical, with little concrete achievement and broad demoralization on the Irish side, especially as it became clear that Ulster Unionists were succeeding in making a separate north a fact on the ground. At the same time, the British realized that it was unsustainable to permanently govern the southern counties as a Crown Colony under martial law.

As a possible solution to the deadlock, an increasing number of British policy advisors advocated for Dominion status that would grant Ireland some autonomy but keep it within the Commonwealth. The following autumn, after a truce between the Irish Republican Army (IRA) and the British Army, Éamon de Valera accepted David Lloyd George's invitation to represent Ireland at a conference in London to determine "how the association of Ireland with the community of nations known as the British Empire may best be reconciled with Irish national aspirations."[15] The resulting Anglo-Irish Treaty of 1921 led to the establishment of a separate Irish Free State the following year. Comprising twenty-six of the thirty-two counties of Ireland, this "free" state was in fact a Dominion of the British Commonwealth of Nations and remained subordinate to the British Parliament until the eventual declaration of the Republic of Ireland in 1949.

Partition in Ireland, then, was a consequence both of decades of negotiation between Ireland, its Protestant settlers, and the British imperial state and of the violent context of the political, economic, and military pressures of global war; and debates about the partition settlement were often concerned with the limitations imposed on Irish nationalist aspirations and the precise meaning of Ireland's allegiance to the Crown and the Commonwealth. Many of its nationalist defenders understood the agreement as a temporary measure, an unfortunate but necessary step toward a different final status. Even the unyielding republican Michael Collins, veteran of long years of military struggle against the British, accepted the principles of the treaty because it gave the Irish "freedom"— not, he explained, "the ultimate freedom that all nations desire and develop to, but the freedom to achieve it."[16] The thankless task of drawing a line on the map separating the two Irelands was left for later and would not be accomplished until after the ensuing civil war finally came to a halt in November 1925.[17] These two peculiar features—seeing partition merely as an interim step on the road to a final settlement and leaving the determination of an actual border until the final stage—would be recurring aspects of twentieth-century partitions, making appearances in the subsequent British divisions of both Palestine and India. Partition, it appeared, led not to the stabilization of conflict but to landscapes of long-term geopolitical deferral.

Nevertheless, its appeal was growing. At the moment of Irish partition, the newly formed League of Nations was engaging in the process of drawing (theoretically) ethnically determined borders in eastern Europe; at the very same time civil war raged in Ireland, the League's representatives at Lausanne were formalizing international support for a de facto ethnic cleansing as a mode of nation-state creation through a brutal forced population exchange between Greece and Turkey.[18] In the interwar era, such large-scale transfers of entire communities came to serve as both a rhetorical legitimation and a practical mode of imperial and/or internationalist intervention; and partition now emerged as a parallel "solution" that was viable precisely because its proponents on all sides spoke the postwar language of self-government and ethnic nationalism.[19] The apparent success of the Irish model—measured primarily by the cessation of war—allowed the abstract idea of partition to enter into the interwar toolbox of nation-building strategies alongside other, related approaches of the moment: population exchanges, mass deportation, forcible denationalization, minority rights treaties, and refugee resettlement.[20]

Thus it happened that following World War II, as Britain prepared to withdraw from Palestine and India under the most favorable circumstances it could manage, the devolution of power onto newly partitioned states emerged as a possible "solution" to the problem of assigning power in the context of disintegrating British authority and an international enthusiasm for ethnic nation-statehood. Subsequent British partitions of these colonial territories would combine the models of Ireland and Lausanne, with proposals for the "transfer" of inconvenient populations in addition to forcible territorial division into separate states—an approach that would exponentially magnify the violence of partition as the task of carving out physically separate political entities on the ground and making them ethnically homogenous devolved onto local actors with everything to lose.

The case of Palestine, where partition was first proposed in 1937 and partially implemented in 1947/1948, echoed Ireland and foreshadowed India. Like Ireland, Palestine's partition involved an important settler colonial element; like India, it involved a longer history of British colonial imposition of communal legal and political distinctions. As in both other instances, partition was proposed at a time of anxiety and violence

both locally and globally; the strikes that inaugurated the 1936–1939 revolt provided the initial pretext for the exploration of partition, and fears
about an approaching war in Europe had much to do with the urgency
of the British desire to put an end to the uprising in Palestine. Once
again, partition emerged as a "solution" to ethno-communal divisions in
the context of an emerging and unstable international/imperial system
built around the rhetorical principle of ethnic nation-statehood.

Palestine began to see Zionist immigration from Europe in the late
nineteenth century, around the same time that the British government
began to explore the possibility of incorporating Palestine into the empire on the grounds of its strategic location vis-à-vis Egypt and India.
The First World War offered the relevant imperial opportunity, and the
Zionist movement seemed a potential ally. In November 1917, a month
before the British Army entered the gates of Jerusalem, British foreign
secretary Arthur J. Balfour penned a letter (with the approval of the British War Cabinet) to the London-based Zionist leader Walter Rothschild
committing the British government to the cause of large-scale Jewish
immigration into Palestine with a view to creating a "Jewish national
home." The use of such vague, open-ended terms provided both British
and Zionist politicians with considerable room for political maneuvering;
Balfour himself, defending what came to be known as the Balfour Declaration to the House of Lords, described it as an exciting "experiment
and adventure," an exercise in imperial imagination and territorial expansion.[21] In July 1922, the Balfour Declaration's commitment to mass European Jewish settlement in Palestine was ratified by the League of Nations
document that incorporated the wording of the declaration into the legal
instrument that gave Britain "mandatory" authority over Palestine. A few
months later, the League endorsed an additional British memorandum
separating Palestine, now defined as the area between the Jordan River
and the Mediterranean, from a newly created Transjordan and exempting
the latter from the strictures of the Balfour promise.

The text of the Palestine mandate maintained some older Ottoman
practices of communally conscious political organization, making provisions for individual communities to maintain schools and religious institutions such as *waqfs* and guaranteeing government recognition of religious

holidays. More radically, it provided a framework of ethno-national sovereignty for the settler population (but not indigenous citizens, unless they happened to be Jewish) and explicitly tied political rights to communal affiliation. Acknowledging and incorporating the Balfour Declaration, the League declared, "The Mandatory shall be responsible for placing the country under such political, administrative and economic conditions as will secure the establishment of the Jewish national home, as laid down in the preamble, *and the development of self-governing institutions*, and also for safeguarding the civil and religious rights of all the inhabitants of Palestine, irrespective of race and religion" (emphasis added). In this context, state- and empire-building were not mutually exclusive projects; and Zionists set to work immediately, with British encouragement, to develop new proto-state institutions of self-government made possible by the new British military occupation of Palestine and supported by the League. In the view of the Palestinian political elite, of course, the Balfour declaration was fundamentally illegitimate from the beginning—as, indeed, was the division of Palestine from Syria, the carving out of Transjordan, the British military occupation, and the mandate itself. For the next three decades, Palestinian activists would find themselves fighting a rearguard action against these founding documents of the Palestine mandate, which legally enshrined the principle that Jewish identity conferred particular political rights not shared by Muslim and Christian Arabs.

As the mandatory state was established, its British architects further formalized and institutionalized this legal and political distinction between the Jewish settler community (the Yishuv) and the indigenous Arab community. Under mandate rule, the Yishuv enjoyed a number of collective rights and privileges not extended to Arabs: a recognized internal legislative assembly, explicitly nationalist schools and language policies, a flag, and a military wing. The attempts made by the first British high commissioner, the pro-Zionist Herbert Samuel, to establish a pro forma legislative assembly immediately became a site of resistance as it became clear that the envisioned government would give the small Jewish minority, representing about 10 percent of the population in 1920, the same number of legislative seats as the Arab majority and would have no right even to discuss the framing of the mandate (i.e., the core issues of

Zionist immigration and land sales).[22] The stated commitment of Labor Zionism, the most important political faction in the Yishuv after 1920, not to employ Arabs in any capacity on Jewish-held settlements and land (though often not successfully enacted) further divided the communities and resulted in a segregated and highly inequitable labor market.[23] Land sales to Zionists dispossessed large numbers of Arab peasants, whose migration to cities in search of work created rings of slums around many of Palestine's major urban centers.[24] In 1929, these tensions led to violence, with the outbreak of Arab-Jewish riots at the Western Wall that killed nearly 250 people and injured hundreds more.

In the spring of 1936, an Arab general strike brought the country to a standstill and quickly turned into huge anti-Zionist and anti-British demonstrations, leading the colonial government significantly to expand its military presence in Palestine.[25] To crush the demonstrators, the British began to deploy some of the "counterinsurgency" methods they had developed in prepartition Ireland, including recruiting former members of the notoriously brutal "Black and Tans" to join the Palestine Police Force.[26] Facing widespread and organized Arab resistance, the British government appointed a royal commission to investigate the causes of the unrest and make a recommendation about future British policy for Palestine. The Conservative politician and former secretary of state for India Robert Peel headed the commission, which arrived in Palestine in November and spent several months traveling around the country and interviewing prominent members of the Zionist and Arab political elites, as well as discussing the situation with local British government officials. In 1937 the commission published its findings, with a nearly four-hundred-page report detailing the increasingly violent and hostile conditions on the ground and proposing a "solution": partitioning Palestine into separate Arab and Jewish states. This particular scheme combined the principles of partition and transfer: it was to be made possible not only by the Zionist acquisition of huge amounts of Arab territory, but also by the forcible expulsion of somewhere on the order of 300,000 Arabs (versus about 1,250 Jews) to create a Jewish majority in the proposed Jewish state (see map 2a).

The idea of some kind of division of territory was not new; it had been mooted before by both Zionist and British officials, as detailed in several chapters of this book, and was predicated on earlier "cantonization" proposals. Broadly speaking, though the delegates of that year's Zionist congress were unwilling to accept the territorial specifics of the Peel Commission plan, believing the land provided for the Jewish state to be insufficient, they accepted the principle of partition and empowered the leadership to continue negotiations with the intention of eventually achieving a more favorable deal. But there were opponents of partition within the Zionist camp, including Revisionist leader Vladimir (Ze'ev) Jabotinsky, whose objections rested equally on his commitment to Zionist claims over the whole of historic Palestine, including Transjordan, and his anxiety about the implications of internationally sanctioned "transfer" for eastern and Central Europe's vulnerable Jewish communities. "From a Jewish point of view," he explained, "[transfer] is nothing short of a crime. While the Royal Commission babbles about the 'instructive precedent' (that is, the expulsion of more than a million Greeks from Turkey) we witness yet another case in which it toys with concepts that none of its members have any idea about."[27]

And, of course, the partition and transfer proposal aroused immediate and implacable opposition among Palestinian Arabs, who viewed it as little more than outright theft. As Palestinian anger and the revolt both intensified, the British administration began to reconsider its position and sent in yet another commission of inquiry (the Woodhead Commission, sometimes mockingly dubbed the "re-Peel" Commission), which eventually abandoned the idea. It was only a decade later, in a very different international and local context, that the almost forgotten scheme was reintroduced. In 1947, the strapped and exhausted British government—facing down right-wing Zionist militias engaged in terrorist attacks against both Arab and British targets in Palestine, and just off its recent imperial experiment in partitioning India—announced its intention to withdraw. The question of Palestine's disposition was turned over to the newly formed United Nations (UN), as the natural successor to the League that had engineered the original mandate. Partition had transcended its original context and transformed from a British imperial tactic into an organizing principle of post–World War II world diplomacy.

The United Nations Special Committee on Palestine (UNSCOP)—made up of representatives of eleven states, including Australia, Iran, Yugoslavia, Sweden, and Guatemala—found itself feted by Zionist leaders making every effort to influence the committee to support the principle of partition and dismissing the many alternative binational and federalist proposals put forward by the Marxist-Zionist movement Hashomer Ha'tzair and intellectuals such as Judah L. Magnes, Martin Buber, and others affiliated with the Ihud (Unity) party.[28] The eviscerated Palestinian Arab political leadership, unanimously opposed to the concept of partition, refused to participate in the undertaking on the grounds that the UN had no legal jurisdiction over Palestine and the question should be turned over to an international court.[29]

Facing this radical imbalance of evidence and opinion, UNSCOP members found it hard to reach a consensus and ended up submitting two reports: a minority proposal recommending a unitary federal state, and a majority proposal, inspired by the decade-old Peel Commission plan, recommending partition. The majority report envisioned a three-way division of Palestine, with an Arab state comprising 43 percent of the mandate territory, including the highlands and one-third of the coastline; a Jewish state encompassing 56 percent of the territory and including the northern coast, the eastern Galilee, and most of the Negev; and a "corpus separatum" including Jerusalem and its surrounds, which would be subject to some form of international authority. In describing the plan, the commission members noted that it suffered from many of the same problems the Peel Commission's proposal had encountered—most centrally, the presence of large numbers of Arabs in the proposed Jewish state.

UNSCOP's partition plan was voted through the UN General Assembly in November 1947, with India and Pakistan against the plan, the United Kingdom abstaining, and the United States and the USSR in favor. The first violent clashes signifying the beginning of the 1948 war—dubbed the War of Independence by Israelis and the *nakba* (catastrophe) by Palestinians—followed immediately. Essentially, the violence unfolded in two stages: first a "civil war" between local Arab Palestinian and Zionist forces between the partition vote and May 1948,[30] when British forces were still in Palestine preparing for their final evacuation, and then

a broader Arab-Israeli conflict following a declaration of war by the surrounding Arab states. Zionist forces moved quickly to secure territory
assigned to them by the UN plan and beyond, working against poorly
organized and poorly armed Arab militias handicapped not only by their
long-institutionalized economic, political, and military disadvantages vis-
à-vis the Yishuv, but also by the virtual decapitation of the Palestinian
Arab political leadership by the British military during the revolt.

By the time Israel emerged as the clear victor, thousands had been
killed on both sides, and Zionist paramilitary groups—transformed into
the nascent Israel Defense Forces during the war—had forcibly expelled
approximately 750,000 Palestinian Arabs from their newly claimed territory, which extended well beyond the bounds of the Jewish state envisioned in the 1947 UN plan (see map 2b). This mass expulsion of
Palestinians created an acute and still unresolved refugee crisis across
the region and effectively partitioned mandatory Palestine into an Israeli state, an Egyptian-occupied Gaza, and a Jordanian-occupied West
Bank.[31] The total incapacity of the newly formed UN to implement the
partition plan led officials to try to recast themselves as mediators and
supervisors of the truce and armistice agreements, a task at which they
proved equally incapable. Partition had turned a difficult local and regional conflict into an apparently insoluble international one.

The simultaneity of partitions in Palestine and British India is striking:
Pakistan gained independence on August 15, 1947, just two months after
UNSCOP's members arrived in Palestine to begin their investigations.[32]
And as in Ireland and Palestine, the eventual partition of the Indian subcontinent emerged, quite suddenly, from both colonial histories and immediate local circumstances. From the late nineteenth century, British
imperial rule over India encouraged a reimagining of often-intermingled
Hindu and Muslim populations as distinct and separate political communities. In particular, a series of British decisions about colonial legislative
representation—including, rather ominously, the communally conscious
division of Bengal into Muslim- and Hindu-majority territories in
1905—helped to encourage a wide range of local communalisms, many
of which made use of indigenous traditions to support the emergence of
communally conscious and even communally exclusive political structures

from the 1920s on.[33] This narrative of separate Hindu and Muslim subject "nations" had parallels in other parts of the empire, from Africa to Iraq, and constituted an important influence on an increasingly explicit international discourse of ethnic nation-statehood in the interwar period.[34]

Though electoral competition and negotiation over Hindu and Muslim interests (broadly represented by the Indian National Congress and the All India Muslim League) had been a main feature of the Indian political landscape since the 1920s, the so-called two-nation theory did not emerge as a central component of Muhammad Ali Jinnah's political program until 1940—like the previous two partitions, in the context of global war.[35] Scholars have debated the extent to which Jinnah's adoption of a language of separatism represented a real claim for nation-statehood or merely a bargaining chip in the negotiations over postcolonial representation; either way, it soon took on a life of its own.[36] In 1946, following a significant electoral victory on the part of the Muslim League and Jinnah's declaration of a "Direct Action Day" to demonstrate the strength of Muslim political feeling, Muslim-Hindu violence broke out in Calcutta.

The bloodshed and the clear and dramatic loss of imperial control influenced the British decision to withdraw from India earlier than originally planned, leaving just a few short months to determine the shape of the postcolonial state or states. Partition now became a topic of intense debate within the Congress-led government as well as among Louis Mountbatten, Jinnah, and Jawaharlal Nehru, with Mohandas Gandhi in vehement opposition. Even at this late date, there was considerable opposition to the idea of partition within the Muslim-majority provinces whose legislators voted on the concept in June 1947.[37] As historian Ayesha Jalal has pointed out, Jinnah now had to choose between a unified Indian state with no safeguards for Muslim political participation or a "maimed, mutilated and moth-eaten" separate Pakistan to be constructed from Muslim areas of the Punjab and Bengal.[38] So, under pressure of time, Jinnah, Nehru, and Mountbatten signed off on a plan to partition the subcontinent into two states (see map 3b), on the assumption that the creation of Pakistan would free the Congress from any requirement to acknowledge Muslim political claims in the new India. The exact geographical disposition of the territory was left to the British lawyer Cyril

Radcliffe, whose new borders were not made public for two days after formal independence at midnight on August 15, 1947. As the details emerged, the subcontinent descended into communal carnage.

The full human toll of the Indian partition will never be known. Its violence displaced something like fifteen million people and killed between one and two million; some seventy-five thousand women and girls were raped, and millions of refugees were left impoverished. Partition permanently altered the landscapes of the territories now labeled "India" and "Pakistan": Karachi, which had been nearly half Hindu in 1941, had almost no Hindus left by 1950, and Delhi's Muslim denizens—once a third of the city's population—largely disappeared. And, of course, like all other partitions, it laid the groundwork for further future conflict. Hindu-Muslim violence has continued to recur in northern and western India; India and Pakistan have fought three wars since 1947, one of which resulted in the bloody secession of East Pakistan (now Bangladesh); and insurgency and unrest continue in the disputed territory of Kashmir. Both states, incidentally, now possess nuclear capabilities.[39]

## INTERPRETING PARTITION: IMPERIAL, NATIONAL, AND INTERNATIONAL APPROACHES

Since Palestine was divided in 1948, there have been any number of further partitions in our sense: Korea, Cyprus, Germany, Yugoslavia, and Sudan, to name just a few. A transnational study of these first three partitions, though, provides the clearest possible view of the *origins* of this idea as a strategy of British imperial rule across different territories, with Zionism as a crucial intellectual linchpin between Ireland and India. It also sheds light on how partition moved from theory to practice as decolonization unfolded and the nation-state became the default mode of political organization. The model of partition as a "solution" to ethnonational conflict was later exported elsewhere—in many cases via the imperially inflected venues of international high politics[40]—and tended to reflect the trajectories and structural features of the Irish, Palestinian, and Indian cases.

In all three of these instances, as in many later iterations, partition emerged as an essentially ad hoc response to local, imperial, and international conditions; was enacted by mass violence; and utterly failed to solve the problems it purported to address.[41] Likewise, in all three instances, partition was interpreted as a necessary evil for the emergence of viable ethno-national states; as a protection for the rights of ethnic or religious "minorities" (itself a fundamentally twentieth-century concept); and as a natural solution that required little in the way of historical explanation beyond the apparent existence of intractable, atavistic ethnic or religious conflict. A study of these three paradigmatic examples thus requires us to think not only about the genealogy of the concept of partition, but also about how it has been presented, defended, and remembered within a postcolonial framework—and, centrally, how it came to occupy its current position as a favored policy option for widely varied situations of ethno-national strife.

Because of the broad application of the idea, the violence of its implementation, and the emotive nature of its memorialization, partition has represented a particularly difficult topic for scholars to approach empirically. Nevertheless, no one could argue that historians have ignored partition; historical scholarship on the individual cases of Ireland, India, and Palestine could fill libraries. Among historians, this literature broadly falls into two camps: national and imperial histories of partition. Imperial histories have traced some of the paths through which partition was envisioned and enacted but have tended to reinforce narratives of top-down action and to neglect local landscapes and local actors. National histories, by contrast, have contributed a great deal of specificity and local nuance to our understanding of partition, but they have shortcomings too; they focus much more on outcomes and aftermaths than on genesis, and they often fail to recognize partition as a transnational political concept arising less out of local circumstance than out of world war and global decolonization.

Initially, the topic did not grab the attention of postindependence national historians. Partition, after all, represented a trauma that stood in bleak contrast with triumphal tales of the creation of homelands and rebirth of nations. Particularly in South Asia, in the years after partition the topic was rarely mentioned except as part of the heavy price of liberation.[42] Not surprisingly, then, the topic was at first left mainly to diplomatic historians studying the reordering of the international system after imperial breakdown. As decolonization brought dirty wars, ethnic strife, and proxy conflict to the high politics of the Cold War years, diplomatic historians began to depict violent partitions as early manifestations of a broader political disorder characteristic of the Global South. This historiography tended to understand partitions as technical rearrangements undertaken by noble-minded but tragically naïve colonial administrators trying to oversee an orderly "transfer of power" in the face of violent nationalisms and religious fundamentalisms—a narrative W. H. Auden famously mocked in his ironic description of Cyril Radcliffe's arrival in India:

> Unbiased at least he was when he arrived on his mission,
> Having never set eyes on this land he was called to partition
> Between two peoples fanatically at odds,
> With their different diets and incompatible gods.[43]

Even more sarcastically, the Boulting brothers' 1959 comedy *Carlton-Browne of the F.O.* (starring Peter Sellers) presented partitions as Solomonic trials imposed in a top-down fashion by bored, cynical men of the British Foreign Office, trying to get rid of antique colonial possessions that had turned into political liabilities.[44] Gradually, though, scholarship recycling these tropes fell into disrepute for its failure to acknowledge the crucial participation of local actors who helped turn partition from an abstract idea to a fact on the ground—and the structures of power that encouraged them to do so.[45] The rise first of area studies and then of subaltern studies and postcolonial theory, and the increasing attention given to communal violence and "history from below," all played decisive roles in dissolving such analyses. As historians began to think about partition as a story of communal and ethno-national imagination and violence, they sought to distance themselves from accounts that deprived local actors of all agency.

These older explanations were also cast aside because of their increasingly evident inability to explain the *persistence* of partition as a phenomenon, tactic, and experience. Partition retained a place in the international arsenal of legitimate political tools for decades after 1948, as international treaties advocating partition in settings from Cyprus to Bosnia made clear. Further, it gradually became clear that partitions had utterly failed to provide the promised solution to communal or ethno-national conflict. Take, for example, the orgy of violence prompted by the assassination of Indira Gandhi by her Sikh guards in October 1984, which led many, including Urvashi Butalia, to start challenging the selective amnesia of the nation-state. "It took the events of 1984 to make me understand how ever-present Partition was in our lives," Butalia writes, and the recurring outbursts of violence in subsequent years further strengthened that conclusion.[46] By the mid-1980s it was no longer possible to regard the Irish, Indian, and Palestinian partitions as closed events; they were clearly ongoing processes, continuing to shape both domestic and foreign politics and leaving their imprint on core aspects of everyday life. In this charged arena, high-politics accounts focusing on the powerful few made way for oral histories and testimonies capturing the voices and memories of the masses "from below."

Decades after the event, then, historians of modern South Asia in particular began to think much more seriously about partition and now arguably have covered 1947 in greater detail and depth than any other event in the region's modern history. Dominated for some decades by narratives of (and by) individuals personally involved in the partition decision and its implementation, the early historiography on partition mainly took as its topic "the dilemma of reconciling the attainment of freedom with national unity," as Gyanesh Kudaisya puts it—an approach that was eventually largely abandoned in favor of more regionally conscious social, cultural, and environmental histories of partition.[47] With the rise of the subaltern studies movement in the 1980s and 1990s, the literature on partition began to concern itself with personal narratives of the violence (often emphasizing the gendered nature of both the experience itself and its later recounting) and with questions of memory, memorialization, and forgetting.[48] Though historians of midcentury South Asia have admirably succeeded in delineating regional, class, and gender differences in the historical experience of partition, they have by and large not sought to ask questions about the genesis of the partition idea outside a South Asian framework.

The literature on the partition of Palestine is still more fraught, complicated by the dispersal of the Palestinian Arab population, the absence of a Palestinian national archive, and the ongoing Israeli military occupation of the Palestinian territories. Early scholarly literature on the 1948 war and its outcomes almost exclusively reflected the Zionist narrative, with Arab accounts of the *nakba* facing serious obstacles to production and distribution.[49] Israeli historiography paid some attention to the intra-Zionist debates concerning partition but was heavily invested in sui generis readings of Jewish nationalism, putting severe restrictions on any attempt to read partition in comparative or transnational contexts.[50] For more than forty years, Israeli accounts of 1948 (which scholarship coming out of Europe and the United States tended to echo) did not highlight partition so much as a narrative of military victory and political independence and often failed to acknowledge how the imperial structures of the mandate framed the history of Zionism and the founding of the Israeli state. During the same period, Arab accounts likewise made use of a fundamentally nationalist framing that forestalled the consideration of partition as a topic in itself, although they did tend to highlight the colonial state as the architect of the conflict and thus provided the beginnings of a more sophisticated approach.[51]

In the mid-1980s, following the opening of at least some of the Israeli archival material from 1948, a somewhat disparate group of Israeli historians began to challenge the earlier triumphalist narrative both by investigating individual instances of expulsion and by reviewing evidence of a concerted plan for the violent mass removal of the Palestinians.[52] Around the same time the Palestinian historian Nur Masalha published his still-important book on the Zionist idea of "transfer" that, for the first time, opened the question of connections between Zionist thinking about partition in Palestine and similar discussions elsewhere of forced migration as a political solution.[53] Though this politically charged scholarship contained a great deal of disagreement and even vitriol, it shared two things: a basic agreement that the Palestine/Israel question was a sui generis history without significant reference points elsewhere, and a strikingly conservative methodology that relied almost exclusively on the most traditional of diplomatic and military archival sources. While the latter has slowly shifted over the intervening thirty years, there are still remarkably few scholars seeking to place Palestine/Israel into a wider imperial or global context.[54] The historiography on 1948, in particular, has continued to exhibit self-referential characteristics and to ignore wider questions of ethnic nationalism, partition, and violence that might link the Palestinian/Israeli experience with other regions and histories.

Further, unlike either Ireland or South Asia, the voices of the victims of 1948—displaced Palestinian Arabs—have been largely absent from the scholarly conversations about partition. This exclusion has been both structural and circumstantial. Because of the scattering of Palestinians in exile and camps across the Middle East and beyond—and because of the European and American complicity in supporting Palestinian dispossession as a "solution" to the "Jewish problem" in the aftermath of the Second World War and the Holocaust—little Palestinian writing on the *nakba* was disseminated, read, or seriously considered in American and European academia for many decades after the fact.[55] More structurally, Palestinian writers and activists considered partition from the beginning as an aspect and symptom of the larger questions of imperial occupation and loss of sovereignty and civil rights, not as a phenomenon in itself. As Palestinian nationalist activist Musa Alami wrote as early as 1949: "We resisted both imperialism and partition and considered them complementary to each other. . . . We used to say that partition was the work of the imperialists."[56] The framework through which Palestinians understood the *nakba* was not the division of their territory along ethno-communal lines but the total and permanent loss of the homeland and the hope of a state; and as such their own writings, conversations, and analyses of both the mandate period and the 1948 war focused on the fundamental illegitimacy of the Zionist settler movement, the Balfour Declaration, the British occupation and mandate, and the military expulsion of a majority of the Palestinian Arab population from the Israeli state. Palestinians did, of course, think, talk, and write extensively about their experiences; but they did not generally consider these experiences within the framework of partition, not least because no division of territory between a Jewish Israel and an Arab Palestine ever emerged.

Indeed, the opposite happened: after the 1967 war, many Palestinians found themselves living under an Israeli military occupation that was, from the beginning, not conceived as merely temporary. The first months of the occupation drew on plans that had been in place for at least a few years, developed first by military advocate general Meir Shamgar and further elaborated by the General Security Service.[57] Moshe Dayan quickly deployed these plans on the ground in the months following the war, hoping to normalize this new situation of Israeli rule, in perpetuity, over a Palestinian population without political rights. This institutionalization and naturalization of occupation, on the basis of a permanent differentiation of rights between Israeli citizens (and settlers) and Palestinian residents, emerged quickly and soon became not a temporary circumstance but a central aspect of Israeli state organization.[58]

Ironically, it was only in this context that the concept of partition—in our terms—became truly central to Palestinian political narratives and analyses. As the Palestinian economy and labor market were forcibly integrated into Israel on radically inequitable terms,[59] the Palestine Liberation Organization (PLO) began to think seriously about the possibility of accepting partition as a mode of political settlement—that is, to accede to the terms of a so-called two-state solution that would provide for a Palestinian nation in the West Bank and Gaza. Though the word "partition" was rarely used, Yasser Arafat's official acceptance of the principle of Palestinian statehood in the territories represented a decades-later agreement to the partition concept first formally mooted in 1937 and proposed again in 1947 (and, of course, soundly rejected by Palestinian nationalists in both instances). Now the old debates were revived in a different political and military context, one in which the painful reality of a physically integrated but permanently and violently politically differentiated regime for Israelis and Palestinians had become, for Palestinians in the territories, the de facto alternative to ethno-national partition.

In its new guise as the "two-state solution," partition now became the stated goal of the PLO, the Israeli left, and any number of external mediators, including (eventually) the United States, though the word itself was notably absent from all negotiations from Oslo onward. In the eyes of the great majority of liberal Zionists—Israeli author Amos Oz remains the most eloquent spokesman of that camp—partition remained the only possible answer to what they saw as a "clash of right with right."[60] After the Oslo Accords, objections to partition came mainly from Israel's right wing and from a newly prominent Hamas, which viewed the PLO's acceptance of partition as having conceded the central premise of Palestinian nationalism without gaining anything in return.[61] The Israeli administration's eventual rhetorical concessions to the idea of partition, in 2009, came only in the context of a settlement movement so entrenched in the territories that it rendered real Palestinian autonomy unworkable.[62] By now, the discussions of the partition solution that formed the backbone of the post-Oslo peace talks have withered on the vine. As historian and political commentator Tony Judt put it so trenchantly just before his death: "To summarize: further pursuit of the old 'peace process' and 'road map' is futile. No one who matters believes in it anymore."[63]

Scholars have approached the partition of Ireland in rather different though equally atomized terms. Though it occurred in the immediate aftermath of the First World War and clearly reflected some of the assumptions about ethnicity and communalism being discussed at the peace talks, historians of Ireland have long tended to explain the partition mainly in terms of the longer local history of Home Rule dating to the mid-nineteenth century.[64] To the extent that they have discussed partition in a comparative imperial framework, scholars of Ireland have based their discussion around Nicholas Mansergh's 1978 argument that partition in both Ireland and India emerged not out of British malice but as a consequence of competing nationalist interests and an imperial desire for an easy form of decolonization—an idea that challenged Irish nationalist beliefs in some important ways but also tended to confine the question of Irish partition to a set of specific local circumstances and players.[65] As in the Palestinian case, some of the reluctance to take on the question of partition derived from the particulars of the contemporary political situation; as historian Margaret O'Callahan notes, "Because addressing the fundamental issue of partition was seen as potentially justifying the Provisional IRA campaign, there was a moratorium on serious historical research on certain kinds of questions about 'the North.'"[66] It is only quite recently, then, that a few scholars of Ireland have begun to make a serious effort to examine the simultaneously imperial and internationalist exchanges in which the idea of partition emerged as a "solution" for the "Irish question."[67] It may be worth noting that Britain's recent decision to withdraw from the European Union has brought the question of Ireland and its borders back to the fore; it seems likely that this development, potentially turning the 310-mile frontier between Northern Ireland and the Republic of Ireland into an international border of the older, pre-EU type, might now encourage broader scholarly and public reassessments of the origins of Irish partition.

Contemporary historiography, then, offers much richer accounts than older diplomatic histories trapped in the rigid teleological paradigms of nation-statehood. But it remains a highly fragmented history. It is invested in recovering distinctive, previously repressed voices and exposing the bloody aftermaths of partition, but it has largely abandoned the attempt to offer a more synoptic view of partitions in plural, to trace their shared contexts and genealogies. In its deep suspicion—if not overt resentment—of *haute politique*, contemporary historiography often makes the recovery of connections among these partitions difficult. (The "new" imperial history, which prefers a networked or webbed conception of imperial space over older analyses centered around colony-metropole and patron-client dynamics, has by and large not interested itself in partition.)[68] To paraphrase J. G. A. Pocock's famous complaint, the historiography of partition has not yet succeeded in presenting a *verità effettuale*—"a reality that determines the present and renders a past intelligible."[69]

The most extensive literature on partition as a political phenomenon has come not from historians but from political scientists, who have in the main approached the question of partition from a prescriptive angle. (The few "international history" approaches to partition have shared this policy-oriented approach, investigating rates of "success" for past partitions.) Such scholarship has taken a for/against perspective, with many participants advocating for externally enforced ethnic partitions as a mode of preventing worse violence or ending civil war and others (fewer in number, it must be noted) arguing against partition as an ineffective tool of international peacekeeping. Both positions take a purely instrumentalist view of partition—that is, they see it as a definable, traceable "solution" whose efficacy can be measured after the fact by applying a set of consistent metrics to measure the recurrence of ethnic violence in each setting. Thus pro-partition political scientists like Chaim Kaufmann can make the case that partition represents a "best solution" to ethnic conflict, with alternative political arrangements like enforced unification or federalism representing options that "would likely have been worse" in terms of casualties.[70] Similarly, in an influential article published in 2007, Thomas Chapman and Philip Roeder argued that if case studies are limited to instances where partition resulted in sovereign states recognized by international authorities, "partition is more effective than alternative institutions at reducing the likelihood of a recurrence of violence."[71] Their interlocutors reject this conclusion but make use of the same premise that partition can be studied as an independently recognizable tool of international diplomacy; as another well-known article puts it, "it is important to assess the risks and benefits of partition" through analysis of concrete empirical evidence—which, this particular study argues, demonstrates that partition actually "does not work in general."[72]

This application-oriented, policy-guiding literature, both pro- and anti-partition, fails utterly to recognize the historical contingencies that served to produce the idea of partition after the First World War and continue to shape its application in the twenty-first century. Above all, it fails to acknowledge that the very concept of ethnic majorities and minorities rests on the emergence of a nation-state order dating back no farther than the First World War and dependent on the new capacity of the League of Nations (backed, of course, by British and French imperial force) to enforce such ethnic boundaries in the war's aftermath.[73] Partition, in other words, is not an independent, free-standing "solution" to anything; it is an idea that was invented in very particular circumstances—specifically, by empires trying to extend their lifespans via a carefully calibrated application of some of the characteristics of nation-states in their colonies—and applied by external actors to colonized spaces. As historian A. Dirk Moses has trenchantly noted, such work "proceeds as if thirty years of constructivist sociology and historiography about nations and nationalism was never written . . . [and] is indentured to a managerial gaze of 'solving' the problems of non-Western peoples, a subject position that smacks of neo-imperialism that in many cases led to the problems in the first place."[74]

Political scientists' wholesale acceptance of the premise of partition as a clear and simple, if morally fraught, preexisting tool of international diplomacy represents at best a misapprehension of and at worst a capitulation to imperial propaganda. A transnational approach to the history of partition, by contrast, provides a demonstrated pedigree of the concept: its origins in specific colonial planners; its expression through particular ethnic nationalist movements, especially those associated with colonial rule like Zionism; and its movement across colonial territories via colonial officialdom and colonial collaborators, rather than through any kind of grassroots ethnic consciousness. This transnational account clearly categorizes partition as a fundamentally imperial idea, one whose origins specifically do not lie in local ethnic or communal conflicts in any of the territories where it was enacted over the course of the twentieth century. In particular, it demonstrates partition's emergence from a British colonial ethnography that emphasized ethno-communal division for the purposes of imperial governance[75]—an analysis that helps explain why partition, touted as a "solution" to ethnic conflict, has invariably been associated with mass violence.

CONCLUSION

Partition has been both extensively explored and inadequately understood. We know a considerable amount about how it unfolded in various places; we have analyses of its rates of "success"; we can read about how it is remembered. But scholars and policymakers alike have by and large failed to understand it as the product of a particular global moment, when decolonization, ethnic nationalism, and new forms of international organization came together to create a kind of toxic miasma around the idea of physically separating ethnically or communally defined populations. Any historical approach to the concept of partition must acknowledge its fundamentally colonial roots and its entanglement with the careful institutionalization of imperial privilege at the heart of an emerging twentieth-century international order.

This volume, then, looks at partition as a "traveling theory"—a notion that Edward Said pioneered in his 1983 book *The World, the Text, and the Critic*, in which he defined the transmission of ideas and theories as having three or four discernable stages: a specific point of origin and a "distance transversed," whereby an idea moves into a new place and standing; conditions of "acceptance or, as an inevitable part of acceptance, resistances" that make the implementation of the idea possible; and a final process by which the "now full (or partly) accommodated (or incorporated) idea is to some extent transformed by its new uses."[76] Here, we adapt this idea to explore the genesis, dissemination, and transformation of the concept of partition. The first part of this book, "Origins and Genealogies," looks at some origin points for the idea of partition: in colonial contexts, in the Zionist movement, and in intra-European power politics. In the second part, "Distances Transversed," the authors examine the development of an abstract language of partition at the international level, which British imperial politicians imagined as broadly applicable to any number of local cases. These essays focus particularly on the colonial dissemination of ideas through a small and tightly knit group of colonial officials whose ideas about how to retain power over the populations under their rule led to a broader conceptualization of partition as a mode of imperial and postimperial control. The last part, "Acceptance, Resistance, and Accommodation," explores a wide variety of reactions to partition, from accommodation to resistance. These essays look at some of the reactions to and depictions of partition from those affected, ranging from internationally focused political activism to intracommunity conversations about collective identity to private familial processes of narration and memorialization. A. Dirk Moses's epilogue, "Partitions, Hostages, Transfer," explores the long-term violence of partition through the emergence of a postpartition logic of collective security and retribution.

The analysis contained in this volume particularly matters at the moment because we have recently witnessed a revival of interest in the idea of partition as a political "solution" to ethnic and religious conflict, especially for the Middle East. In 2009, journalist Geoffrey Wheatcroft (responding to an article by Christopher Hitchens deploring the consequences of colonial partitions) declared it a viable and justifiable conceit:

"Over and over again partition has been the entirely inevitable solution; not a good remedy, but the least bad remedy in the objective circumstances. . . . Over and again partition has averted civil war and made possible the establishment of orderly states."[77] In 2012, the well-known journalist and commentator Dilip Hiro wrote an article in which he made the case that the partition of South Asia constituted a successful model of state-building to which diplomats seeking solutions for Syria might turn. "The Indian subcontinent is about 5000 kilometers away from the cockpit of the Middle East's latest upheaval," he wrote, "but analysts would do well to examine the subcontinent's recent history to gain insight into Syria's intractable conflict. . . . The 1947 partitioning of British India into India and Pakistan eased communal violence dramatically. And so Syria, too, could be on the way to a solution by partition."[78] Claims like these are by no means unusual in the current political climate, which has seen repeated suggestions from a variety of quarters that partition might represent a viable path forward for a Syria mired in violence and a collapsing Iraqi state.[79]

Such propositions represent a dangerous misreading of history. Partition is not a long-standing or natural solution to a problem of pluralism; it is a consequence of a particular alignment of global interests, dating from the interwar period, that privileged ethnic nationalisms and ethnically purified nation-states as the building blocks of a modern world order. Further, its imposition has without exception been accompanied by violence of the most extreme kind; only a radical ignorance of the historical facts could allow for the claim that the 1947 partition of South Asia "eased communal violence dramatically." There is no historical evidence that partition as a political practice has done anything whatsoever to provide a "solution" to ethnic conflict—or indeed that it was ever intended to do so; its primary rationale was to smooth the path for imperial powers to create new forms of informal authority and friendly client states for a new postcolonial era, without regard for the human costs. If a historically informed examination of the concept of partition tells us anything, it is that past attempts to enforce ethnic homogeneity as a condition of viable statehood—in Ireland, Palestine, and India alike—now stand as some of the greatest tragedies of the twentieth century.

*Part I*

ORIGINS AND GENEALOGIES

## CHAPTER 1

# FROM MINORITY TO NATION
Faisal Devji

OCCURRING WITHIN months of each other, and as part of Britain's gradual retreat from empire, the partitions of India and Palestine have much in common. Both Pakistan and Israel, after all, emerged from situations in which minority populations dispersed across vast subcontinents sought to escape the national majorities whose persecution they rightly or wrongly feared. For it was only the emergence of national majorities in nineteenth-century Europe and India that turned Jews and Muslims there into minorities, whose apparently irreducible particularity posed a "problem" or "question" for states newly founded on notions of shared blood and the ancestral ownership of a homeland.[1] As a result of representing such a problem or question for the national movements within which they were formed, both Zionism and Muslim nationalism held such forms of collective belonging to be deeply suspect, even as they sometimes attempted to fashion similar nationalities for themselves elsewhere. Or as Jacqueline Rose puts it in *The Question of Zion*, "Israel inscribes at its heart the very version of nationhood from which the Jewish people had to flee."[2] Yet the effort to make oneself at home in a new land, in the same way that one's oppressor had in the old, remained an incomplete and ambiguous one among Zionists as much as Muslim nationalists.[3] But whatever their "objective" similarities, I am interested here in the way in which the history of Jews as a minority came to serve as

a complex site of reflection and identification among Muslim nationalists in India, well before the partitions that founded Pakistan and Israel.
In particular, I look at how an important Muslim thinker deployed this
comparison in order to put the nation-state itself into question.

## AN INTERNATIONAL IMAGINATION

The Pakistan Movement was heir to a tradition of antinationalist think-
ing, one that drew upon the widespread disenchantment with Woodrow
Wilson's notion of self-determination in the wake of the First World
War. For as the historian Beni Prasad put it in his 1941 book *The Hindu-
Muslim Questions*:

> It was perhaps inevitable that the controversy over group adjustments in
> India should be influenced by similar debates in Europe. A militant nation-
> alism created serious minority problems there in the 19th century by en-
> couraging a policy of suppression and assimilation on the one hand and by
> reviving racial or nationalist feeling on the other. The post-war attempt to
> protect minorities took the form of international and constitutional guaran-
> tees of civil rights and for a while evoked a sympathetic response in India but
> it broke down within a few years.[4]

The rise of transnational ideological movements like communism and
fascism during the interwar period, and the collapse of the international
order itself during the Second World War, only intensified this suspicion
that the nation-state was neither indispensable nor inevitable for modern
politics. As it turns out, the greatest critic of nationalism in India was
also the man known as the spiritual father of Pakistan. By the time he
died in 1938, nearly ten years before that country's founding, the poet
and philosopher Muhammad Iqbal had been recognized as India's most
important Muslim thinker. Hugely popular among all classes of people,
his poetry was declaimed in the streets of cities like Lahore, and his apparent support for Muslim nationalism gave the Pakistan Movement an
intellectual credibility it otherwise would have lacked.

Muslim efforts to avoid being defined as a minority in India resulted
from the nineteenth century in a politics that was often directed along
international lines, though in a way that tracked Britain's world empire

so closely as to make it unclear whether it was pan-Islamism or British imperialism that provided one as a model for the other. Before the First World War, Iqbal's antinationalism was also internationalist in character, and it, too, adopted the British Empire as a model for the working out of democracy as a purely human destiny. So in "Islam as a Moral and Political Idea," an essay published in the *Hindustan Review* in 1909, he writes:

> The membership of Islam as a community is not determined by birth, locality or naturalisation; it consists in the identity of belief. The expression "Indian Muhammadan," however convenient it may be, is a contradiction in terms; since Islam in its essence is above all conditions of time and space. Nationality with us is a pure idea; it has no geographical basis. But inasmuch as the average man demands a material centre of nationality, the Muslim looks for it in the holy town of Mecca, so that the basis of Muslim nationality combines the real and the ideal, the concrete and the abstract.[5]

But this ideal, suggested Iqbal, could also be seen operating in the British Empire, "since it is one aspect of our own political ideal that is being slowly worked out in it. England, in fact, is doing one of our own great duties, which unfavourable circumstances did not permit us to perform. It is not the number of Muhammadans which it protects, but the spirit of the British Empire that makes it the greatest Muhammadan Empire in the world."[6]

Iqbal's political imagination, it will immediately be recognized, is nothing if not historical. Yet its detailed and loving embrace of the past does not in the least make for a national history, only a universal one in which Islam itself can become nothing more than a precedent for a rival tradition. So in his *Stray Reflections* of 1910 Iqbal could write: "As a political force we are perhaps no longer required; but we are, I believe, still indispensable to the world as the only testimony to the absolute unity of God. Our value among nations, then, is purely evidential."[7] We shall see shortly how this very "Jewish" theme, at least of the pre-Zionist period, is recognized as such by Iqbal in other parts of his work.

What is interesting about his rejection of Islam's political history, however, was the simultaneous turn to events from the life of the Prophet, when that religion could be studied in its republican or preimperial phase.

I argue that this retrieval of Islam's origins did not indicate a properly historical inquiry, and even less an historical identification for Iqbal. Like other Muslim thinkers of the time, he was concerned with Muhammad's life more as a constitutional model for a future society freed from its grandiose past, of the kind that Periclean Athens or republican Rome played in the West, than as a site of historical analysis or imagination. The Prophet's life was not to become some alternative vision of nationalism's historical romance. As an admirer of the French philosopher Henri Bergson, Iqbal looked askance at what he termed "serial time," seen as a kind of space, a continuum in which individuals and groups might be placed, and spoke instead of time as a form of "pure duration" that was only predicable of historical subjects and did not define them.[8] And this meant that the origins of Islam belonged not merely to the past but could also be posited in the future, constituting a destiny rather than a moment in serial time. Indeed, he even thought that this notion of time was linked to a specifically Semitic view of the world, and when he met Bergson in Paris in 1932, Iqbal, in referring to the former's Jewish background, spoke of the Semitic spiritual affinity that he had for Bergson's work.[9]

In addition to rejecting a national history, which, after all, could be written only in serial time, Iqbal also dismissed geography as a basis for political life, favoring instead a foundation made up of ideas alone, which he lauds insofar as they are universal in scope. In fact, he was severely critical of space as a category, preferring, like Bergson, to see it as a dynamic structure of events instead.[10] In other words, he tried to dismantle space itself in philosophical terms, for to Iqbal this entity simply indicated one form that the "idolatry" of race, geography, and indeed matter took. Islam, therefore, constituted nothing more than an example of a nonmaterial claim to universality, though like previous attempts made by the Greeks and Romans to create a world-state on this principle, the Arab conquests also proved to be a failure. For as Iqbal put it in his essay "Political Thought in Islam," published a year later in the *Hindustan Review*: "The life of early Muslims was a life of conquest. The whole energy was devoted to political expansion which tends to concentrate political power in fewer hands; and thus serves as an unconscious handmaid of despotism. Democracy does not seem to be quite willing to get on with

Empire—a lesson which the modern English Imperialists might well take to heart."[11] Nevertheless, he thought that such an ideal was still capable of realization, since "the life of modern political communities finds expression, to a great extent, in common institutions, Law and Government; and the various sociological circles, so to speak, are continually expanding to touch one another. Further, it is not incompatible with the sovereignty of individual States, since its structure will be determined not by physical force, but by the spiritual force of a common ideal."[12]

By the end of the First World War, Iqbal had become a stern critic of imperialism and now considered communism to be Islam's greatest rival in the establishment of a universal polity based upon a common or ideological understanding of the world. His arguments against nationalism, too, had come to be couched in vaguely Marxist terms, with the nation-state, being itself a mythical form of collective ownership, seen as representing the apotheosis of private property in social life. Nevertheless, he thought that communism, by transferring all property to the state, actually made it an even more oppressive presence in society, thus smuggling back into everyday life the very forms of alienation that it criticized in private ownership. Iqbal maintained that territorial belonging, in the populist form it assumed with the nation-state, destroyed or at the very least enfeebled all ethical or idealistic imperatives in political life, making for an international regime of parochial and so continuously warring interests. In other words, he argued that the "interests" to which historians routinely attribute all actions and ideas were themselves the products of history and could not have existed before the establishment of property as the foundation of social order. For it was only in such an order that interests could even be conceived in terms of the ownership of some substance, whether in the form of land, rights, or indeed religion. Interests, after all, had meaning only in general terms, as defined by historical categories like class or any other form of identity, and did not possess a natural or individual reality.

For Iqbal, then, moral ideals were as real as any interests in a society not regulated by private property, as he thought was still mostly the case in India. And his politics was therefore dedicated to preventing the disappearance, or rather the powerlessness, of such ideals, which would lead in India to the kind of conflict and exploitation that Iqbal saw in modern Europe. He believed that this condition was brought into being there by the Protestant Reformation, whose individualization of religion and revolt against the universality of the Roman Catholic Church ushered the nation-state into history. And within the modern state, religion now occupied the fading realm of spirit as opposed to the ever-expanding world of matter, a purely metaphysical dualism that Iqbal argued was itself inherited from Christianity, saying in his presidential address of December 29, 1930, to the Muslim League in Allahabad: "If you begin with the conception of religion as complete other-worldliness, then what has happened to Christianity in Europe is perfectly natural. The universal ethics of Jesus is displaced by national systems of ethics and polity. The conclusion to which Europe is consequently driven is that religion is a private affair of the individual and has nothing to do with what is called man's temporal life."[13]

Nationalism therefore represented the metaphysical domination of matter over spirit, rather than some merely functional division between social spheres. And by vesting itself in land, race, language, or religion, all seen as forms of collective property, nationalism sought to efface both the moral idea and its purely human universality from politics. All of this, of course, posed a problem for Muslims especially, whose principle of solidarity, Iqbal thought, was based on the universality of an idea that demanded some manifestation in society. In India, furthermore, where Muslims happened to be in a minority, Muslim forms of solidarity could only be threatened with extinction by nationalism. For of all their coreligionists the world over, the Prophet's dispersed and scattered Indian followers were the only ones to be united on the basis of an idea alone. Or as Iqbal said in his presidential address to the League in 1930:

> It cannot be denied that Islam, regarded as an ethical ideal plus a certain kind of polity—by which expression I mean a social structure regulated by a legal system and animated by a specific ethical ideal—has been the chief formative factor in the life history of the Muslims of India. It has furnished those basic emotions and loyalties which gradually unify scattered individuals and groups and finally transform them into a well-defined people. Indeed it is no

exaggeration to say that India is perhaps the only country in the world where Islam as a society is almost entirely due to the working of Islam as a culture inspired by a specific ethical ideal.[14]

It was because India's Muslims represented the Islamic principle of solidarity more than their coreligionists elsewhere that Iqbal considered their fate to be that of Muslims the world over. Indeed, he spoke in the same address of India being Asia in miniature, with the working out of a solution to the problem of nationalism there serving as an example for the continent, if not the world as a whole. And this meant, he told his audience: "We have a duty towards India where we are destined to live and die. We have a duty towards Asia, especially Muslim Asia. And since 70 millions of Muslims in a single country constitute a far more valuable asset to Islam than all the countries of Muslim Asia put together, we must look at the Indian problem not only from the Muslim point of view but also from the standpoint of the Indian Muslim as such."[15] But this patriotic, if not quite nationalist, position of seeing the world as India writ large also entailed conceiving of Muslims in this world as a minority, as indeed they were from a purely demographic point of view.

And it is from this world perspective that Iqbal can compare the fate of Muslims to that of Jews, his attempt to escape the status of a national minority by turning to the world outside, therefore, resulting in a much more fearful vision of virtue outnumbered. So in his *Stray Reflections*, Iqbal followed up one of his typical repudiations of the nation-state as an idolatrous political form destructive of Muslim solidarity by noting: "From what I have said above on Islam and patriotism it follows that our solidarity as a community rests on our hold on the religious principle. The moment this hold is loosened we are nowhere. Probably the fate of the Jews will befall us."[16] This line of argument is pursued more elaborately in his long Persian poem of 1918 called the *Rumuz-e Bekhudi* (Mysteries of Selflessness), where Iqbal invokes the Jews' fate in diaspora first as an example of endurance that Muslims might have to follow:

*Ibrat az ahwal-e israil gir*

*Garm-o sard ruzgar-e u nagar*

*Sakhti-ye jan-e nazar-e u nagar*

*Khun-e giran sir ast dar ragha-ye u*
*Sang-e sad dahliz-o yek sima-ye u*
*Panjah-e gardun chu angurish fashard*
*Yadgar-e Musa-o Harun namard*
*Az nawa-ye atishinish raft suz*
*Lekin dar sineh dam darad hanuz*
*Zankeh chun jam'iatish az ham shikast*
*Juz barah-e raftagan mahmal nisbat*

(Take warning from the Israelitish case;
Consider well their variable fate,
Now hot, now cold; regard the obduracy,
The hardness of their spare and tenuous soul.
Sluggishly flows the blood within their veins,
Their furrowed brow sore smitten on the stones
Of porticoes a hundred. Though heaven's grip
Hath pressed and squeezed their grape, the memory
Of Moses and of Aaron liveth yet;
And though their ardent song hath lost its flame,
Still palpitates the breath within their breast.
For when the fabric of their nationhood
Was rent asunder, still they laboured on
To keep the highroad of their forefathers.)[17]

But second, this fate also served as a warning for Muslims, who like them were bound by an idea, monotheism, that was uniquely powerful while at the same time being vulnerable to the seductions of polytheism in the form of attachments to different lands and languages:

*Ibrati ay muslim-e rowshan zamir*
*Az amal-e ummat-e Musa bagir*
*Dad chun an qawm markaz ra za dast*
*Rishtah-e jam'iat-e millat shikast*
*An keh balid andar aghosh-e rasal*
*Juzv-e u danandah-e asrar-e kul*
*Dahr sayli bar bana gushish kashid*

*Zindagi khun gasht va az chashmish chakid*
*Raft nam az risheha-ye tak-e u*
*Bid-e makhbun ham narawid khak-e u*
*Az gil-e ghurbat zaban gum kardahi*
*Hamnawa hamashiyan gum kardahi*
*Sham' murd-o noha-khwan parwaneh-ish*
*Musht-e khakam larzad az afsaneh-ish*

(Take heed once again,
Enlightened Muslim, by the tragic fate
Of Moses' people, who, when they gave up
Their focus from their grasp, the thread was snapped
That bound their congregation each to each.
That nation, nurtured up upon the breast
Of God's apostles, and whereof the part
Was privy to the secrets of the whole,
Suddenly smitten by the hand of Time
Poured out its lifeblood in slow agony.
The tendrils of its vine are withered now,
Nor even any willow weeping grows
More from its soil; exile has robbed its tongue
Of common speech; dead the lamenting moth—
My poor dust trembles at the history.)[18]

It is entirely in keeping with the nature of Muslim politics during this period that Iqbal's verses on the Jews, which are only some of several similar scattered throughout his work, should be so close to Zionist sentiments as to easily be mistaken for them. For even his rejection of nationalism does not contradict the world-historical role that Zionism would attribute to its homeland. The fate of India's Muslims, then, like that of Jews around the world, was intimately tied to the future of monotheism itself as a global fact, and in this way to the political future of humanity as a whole. All of this made the question of nationalism in India much more important than one defined merely by its domestic politics. Despite or perhaps because of their much-contested position as a minority, in other words, India's Muslims were able to look upon themselves from a world-historical perspective that diverged significantly from any vision retailed by the Indian National Congress, bringing to the politics of nationalism a set of ideas whose dimensions were so great they risked overwhelming its categories altogether. Not that men like Iqbal were unable to deal with the everyday reality of such a politics. In his Allahabad speech, for instance, the "Poet of the East" pinned his hopes to what he saw as the antinational spirit of Indian society in general:

> "Man," says Renan, "is enslaved neither by his race, nor by his religion, nor by the course of rivers, nor by the direction of mountain ranges. A great aggregation of men, sane of mind and warm of heart, creates a moral consciousness which is called a nation." Such a formation is quite possible, though it involves the long and arduous process of practically remaking men and furnishing them with a fresh emotional equipment. It might have been a fact in India if the teachings of Kabir and the Divine Faith of Akbar had seized the imagination of the masses of this country. Experience, however, shows that the various caste-units and religious units in India have shown no inclination to sink their respective individualities in a larger whole. Each group is intensely jealous of its collective existence. The formation of the kind of moral consciousness which constitutes the essence of a nation in Renan's sense demands a price which the peoples of India are not prepared to pay.[19]

Nevertheless, Iqbal feared the destructive forces that he thought nationalism had unleashed in India, and which he considered even more fatal to Hinduism, held together as it was by the complex structure of caste, than they were to Islam. And it was in order to defend themselves against such forces that Iqbal advised Muslims to support the League, either by insisting on the autonomy they already possessed in the form of separate electorates and other protections guaranteed by the multiple jurisdictions of the Raj, or by seeking another kind of unity in territorial adjustments that would create Muslim provinces within an Indian federation. Historians have done little more than follow Indian or Pakistani nationalists in arguing whether Iqbal's conception of territorial autonomy can be seen as a precursor to the subcontinent's partition, but what is of real interest in his always ambiguous pronouncements on the subject are his reasons for making the demand. If Muslims were given the political and economic power to organize and administer their own societies, such autonomy, he thought, would allow them to remake Islam itself, or rather address the challenge that modernity posed to it. In his Allahabad address, then, Iqbal put his demand like this: "I therefore demand the formation of a consolidated Muslim State in the best interest of India and Islam. For India it means security and peace resulting from an internal balance of power; for Islam an opportunity to rid itself of the stamp that Arabian imperialism was forced to give it, to mobilize its law, its education, its culture, and to bring them into closer contact with its own original spirit and with the spirit of modern times."[20] It will be noted that the Muslim territories of Iqbal's imagination had nothing of the national about them and were indeed dedicated to the rejection of history as much as to its recovery. And in this way these lands, together with their inhabitants, constituted nothing more than instances of Islam as a form of the universal idea. It is not surprising, therefore, that Iqbal should have seen communism alone as Islam's competitor in this paradoxical enterprise. So in his epic poem of 1932, the *Javid Namah* (Book of Eternity), Iqbal has the famous pan-Islamist Jamal al-Din al-Afghani address the Russian people as potential successors of the Muslims, who broke up the empires of antiquity only to create one of their own. On one hand, then, he is afraid that God's favor will be lifted from these Muslims to be given to the Bolsheviks:

> *Zikr-e haq az ummatan amad ghani*
> *Az zaman-o az makan amad ghani*
> *Zikr-e haq az zikr-e har zakir judast*
> *Ihtiyaj-e rum-o sham u ra kujast*
> *Haq agar az pish-e ma bar daradish*
> *Pish-e qawm-e digari baguzaradish*
> *Az musalman dideh-am taqlid-o zann*
> *Har zaman janam ba-larzad dar badan*

(God's remembrance requires not nations,
It transcends the bounds of time and space.
God's remembrance is apart from the remembrance of every remembrancer—
what need has it of Greek or Syrian?
If God should remove it from us

He can if He will transfer it to another people.
I have seen the blind conformity and opinionatedness of Moslems
and every moment my soul trembles in my body;
I fear for the day when it shall be denied to them,
and its fire shall be kindled in quite other hearts.)[21]

But on the other hand Iqbal is keen to invite the communists to complete the work of Islam by joining with the struggles of colonized Asian peoples and identifying with their non-Western history, for he thought that Marxism's focus on European thought could only provincialize and turn it into an accomplice of imperialism:

*Tu ke tarh-e digari andakhti*
*Dil za dastur-e kuhan pardakhti*
*Hamchu ma islamiyan andar jahan*
*Qaysariyyat ra shikasti astakhwan*
*Ta bar afruzi chiraghi dar zamir*
*Ibrati az sarguzasht-e ma bagir*
*Pa-ye khud mahkam guzar andar nabard*
*Gird-e in Lat-o Hubal digar magard*
*Millati mikhahad in dunya-e pir*
*Anke bashad ham bashir-o ham nazir!*
*Baz miyayi su-ye aqwam-e sharq*
*Basteh ayyam-e tub a ayyam-e sharq*
*Tu ba-jan afgandahi suz-e digar*
*Dar zamir-e ti shab-o ruzi digar!*
*Kuhneh shud afrang ra ain-o din*
*Su-ye an dayr-e kuhan digar mabin*
*Kardehi kar-e khudawandan tamam*
*Baguzar az la janib-e illa khiram*
*Dar guzar az la agar juyandahi*
*Ta rah-e asbat giri zindahi*
*Ay ke mikhwahi nizam-e alami*
*Justehi u ra asas-e mahkami?*

(You who have set forth another way
Dissociated your heart from the ancient usage

In the world like us Muslims

Have broken the very bones of empire

So that you might illumine yourselves

Take warning from our history

Set your foot firmly in the battle

Circle no longer about this Lāt and this Hubal

This decrepit world needs a community

To be both herald and warner

So turn again to the peoples of the East

For your battles are tied up with the battles of the East

You who have lit another fire of the spirit

In your souls resides another kind of night and day

The law and faith of Europe have grown old

Do not look to that ancient cloister again

You have finished up the work of lordship

Now pass from the negation of "no" into the affirmation of "but"

Pass onwards of "no" if you are a seeker

So you might follow the path of living affirmation.

You who desire world dominion

Have you found for it a sure foundation?)[22]

The negation and affirmation Iqbal refers to are taken from the first line of the Islamic credo "no god but God." Iqbal often cited this line as an example of his view that negation was the principle of movement in Islam, and had to precede affirmation, by stressing the paradoxical way in which the credo can be read as a denial of the very deity who is then to be accepted. Negation, of course, is also the mark of the devil, who had, not coincidentally, become a heroic figure for Iqbal, representing a new kind of political ideal for a free-floating and self-possessed nation that rejected its grounding in nature or history.

## A POLITICS OF NEGATION

As early as 1909, in the essay "Islam as a Moral and Political Ideal," published in the *Hindustan Review*, Iqbal had written: "I hope I shall not be offending the reader when I say that I have a certain amount of admiration for the devil. By refusing to prostrate himself before Adam, whom he honestly believed to be his inferior, he revealed a high sense of self-respect, a trait of character, which, in my opinion, ought to redeem him from his spiritual deformity, just as the beautiful eyes of the toad redeem him from his physical repulsiveness."[23] In subsequent years Iqbal would go on to praise Satan's tragic independence of mind as a model for Muslims, for it was their dissociation from any given foundation, including even religion itself, that allowed Satan to become a Muslim ideal. So in one of his "Stray Thoughts" published in the *New Era* of August 1917, Iqbal could say: "At least in one respect sin is better than piety. There is an imaginative element in the former which is lacking in the latter."[24]

Unlike Iqbal's rather conventional praise for Muslim heroes through the ages, his verses on Satan cut to the heart of his philosophy, in which humans are meant to partner and even compete with God. In the *Jawab-e Shikwa* (Complaint's Answer) of 1913, for example, God ends up resigning to humankind the stylus and tablet upon which destiny is written, while the prelude to the *Javid Namah* ends with the angels singing about humanity's challenge to God as constituting the final act of freedom:

*Furugh-e musht-e khak az nuryan afzun shawad ruzi*
*Zameen az kawkab-e taqdir-e u gardun shawad ruzi*
*Khayal-e u ki az sayl-e hawadis parvarish girad*
*Za girdab-e sipahr-e nilgun birun shawad ruzi*
*Yeki dar ma'ani-e adam nagar az ma che pursi*
*Hunuz andar tab'iat mikhalad mawzun shawad ruzi*
*Chunan mawzun shawad in pish pa uftadah mazmuni*
*Ki yazdan ra dil az tasir-e u pur khun shawad ruzi*

(The lustre of a handful of earth one day shall outshine the creatures of
    light;
earth through the star of his destiny one day shall be transformed into
    heaven.
His imagination, which is nourished by the torrent of vicissitudes,
one day shall soar out of the whirlpool of the azure sky.
Consider one moment the meaning of Man; what thing do you ask of us?
Now he is pricking into nature, one day he will be modulated perfectly,

so perfectly modulated will this precious subject be

that even the heart of God will bleed one day at the impact of it!)[25]

While such verses can be taken as being atheistic, of course, and are deliberately provocative in a way acceptable to the literary tradition of Persian and Urdu, they were probably meant to indicate what Iqbal thought was a higher stage of religion, where humans recognized their own divinity and God came to exist through them rather than the reverse.[26] But it is interesting to note that in his Urdu poem "Jibreel-o Iblis" (Gabriel and the Devil), Iqbal uses the same image, of a prick, that ends the verses above, but one that now entered the heart of God rather than nature. The poem is composed as a dialogue between the Archangel Gabriel and the fallen angel who has become Satan. Gabriel asks whether his former companion can return to paradise by seeking God's forgiveness, only to be told that Satan's exile on earth has intoxicated him, making the silence and eternal stillness of heaven tedious by comparison. The devil then tells Gabriel that he has a far more exalted role now than when he was an angel, exclaiming that it was his blood, after all, that gave color to the story of Adam, and ending the poem with the following lines:

*Main khatakta hun dil-e yazdan men kante ki tarah*

*Tu faqat Allah-hu! Allah-hu! Allah-hu!*

(I prick into the deity's heart like a thorn;

All you can do is sing hosannas to his name.)[27]

Satan's rejection of paradise represented for Iqbal the power of negation as a principle of movement, one that he described most often in the fairly traditional images of stars in eternal motion, ships that never find a shore, lovers who pine in endless separation, and mystics who refuse union with the divine. All these familiar negations in Urdu and Persian poetry produced beauty and made life into a boundless journey. And the negation of a national homeland was only one instance of this desire for the infinite, which Iqbal described repeatedly, as in the following couplets from the *Javid Namah*:

*Rahrave ku danad asrar-e safar*

*Tarsad az manzil za rahzan bishtar*

(The traveller who knows the secrets of journeying
Fears the destination more than the highwayman.)

*Ishq dar hijr-o visal asudah nist*
*Be jamal-e laziyal asudah nist!*

(Love does not reside in separation or union
For there is no residing without beauty eternal!)

*Ibtida pish-e butan uftadagi*
*Inteha az dilbaran azadagi!*

(In the beginning falling down before idols;
In the end freedom from all beloveds!)

*Ishq be parwa-o hardam dar rahil*
*Dar makan-o lamakan ibn-e asbil!*

(Love cares not and is always on the move;
A journeyman in place and non-place!)

*Kesh-e ma manand-e mawj-e tez gam*
*Ikhtiyar-e jadah-o tark-e maqam!*

(Our custom is like the swiftening wave—
A willing for the road, a departure from the lodging!)[28]

It should by now be clear how the negation and abandonment of all
that is given constituted, in Iqbal's work, a philosophical vision of life in
general, one that provided an expansive and layered context for particular
themes in Muslim nationalism. And though it was no doubt linked to
the specific history of Muslim minority politics in India, this vision also
possessed its own integrity and cannot be reduced to such sociological
facts, making Iqbal, for instance, a hugely popular poet among Muslims
outside India. Indeed, Iqbal's vision was so expansive and his distrust of
the nation-state so deep that, like many others in the League, he, too, had
a most ambiguous attitude toward ideas such as a Muslim state. Though
he died a couple of years before the Muslim League adopted Pakistan as
its goal, Iqbal, who was claimed as an early proponent of the idea, seems

to have rejected it in the end. Not only did he praise Motilal Nehru and Jawaharlal Nehru in the *Javid Nama* as "keen-sighted Brahmins" imbued with the desire for India's freedom, the poet of Muslim nationalism also repudiated Pakistan in his correspondence with the historian Edward Thompson, who had invited him to deliver the Rhodes Lecture at Oxford, writing in a letter dated March 4, 1933: "Pakistan is not my scheme. The one that I suggested in my address is the creation of a Muslim Province—i.e. a province having an overwhelming population of Muslims—in the Northwest of India. This new province will be, according to my scheme, a part of the proposed Indian Federation."[29] We should be clear that this denial was by no means a vote of support for Indian nationalism but instead an example of the long-standing efforts on the part of India's Muslims to refashion India into a country without a nation. This world-encompassing vision of a nonnational future, however, by the same token made for a "fanatical" politics, and I close with an egregiously violent instance of it.

## SPINOZA IN THE PUNJAB

In his book *The Returns of Zionism*, Gabriel Piterberg writes about how Gershom Scholem, the founding figure of studies on Jewish mysticism, wrote what he calls a proleptic history of Zionism by identifying its myth of return in the past of Judaism's heretical tradition.[30] Scholem's major work was focused on the extraordinary story of Sabbatai Sevi, a seventeenth-century Ottoman Jew who claimed to be the messiah, giving rise to a wide-ranging movement in his support. At the behest of worried rabbinical authorities, Sevi was eventually arrested and converted to Islam. But this repudiation of Judaism was seen by many of his followers as demonstrating the truth of Sevi's mission, since he could save his people only by sinning against his religion and thus spiritualizing it as an internal force rather than a set of outward observances. Putting aside the complex theology behind this assertion, what interests Piterberg is not only Scholem's desire to read back the messianic element of Zionism into the Jewish past, but to do so precisely by breaking the hold of rabbinical Judaism, which he thought had normalized exile and degenerated into a set of ritual prescriptions. And yet despite his concern with heresy,

Scholem ended up, says Piterberg, the spokesman for Zionism as a new form of Jewish orthodoxy. A similar tale might be told about Muhammad Iqbal, who, incidentally, shared the same academic supervisor as Scholem at Munich's Ludwig Maximilian University, though the two men were separated by a gap of more than a decade. Fritz Hommel, a Semitic expert, also seems to have played little role in the intellectual development of either of his more illustrious students. Iqbal is today accepted as an impeccably orthodox Muslim, as indeed he more or less was in his own practices, though his ideas, we have seen, draw from very heterodox and mystical traditions indeed. In some ways Scholem's notion of an apostate messiah fits rather well with Iqbal's idea of a heroic Satan. For both men saw in traditional religion an obstacle that had to be removed if a new society were to emerge, one that was faithful to its revolutionary origins.

But what particularly interests me about these men is how they managed to make a norm out of heresy by attacking the heterodoxy of others. In Scholem's case the enemy was exilic Judaism itself as a norm, and in Iqbal's it was a traditional theory of Muslim authority that in the twentieth century came, above all, to be identified with a supposedly "deviant" community called the Ahmadis. What makes the comparison so fruitful, however, is the fact that in his attacks on the Ahmadis, Iqbal takes recourse to exilic Judaism, with which he compares Indian Islam, thus returning to the fearful identification with it that we have already seen manifested earlier in this chapter. Founded in nineteenth-century Punjab by Mirza Ghulam Ahmad, this group quickly became known for its proselytizing zeal and willingness to engage in polemics with Hindu revivalists, Christian missionaries, and others. Indeed, Iqbal had once even praised them as examples of Islam's modern revival. Outwardly conservative in the extreme, and in fact indistinguishable from the most orthodox of Sunnis, the Ahmadis were soon marked in Iqbal's eyes by one belief in particular: their attribution of prophetic status to Mirza Ghulam Ahmad. This sort of attribution, along with other claims of supernatural favor made by the Mirza, was part of a long messianic tradition in Islam, one that had sometimes produced controversy but never the kind of public obloquy and eventually violence that the Ahmadis were soon subject to. So apart from the role that mass communication and mobilization in the twentieth century played in expanding this controversy, what made it conceptually different from previous religious altercations?

Soon after Pakistan was established, religious organizations like the Jamat-e Islami started an agitation against the Ahmadis that resulted in extensive riots and eventually a judicial declaration that they were not Muslim and so could neither call themselves by that name nor, indeed, invoke God and the Prophet in Islamic fashion; they could not even have their places of worship look like mosques. This anxiety to stop people from appearing or behaving like Muslims is not only novel, but also interesting because it suggests that Islam can easily be usurped by others and become a kind of simulacrum seducing true believers from the religion. In an essay on anti-Ahmadi discourse in Pakistan, the anthropologist Naveeda Khan has made the point that the judgments against them drew upon the law of patents and copyright, arguing that an "original" Islam had to be protected from false imitations or its distinctiveness might itself be lost.[31] Islam, in other words, was legally defined as the intellectual property of its believers. Apart from illustrating the rather modern character of this controversy, which in this sense only follows the precedent set by the Ahmadis' own "modernization" of religious debate, what is interesting about it is the reliance on inner belief as a criterion of veracity, since outward appearances were no longer trustworthy. Given the fact that Sunni tradition had always been concerned with outward conformity rather than inner belief as a criterion of orthodoxy, this turn to the latter was itself curiously heretical in character, for such an emphasis on the esoteric had always been associated with mystical and sectarian groups in the past. I would argue, however, that this focus on an invisible doctrine had something to do with the importance of ungrounded ideas and unmediated principles in Muslim nationalism.

The judicially authorized persecution of the Ahmadis in Pakistan has opened the door to increasingly murderous attacks on all other "deviant" groups there, especially the Shia, to say nothing about the oppression of those, like Hindus and Christians, who make no claim on Islam. And though Iqbal would no doubt have been horrified by this situation, it is his reasoning on the Ahmadi issue that has come to define these various forms of intolerance. Indeed, during his own lifetime, Jawaharlal Nehru

had pointed out that as far as heretics went, as prominent a Muslim figure as the Aga Khan and his Shia subsect were no less "extreme" than the
Ahmadis, as if to warn Iqbal that targeting one group could end up in a
more general denunciation, as indeed has been the case in Pakistan. But
Iqbal, in an open letter responding to Nehru, defended the Aga on rather
formalistic grounds, while at the same time regretting the errors of his
sect. For Iqbal, then, it was not the highly visible missionary efforts of this
largely middle-class group, comparable in some respects to Scientology in
the United States, that posed a problem; nor was it so much Mirza Ghulam Ahmad's declaration that other Muslims were unbelievers, though
he didn't much like that either. Crucial, rather, was their supposed denial,
at a purely doctrinal level, of Muhammad as the final prophet.

Of course the finality of prophecy is an important part of Muslim belief, though it had never stopped kings, saints, and others from claiming
to share in or inherit Muhammad's mission throughout Islam's history.
But I argue that Iqbal's defense of this finality is in some ways far more
heretical than Mirza Ghulam Ahmad's alleged repudiation of it. The man
claimed as Pakistan's spiritual father saw Muhammad as standing with
one foot in the ancient world and the other in the modern. The Prophet
belonged, he thought, to the ancient world insofar as he was the recipient
of revelation. But Muhammad was a modern man insofar as he put an
end to this occult form of knowledge, both by disclaiming any miraculous
abilities and by announcing the end of prophecy with himself. By stopping all access to divine knowledge in its occult form, then, the Prophet
freed humankind from such "leading strings" and for the first time made
of it history's unique actor. And we have already seen how Iqbal cele-
brates the rise of humanity's "maturity" with Islam by describing God
resigning the stylus and tablet of destiny to human beings, as well as in
contemplating humanity's partnership and indeed rivalry with the deity.

The idea of divine partnership was in fact one of the great themes of
Iqbal's thought, whose "heretical" origins he made clear in his thesis *The
Development of Metaphysics in Persia*, which placed the origins of Muslim
philosophy in Zoroastrianism and saw its ultimate fulfilment in Baha-
ism. In this text Iqbal attributed the most fulsome enunciation of such a
partnership to the ancestor of the Baha'i faith, Siyyid Ali Muhammad,

known as the Bab, who pointed out that "the Quranic verse, that 'God is the best of creators,' implies that there are other self-manifesting beings like God."[32] Though he would omit his source in future discussions of this theme, itself a classic mode of mystical and heretical writing, Iqbal continued making use of the Bab's favored interpretation of this verse from the Quran to the end of his career, which suggests that his self-proclaimed orthodoxy needs to be approached with a great deal of suspicion. Indeed, given the fact that the Babis and later Baha'is represented a similar "threat" to Shia Iran as the Ahmadis did to Sunni India, and that, too, at the same time, it is curious how well-disposed Iqbal continued to be toward them, despite being clear that they were no longer Muslim in any strong sense. Iqbal lauded in particular the female Babi martyr Qurratul-Ayn in his poetry, and in this he followed the example of many Indian Muslims, for whom she was a great heroine whose name became a popular one for young girls. In some sense, then, Iqbal was interested in the figure of the god-man, prefigured most strikingly by Jesus as God become man, but also in the messianic figures of Judaism and Islam, though he used the old mystical term of the "perfect man" (*insan-i kamil*). Indeed, there are many places in his verse where Iqbal speaks of humans becoming like God, otherwise an unpardonable sin in Islam, verses that, unlike the Christian emphasis on incarnation, assume the ascent of humanity to divinity rather than God's descent into humanity. The Ahmadis, then, were dangerous because they would drag humans back into the mists of occult wisdom while at the same time refusing to let them assume divinity by reserving this attribute for Mirza Ghulam Ahmad alone.

Stripping the Mirza of his divine attributes, then, had nothing to do with reserving these for Muhammad, since the Prophet, too, was increasingly seen by many Muslims, reformers as well as revivalists, as being a mere mortal. Iqbal's views about prophecy, in other words, might have been idiosyncratic in one sense, but they were commonplace in another, since his conception of prophetic finality also emphasized the human element in Islam. Being deprived of miracles and other signs of grace, however, did not lessen Muhammad in the eyes of his followers, but rather the contrary, as he could now become a model for them in a new, even "secular" way. Indeed, once the Prophet had become merely human, he suddenly became vulnerable to attack and thus required the defense of Muslims as in some sense their property, as the Pakistani court forbidding the Ahmadis from calling themselves Muslim in fact argued. So while Iqbal could treat God in a rather cavalier fashion in his poetry, accusing God of infidelity, he would tolerate no such playful dealings as far as Muhammad was concerned, and this is true even of Muslims who protest against insults to the Prophet today, for whom God is never in need of their defense.[33] In the *Jawab-e Shikwa*, for instance, after humanity is offered the stylus and tablet of destiny, God says that keeping faith with Muhammad is the only requirement of Islam. For the Prophet, as we have seen, is the founder of humanity as history's true actor, representing therefore the vanishing moment of particularity out of which Islam's universality emerges, and it is this that calls for his protection, whereas God requires none. Iqbal took this peculiar faith in a "disenchanted" messenger so seriously as to praise the Muslim assassin of a Hindu publisher who had printed a scurrilous and immensely controversial attack on Muhammad in 1927, and, it is rumored, even served as a pallbearer at the assassin's funeral after his judicial execution in 1929.

It is a curious defense of orthodoxy that Iqbal mounts against the Ahmadis, in other words, premised as it is on a certain vision of Friedrich Nietzsche's thesis about the "death of God," given the fact that the German philosopher was one of his favorite writers. But why did a small if persistent group like the Ahmadis in the Punjab pose such a threat to Iqbal's world-historical vision of Islam? Because having been divested of all materiality to become a pure idea, it was uniquely vulnerable to disruption. The very quality that made Islam universal and gave it power, in other words, also imperiled it and required of Muslims a touchy and even aggressive defensiveness. So in a 1934 article titled "Qadianis and Orthodox Muslims," Iqbal writes: "Islam repudiates the race idea altogether and founds itself on the religious idea alone. Since Islam bases itself on the religious idea alone, a basis which is wholly spiritual and consequently far more ethereal than blood relationship, Muslim society is naturally much more sensitive to forces which it considers harmful to its integrity."[34]

Rather than having anything to do with old-fashioned religious disputation, in other words, this is the kind of doctrinal struggle that characterized twentieth-century ideologies, and communism in particular, with its show trials and excommunications, whose meaning cannot be exhausted by sociological factors and bureaucratic politics alone.

And it is the unique vulnerability of a community built on an idea alone that Iqbal goes on to describe in entirely Jewish terms. But rather than take the part of Judaism's heretical tradition, as Gershom Scholem did, Iqbal sides with rabbinical Judaism instead, thus secreting his own heterodox position in the heart of orthodoxy in a truly mystical way. So, he can write about Ahmadism: "Its idea of a jealous God with an inexhaustible store of earthquakes and plagues for its opponents; its conception of the prophet as a soothsayer; its idea of the continuity of the spirit of the Messiah, are so absolutely Jewish that the movement can easily be regarded as a return to early Judaism. The idea of the continuity of the spirit of the Messiah belongs more to Jewish mysticism than to positive Judaism."[35] Indeed, he even compares the rise of Ahmadism in colonial India to the emergence of Christianity as a Jewish heresy in Roman Judea, both representing, in Nietzsche's sense, "slave moralities" that accept and religiously legitimize tyranny:

> This country of religious communities where the future of each community rests entirely upon its solidarity, is ruled by a Western people who cannot but adopt a policy of non-interference in religion. This liberal and indispensable policy in a country like India has led to most unfortunate results. In so far as Islam is concerned, it is no exaggeration to say that the solidarity of the Muslim community in India under the British is far less safe than the solidarity of the Jewish community was in the days of Jesus under the Romans. Any religious adventurer in India can set up any claim and carve out a new community for his own exploitation. This liberal State of ours does not care a fig for the integrity of the parent community, provided the adventurer assures it of his loyalty and his followers are regular in the payment of taxes due to the State.[36]

Iqbal elaborated his argument about Ahmadism providing, as he saw it, a religious basis for colonial rule in his article "Reply to Questions

Raised by Pandit Jawahar Lal Nehru," in which he described the group's refutation of holy war and accommodation with the state as being, if not unusual and even expedient in politics, then at least novel in its reliance upon occult knowledge, saying that "the function of Ahmadism in the history of Muslim religious thought is to furnish a revelational basis for India's present political subjugation."[37] But the strangest comparison he draws in this extended meditation on Jewish mysticism is between Mirza Ghulam Ahmad and the philosopher Spinoza, who, Iqbal nevertheless hastens to say, was far superior to the founder of Ahmadism. Quoting from Will Durant's *The Story of Philosophy*, Iqbal writes:

> Furthermore, religious unanimity seemed to the elders their sole means of preserving the little Jewish group in Amsterdam from disintegration, and almost the last means of preserving the unity, and so ensuring the survival of the scattered Jews of the world. If they had had their own State, their own civil law, their own establishment of secular force and power, to compel internal cohesion and external respect, they might have been more tolerant; but their religion was to them their patriotism as well as their faith; the synagogue was their centre of social and political life as well as of ritual and worship; and the Bible whose veracity Spinoza had impugned was the "portable fatherland" of their people; under these circumstances they thought heresy was treason, and toleration suicide.[38]

While the difference between Jews in diaspora and Indian Muslims might seem very great, for Iqbal their similarity was based upon each community's dependence on an ideal or, as he would say, "ethereal" form of solidarity, which made both groups vulnerable and strong at the same time. And so Iqbal could conclude his train of thought by saying: "Similarly the Indian Muslims are right in regarding the Qadiani movement, which declares the entire world of Islam as *kafir* and socially boycotts them, to be far more dangerous to the collective life of Islam in India than the metaphysics of Spinoza to the collective life of the Jews."[39] Iqbal, in other words, managed in his anti-Ahmadi writings to adopt an orthodox mien in a specifically rabbinical way, while at the same time upholding a radically mystical vision of Islam. But this had to be compensated for by the most rigorous conservatism, since the "portable fatherland" of Islam, too, otherwise risked destruction in a world context where Muslims were increasingly seen, as in India, to be nothing more than a minority. And so the very radicalism of Iqbal's thought impels him toward a conservative protection of Muslim practice in a gesture that can be seen as paradoxical if not a sign of bad faith.

## CHAPTER 2

# THE ARCHITECT OF TWO PARTITIONS
# OR A FEDERALIST DAYDREAMER?
### *The Curious Case of Reginald Coupland*
#### Arie M. Dubnov

## INTRODUCTION

The present anthology takes the similar historical trajectories of the three paradigmatic twentieth-century British partitions—namely, those of Ireland, India, and Palestine—as its point of departure. The bloody aftermaths of all these partitions, specifically in Mandatory Palestine and the British Raj in India, deserve our attention. Not only the fact that these spaces were partitioned almost simultaneously is striking, but also their astonishingly similar postcolonial trajectories. The list of historical resemblances includes a political vocabulary used to describe the ethnic and religious conflict in those areas as unsolvable and incompatible; an inherent, innate association of division and separation with national sovereignty and independence; similar types of violence exercised in order to turn partition from an abstract idea to a fact on the ground; and a considerable degree to which subsequent, even contemporary political life in these postcolonial spaces is still dominated by the "unfinished business" of 1947–1948. They suggest a pattern; far more, however, they reveal the ongoing, disturbing legacies of partition.

But do these partitions also share a genealogy? Switching gears from comparative to transnational intellectual history, the present chapter approaches the history of partition from a different angle: it does not aim to put the three partitions side by side but to begin tracing the connections and common features among them, and to understand how partition became a "traveling theory."[1] The chapter attempts to steer our conversation in that direction in two ways—first and foremost, by bringing the British Empire back into the picture. So far, too many discussions on the meaning and history of partition have been guided either by political scientists, who imposed abstract models on a reality that resists such neat schemas, or by area experts, who added much nuance and detail but paid little attention to the imperial backstory and to similar developments elsewhere. In contrast, this chapter argues that the idea of partition was conceived in a British imperial context. It was introduced as part of a larger effort of neoimperial thinkers to restructure empire and prepare it for twentieth-century challenges. It never remained a conversation of the imperial metropole alone, however. The empire was the one to offer a shared platform for translocal conversations, a global framework that connected these separate areas. Put otherwise, more than a political structure, empire provided vital channels for communication and the dissemination of political practices and ideas. Furthermore, the story of partition is revealed as a tale of unintended consequences—a scheme developed in the service of imperial reconfiguration and designed to counter secessionist nationalism and promote a federalist-imperial vision that became, contrary to the authors' original plans and aspirations, a symptom of the postwar imperial breakdown. In that process, both the meaning and function of partition changed radically.

Second, the chapter employs the tools of intellectual history in attempting to decipher the dynamic that allowed the idea of partition to travel such great distances. Our "traveling theory" conversation can benefit from methodological sensitivities: we should not forget that ideas are not free-floating atoms, existing independently. Instead, ideas require human agents who can develop them as "answers" to given "questions"; and far more significantly, ideas need humans who can serve as "idea carriers," disseminating them and applying them in different contexts. Partition is not different in that respect from any other theoretical construct. Still, when carried from metropole to the colonies, the theory of partition was not simply "imported" or "implanted" as is, but negotiated and adapted to different conditions. Here again, the meaning and function of partition did not remain fixed. It changed as it was applied to new lands and different circumstances.

In what follows I demonstrate these two claims by tracking the trajectory of a single individual, Sir Reginald Coupland (1884–1952). Fellow of All Souls College and second Beit Chair of Colonial History at Oxford University (1920–1948), Coupland served for many years as editor of the *Round Table*, the influential neoimperial periodical founded by members of "Milner's Kindergarten," who served under Lord Milner in South Africa. Like many of his peers, Coupland portrayed the Union of South Africa as a remarkable historical achievement to be emulated throughout Britain's vast empire. It was from this vantage point, as we shall see, that he developed many of his subsequent ideas. In addition to being an academic historian, Coupland acquired some broader recognition thanks to a series of popular historical biographies—including *Wilberforce* (1923), *Raffles* (1926), and *Kirk on the Zambesi* (1928)—following the journeys of Britain's colonial heroes. Read like novels, these books reveal that Coupland's talent as an author lay in his ability to transform the abstract ideals of empire into enthralling, flesh-and-blood stories of captivating personalities. They also disclose the extent to which he was an unapologetic mouthpiece for the interwar colonial elite.

Most remarkably, at least for our purposes, Coupland served as an astonishing *connecteur*: first, as a central figure at the Round Table group, he worked closely with Lionel G. Curtis, one of the masterminds of the Anglo-Irish Treaty of 1921 and special advisor to the colonial secretary on Irish affairs until October 1924, thus overseeing, albeit from a distance, the creation of an Irish Free State and the carving out of a separate Northern Irish entity; next, in the summer of 1936, Coupland was appointed a member of Lord Peel's Royal Commission of Inquiry, sent to Palestine to look into the underlying causes of the Arab Revolt and advising, in July 1937, the division of Palestine into two separate federal states, one for Jews and the other for Arabs; and last, he was a leading expert of Indian politics who joined Sir Stafford Cripps on his special mission to India in March 1942, which failed to negotiate an agreement that would appease Muslim and Hindu nationalist leaders and keep an integrated Indian jewel in the Crown. Typical of Coupland, he was also the first to produce the authoritative account of that special task force.[2] Shortly thereafter, he authored the monumental three-volume *Report on the Constitutional Problem in India*, which examined the applicability of partition to the British Raj in India.

If partition was indeed a traveling theory, Coupland was one of its most important couriers, connecting the dots between interwar Ireland, Palestine, and India. Yet, his voluminous writings on India do not disclose a mechanical, "copy-and-paste" attempt to employ the same methods on the British Raj. Rather, identifying the impracticality and potential destructiveness of partition, they indicate a desire to steer clear of it. Indeed, for Coupland the appeal of partition for Ireland, Palestine, and India lay not in its separation of warring populations, but in its possibilities for offering federation, cooperation, and even unity across the empire.

## THE MOOT'S FEDERALIST DREAM, OR, HAMILTON IN IRELAND

Although little is known about Reginald Coupland's life up to 1912, when he joined the Round Table movement, his intellectual voyage can be readily reconstructed. A sickly, bookish young man educated at the prestigious Winchester College, Coupland attended New College, Oxford, where he studied classics. He was a talented student and quickly rose to the top of his cohort—he obtained second class in classical honor moderations in 1905 and first in Greats in 1907—and was eventually elected to a fellowship and lectureship in ancient history at Trinity College, Oxford.

It was during these early years that Coupland befriended Alfred Eckhard Zimmern (1879–1954), who later became a leading proponent of liberal internationalism, and Lionel George Curtis (1872–1955), the newly appointed Beit lecturer in Colonial History who, in 1912, spearheaded the Round Table movement. Both men had an enduring influence on Coupland: in the early 1910s, Zimmern, who served as one of Coupland's tutors at New College, began developing a "presentist" reading of the chronicles of fifth-century Athens, depicting it as an ancient precursor of the seafaring and democracy-loving British Empire. The Greek city-state system, Zimmern came to believe, offered an exemplary model of a "loose" empire, which fell short of achieving full unification because of its members' stubborn local patriotism but was able nonetheless to sustain a deep-seated sense of shared fate, identity, and citizenship. Not only Athens's success but also its apparent failure to become an empire, Zimmern argued in *The Greek Commonwealth* (1911), provided critical lessons for modern Britain: On one hand, Britain's imperial architects had to learn from the ancient Greeks—and not the Romans—how to balance between self-government and empire. Britain, in other words, was to become the Thalassocracy of the future. On the other hand, there was always the danger that the two vectors of development would create a tension too sharp to contain. After all, once Athens took the lead and became "a metropolis or mistress of some 250 dependent communities," Zimmern argued, the ideal of freedom was surrendered, and the spirit of unity was replaced by intensifying conflict between separate city-states. From there, the road to demise was short.[3] As Jeanne Morefield and Reba Soffer have already pointed out, Zimmern's teachings, on the verge of moralistic parables, show how the classicist-centric *Literae Humaniores* was prescribed as a guide to engage with present dilemmas and to design future visions.[4] Coupland, like many others, could detect a subtle warning hidden beneath the pathos of Zimmern's narratives—in order to survive, the British Empire needed to move in the direction of increasing levels of self-government and to transform itself into a more open and liberal "commonwealth of British nations." Crucially, in his vision, Britishness was reimagined as a hallmark of a translocal spirit of unity and a sense of common purpose, capable of tying together remote colonies and imperial possessions.

The young Coupland, who followed the traditional Oxonian *Literae Humaniores* course of training, listened carefully to Zimmern's advice. In an early letter sent to Gilbert Murray he explained with a characterizing authority that the decline of Hellenic power was an unfortunate but unavoidable outcome of "the fact that for all their internal patriotism the city-states could never combine."[5] Furthermore, among Coupland's papers we find early sketches for an unpublished work on the Greek commonwealth, providing yet another example of his early classicist appetites. Instantly, he began searching in these classicist lessons for guidelines to rulers. Thus, in May 1915, at the midst of the Gallipoli Campaign, he reached out to Winston Churchill (First Lord of the Admiralty at the time) and sent him a copy of the writings of Thucydides accompanied by Zimmern's book, which he described as "a brilliant introduction" to the subject. "Though you will not read them now," Coupland explained, "I still venture to send you the books as a feeble token of an Englishman's gratitude for your services to England."[6]

When shifting his gaze to colonial history shortly thereafter, Coupland could not but combine Zimmern's ideas with those of J. R. Seeley and Hugh Edward Egerton, the two founding fathers of Britain's colonial history. Seeley's lofty vision of "Greater Britain" was key in that respect: the oft-quoted phrase he coined, comparing Britain to an organism in the process of expansion, an "enlargement of the English State and not simply English nationality," provided an important guideline for future colonial historians who reimagined Britain and its empire as a single entity, a unity. Discarding the image of a hierarchical axis of metropole versus colony, this Seeleyian vision of unity was well suited to the age of increasing global connectivity. Empire was not understood as a centralized, asymmetrical system of control and exploitation but as a worldwide network that "carries across the seas not merely the English race, but the authority of the English Government."[7] Though less dramatic, the historical surveys produced by Egerton, Seeley's heir, were based on similar premises, purporting to unveil the hidden evolutionary processes that gave rise to that spontaneous, wide global net called the British Empire.[8] Egerton's 1911 historical survey *Federations and Unions Within the British Empire*— published not long after Zimmern published *Greek Commonwealth*— brought the Victorian discourse of imperial federalism back to life and concluded that federation was a historical necessity. "A federal form of government," Egerton explained, "is found where communities, which possess for certain purposes a distinct political existence, join together to form a common whole, without losing their separate organization."[9] Using history as a tool for prognosis, he prophesied that the future federation would emerge "organically," not from the imperial metropole, but from the colonies that would demand it. Federalism of this kind, he insisted, was the expression of a desire for union, not a desire for unity.

Much of this political language rested on preexisting late Victorian notions of liberal imperialism.[10] Yet, this liberal imperialism was further developed by men like Zimmern and Coupland: both moved beyond Atlanto-centric visions of empire and took the globe-spanning British polity or commonwealth to be a vehicle for promoting "responsible" self-government around the world, believing they could avoid making the contrast between empire and regional nationalism too sharp. As we shall see next, by the late 1920s both considered the processes of "dominionization"—the transformation of former colonies or new territories to self-governing dominions—to be the safest course of development for their imagined federated empire. They were not alone. This shared impetus led Zimmern and Coupland to accept Lionel Curtis's invitation to join the newly founded Round Table group. Curtis, it has been suggested, was eager to recruit the two precisely because of their reputations as democrats. He hoped that they would broaden the range of opinions within the group that was formed around 1910 and consisted predominantly of Oxford alumni who served under Sir Alfred (later Lord) Milner in South Africa.[11] Ultimately, this was a happy marriage: the classicist appetites, the vocabulary, and the political imagery the two brought with them into the group ultimately helped the Round Table group to develop what Max Beloff has described as its "staple doctrine"—a transition from "empire" to "commonwealth," imagined as a form of a translocal voluntary cooperation of separate colonies in matters of common concern.[12]

The Round Table group has been a subject of many solid historical studies and even a larger number of conspiracy theories. The full story of the group will not be rehearsed here. Its social makeup and the way the group expanded its outreach and language are significant, however. Initially the group consisted of about a dozen men, all of whom served under Milner, including Philip Henry Kerr (later Lord Lothian) (1882–1940, who is particularly well known thanks to his short but decisive tenure as ambassador to the United States [1939–1940]),[13] Richard Feetham (1874–1965; chairman of the Feetham Function Committee on Constitutional Reform in India [1918–1919] and of the Irish Boundary Commission [1924–1925]),[14] Geoffrey Robinson (1878–1944; later Dawson; the editor of the *Times*, 1912–1919 and 1923–1941), Patrick Duncan

(1870–1943; future governor-general of South Africa),[15] Robert Brand (1878–1963; a future prosperous banker and governmental advisor), John Dove (1872–1934; director of the Commonwealth Trust and from 1920 editor of the *Round Table* journal),[16] and Lionel Hichens (1874–1940; chairman of the board of the steel firm Cammell Laird & Company, architect of the Imperial Munitions Board of Canada, and director of the Commonwealth Trust Company). It started off as an informal fraternity, dubbed "Milner's Kindergarten" or "The Moot," which occasionally met to discuss foreign policy and imperial politics.[17] Curtis was recognized as the group's unofficial leader almost immediately. Soon after his return from South Africa, he reached the conclusion that the creation of an "Imperial unity" would best guarantee Britain's imperial defense and foreign policy alike. Intimates since their days in South Africa, Curtis and Feetham played crucial roles in the deliberations leading to the division of Ireland (1921–1922) and creation of the Dominion of Ireland (1922–1932).

Initially, Curtis and his peers imagined the empire as based on an "organic unity." Yet by the time the group became the main advocacy organ in Edwardian Britain pushing for imperial federation and imperial citizenship, new buzzwords such as "imperial federalism," "cooperation," and "self-government" gradually began to crop up in their writings. "Commonwealth," of course, was one of these buzzwords. "Dominion" was another: not colonies, but autonomous dominions—political entities running their own business, independent in almost all but name, yet loyal to the Crown and accepting its sovereignty—were to lead the way. A mechanism for governance was still lacking, Curtis and his peers knew. But once their proposed Imperial Parliament would come to life, they believed, the dominions would enjoy proportional representation and would be able to shape foreign policy.

In March 1917, Coupland became the editor of the group's influential quarterly (a position he held until June 1919 and again between December 1939 and March 1941).[18] His exemption from military service due to poor health may have left him in an inferior position vis-à-vis the older founders of the group, who had seen battle in Africa, but it also allowed him to retain his academic job. His letters from this immediate postwar period, brimming with patriotic spirit, laud the works of Curtis and Zimmern.[19] They epitomize Jeanne Morefield's claim regarding the two "interrelated rhetorical strategies" that the Round Table members cultivated, rechristening the empire as a liberal commonwealth (contrasted with "Prussianism") and developing a historicist reading of its origins, in a way that naturalized the empire's origins and presented it as a "special genius" that was unique to the Anglo-Saxon mode of government.[20] At the same time, Coupland also launched an ambitious research project inspired by his academic mentor Egerton and sponsored by Curtis, culminating in a manuscript titled "Canada and the British Commonwealth: An Historical Study of Self-Government and Nationality."[21] Coupland did not disguise the fact that his historical inquiry was geared toward contemporary discussions. He hoped that the American intervention in the war in Europe might signify that the "far-off schism between the colonies and mother-land" that created the great rupture of 1776 would be repaired and that the "deep-rooted" and shared "instincts of their race" would bring the British and Americans together again.[22] The same hopes found their way into his early visions for the future of the empire: his 1917 article "Freedom and Unity," for example, linked the Dominions of Canada and South Africa, which he considered success stories, happy results of the "doctrine of colonial self-government initiated by Lord Durham and his little school of Radical Imperialists," and a masterful balance of freedom and unity.[23] The Canadian achievement captivated Coupland, the same way it fascinated Egerton. Being the first Dominion, Canada became a signpost, a positive precedent. Coupland was particularly fond of quoting Durham's description of Canada as "two nations warring within the bosom of a single state."[24] Famously, he would later paraphrase Durham's phrase in his report on Palestine.

A direct line can be drawn between the Round Table group and the deliberations leading up to the Anglo-Irish Treaty of 1921. Serving as Lloyd George's main Irish advisor, Curtis followed avidly the low-level guerilla war that began in pockets across the country after the brutal crash of the Easter Rising of 1916, and the increasing appeal of republican slogans for large swaths of the population. His appointment as second secretary (and in effect constitutional advisor) to the British delegation at the Anglo-Irish treaty talks during October–December 1921 put Curtis in a position to promote the idea of partition. As advisor to the colonial secretary on Irish affairs until October 1924 and a close friend of Round Table member Richard Feetham, who was appointed chairman of the Boundary Commission, Curtis oversaw much of its implementation.[25] He quickly concluded that the Anglo-Irish conflict would be solved by declaring Ireland "independent" de facto, without allowing it to divorce itself from the empire in toto. Renaming the south a free state, not a republic, was crucial, for "republic" remained a political arrangement incompatible with constitutional monarchy and the unyielding demand that imperial affinity be maintained by oaths of allegiance to the Crown. The belief that jumpstarting a devolution process and granting the new state the fullest measure of dominion self-government would solve the problem was founded on naïve assumptions. In fact, it was one of Curtis's attempts to have the cake and eat it too.

The separation between the north and south, in other words, was premised not only on the idea that it could offer a durable settlement that would satisfy both Irish nationalists and Unionists, but also on the idea that Irish nationalism could be "contained." As David Harkness has observed, this was a political scheme that rested on the unverifiable assumption that the Irish, like all other dominions, would be prepared to "settle for something less than independence: to deny themselves the sovereign right to unfettered individual decision in foreign affairs, in the pursuit of an alternative form of common security, based upon common policymaking."[26] The contemporary jargon of "conflict resolution" by which we describe partitions misses that crucial dimension. It also overlooks the overtly optimistic, evolutionary imagination of Curtis and his peers, who believed that he deciphered the code that would allow one to reconfigure intraimperial relations without introducing radically new concepts but rather by following the Canadian model, and, of course, the South African example. The "solution," in other words, was concealed in the past chronicles of the empire, and the prognosis could be derived from there.

Nor should we confuse politics with cartography. Partition was never simply about mapmaking. On the contrary, the Irish precedent is intriguing not only in that partition was imagined as a federalist political formula, but also because of the considerable chronological gap between the negotiations leading to the acceptance of the political formula and the act of drawing lines on maps to establish a physical international border. In fact, in Ireland, the maps had to wait for four years, until the Boundary Commission finally completed its mission of carving out the new borders in 1925. The dynamic was therefore based on two steps: partition first had to be endorsed as a principle, with decisions about geographical demarcations coming only later. The very same dynamic—accepting the idea first and referring to maps on which boundaries would be sketched later—would reappear in later partitions and establish itself as a pattern in both the Middle Eastern and South Asian contexts.

Coupland followed the Irish developments closely. Up to the summer of 1921, that is, until an Irish Free State was already a fait accompli, Coupland continued supporting those who advocated "Home Rule All Round," the code name given to the federation of the four nationalities of the British Isles, as a solution to the Irish Question.[27] Like his mentor, his support of the Unionist cause was couched in the language of federation and dominionization, not separation. He considered Sinn Féin separatists, who demanded sovereign independence, to be unimaginative sectarians who failed to understand that dominions enjoy the full freedom to "develop and control their national life." The fact that they would remain connected to Britain is an asset, he wrote, not a liability:

> An independent Ireland could enjoy no real freedom in its foreign relations without the protection of the British or some other fleet: nor could it justify its independence by rendering through it any better service to humanity. Its weakness would endanger the security of Great Britain and the whole Commonwealth: and it would directly injure the cause of peace and freedom throughout the world by thus impairing the strength of the strongest Power that defends it. It might be said, in fact, that Sinn Fein is fighting not so much for freedom as against unity; and if *Myself alone* is not the noblest watchword for an individual, *Ourselves alone* is little better for a nation.[28]

As already mentioned, the notion of a federalist reorganization of the United Kingdom was not a new one. When it was first proposed in the mid-1880s by Joseph Chamberlain, it was swiftly rejected. It resurfaced in 1918, with the breakdown in negotiations over Home Rule. With respect to the attraction it held for Coupland and the Round Table group, the writings of Frederick Scott Oliver (1864–1934) also played a role in the run-up to partition.[29] Though he joined the Round Table group at a very early stage and was an influential figure, this hard-nosed Scottish businessman is a somewhat neglected figure. It was Oliver, however, who subscribed to the Chamberlain Unionist precepts making federalism—or "Home Rule All Round"—the counterweight to Gladstone's first Home Rule Bill—and the one to connect this conversation with the federalist vision.[30] The highly popular biography of Alexander Hamilton published by Oliver in 1907 is a key text in that respect: it attempted to recover the extraordinary historical process by which a feeble federalist theory succeeded in bringing into fruition the "organic unity" that was so dear to Curtis.[31] Once again, federalism, not a strong centralized empire, was to him the antidote to separatism: a loose federation was more likely to turn into "a nation or an empire," he held, because "the instinct of civilization, seeking security and justice, is towards co-operation."[32]

Evidence suggests that Coupland, who was fascinated by the US federal arrangements as soon as 1916, endorsed Oliver's views on this matter.[33] Coupland's last, posthumously published, book, *Welsh and Scottish Nationalism* (1954), written long after the stormy events of 1920–1921 had passed into distant memory, praised Oliver for his clear-headed advocacy of a federal settlement for Ireland and portrayed him as the voice of nonpartisan, sober reason.[34] Coupland's 1921 inaugural lecture as Beit Professor drew heavily on Curtis's ideas and prophetic language. The Great War, he insisted, only revealed the extent to which "human society . . . has become so close-knit, so complex an organism"—a fact that escaped the separatist nationalists, who followed an outdated, "shallow nineteenth-century doctrine," a form of "jealous 'particularism'" that threatens a global drift into "race-schism."[35] In the stormy events of the 1920s in Ireland, he saw a deplorable separatist movement, accentuating minute, insignificant differences to distinguish itself from the culturally dominant group. Falling back on a paternalistic and haughty British view of the Irish, he returned to the subject in 1935: how sad it was to realize that the Irish—unlike the Welsh and the Scots—were not "responsible" enough, inflamed much too easily by "Continental" ideas. They failed to grasp the benefits that would accrue to them from cooperation between different nations. Ultimately, they substituted the intranational with the international, rejecting integration, and tarnished the noble dream of creating a democratic "super-national state."[36]

## PALESTINE: PARTITION AS A PACKAGE DEAL

It was in the summer of 1936—around the same time George Orwell published his anticolonial short story "Shooting an Elephant"—that Coupland was appointed a member of Lord Peel's Royal Commission of Inquiry, which was sent to Palestine to investigate the underlying causes of the anti-British rebellion that had broken out a few months earlier. The commission published its report only a year later, in July 1937, suggesting that territorial partition into two separate sovereign states would be the best long-term solution to the Palestine problem. Many have detected Coupland's fingerprints on the commission's report. Its resounding rhetoric and extensive historical exegesis have long prompted scholars and journalists alike to speculate that it was the Oxford professor who penned the political paradigm of partition. The suspicion was confirmed thanks to Penny Sinanoglou's meticulous research, which demonstrated definitively that Coupland was the main driving force behind the 1937 Palestine partition plan.[37] Nonetheless, as we shall see shortly, this does not mean that Coupland was acting alone. More than a sole originator, Coupland introduced partition in response to suggestions and ideas he was exposed to through his British contacts as well as his contacts with local actors and leaders.

Scholarship has seen the application of territorial partition in Ireland as a model of sorts for Palestine and, later on, for India. This is true to some extent. Yet, Ireland failed as a viable precedent in at least three senses. First, although the Anglo-Irish Treaty of 1921 granted dominion status for the twenty-six counties of the new Free Irish State, the colonial administrators in Palestine were reluctant to apply such a formula to the Yishuv (the Jewish population in preindependence Palestine) or to the local Arab population, formally admitting them into the Commonwealth. Second, constrained by the League of Nations in Geneva and by the mandate covenant, in Palestine the British had a far more limited space in which to maneuver. For this reason, Coupland resorted to impressive interpretive acrobatics to redefine the term "mandate" in a way that would better fit his vision. Third, and more significantly, the Palestine partition was never about geographical divisions alone; it was a package deal, which included, alongside the idea of territorial division, the notion and vocabulary of population transfer. In this respect, the partitions of Palestine and India, unlike the Irish one, were fundamentally post-Lausanne partitions.

Along with the redrawing of Europe's political map and the introduction of a new language of national self-determination, the post–World War I settlement also released a deluge that Matthew Frank has called "fantasies of ethnic unmixing."[38] Perceiving the intermingling of ethnonational groups as a dangerous source of friction, the notion of population transfer—that is, forced displacement of mass populations—came to be seen not only as a legitimate "vaccine," but also as a "progressive" solution for the crises taking place in Europe's postdynastic backyard. These theories, Frank shows, can be traced to the 1860s, but a new and crucial feature was added to them in the early interwar years: the compulsory resettlement of national minorities would be organized and regulated by international treaties. From a British vantage point, the 1923 Greco-Turkish exchange of populations was an important precedent. The young Arnold J. Toynbee, who was affiliated with the Round Table at this stage of his career and who had befriended its key figures, witnessed it firsthand. For him, the realization that the non-European Greece (embodying the "Near East") and Turkey (the "Middle East") were homogenizing themselves, curiously enough, under the auspices and with the blessing of the new internationalist regime indicated that "inoculation of the East with [Western] nationalism" set the stage for a new type of clash of civilizations.[39] He was deeply disturbed that the war had made Britain a Middle Eastern power; this marked, in his view, a decisive shift in the policy of the British Commonwealth, which was "strategically a combination of islands, varying in size from fortresses to continents and scattered all over the world, but all capable of adequate defence by sea power," as he wrote in an essay he published in the *Round Table* quarterly. The essay ended on a pessimistic note, with Toynbee prophesying an approaching apocalypse: "whatever decision we [the British Commonwealth] take, let us take it with open eyes, for we are possibly approaching either our greatest political achievement or a catastrophic conflict between the British Commonwealth and the Oriental world."[40]

Coupland's view of the interwar predicament was more hopeful. Although as early as 1917 he suspected that Turkey would turn increasingly irredentist and hostile toward its minorities, its problem was not that it was an "Eastern" power absorbing uncritically alien "Western ideas" but that the nation-building project it had decided to undertake was outdated.[41] Besides, this shift toward inflamed chauvinism that requires the removal of "demographic misfits" was the exception, not the rule. The war, Coupland argued in his inaugural lecture, had demonstrated the degree to which interconnectedness became the distinguishing feature of the world today, that "human society . . . has become so close-knit, so complex an organism." This was yet another fact that escaped the separatist nationalists, who were nothing but followers of an outdated "shallow nineteenth-century doctrine," subscribing to a form of "jealous 'particularism'" that threatens drifting the world into "race-schism."[42] In a different lecture delivered to an Indian audience in 1924 (in memory of a certain Captain Charles Russell, who was killed in action in the battle of Nebi Samwil in Palestine in November 1917), Coupland went on to explain, in a somewhat suspicious Hegelian terms, that "Time-Spirit is against the feud [called nationalism]. It will steadily become more and more of an anachronism. Before our generation passes, I believe it will be dead."[43] Since he held to his stance that a true Commonwealth—unlike the excessive linguistic nationalism—transcended ethno-racial differences, he further amplified his earlier proclamations that global peace could not be maintained without a strong British Commonwealth masterfully balancing centrifugal and centripetal forces, providing a counterweight to balkanization.

It was not enough to fall back on old slogans, however. Under such bleak circumstances, it was vital to transform federation, a speculative framework before the war, into a matter of practical politics. Promoting a different theoretical apparatus, Coupland coupled two key concepts—

"trusteeship" and "mandate"—and reconceptualized them. Trusteeship, unlike mandate, was a concept with a long pedigree. Carrying heavy Edmund Burkean echoes, it was based on the paternalist notion that morally and practically sound political representation posited representatives who follow their own understanding of the best action to pursue.[44] Subsequently, trusteeship was understood as an unwritten law granting to a superior civilization (measured by political organization, economy, technological might, and Protestant belief) the right to manage less-advanced societies, yet without ever claiming sovereignty. Trusteeship was about the rule of law, making the trustee accountable for its acts. Yet, as Peter Lyon has put it, the trusteeship had nothing to do with whether or not "the recipients of this rule had ever requested such stewardship."[45] As a form of political discourse, trusteeship had been advanced and perfected, as Kevin Grant showed, during the last decades of the nineteenth century, when the discovery of coercive systems of labor taxation and indentured servitude in the colonies prompted a series of British humanitarian campaigns against "new slavery."[46] Armed with a strong sense of moral calling, the new abolitionists absorbed the idea that in their struggle they helped bring local people to a degree of "maturity" and "responsibility." The resulting trusteeship was a fusion of evangelical and philanthropic discourse.

The interwar reconceptualization of trusteeship, however, took a slightly different tack, especially once the concept had been associated with the new principle of mandate rule. Coupland downplayed the novelty of these international standards. The mandate, he argued, was nothing but a new name given to a "principle . . . as old as the days of Burke and Wilberforce":

> For the principle of the Mandate is simply the doctrine of trusteeship—the doctrine that implies (1) that a native territory must not be regarded as the private estate of its European rulers; that the economic development of it is undertaken for the benefit of the world at large; and therefore that the subjects of other States shall be as free to share in its development and trade as the subjects of the ruling State—i.e. the principle of the Open Door: (2) that the natives, on their part, must not be regarded as so much labour-power for

their rulers' plantations, nor as so much "cannon-fodder" for their armies, nor as so many clients for their liquor-trade; but in spirit, if not yet in political capacities and duties, their fellow-citizens, as free as they themselves to traffic in their property or labour; and (3) that not only should their moral and material interests be upheld against all other interests that conflict with them, but positive efforts should be made to raise them by wise education and in other ways to a higher and wider life. And since on all these heads, with one or two exceptions, with hesitations and backslidings here and there, British ministers and British officials have observed the doctrine, Britain can claim to have been a Mandatory State for many years past.[47]

In September 1934, he returned to the parallel in a *Round Table* essay, "The Future of Colonial Trusteeship," arguing that before our eyes "a new colonial doctrine seems to be taking shape, a doctrine that tends to regard colonial territories less as a class in themselves, and more as an integral part of the Empire, and to identify their interests more closely with those of the Empire as a whole. It suggests that their new path of progress lies in imperial co-operation."[48]

Coupland was not alone in perceiving Article 22 of the Covenant of the League of Nations—an article considered by its architects as a "special regime" for Palestine and the internalization of the German colonies—as a Burkean fruit. Most significantly, British mandatory officials, who were supposed to promote "self-government," postponed indefinitely the creation of representative institutions in Palestine. One of the reasons for doing so, as Sir Herbert Samuel, the first high commissioner, explained to the Permanent Mandates Commission in 1924, was the fear that if the Arabs had a majority, they would use it to oppose the establishment of a Jewish national home, and therefore a postponement was necessary to prevent giving them "an opportunity of acting in a way that was hostile to this requirement of the mandate."[49]

Yet, what remains unclear is the degree to which Coupland was aware of the mishandling of affairs in Palestine and the growing tensions on the ground before the summer of 1936, when he was sent to Palestine as an official representative. It was not only because Palestine remained a rather peripheral issue as far as the *Round Table* journal was concerned.[50]

The violent events commonly referred to today as the Arab Rebellion or Arab Revolt were not understood immediately as constituting a shift in the eyes of many mandatory officials. The British still dubbed them "disturbances"—that is, short of a full-fledged nationalist awakening, more akin to yet another episode of "sectarian violence" or "intercommunal friction."[51] This self-comforting language suggested that such events could be managed and calmed, if approached prudently. For a diehard imperialist like Coupland, it meant that the violent atmosphere could be rationalized as birth pangs of a stronger union. Furthermore, given the fact that Coupland was observing the developments in Palestine at this time from his Oxford vantage point, he had good reasons to believe that the spirit of union would prevail. The activities of the now almost entirely forgotten Seventh Dominion League, founded in 1927 and calling openly to transform Palestine into a Dominion of the British Commonwealth of Nations, provided one positive indication. How apt that the presiding spirit behind the movement—Colonel Josiah C. Wedgwood (1872–1943)—was the great-great-grandson of the famous potter who supported Wilberforce's abolitionist campaign that had inspired Coupland the historian.[52] Surely the fact that Wedgwood's proposal was advanced by non-Jewish supporters of Zionism (including, it seems, Robert Cecil and Philip Kerr) and leading Zionists alike was a source of encouragement. A few months later, in May 1928, Robert Cecil became president of the Palestine Mandate Society, a new organization set up by non-Jewish supporters of Zionism to foster stronger relations between the Zionist movement and the empire.[53] All this seemed to be indicating a consistent line of development: from the 1917 Balfour Declaration, calling for the establishment of a Jewish national home, to the "Balfour formula," presented at the Imperial Conference of 1926, defining all Dominions as "autonomous Communities within the British Empire, wholly equal in status and united by a common allegiance to the Crown, freely associated as members of the British Commonwealth of Nations."[54] For Coupland, these plans pointed explicitly toward a supranational imperial federation.

On the eve of his Palestine mission, then, Coupland was an archimperialist, vehemently opposed to the idea that nationhood is to be defined solely by independent nation-states. Such views account for why his younger All Souls colleague Isaiah Berlin, a Zionist sympathizer, panicked upon learning that his colleague had been appointed a member of the Palestine Royal Commission. Berlin was quick to warn his relatives in Jerusalem that this "very suave, smooth, silver-tongued . . . imperialist," a "professional compromiser" who was probably also an anti-Semite, was destined to be hideously critical of Zionism.[55] Yet, it was none other than Coupland himself who eventually recommended the division of Palestine into two sovereign states, a Jewish one and an Arab one (with a corridor to the sea at Jaffa, and Nazareth remaining under the British Mandate).

How this shift came about remains a riddle. Penny Sinanoglou and Motti Golani, for their part, have demonstrated two important points: first, that earlier proposals for local autonomy and cantonization, modeled after Switzerland and other places, had already introduced the idea that a territorial division would resolve the Palestine impasse; thus, a partition of some sort was on everyone's mind *before* Coupland and his colleagues arrived in Jerusalem. In this light, the 1937 Peel Commission report "gave a concrete and consequential shape to ideas that had been developing in diffuse form and debated in the Palestine administration for years before the outbreak of the 1936 Arab revolt."[56] Second, Coupland's unfamiliarity with Palestine and the exceptionally wide terms in which the mission of the commission was defined inclined him to be open to ideas from different sources.[57] Thus, during the short but decisive period Coupland stayed in Palestine (November 1936–January 1937), a close dialogue was forged between him and representatives of the Jewish Agency, Chaim Weizmann the most senior among them. Hence, we need to rethink previous narratives that have presented partition as Coupland's brainchild, later to be "launched" to Weizmann. As Golani argues, in all likelihood, the idea was launched in the opposite direction.[58]

The compound conceptual and practical connection between the canonization proposals and the partition plan reveals an interesting dialectic, parallel to the conceptual tension animating the federalist imagination of the Round Tablers. Before Coupland entered the room, it was L. G. Archer Cust, the assistant district commissioner in Nazareth, who played the central role in the story. The long memorandum on cantonization he prepared for the Colonial Office on January 18, 1935, spoke specifically of a "delimitation of Arab and Jewish areas" in order to create "autonomous administrations [enjoying] as much legislative and executive authority as possible." These, he explained, would "replace the direct government by Mandatory [forces] by a supervision and inspectorial system."[59] Not making a single reference to independent sovereign states, Cust's proposal fitted perfectly the federalist schema of colonial dominance. Importantly, in addition to the drawing of new demarcation lines, Cust also proposed the "abolition of the unnatural and unnecessary Jordan frontier" in order to link up the Arab regions west and east of the Jordan River. The erasure of the borderline established between Palestine and Transjordan by the British had significant demographic implications: even if substantial Jewish immigration were to be permitted into Palestine, Jews would still remain a minority in the new federal entity that would emerge. The Zionists sent angry letters to the editor of the *London Times* in response, condemning Cust, debating whether the proposal violated the principle of the mandate. It was only a matter of time until the Zionists would come up with an alternative proposal.[60] British colonial authorities not only expected such a counterproposal to land on their desks but practically commissioned it: on June 29, 1936, Assistant Under-Secretary of State Sir (Arthur Charles) Cosmo Parkinson (1884–1967) wrote in a minute submitted to Colonial Secretary William Ormsby-Gore that although the cantonization proposals "may ultimately form a basis of a solution of our difficulties . . . it would be a big advantage if Dr. Weizmann were to spontaneously and of his own accord make some suggestion on these lines, for I think the proposal would lose some of its force, and possibly effect if he were in a position to say that the original suggestion came from either the High Commissioner or the Colonial Office."[61]

Unsurprisingly, cantonization plans surfaced time and again during the sittings of the commission. When giving their testimonies, J. C. Wedgwood and Vladimir (Ze'ev) Jabotinsky voiced their objections to cantonization, with Jabotinsky "prepared to advise the Jews, who would eventually be in the majority in Palestine, to sit down at a round-table conference—a happy family of three, the Jews, the Arabs, and the English adviser."[62] From these deliberations, we see that the idea of division of some kind was already in the air when Coupland arrived in Palestine, but also that partition was the result of a complex pull-push dynamic in which "outsider" colonial administrators and "insider" actors negotiated different deals. Such dialogue was made possible by the hesitance of the very colonial rule that is often considered efficient, potent, and confident. But the commission's meetings also exposed the degree to which the Palestine triangle of Jews, Arabs, and British was not equilateral. The Arab representatives never enjoyed the degree of access to and respect from the British authorities enjoyed by the Jewish Agency, and the Arab decision to boycott the committee only increased the asymmetry. Equally clear was the fact that the idea to divide Palestine was not a simple "colonialist invention" violently imposed upon the inhabitants of the land in a top-down manner. The Palestine partition plan was the result of extended deliberations between outsiders and insiders, and the report's insistence that the two postpartition sovereign states would be linked to Great Britain by a treaty system discloses a very different sentiment than that which we find in India and ultimately also in Palestine itself a decade later, in 1947.

The proposal was not received enthusiastically. In the protracted and provocative public hearing that ensued, Coupland took upon himself the role of being the preeminent British advocate in defense of partition. It turned out to be a lonely crusade. The problem was not only that the Arabs and the Jews were upset and that the Foreign Office officials were baffled; even Coupland's peers and colleagues at the Round Table remained unconvinced. "The [Peel Commission] report is a great state paper which is full of character," wrote Toynbee in the *Round Table*, outstanding in "its extreme intellectual ability" and "moral courage in facing facts." Nonetheless, it had done too little too late. No matter how the "surgical operation" would be performed, a considerable Arab minority would remain trapped within the Jewish state. Unlike in Central Europe, there would be no Saar, Polish Corridor, Danzigs, and Memels in "a country the size of Wales"; and besides, granting full national independence to the two clashing communities would not remedy the situation but set the stage for international wars. The very term "partition" chosen by the committee, he argued, is a misnomer, "for the word 'partition' implies the destruction of some historic or natural unity." Palestine was

nothing but a label given to the territory that was placed in the peace settlement under a British mandate, with artificial frontiers that "represent
neither natural geographical boundaries nor historic political divisions."
That "natural" space as far as the Arab is concerned, Toynbee argued, was
the entire Dar-al-Islam, or the entire Fertile Crescent. What is needed
instead, Toynbee concluded, is a "more ambitious piece of political architecture" that would solve the problems of the entire Middle East, not
Palestine alone.[63]

Toynbee's critique was a powerful one. Echoing old Round Table fantasies of large-scale, supranational unities, it was shaped by the original
sweeping spatio-historical vision he perfected after 1923. From his perspective, the violent act of cutting into the flesh, the partition of a "natural" space, was not a future shock but a past one: it had occurred when
the European colonial powers had cleaved the territories of the Ottoman
Empire. The primal partition, if one wishes to subscribe to Toynbee's vision, happened in 1916, when Mark Sykes and François Georges-Picot
drew lines between French and English spheres of influence and control
in the Middle East. That is an outlook that Coupland could not endorse.

Coupland, unlike his critics, was less concerned with the practicality
of the borders proposed by the Peel Commission and more concerned
with whether a successful partition would require population transfer.
Both questions were mishandled, he argued, because critics ignored the
important proviso that was included in the report, which stipulated that
these issues would be addressed later as part of a proposed future agreement between Arab and Jewish leaders.[64] There were two leitmotifs to
Coupland's post-1937 campaign to resuscitate the partition plan: first
was his insistence that partition, unlike cantonization or the formation
of a pan-Syrian federation, had the potential to resolve a demographically *unbalanced* condition;[65] next was his firm conviction that the nascent Arab nationalism was not yet capable of generating responsible
self-government.

Clearly, the Central European model, based on minority treaties, was
out of the question in his view. But federalism was still very much relevant: in May 1939, four days after the British government issued its
White Paper on Palestine, which restricted Jewish immigration into

Palestine and promised to set up an independent Palestinian state within a decade, Coupland, along with the other remaining members of the Palestine commission, published a lengthy letter in the *Times* defending the recommendations of the 1937 report yet without rejecting altogether an alternative "federal treatment" of the issue.[66] The next time the issue resurfaced, with the Morrison-Grady Plan and the Anglo-American Committee of Inquiry report of 1946, the federal alternative was muted. Criticizing the Anglo-American report, Coupland tried to reintroduce the notion of trusteeship and to couple it with a standard liberal imperialist argument—that fair political representation has little to do with the arithmetic of counting votes:

> But is it not a mistake to regard [the term] "domination" as only a matter of numbers? One educated, forcible, westernized Jew is more than a match for one ignorant, old-fashioned Arab peasant; and Arab nationalists, less extremist than the Mufti, would have agreed with him when he told the Peel Commission that Palestine could not digest the number of Jews already there. Long, indeed, before the Jews were actually more numerous the Arabs would feel—and in fact would be—dominated whatever the constitutional balance might be. Meanwhile both Arabs and Jews would be subjected to "a long period of trusteeship" while Arab standards of life were gradually being leveled up to Jewish [standards]. . . . The trusteeship is to last till Arab-Jewish antagonism has disappeared and the independence of a harmonious bi-national State has thereby been made possible. But is such a happy outcome probable? The Peel Commission were convinced that it was not, and they did their best to combat the evasive, comforting belief in the possibility of Arab-Jewish reconciliation in an undivided Palestine because they regarded it as the greatest and most persistent obstacle to a real and durable settlement. . . . Ten years ago, the writer [Coupland] had a lively talk with a passionate anti-Jewish Arab patriot in Palestine. "Tear us apart," he said, "and then we may learn in time to come together again."[67]

Edmund Burke was revived, now resettled in Palestine. Partition, a novel idea, was now paired with older notions of tutelage for self-government. Perhaps partition and federal union were not inimical concepts after all. At the end of the day, Coupland justified partition as a form of federalist eschatology: the End of Times would witness the re-unification of the Jew and the Arab, who would outgrow their tribal idio-syncrasies and join the Commonwealth of Nations.

## THE END OF THE RAJ: "UNITARIANISM HAD BEEN
MET BY SEPARATION"

On November 30, 1941, Coupland arrived in Karachi to gather informa-tion for a special report on India's constitutional problem that he had promised to prepare for Nuffield College. By March 1942, he visited eight of the eleven provinces of the British Raj, keeping a daily diary.[68] He was poised to return home to England when the Cripps Mission was announced, and Leo Amery asked Lord Linlithgow, India's longest serv-ing viceroy, to persuade Coupland to stay on with the young and ambi-tious politician. In this way, Coupland became an observer-participant in the last British effort to keep the Raj intact within an imperial system.

This was not Coupland's first visit to India. He had gone to the coun-try for the first time in 1924 as a member of the Lee Commission, sent to investigate a possible reform of the Indian civil service, and he had been fascinated by the subcontinent ever since. If in 1924 he found himself advocating the transfer of more responsibilities from the civil service to the all-Indian provincial services, by 1931 he explicitly discussed India's future as "Dominion in our commonwealth of nations, linking East and West together in the service of mankind." In a letter sent to the *London Times*, he defended this idea and criticized Winston Churchill, who in-sisted that Dominion status should remain a "vague, remote, and largely ceremonial aspiration," not a concrete plan of action in the Indian's grasp.[69]

During Coupland's 1941 visit, however, a completely different atmo-sphere prevailed. Shortly after the outbreak of the Second World War, the Indian National Congress declared that "Indian freedom cannot exist within the orbit of imperialism, and Dominion status or any other status within the imperial structure is wholly inapplicable to India," in what was seen as an exploitation of Britain's weakness and need for support from its Dominions and colonies during the war.[70] Things went from bad to worse during the first months of 1942, when the British lost Malaya and

Singapore to the Japanese, and imminent attacks on India, Ceylon, and Australia were anticipated. Coupland was deeply disappointed when a speech he gave to a group of professors and students in Calcutta in January 1942 was met with severe criticism, including an accusation that he was nothing but "a propagandist . . . posing as a socialist." When Gandhi informed him that "Hitler was not so bad as he was painted and that an Allied victory would not make a better world," his angst increased.[71] Muhammad Ali Jinnah, who had little patience for Coupland's predictions that the war would ultimately lead to political integration, interrupted his discourse with the exclamation, "Oh, you dreamer!"[72] As the failure of the Cripps Mission demonstrated, Dominion status for India was no longer considered an attractive consolation prize, even with the British promise of permission to secede from the Commonwealth later on. By that stage, partition was already on everyone's mind.

Coupland's South Asian writings make it clear: although he had helped to engineer the Palestine partition, Coupland categorically dismissed the idea of partition in India. The dense intermingling of Hindus and Muslims, he insisted, made the idea impractical, if not completely senseless. Economically, it would be harmful, deepening the subcontinent's endemic poverty. Above all, it would make India into a symbol of Britain's failure, setting Britain up as responsible for division. He insisted instead that unity, which had been Britain's greatest gift to India, should provide a horizon for the future and that such a unity could be preserved through a federal compromise, despite national strife. Citing other examples—Canada, Switzerland, England, Scotland, and the Soviet Union—Coupland advocated "the loosest possible federation," with minimal power allotted to the center, whose spheres of responsibility would include foreign policy, defense, and some financial issues only.[73] Neither Nehru nor Gandhi was impressed. The detailed account of the Cripps Mission that Coupland published in 1942 reflected his anxieties and anti-Congress stance. Manifestly, the mistrust was mutual.

As far as structure is concerned, the three thick volumes of the Nuffield College report—beginning with a survey of the history of India, moving to the present political impasse, and concluding with recommendations for the future—paralleled the organization of the Peel Commission report. The massive study afforded Coupland ample space to air his frustrations. Partitioning the Punjab, he insisted, made no sense. With no natural barriers or boundaries, any line that would be drawn on the map will require "cut[ting] in two the system of canals on which the productive capacity of the whole area largely depends." It would not achieve a desired "balance" but create a Muslim state that most likely would be militarily weak and economically poor, satisfying neither Muslims nor Hindus. Far worse, it would inevitably create a new problem for the Sikhs, the third group in the province, who were ready to fight to avoid the prospect of becoming a minority in an independent Muslim state. Thus, partition would probably end up fueling future struggle, Coupland anticipated, since "the Sikhs would insist on their own right of self-determination."[74]

A large-scale transfer of the population, he argued, was also impractical:

> If frontiers can be shifted, so, with more or less hardship, can people. The compulsory exchange of Greek and Turkish populations in 1923–4 under the auspices of the League of Nations has often been cited as an example of a method of dealing with a minority problem which, harsh as it is for the existing generation, offers a better prospect than any other method of peace and happiness in the future. . . . But it must not be supposed that the minority-problem in India could be eased by this method to anything like the same extent as it might be eased in small European countries. But a separation so complete is quite impossible. Numbers and distance alike forbid it. Mass-transfer would involve not hundreds of thousands but millions or tens of millions, and in many cases it would mean an unbearable change of climate and of all the ways of life which climate has dictated. Nor would it bring about in India, as it would in the Balkans, the union of homogeneous folk. The transferred multitudes would find themselves among people of a different stock, speaking a language they could not understand.[75]

The suggestion that partition would be a solution to the Indian deadlock was considered but rejected. The three books, like the 1945 sequel *India: A Re-Statement*, revealed once again an optimistic if not complaisant Coupland, willfully ignoring the fact that the Congress had already launched the "Quit India" movement, falling back instead on the old idea that unity would prevail. The books demonstrated how diligent and scrupulous was Coupland the scholar; they also demonstrated how stubborn and out of tune was Coupland the Round Tabler: the diehard unity-through-constitution believer was repeating old mantras, refusing to respond to the radical escalations of crude nationalism happening before his eyes and failing to recognize the depth of Hindu-Muslim hostility.[76] Producing erudite disquisitions, he remained blind to the ways in which British administrators had earlier instigated this hysterical animosity, internalized by the local actors who could no longer consider seriously any federal proposal, even a fairly reasonable one.[77] Federalism was restarted, but the partition model was not replicated.

## CODA: "TEAR US APART, AND THEN WE MAY LEARN IN TIME TO COME TOGETHER AGAIN"

It is both striking and troubling to note, as historian Margaret O'Callaghan has observed, that "the impulse to partition seems not to have been restrained by its apparent failure to address the divisions that were allegedly its *raison d'être*." More than lines drawn on maps, partition is first and foremost the brainchild of intellectuals begging for a Gramscian intervention: only by tackling its epistemology, definition, and conceptualization can we hope to grasp its function and its abiding appeal. That is, we are called upon to reconstruct how academically trained "cohorts of governance in various imperial locations," as O'Callaghan has called them, relied on commonly held assumptions, employed tropes and preexisting theories, and invented new vocabularies and modes of representation to describe, analyze, and subsequently "solve" the problem of "warring factions."[78]

How did Coupland's story end? In June 1945, shortly after publishing his India sequel, Coupland was invited to deliver the Ludwig Mond Lecture at Manchester University. In the talk, titled "Nationalism in the British Commonwealth" and chaired by Lewis B. Namier, his old Oxford classmate, Coupland offered a trenchant transnational and transhistorical analysis of the centripetal and centrifugal powers of separateness and unity that shaped colonial history and contemporaneous politics. He began with the unification of Great Britain—"once a little Balkans"—

praising the people of Wales and Scotland who were "far too level-headed to contemplate a Welsh or Scottish 'Pakistan.'" Next, he compared the Irish problem to the French–Canadian one, praising the latter for overcoming animosity by a wise and liberal settlement. He moved on to juxtapose Palestine and India, explaining that Jews could not be surrendered to the rule of an avowedly hostile Arab majority and that Muslims "have met the logic of democracy with the logic of nationalism." He ended on an optimistic note, rejecting the view of J. S. Mill that "free institutions are next to impossible in a country made up of different nationalities," an important reminder that "there are cases where simple majority rule is not itself sufficient."[79] It was an impressive summary of a liberal imperialist philosophy perfected over a life's journey. Two years later, the partition of India and Pakistan took place *despite* his recommendations, not because of them.

Usually discussed in the context of post–World War II decolonization, partition ought to be resituated in its interwar context and reassessed as a theory that was developed as part of a new intraimperial political strategy. Partition politics were the obverse of the "unity-through-dominionization" model that men like Coupland developed and promoted. Coupland's case reveals also the extent to which this model was anchored in a very British kind of historical self-understanding. When partition is restored to its early, interwar context, it becomes easier to appreciate it as one technique in an arsenal developed to counter—and not to surrender to—nationalist separatism. Our genealogy thus confirms Brendan O'Leary's categorical imperative that partition is to be distinguished conceptually from secessionism.[80]

Let us also bear in mind that Coupland never perceived the British Empire as a stable, unchanging political structure but rather as an evolving organism, adapting to new conditions and conceptual climates. For that reason, his historiographical writings also merit scholarly consideration. Taken together with his political writings, they provide a singular snapshot of the nonlinear, ultimately paradoxical genealogy of British partition politics. Once restored to this context, we can see that partition was neither a new formulation of the old imperial *divide et impera* (divide and rule) technique nor a precursor of postimperial fragmentation.

Instead, it was a method of intraimperial political rearrangement based on further expansion of self-government and increasing "dominionization" on one hand and new, interwar ideas of ethnic unmixing and population exchange on the other. Put differently, partition finds its origins in both the now-forgotten imperial federalist vision of bringing to life a Third British Empire and to the interwar discourse that considered population transfer a pragmatic, liberal, and legal mechanism for overcoming ethno-national strife. In this light, the longevity of this concept of political rearrangement—outliving empire and shaping the afterlife of postcolonial states to this day—is nothing short of astonishing.

By the 1940s, this model lost its appeal. Coupland's centrality to the history of partition notwithstanding, he was, at the end of the day, more a transmitter of ideas than a single, strong-willed author of political "solutions," as it may seem initially. He was unable to force his theories upon the "natives" and the "settlers," in both the Far East and the Near East, and not even in the Irish backyard. Rather, Coupland's success stood in direct correlation to his ability to communicate and negotiate these ideas with local national leaders. Often, local actors, resisting the top-down imposition of ideas generated in London, opted not to follow his advice. At other times, at least as far as the Palestine case is concerned, these were the local actors who took it upon themselves to develop partition schemes in response to earlier proposals for local autonomy and cantonization.

The postwar years saw a dramatic shift in the meaning of partition. In the context of rapid imperial breakdown, partitions ceased to function as tools of intraimperial governance and became engines for generating independent nation-states. Ultimately, the demise of the grand dream of fashioning a Third Empire coincided with the strange death of imperial federalism as a form of national cohabitation in an increasingly antagonistic world.

## CHAPTER 3

# "THE MEAT AND THE BONES"

*Reassessing the Origins of the Partition of Mandate Palestine*

Motti Golani

IN JULY 1937, an official political body—the Government of Britain—proposed the partition of Palestine into three territories: a Jewish state, an Arab state associated with Transjordan and under its auspices, and Greater Jerusalem under British rule. The government thus adopted the recommendation of the recently submitted report of the Palestine Royal Commission of Inquiry. The principle espoused in 1937 would become the basis of the partition plan approved by the United Nations in November 1947. Ultimately, the basic elements of that plan would also become the foundation for British policy in seeking the partition of Palestine between nascent Israel and the Kingdom of Jordan in 1948. Although the 1937 plan was not implemented at the time, it has remained a bedrock precedent on the Zionist, Palestinian, British, and afterward international agendas to our own time.

As in earlier milestones—from the Uganda episode (1903–1905) through the Balfour Declaration (1917) and the MacDonald Letter (1931)—the developments of 1937 were moments of potent historical interface between British and Zionist interests. And here, too, as on the eve of the Balfour Declaration and often thereafter, it was Dr. Chaim Weizmann—the president of the World Zionist Organization (WZO) since 1920—who was the connecting link, at times in a very personal manner, between the Zionists and the British. Indeed, in large measure, he was instrumental in bringing about this convergence of ideas on both sides. Weizmann's political and diplomatic strength, both in Britain and within the Zionist movement, was dependent on his ability to maintain the Anglo-Zionist connection.

Weizmann's role in inculcating the partition idea in both the British and the Zionists was far more significant than he himself was inclined to relate. In fact, David Ben-Gurion, who frequently rewrote history, in some cases while it was still occurring, had already appropriated the partition idea by July 1937.[1]

The deliberations of the Palestine Royal Commission of Inquiry (the Peel Commission, October 1936–June 1937) were not the first occasion in which the partition idea, still more its conceptual underpinnings, had arisen. They had been mooted, in greater or lesser clarity, since the First World War and more intensively since the issuance of a series of official documents—the Shaw Report, the Hope-Simpson Report, and the White Paper of Lord Passfield, the colonial secretary—in the early 1930s, following the violence that rocked Palestine in the summer of 1929.[2]

For the Zionists, the events of 1929 ignited a debate over the feasibility of implementing the movement's policy. The cardinal questions in this regard were what constituted a "national home" and whether the aim was to achieve a Jewish majority and a state in Palestine. On the left—within moderate circles such as Brit Shalom and notably in the German Zionist movement, certainly among the non-Zionists who had recently joined the fledgling Jewish Agency, and even among some of Weizmann's sympathizers in Britain—the tendency was to forgo the demand for a majority and a state, at least publicly. Zionism, this approach held, would make do with a national home—a cultural and national center—and would not rule the Arabs. Indeed, the advocates of this approach argued that the Arabs were amenable to dialogue and that Zionism must not thrust them into a position in which their only recourse would be violence. The Zionist interest would not suffer by recognizing the Arabs' rights—on the contrary, it would gain. At the same time, the Zionist right felt vindicated by the grim events of 1929; Ze'ev Jabotinsky and his followers pressed their demand for a Jewish state on both sides of the Jordan, under British auspices.[3]

Weizmann, though, was more perturbed by those who would flank him from the left. He had no intention of abandoning the arena to an ideology that he feared would agree to forsake the essence of Zionism in order to obtain the goodwill of the Arabs. Thus, following the events of the summer of 1929 he made a first concentrated effort to engage the Arabs in a dialogue. Equally important, he sought a future political solution that, while not giving up the Mandate, would display a new understanding that the Arabs constituted a national group with its own claims, not only individuals whose rights would have to be addressed within the framework of the Jewish national home. The very recognition that it was necessary to talk to the Arabs—initially with those outside Palestine and afterward with the Palestine Arabs—would lead Weizmann to arrive at a more moderate interpretation of both the Balfour Declaration and the Mandate document.

Weizmann's two basic assumptions were powerfully illuminated in the wake of the crisis of the late 1920s in Palestine. Nor did he deviate from them afterward. The first involved taking action along binational lines. "Now we should be content with [a] bi-national State, provided it was truly bi-national," Weizmann wrote in January 1930 to James Marshall, his non-Zionist American colleague in the Jewish Agency. The "parity" idea, as it was known, was adduced from the beginning of the 1930s. However, in Weizmann's view, parity did not necessarily entail a binational state; it meant recognition that any future political solution would be based on the existence of two national groups.[4]

The second key assumption was a principle to which Weizmann would return repeatedly, and in a more complex fashion later: "it is absolutely essential . . . to make it perfectly clear to the Arabs that we do not want to dominate them, and we do not want to drive them out of their country. We recognize that it is their country as much as it is or will be ours, and that we can live in Palestine with them." He articulated this approach publicly, as WZO president, in a talk to the Central Asian Society, in London, as early as November 1929.[5] This line of thought could have been a basis for various follow-up ideas, including that of "two states for two nations"—that is, partition.

The wellsprings of this new perception lay less in the events in Palestine than in developments in London and within Weizmann himself, in the light of the perilous situation of his political career. The report of the British Commission of Inquiry that investigated the violence of 1929 in Palestine (the Shaw Commission), the subsequent expert's report (Hope-Simpson), and the dramatic shift in Britain's Palestine policy in October 1930, upon the publication of the Passfield White Paper, came as a severe jolt to Weizmann.[6] Very briefly: In late 1930, the British government turned its back on the Mandate idea as underpinned by the Balfour Declaration. The effect was to topple the central pillar of Weizmann's policy in the 1920s. In Weizmann's perception, the crumbling of the mainstay of his political might—the alliance with Britain revolving around the Mandate in the spirit of the Balfour Declaration—threatened the entire Zionist enterprise as well as his status as president of the WZO. This potential debacle set him on a search for new ideas, or for ways to develop already existing ones.

At least until the beginning of 1932, Weizmann had not thought in terms of partition—at any rate, no explicit evidence to this effect exists. On the contrary: he constantly declared, in particular to external groups and individuals connected with Britain, his exclusive loyalty to the principles of the Mandate, namely, a national home for the Jews in Palestine—no less but also no more. His concern was sincere, as he believed that without British auspices a Jewish national home, and certainly anything beyond that, was out of the question.[7] Furthermore, his disbelief in the Arabs' ability to conduct authoritative negotiations, their intoxication of power after the unrest of 1929, and their growing activism in Palestine, combined with his reading of the international political map, led him, as of January 1930, to a conclusion that he set forth with unabashed frankness in a letter to Felix Warburg. This conclusion reflected the apprehensions of the non-Zionists in the newly created Jewish Agency that Weizmann was pushing for a "state now" under the table: "If Palestine were an empty country, the Jewish State would have come about, whether we want it or not. Palestine being what it is, the Jewish State will not come about, whether we want it or not, unless some fundamental change takes place, which I cannot envisage at present."[8]

He did not tell his correspondent that after the events of 1929 and more intensively after the "Passfield crisis" and the dangers posed, in his view, by those seeking shortcuts on both the left and the right in the Zionist movement, he himself was searching desperately for precisely the kind of change that he could not "envisage at present." By a process of trial and error, and without his necessarily being conscious of it, Weizmann oriented his approach, in response to the events of the hour, toward what would shortly become the "partition idea." Already in November 1929, he believed that "they [the Arabs] know that if we speak of Jewish Palestine we mean those parts of Palestine which are in Jewish hands."[9] Along with this, Weizmann could definitely agree with a call issued by the German Zionists, who held that "we will not be showing any weakness or be conceding anything if we enter into negotiations with the Arabs." This was understood to refer to negotiations that would recognize the Arabs of Palestine as a national community and give up the idea of the Jews either ruling or being ruled, which was a guiding principle for Weizmann.[10]

In January 1930, Weizmann wrote to his new colleague in the nascent Jewish Agency, James Marshall: "If we enter Palestine, we cannot live in the air, or on air; we must have firm ground. Where is the Jew to build his farm, grow his wheat. And plant his trees, the Arabs cannot do the same thing at the same time [and in the same territory]."[11] In other words— words that were not yet in currency at the time—he was writing about the partition of Palestine.

But at the beginning of the 1930s, Weizmann was still doing battle against the demand of the left to dissociate Zionism from the Balfour Declaration and against the call from the right to establish a state on both sides of the Jordan immediately, even without a majority. From the left, Weizmann had to cope with calls to act that he found unconscionable. He was urged to give up the state as a goal and openly advocate the creation of a national home that would not pose a threat to the Arabs, who were concerned that the Jews would seize control of their land.

But even earlier, the idea that mandatory Palestine should be divided between Jews and Arabs necessitated a consideration of some basic new assumptions by everyone involved, mainly Zionists and British, and perhaps also Arabs. First was the assumption that the Jewish national home would be established only in part of mandatory Palestine between the

Jordan River and the Mediterranean. Second was the assumption of explicit and official Zionist recognition, which was not yet in the cards, of Palestinian Arab nationalism. And third was the assumption that Britain and the Zionist movement would need to forgo the spirit of the Balfour Declaration, which was enshrined in the Mandate document as received from the League of Nations in 1922, and redefine Britain's role in Palestine.

Weizmann emerged strengthened from his success, in February 1931, at forcing the British prime minister, Ramsay MacDonald, to annul the Passfield policy (the MacDonald Letter). At the same time, in his battle with the British government in the fall and winter of 1930–1931, Weizmann made successful use of by-now outmoded tactics. The thrust of his argument, which MacDonald ultimately accepted, was thoroughly imperialist in character and rested on the underlying assumptions of the Mandate in the spirit of the Balfour Declaration. His case, in short, was that a national home for the Jews in Palestine was in the British imperial interest.[12] His insistence until 1931 on the principle that a Jewish state must be preceded by the existence of a Jewish majority in Palestine meant that it was not necessary to press the British for the establishment of a Jewish national home immediately. Like many of his allies/rivals in the Labor movement, Weizmann believed that significant immigration and the creation of a firm economic and political infrastructure were preconditions for the establishment of a state.

Yet for some time, despite his success from 1922 in persuading British governments that it was in their interest to fulfill the terms of the Balfour Declaration, he had been under no illusions about where Britain was headed on the Palestine question. That perceived danger, intertwined with the setbacks to his political career, drove Weizmann to revise his approach. Nevertheless, it is not clear whether he had already articulated to himself the partition idea as an operative platform by the summer of 1931.

Certainly the new orientation was apparent, even if not yet fully formulated. What remained was to forgo the principle of a Jewish majority throughout the whole of mandatory Palestine and hint at the option of a Jewish state in part of the territory. In mid-1931, Weizmann took another step in this direction when he made an unexpected declaration that perplexed his contemporaries and was politically unfortunate for him, at least in the short term. During a press interview on the eve of the Seventeenth Zionist Congress, in July 1931, he stated that although all his work was aimed at making the national home a reality and he could not compromise in restricting Jewish immigration to Palestine, his heart was not with those who were demanding a Jewish majority in the country. That, he said, would be tantamount to declaring that the Zionists were out to rule the Arabs or even to expel them, and even if incorrect, that interpretation was harmful to the Zionist cause internationally.[13] There is an echo here of his struggle for the revocation of the Passfield White Paper. What Weizmann had seen and heard in the backrooms of the give-and-take on the eve of the MacDonald Letter was unknown to, and still less understood by, his colleagues in the Zionist leadership.

Weizmann's declaration undoubtedly contributed to the serious personal defeat he suffered at the Zionist Congress that summer. Despite his amazing successes in establishing the Jewish Agency and getting the Passfield White Paper revoked, he was not reelected president of the WZO. Yet his declaration had not been the utterance of a politician intoxicated with victory who had triumphed over the British government in February 1931. In retrospect, Weizmann's espousal of parity and his rethinking of the question of a Jewish majority should be seen as a stage—not conscious, perhaps, but necessary—in the direction of the partition idea. In the years ahead, the parity concept, originally a goal in itself, was transformed in Weizmann's thought into a means aimed primarily at promoting governmental development plans in mandatory Palestine and as an approach that would set at ease the minds of both the British makers of colonial/Mandate policy and Weizmann's Zionist colleagues. By the beginning of 1937, when it was already clear to him that the only solution was partition, he reminded the members of the Royal Commission of Inquiry that the parity principle had been put forward originally in order to consolidate a situation in which the Jews in Palestine would neither control nor be controlled.[14]

Parity was not the only hindrance Weizmann faced on the road to partition. He also had to address the principle of cantonization in Palestine

under a federative-type central administration, or preferably confedera-
tive and British. Within the Zionist movement, the pioneer advocates of
the canton approach, each proposing different levels of autonomy, were
Arthur Ruppin, the head of the WZO's Palestine office from 1907, and
Itamar Ben-Avi, a journalist, who first broached the idea in 1920 and re-
prised it in 1930–1932. In the 1920s, David Ben-Gurion, then the secretary of the Histadrut federation of labor, referred to "territorial autonomy."
Paltiel Dickstein, a member of the Jewish Agency Executive, raised similar
ideas in the 1930s. They were joined in 1933 on the Arab side by the moderate Palestinian leader Musa al-Alami and Ahmed al-Khalidi, the deputy
director of the governmental department of education and headmaster
of the Arab College in Jerusalem. Cantonization received a major boost
when it gained the support of British public figures. At the beginning of
1935, the idea was put forward by Sir Archer Cust, a senior official in the
civil and afterward Mandate administration from 1920 to 1935.[15] Stafford
Cripps, a Labor member of Parliament, adduced similar ideas in a letter
to the *Manchester Guardian* of September 8, 1936, on the eve of the Peel
Commission's departure for Palestine. Another advocate was the Mandate
administration police officer Douglas Duff, who said of partition in his
memoirs of 1936, "Better half a loaf than none at all." (The Peel Commission repeated this proverb without crediting Duff.)[16] The idea of binational parity and the cantons principle—referring to a mosaic of district
autonomies under one political umbrella—appeared in a number of plans
that came about as a response to the situation that emerged with growing
clarity during the decade of the 1920s. At that time, it became increasingly
apparent that two national movements were pitted against each other in
Palestine. But besides bearing separate national identities, they were also
radically different in character, culture, and territorial aspirations—even if
both sides sought the same territory. The cantonization idea evolved rapidly into partition. The principal difference between the two concepts was
that cantonization presupposed autonomous blocs without full sovereignty
based on a regional demographic majority, whereas partition presupposed
two separate territorial blocs, each sovereign in its territory and possessing a distinctive identity. Sovereignty under cantonization—an idea that
was a response to demographics—was restricted by its basic assumption of

autonomous units above which was a federative state. Partition, however, assumed territorial sovereignty a priori, and therefore it also held out the possibility of a population transfer and the option of a confederation between the two states that would be created in Palestine.

The two conceptions, cantonization and partition, sprang from the inherent difficulty of realizing the terms of the Mandate in their original spirit—that of the Balfour Declaration. More specifically, the two proposed solutions emerged from the failure of the Balfour Declaration's "national home" idea—indeed from the failure of the Mandate as such. Its emphasis, even if not formally, lay on the British "dual commitment" to the Jews and the Arabs, and to a state that would be founded on civic partnership and binationalism. However, the concept of a legislative council based on a democratic majority broke down and metamorphosed into the parity idea, which naturally gave rise to the cantonization proposal and then to partition. It was not by chance that the notion of a Royal Commission of Inquiry—that is, a reassessment of the Palestine question—first arose in London in February 1936, just before the final collapse of the legislative council. The sporadic waves of violence that swept the country (1933, 1935, and the Arab Revolt of 1936–1939), though a result, not a cause of those failures, played a part in advancing the partition idea to the front of the political and diplomatic stages. The decision to establish the Royal Commission of Inquiry was finalized in May 1936 in response to the Arab uprising, which had broken out in the previous month. The expectations held out for the commission went far beyond the question of how Britain would respond to the Arab general strike and its accompanying violence.

.   .   .

In the light of these developments, and in the light of his declining status in the Zionist movement beginning in the summer of 1931, Weizmann carved out a secret path of his own. His personal political difficulties necessitated action, especially when taken in conjunction with the worrisome falloff in British-Zionist relations. It emerges, then, that the idea of partition, or at least the thrust to make it the centerpiece of Zionist and British policy, was not only due to the failure of the Mandate. Its genesis was also very much a function of a personal setback for Weizmann: the loss of the presidency of the WZO in July 1931. Above all, though, partition sprang from the interplay between the two developments, not least because Weizmann's political fortunes depended on the Anglo-Zionist connection. From the perspective of Weizmann's approach, it was a short road from the ideas described above to partition.

In January 1932, Dr. Victor (Avigdor) Jacobson, a member of Weizmann's inner circle, drafted an explicit partition plan of his own. For the first time, this went beyond the principle involved and addressed concrete practicalities (including the geographical aspect). Jacobson was one of the leading Zionist diplomats of his time. A member of the Zionist Executive from 1911 to 1920 and again from 1932 to 1934, he gained prominence as the envoy to the powers that were sovereign in Palestine. He was in Constantinople from 1908 to 1914 and afterward in Paris and Geneva as the Zionist representative to the institutions of the League of Nations. Briefly a member of Brit Shalom (1927–1929), which rejected a territorial solution in favor of a spiritual center in the Land of Israel, Jacobson later broke with this approach and was one of the envoys who acted in the spirit of Weizmann.[17]

Under the Jacobson plan, the Jews would get "the meat," as Weizmann put it. By this he meant the plain and the valleys, which would later be called "the N settlement" (referring to a sequence of Jewish settlements that followed the contours of the letter *N*): the coastal plain, the Valley of Zebulun, the Jezre'el Valley and Lower Galilee, the Beit She'an Valley, the Jordan Valley, and the eastern Upper Galilee, together with two additions in sparsely populated areas—the Negev and uninhabited regions in northern Transjordan, in Hauran and in the Golan Heights. These additions reflected Weizmann's tendency to expand the area of the Jewish state east of the Mandate territory as compensation for the loss of sections of Palestine through partition. The Arabs, Weizmann noted, would get "the bones": the hills of Judea, of Samaria, and of Galilee. Jerusalem would become the capital of a confederation that would encompass the Land of Israel and Palestine (as Jacobson referred to the Jewish and Arab states, respectively), together with Transjordan, Syria, and Lebanon, all under British auspices, of course.[18]

Jacobson in effect laid down the partition principle that would re-appear in the plans that followed: namely, two states and a separate arrangement for Jerusalem. Similarly, his territorial plan for a Jewish state would form the backbone of most of the subsequent versions of partition. This consisted of the coastal plain from Gaza to Haifa, eastward to the Jezre'el Valley and northward to encompass the Beit She'an Valley, the Jordan Valley, and the Galilee Panhandle. The "Jacobson-Weizmann plan" spoke for the first time in terms of finality—independent states. It spurned the British version of partition, which separated Palestine from the territory east of the Jordan. And, in contrast to subsequent partition concepts that were developed on both the Zionist and British sides, the Jacobson-Weizmann plan considered the Palestinian Arabs a distinct national group.[19]

The Jacobson-Weizmann plan came from within the Zionist establishment. It was attentive to the Arab posture without forgoing the Zionist idea. Contrary to many of his colleagues, who were wont to despair of political Zionism following the events of 1929–1931, Jacobson, in the spirit of Weizmann, leaned toward political activism without advocating territorial maximalism.[20] Even though Jacobson was slightly older than Weizmann, and at least until the late part of World War I was senior to him in the Zionist establishment, the relations between the two were those of revered teacher and reverential pupil.[21]

Like Weizmann, Jacobson preferred to work clandestinely, pursuing activity done behind the scenes that need not be spoken aloud. Jacobson's loyalty to Weizmann made him an excellent partner for backroom collaboration. In addition, the two shared an awareness that the "Jewish state" idea had long since become an empty slogan in the Zionist movement—on both the right and the left—and that few genuine efforts were being made to realize it concretely.[22]

Before disseminating his plan, Jacobson consulted with several prominent members of the Zionist Executive. Their responses were generally negative. Thus, Dr. Chaim Arlosoroff, the head of the Jewish Agency's political department, rejected the plan, not on principle, but because he believed it to be unworkable. However, as his objections were not unequivocal, he was probably a good candidate for persuasion. Arlosoroff put the idea to former Brit Shalom circles: "I put forward the subject of a 'small state,' as proposed by Dr. Jacobson, which for some reason is giving me no rest. His idea rests on a healthy foundation and possesses great attractiveness." Arlosoroff also succinctly set forth the innovation that inhered in Jacobson's concept: "A Jewish state in the Land of Israel, instead of the Land of Israel as a Jewish state."[23]

The other senior figures in the WZO largely ignored Jacobson's plan. Jacobson himself almost despaired of it but then was surprised to discover that it had a quiet, off-the-record supporter: none other than Weizmann himself. From afar—during a lengthy fundraising mission in South Africa at the beginning of 1932—Weizmann signaled to him that the plan was consistent with his own approach. Thrilled, Jacobson replied:

> I did not send you the memorandum [about the partition plan] we talked about, because, to tell you the truth, I am pessimistic about its fate.... My experience with the Zionists has been almost entirely negative. To tell you the truth, I thought you had asked me for the memorandum out of friendship or pangs of conscience, without attaching any importance to it. But as you asked me again to send you the memorandum, I am very happy to do so, together with general lines of the plan's guiding principles, and I will send you a more detailed survey later.[24]

With Weizmann's encouragement, Jacobson rejoined the Zionist Executive in 1933 in order to promote his plan. In the spring of 1933, he visited Syria and Lebanon—now in his capacity as a member of the Zionist Executive and at its behest—to examine the feasibility of the confederation idea and of a Jewish state. He returned with a complex but essentially optimistic assessment.[25]

Weizmann set about promoting partition quietly, not to say secretly. In part, this approach was required by the fact that he remained far from certain about the plan's reception by the British and by his colleagues in the Zionist movement, still less by his political rivals, who believed he was prone to dangerous ideas of peace and compromise.[26] As for the British, Weizmann did not want to aggravate the already sensitive relations with them. A flawed Mandate was better than no Mandate. Weizmann was a practitioner of secret diplomacy—making a full report to his colleagues was not his style. The truth must serve the goal, certainly not the other way around.

Did either Weizmann or Jacobson go to the British with the partition idea? In late March 1932, the Revisionists spread a rumor to the effect that in the fall and winter of 1931–1932 a plan to partition the country had been circulated among the relevant ministries in London and within the British administration in Jerusalem. The British denied this. The Revisionists, like conservatives everywhere, tended to circulate reports not to their liking in the hope of getting them removed from the agenda. In this case, the reports were probably an echo of the ideas that Jacobson conveyed to the leaders of the Zionist movement around this time.[27]

An illuminating example of Weizmann's activity during this period to advance the partition idea—even as he scattered half-truths and kept his cards close to his chest, so much so that he misrepresented the situation to Britain and to his Zionist colleagues—can be seen in the contacts he maintained with the Italian dictator Benito Mussolini. Weizmann spoke to Il Duce about partition twice: in April 1933 and in December 1934. He concealed the first meeting but not the second—and not because of Mussolini's later alliance with Hitler or the race laws promulgated in Italy. Weizmann, it turns out, was concealing something else: his effort, undertaken in close collaboration with Jacobson, to advance the partition idea through Mussolini. The two wanted to create the impression that it was Mussolini who raised the partition concept in the meeting of February 1934. However, the idea of partition in Palestine was apparently first broached to the Italian leader in a previous meeting with Weizmann in April 1933.

At the time, Weizmann and Jacobson were conducting intensive discussions at the League of Nations with Italian representatives who headed the organization's Mandates Commission—the sovereign power in Palestine. Mussolini's inclination, inspired by the ideas of Jacobson and Weizmann, to a territorial solution in Palestine under Italian auspices and, as he believed, at Britain's expense was enthusiastically picked up by his diplomats at the League of Nations. They were eager to take action in the spirit of their leader and even to move farther ahead in the direction they believed Il Duce favored. In November 1933, Jacobson wrote to Weizmann that the head of the Mandates Commission, Count The-odoli, who was Mussolini's man, had told him that "it is impossible to force a marriage to last when the husband and the wife do not want each other."[28] In December, while negotiations were taking place ahead of an-other Weizmann-Mussolini meeting, Weizmann wrote, in a thoroughly personal letter to his wife that "if I were to negotiate as in 1917 I would certainly demand a *separate territory for the Jews in Palestine and Trans-jordan* or even a reserve!!! [emphasis added]."[29] Unable to get to Rome for another meeting, Weizmann suggested sending Jacobson, with whom he maintained close ties at this time. But when Mussolini balked at this suggestion, Weizmann went to Rome for a second meeting, in February 1934. Jacobson, who was present at the meeting, wrote a summary of the proceedings that was worded vaguely to avoid arousing suspicion that Weizmann was behind the partition initiative. However, he did not suc-ceed in blurring altogether the fact that the partition idea that Mussolini talked about in 1934 was based on ideas originally broached by Jacobson and Weizmann. According to his report of the meeting, Mussolini practi-cally recited the partition idea, which he raised in connection with a dis-cussion about Jerusalem's status in the event of a "two-state solution." He was not troubled by the idea as such. "You must establish a Jewish state," he said. "I have already spoken with the Arabs. I believe an agreement can be reached. The difficulty could arise from the question of Jerusalem. The Arabs are of the opinion that the Jews should make Tel Aviv their capi-tal." Weizmann, instead of responding to the Jerusalem issue, chose to re-mind Mussolini of the broader picture: "The idea you have just expressed is a great one. In my opinion, a state, even a small one, is an Archimedean point of support."[30]

After the meeting, Weizmann exulted, "We have got quite friendly." He requested and received a photograph with a dedication in Musso-lini's hand and placed it, framed, in his study in Rehovot, his immediate destination after Italy. The photograph is still there. It was far from clear whether Mussolini "can influence the course of the illness very much judging by what he himself believes," Weizmann wrote, apparently in ref-erence to the burning question of German Jewry, "but he can be useful in a few other ways."[31] In sum, this was an attempt by Weizmann to place the partition idea on the agenda of the League of Nations through Il Duce. Indirectly, he wanted to put pressure on the British and the French, as well as on his colleagues in the Zionist leadership. He lost no time in reporting—not fully, of course—to the British ambassador to Rome, emphasizing that the Zionists' loyalty to Britain was not in doubt. The partition idea was no longer the sole preserve of Weizmann and Jacobson.[32]

Weizmann refrained at this stage from sharing his partition ideas with others in the Zionist leadership. At the same time, whether because he found it difficult to keep these thoughts to himself, or out of a desire to examine or prepare the ground, or both, he occasionally hinted at them to individuals whose views carried weight, even if they were not among Zionist policymakers. In doing so, he was probably also seeking to reassure himself about his new path. In March 1934, after his meeting with Mussolini in Rome, Weizmann returned to Rehovot to inaugurate the Daniel Sieff Research Institute, which was his handiwork. The partition concept apparently arose in conversations at this time with various personalities in Palestine. Remarks made by the "national poet," Hayyim Nahman Bialik, at a reception held in Weizmann's honor, clearly suggested approval of partition: "Externally, toward other nations, we must set forth our aspirations in their full scope: that the Jewish people, if it is to fulfill the idea, must necessarily contract, recognize reality. Contracting is a deep instinct. . . . Flowery political speech must be fought."[33] A sharply contrary view was expressed by Moshe Smilansky, a prominent farmer-landowner:

And do not say that only the Revisionists are trying to rush things. Revisionism, in one form or another, is the sickness of this generation. [But] one famous veteran leader, who is known to "eat up" Revisionists, informed me frankly in the past few days that he is praying now for a state—even an olive-sized [small] one. . . . This important statesman has forgotten that an olive-sized state is nothing less than the desecration of the idea behind our policy, and that the fire of envy and hatred will surely not be lacking in an olive-sized state, but the fire of creativity will be lacking in it, unable to be lit.[34]

In the summer of 1935, Weizmann resumed the presidency of the WZO, but in a very different political situation from that during his previous term. Above all, he was dependent on the Labor movement, which now held power in the organization. "We are here being reduced to an Embassy," Weizmann complained.[35] Caught in this intolerable political reality, Weizmann was impelled to embark on a two-pronged attempt—in which each element was inextricably linked with the other—to rehabilitate his status as the senior figure in the movement and at the same time to rescue the Zionist-British connection by putting forward partition as an alternative to the "old Mandate." From his vantage point in the second half of the 1930s, this approach seemed more valid than a binational state or cantonization, on the condition that the Zionist connection with Britain would be maintained.

. . .

The First World War and the recognition of nationality as such—which underlay the creation of the League of Nations and Irish independence, as well as the establishment, for example, of Turkey and Poland as states possessing old/new nationality—had a resounding impact on the British Empire. The national unrest that flared up in India and the Middle East are among the best-known examples. This new mindset produced a retreat from empire, or at least an unmistakable change in the mode of British influence, as could be discerned in London's policy of the 1930s. The incipient elimination of the Class A Mandates in Iraq, Transjordan, and the Levant should be seen in the same context. Indeed, Palestine would shortly become the last Mandate of this type. Hence, also, we see Britain's intention to promote the creation of one state possessing an Arab majority but with a binational legislative council.

Around this time, Sir Archer Cust renewed his advocacy of the cantons plan, originally presented, as already noted, in January 1935. Having left the civil service in the meantime, Cust decided to publicize his ideas through the press and in lectures to selected audiences.[36] Weizmann, who was alert to every development in Britain in the spirit of a solution based on territorial separation, asked Cust to send him a copy of a talk he had given at the Royal Central Asian Society. Cust sent the text on May 28, 1936, together with a timetable for implementing his ideas and a map showing the borders of the proposed Jewish canton. It was important for Weizmann that Cust, until very recently a British civil servant, might be acting on behalf of the colonial secretary. He may have thought, not entirely mistakenly, that the Colonial Office was encouraging the initiative. Certainly Cust made full reports of his activity to the Colonial Office. From Weizmann's perspective, it was crucial that every idea for a solution in Palestine that was territorially based and specified Jewish autonomy should come from the British, not the Zionists, and still less from him.

After perusing Cust's ideas, Weizmann asked for a meeting. It took place on June 26, 1936, at the London office of the Zionist Executive. The discussion, held as the two pored over a map of Cust's plan, was eminently practical. Weizmann was by now past the stage of soul-searching about the principle of territorial separation between Jews and Arabs in Palestine.[37]

On June 9, Weizmann attended a public lecture by Cust. At its conclusion he could not restrain himself and noted, "There is something to it." Weizmann could hardly help but notice that Cust's plan, though it referred to cantons and not to a state, was similar to his ideas, at least in terms of the "meat and bones" principle that Weizmann sought to promote in the spirit of Jacobson's plan. Thus, the Jewish canton would include the coastal plain, the valleys, and the eastern Upper Galilee, with a foothold in the Negev. The Arabs would receive the hilly spine, with outlets to the sea in Gaza, Jaffa, and Acre. The plan's primary shortcoming, from Weizmann's viewpoint, lay in the fact that even though Cust, like him and like Jacobson, would abolish the border between Palestine and Transjordan, the Zionists' plan would append parts of western Transjordan to the Jewish state, whereas Cust would connect Transjordan with the Arab canton. Weizmann, elliptical in his way, posed difficult questions to Cust—the very questions he himself feared, if and when he was to make his ideas public. He put it to Cust, for example, that separating the narrow but relatively rich coastal plain from the rest of Palestine was economically unrealistic. Concurrently, and again on the assumption that Cust was working on behalf of the Colonial Office, he sent aides to assail the notion of detaching the Jewish canton from Transjordan. However, it soon transpired that at the heart of the territorial dispute between the two (beyond the question of whether the entity under consideration was a canton or a state—a non-question, really, as Weizmann studiously avoided sharing his ideas with Cust) was the "meat," namely, the valleys, which would constitute the bulk of the Jews' territory. In the spirit of the Jacobson plan of 1932, Weizmann demanded the coastal plain from the Gaza Strip (inclusive) to Rosh Hanikra in the west and the Jordan Valley in the east. Under the 1932 plan, the Arab state would in any case lie exclusively in Palestine. Cust, though, balked at Weizmann's ideas, because they would drive a wedge between the two parts of his proposed Arab canton, which would lie on both sides of the Jordan River.[38]

The real problem, though, resided in the principle, not the map. Cust was referring to cantons within a one-state framework, and Weizmann, to partition. Weizmann informed Cust that he rejected his plan, but at the same time he addressed it in immense detail. Cust's direction was positive, but Weizmann preferred partition into two independent states. Cantonization called for a level of cooperation that was too close to be sustainable by the two sides. Pursuing his penchant for secrecy and deception, Weizmann kept his preference secret. His aides let it be known that he was uncomfortable with Cust's ideas.[39]

Cust was not the only one who was baffled by Weizmann's habit of keeping his cards close to his chest. His colleagues in the leadership, particularly Ben-Gurion—who was always suspicious of Weizmann—were equally bewildered. Ben-Gurion, the chairman of the Jewish Agency Executive, was in London at the time in order to apprise himself firsthand of the government's frame of mind and, no less, to see what Weizmann was up to. Around this time, Weizmann met with Nuri al-Said of Iraq. Ben-Gurion thereupon demanded the resignation of the president of the WZO, claiming he had agreed in the meeting to a temporary stoppage of Jewish immigration to Palestine. Weizmann did in fact discuss the territorial question with al-Said. In the spirit of the Jacobson plan, Weizmann calculated that the Iraqi statesman's advocacy of a federation would induce him to support an autonomous Jewish territorial unit as part of the Arab federation. Ben-Gurion could not have known this. Excluded and distraught, he wrote to Moshe Shertok, "I saw not only the calamity we can expect from this man [Weizmann] now—the entire political debacle of previous years is now clear to me."[40]

.   .   .

By the time the Arab Revolt erupted, in April 1936, followed a month later by the announcement that a Royal Commission of Inquiry would be established, Weizmann was wholly devoted to partition. It was clear to him that the idea for partition must originate from the British, if not the Zionists themselves, and of course the Arabs were to take it under consideration. He was pleased to discover, after a time, that this approach was also acceptable to the leaders of the Labor movement in Palestine, without whom no binding decisions could be arrived at. By 1936, it was no longer possible to ignore the dramatic fact that the Jews, owing to massive immigration since 1932, now constituted 37 percent of the population of Palestine, more than double the percentage four years earlier (17 percent).

Accordingly, during this period Weizmann continued to deal with partition as though a device to erase footprints were strapped to his back, eliminating all "incriminating" signs. The opportunity he was waiting for soon presented itself. Reginald Coupland, a historian and an expert on the contemporary British Empire, was co-opted to the Royal Commission of Inquiry. The encounter between Coupland and Weizmann would thrust the partition idea into the light of day in the commission's recommendations of June 1937, which would be adopted by the British government in July.

Arriving in Palestine in late October 1936, the Peel Commission spent almost three months there. On Saturday, January 16, 1937, just before the commission concluded its work and left the country, Coupland was absent from its meeting in Jerusalem. Unbeknownst to the others, he had accepted a secret invitation from Weizmann for a private, informal meeting in Nahalal, the first Jewish *moshav*, or workers' cooperative (founded in 1921), which lies in the western part of the Jezre'el Valley, south of the Haifa-Nazareth road. There was nothing unusual about Weizmann's visit to the settlement. He customarily passed through Nahalal when leaving and entering the country via Haifa and often hosted high-ranking visitors there, to show them the "new Jew" in action. On the day after the secret meeting, after spending the night in Haifa at his mother's home, Weizmann left for London. Coupland and his colleagues departed on the same day.[41]

It was difficult to hide Weizmann's arrival in Nahalal. Though far from rare, a visit like this would still be the main topic of conversation in the Jezre'el Valley and beyond. Nor could Weizmann prevent what would now be called a paparazzo—who hid behind a convenient bush—from photographing him with Coupland. A report about the meeting also appeared in the newspaper *Davar*. The two emerged from the room in which they met after about two hours. Coupland left at once; Weizmann lingered to tell curious onlookers what he wished to tell them. So the fact of the meeting was known—but not its content.[42]

Years later, in February 1950, shortly after the publication of Weizmann's autobiography, *Trial and Error*, Coupland wrote a letter to Weizmann whose extremely polite tone did not conceal his anger at the Zionist leader for violating an unwritten agreement between them.[43] Coupland, a historian of repute, had received an advance copy of the manuscript from the book's publishers in the United States and Britain so that he could write a blurb. Instead, Coupland wrote to Weizmann:

> I do not at all regret that your reference to me is brief . . . when I came to your account of the Peel Commission; I was somewhat disquieted at your reference to our meeting at N ____ [Nahalal] (I can't spell it). While I felt proud that you should have thought it sufficiently important to mention it in your Autobiography, I was afraid it would—or at least might—affect my reputation in England. There are pro-Arabs who think that my share in the Peel Report was biased in favor of the Jews, and, if they read your account of our meeting, they would say that not only had I been "nobbled" by you but had also gone behind the back of my colleagues. . . . I'm sure you'll understand it and will forgive me for asking those Jewish friends in America to whom you had entrusted the publication of the book, if they could see their way to cutting out the story of our meeting. They at once most kindly agreed. . . . There would, of course, be no harm in your saying anything you like about my understanding of the problem as revealed in the public proceedings of the Commission or that the *first and third parts of the report were drafted by me or that the idea of partition was first broached by me* [emphasis added]. The only

thing I would wish to be avoided is any reference to private contact between you and me.[44]

Amid all of the above that was "not for publication," Coupland revealed his participation in the secret meeting at Nahalal. Weizmann, the well-known tempter, had pulled out all the stops this time. He had enticed Coupland, the most promising link on the Royal Commission from his viewpoint, to his turf in order to spell out what he wanted without beating around the bush. It was a one-time opportunity, just before the commission members were to leave the country. Weizmann's intuition and experience, the pressing political hour, and his personal need to regain control of the Zionist-British agenda on the way to restoring its former pride of place called for a dramatic move. In his appearances before the commission, Weizmann had noticed that Coupland leaned toward a solution of complete separation of Jews and Arabs. He also knew that Coupland was an authority whose opinions on questions about the empire's past and future were listened to respectfully. He therefore acted, as he had so often, on his own, without reporting to his colleagues. Nor did he hesitate to "embroil" a member of the Royal Commission by getting him to act behind the backs of his colleagues. Inviting Coupland to a place that lay at the margins of consciousness of his associates was intended to enable a free conversation that would persuade Coupland to take the lead in advocating partition. The "culprit" himself apparently was not required to offer explanations for his absence from the commission's session that day. British commissions of inquiry often operated in smaller, parallel groups that met separately.[45] Moreover, Coupland, an academic who was not from the British establishment, was less politically beholden than his colleagues.

In their meeting at Nahalal, Weizmann and Coupland strengthened each other's awareness of the need for an agreed partition plan—agreed, at least, between Britain and the Zionists. Coupland remarked that the high commissioner's objection to partition should be disregarded. Weizmann, according to his account, explained to Coupland that the idea would probably be feasible if the commission were to recommend the legal immigration of fifty thousand Jews a year in the coming twenty years. Weizmann wanted to ensure that the commission's report would put forward the idea of partition as having originated within the commission and not having been proposed by him or by anyone else in the Zionist movement. The developments in the months that followed suggest that Weizmann tried to exert pressure on Coupland to ensure that he would write the section of the report dealing with the political solution, in which the daring proposal to terminate the Mandate and divide the country would be put forward. Coupland, for his part, wished to ensure general Zionist support for the partition clause, if he should succeed in getting it incorporated into the report, particularly in light of the well-known opposition by Weizmann and his movement to the annulment of the Mandate. Though manifestly hesitant about this course of action, Coupland remained in quiet touch with Weizmann during the months that followed, though he was still a member of the commission. Other members of the commission refused to see Weizmann as long as the final report was not yet completed—to do otherwise would be untoward.[46]

Weizmann's excitement at the conclusion of the meeting in Nahalal was apparently sincere: he had been able to persuade Coupland that the Zionist movement would support partition, while Coupland had promised that the idea would be put forward as a British initiative, to which the parties would be called upon to respond. Weizmann pounced on the opportunity to exploit for his personal benefit a convergence of views that would benefit the Zionist cause—in his perception, the two were one and the same.

Weizmann's sense was that an alliance—the "Nahalal alliance"—had been forged between him and the Oxford professor. This, he thought, made Coupland an interested party not only on the question of Palestine's status from the British imperial perspective, but also in regard to internal Zionist developments. After all, that too had been part of the "Nahalal pact": Coupland would give expression to the British acceptance of partition, and Weizmann to the Zionist acceptance. In the immediate aftermath, Weizmann, once he had garnered the support of the majority of the Mapai leadership, was able to be more forthright toward Coupland, believing that his forceful words would fortify the British academic in his formulation of the partition proposal:

Since we met last I have had an opportunity of thinking over the Question we discussed, and of discovering somewhat more than I knew then of general Jewish and Zionist opinion with regard to them. I do not know whether you would be interested to hear something of the results of all this (I need hardly say that I am anxious not to suggest anything that might prove embarrassing to you), but if you would care to see me, I should be happy to come to Oxford."[47]

Coupland, who had known since April 1937 that he would write the Royal Commission's report, was concerned that an overenthusiastic reception by the Jews to partition would be detrimental to the prospect of its acceptance by the Arabs and by some in Britain.[48] Still leery, he reported to Weizmann secretly about the commission's internal deliberations. On May 29, 1937, for example, he informed Weizmann that last-minute changes had been introduced into the draft report on the subject of the border between the two states. Weizmann, who was in Paris when he received this information, returned to London that same day and met with Coupland in private on the following two days. The interaction between them was intense. Weizmann closely followed Coupland's work on the report. It is unclear, as intimated in Coupland's letter from February 1950 cited above, how much input Weizmann actually had in drawing up the partition section of the report. What is clear is which side Coupland was on: he would, he told Weizmann, do his best to accede to the Zionists' demands.[49]

In the case of partition, as previously with the Balfour Declaration, Weizmann was not necessarily the progenitor of the idea, but without him it is difficult to account for its appearance for the first time as an official British plan. As Moshe Shertok, the head of the Jewish Agency's political department, noted in June 1937, the key to understanding Weizmann's role in regard to partition lay in the assumption at the time that the idea must be seen to have come from Britain. "As long as Weizmann heads the movement," Shertok observed, "no important Englishman in London will heed the words of anyone else if they conflict with Weizmann's views."[50] David Remez, the general secretary of the Histadrut federation of labor at the time, aptly summed up Weizmann's role in the debate over partition: "Displaying the faithful intuitive sense with which he forged the Balfour Declaration, [Weizmann] has now seen to it that the idea of the Jewish state appears as a concrete issue on the international stage."[51]

We can't truly understand the history of the partition of Palestine without understanding that the idea of partition not only originated as part of the Zionist strategy, well before the British ever considered it, but also that this very concept was devised by the major Zionist leader of the time—Chaim Weizmann—and his senior aides. This conclusion helps us better understand Weizmann's historic role and the way he worked. It helps us identify a pattern in his behavior. Weizmann liked to work under the radar. But sometimes, when he was working on something really big, he became more like a rogue agent, often working against the policies of his own movement. In the end, however, he always returned home, to the Zionist movement, to lead it, usually extremely effectively, in the directions that he believed were right. He did this during and after the First World War with the Balfour Declaration, and he did it again in the 1930s with the partition plan.

But more importantly, and perhaps more dramatically, this conclusion gives us critical new insight into the evolution of British policy in mandatory Palestine—and that is, that both fundamental pillars of British policy in Palestine until the Second World War—the Balfour Declaration and the partition plan—were actually devised by the Zionist leadership and "sold" to the British, who then presented it as their own policy.

*Part II*

DISTANCES TRANSVERSED

## CHAPTER 4

# "INDIAN ULSTERISATION"—IRELAND, INDIA, AND PARTITION

*The Infection of Example?*

Kate O'Malley

THE PARTITIONS of Ireland and India were different: in the manner they were carried out, in the geography of the partitioning, and in their immediate and long-term outcomes. Ireland's partition came about as a result of the Government of Ireland Act of 1920, but this was thought at the time to be an interim measure. The Anglo-Irish Treaty the following year provided for a "Boundary Commission" revision of the partition. This commission met finally in 1924 but without Northern Irish cooperation, and, controversially, no changes to the boundary were implemented.[1] India's partition was mooted during the war years and was not unexpected when the official announcement came from Louis Mountbatten in 1947, popularly known as the 3 June Plan.[2] It was, nonetheless, a sharp, sudden shock in contrast with Ireland. Arguably, British administrators had learned from their Irish experience and did not drag out the process, and partition was definitive and was not reviewed afterwards. The partition of Ireland coincided with a war of independence and a civil war, but partition was not the cause of these nor did they result in much bloodshed. The partition of India, however, was one of the bloodiest and most shocking events of the twentieth century. It was prefaced by almost a year of communal riots on an unprecedented scale in Calcutta, East Bengal, Bihar, the United Provinces, and Punjab. The estimated number of casualties runs from two hundred thousand to one million, but there is little disputing the fact that its aftermath saw one of the largest, swiftest, and most violent population transfers in history.

Even a cursory glance at the history surrounding both partitions reveals many similarities. In both cases the demand for partition developed in the wake of a world war, when Britain, after a protracted struggle with the respective nationalist movements, decided to withdraw. In Ireland's case the British left behind a loyalist community whose interests they wished to protect. This loyalist minority, for historic reasons, was mainly Protestant and was chiefly located in the northeast of the country. In India's case, and also for historic reasons (although ones that did not implicate Britain) the minority community was also of a different religion, with larger clusters of Muslim populations in the northeast and northwest of the country. No one party in this "triangular narrative" escapes accountability for the evolution of the demand for partition. In both Ireland and India the majority communities' emphasis upon the link between culture and nationality contributed significantly to the closing of the anti–Home Rule ranks—in Ulster in order to save them from "Rome Rule," and for the Muslims their resolve to mobilize behind the Muslim League lest they end up in a "Hindu Raj." In both cases also the minority community leaders were culpable by awakening and heightening centuries-old religious antagonisms.[3] From a British perspective the "need" to partition was equated with the need to safeguard minority communities, deeming it the only means of reconciling "irreconcilable people."[4] Such reasoning adds fuel to an established argument in the historiography of British decolonization: that there was an inherent reluctance on the part of the British to devolve power in the colonies, as they believed the indigenous populations to be simply unfit to rule. The "need" to partition, therefore, provided British politicians and administrators with a *res ipsa loquitur.*

This chapter looks at the ways in which several appropriated narratives of the partition of Ireland surfaced at the time of the partition of India. It will become apparent that the partition of Ireland was used as a point of reasoning by all three parties to the partition of India, with Indian economist Samar Sen referring to the partition of the subcontinent as "Indian Ulsterisation,"[5] and in Ireland also it provided a fresh opportunity to resurrect the topic of the long since established, if still contested, partition of Ireland.

## THE IRISH ANALOGY

The parallels between the nationalist movements in Ireland and India, as well as the similarities in British imperial policymaking in both spheres throughout the nineteenth and early twentieth centuries, are well known.[6] In particular, throughout the 1920s and 1930s Ireland as an example had been used regularly by Indian National Congress leaders as hyperbolic fare in speeches and meetings and in negotiations with the British. An Indo-Irish nationalist nexus had been established, with many well-known agitators and figures from both countries meeting and exchanging ideas, including Éamon de Valera, Maud Gonne, Frank Ryan, and Peader O'Donnell on the Irish side and Jawaharlal Nehru, V. J. Patel, and Subhas Chandra Bose on the Indian, to name but the better known. In India, Congress leaders often cited the establishment of the Irish Free State in the wake of the Irish War of Independence and its status as an independent dominion within the Commonwealth as a precedent for their own situation. However, the attainment of dominion status was an outcome only reluctantly accepted by a bare majority of the Irish revolutionary elite, and the lesson of Ireland was flawed in more ways than this. It begged the question from British Indian civil serviceman and later historian Hugh Trevor Lambrick: "Why do not Congress speakers see the irony, and indeed absurdity, in their invoking the example of Ireland—her long struggle for Home Rule, and England's eventual surrender? Nothing could be more damaging to their-own [*sic*] cause. The lesson of Ireland for India can be summed up in one word—Ulster."[7] The Muslim League began to pick up on these pertinent parallels and in so doing would steal one of the Congress's kindred causes. Increasingly, Muhammad Ali Jinnah and lesser well-known members from among the League's ranks began to use the partition of Ireland to legitimize their own demands for the creation of Pakistan. At the famous Minto Park meeting in March 1940, when the Lahore Resolution was adopted, Jinnah compared the unhappy union of Britain and Ireland to the yoking together of Hindus and Muslims. The war years had seen the rapid rise of Jinnah's Muslim League, which articulated quite specific demands and declared that "Pakistan is a question of life or death for us."[8] The day after the Lahore Resolution was publicized, the *Times of India* was drawing comparisons with Ireland in a manner that already implied tacit approval of partition: "only once before was Great Britain confronted with a similar situation; that occurred in Ireland where the country had to be divided to permit self-government to function."[9] In 1945 Jinnah was again referring to Ireland as India was drawing closer and closer to independence: "Differences between the Irish and the British are nothing when compared with the differences between the Hindus and Muslims. When after three and a half centuries, Ireland remains separate, why not the Hindus and Muslims? What is there to frighten us?"[10] In response to Jinnah, Sir Hari Singh Gour pointed out that it was a well-known constitutional fact, emphasized by the League of Nations in its report on the minority question, that no country could be partitioned at the insistence of any group or groups of people:

> Suppose all the Hindus of India were to demand its partition, it would not be constitutionally feasible because India is interdependent and unless in a referendum a vast majority of its people claim a partition, no partition of the country is legally or constitutionally possible. Ireland is an example. Its partition was not unilaterally decided and, therefore, the Muslim League's demand for partition is as unsound as is its claim to call Muslim India, Pakistan. In other words, the demand for Pakistan is merely a bargaining counter and my fellow-countrymen should remember it.[11]

The constitutionality of the demand for Pakistan was less of a concern for the Muslim League followers, and Jinnah's own words became more urgent as the transfer of power approached. The Irish *Sunday Independent* in 1946 commissioned a piece on Indian political developments from the London editor of the United Press of India, journalist and author D. V. Tamhankar. With his Irish readers in mind Tamhankar was bound to quote Jinnah and make parallels with Ireland: "In one message of exhortation to his followers Mr Jinnah used almost the very words of Lord Carson to his Ulster Volunteers in 1913–14. He has asked the Moslems to organise, consolidate, and be prepared to face any eventuality."[12]

There are earlier examples than this of Ireland being cited in relation to communal tensions in India. In the *Times of India* in April 1940 economist and lecturer at Presidency College, Calcutta, Sir Jehangir C. Coyajee contributed an opinion piece titled "The Demand for Independence: Ireland's Lesson for India." He offered a word of caution in advance of India attaining independence by recommending some essential preliminary conditions. The first and obvious one he listed was unity of political opinion. He invoked Alfred Balfour's definition of a democratic nation by telling his readers that "our whole political machinery presupposes a people so fundamentally at one that they can safely afford to bicker."[13] This description was clearly not one applicable to India of 1940, where growing communal tensions were grabbing international headlines. Coyajee went on to relate how "the cry for independence . . . had a strange echo in Northern India—a cry for partition. . . . [W]hat other threat or challenge, short of partition, could have made either the Congress or its leader pause for a moment in their headlong stampede towards the fatal status of independence?" He thought the demand for partition enough of a punctuation in the march for independence to stop any patriotic Indian in their tracks: "for India seems to be rapidly following in the footsteps of Ireland," he said, where a minority that "had traditions of having governed the country for centuries chose to separate itself and has continued to throw constant obstacles in the way of union. The intensity of the alarm expressed by the Protestants of the North at being ruled by a Catholic majority is finding a close parallel in Muslim India."[14] The crux of Coyajee's "Ireland's Lesson for India" becomes apparent toward the end of his piece, and it gives lie to his Anglophile background. He believed that the answer to all of India's problems lay in Commonwealth membership, a theme that will be returned to later. He thought that the only way the threat of partition could be nullified was by Gandhi reconciling "the idea of Commonwealth citizenship with the claims of Indian nationality." How this would reconcile minorities' concerns was not made clear, however. Later that same week a more robust argument, this time in favor of partition, was put forward in the *Times of India* by Muslim League stalwart Sir Ali Mahomed Khan Dehlavi, then leader of the Bombay Provincial Legislature. Dehlavi used a simple but effective comparison with Ireland. The "division of India into Hindu and Muslim States is the only panacea for all our political ills," he told readers, and such early and overt references to a strict partitioning of India in 1942 were coupled with a bleak and rhetorical argument about the partition of Ireland:

> The reason why all efforts to reach a solution of the Hindu-Muslim deadlock had proved abortive . . . was that the union of the two was unnatural. . . . Mr Gandhi looked upon complete independence for India as a possibility. Why then should the more feasible step of dividing India in to two, for internal peace, tranquility and safety, be considered an impossibility. . . . [W]as the division of Protestants in the north and Catholics in the south of Ireland an impossibility?[15]

The British had transferred power before to a country with minority concerns, and as far as the Muslim League was concerned, it had been a success.

As these cursory and early references in India to Ireland's partition illustrate, it was used on both sides of the argument, and whether one deemed the division a success or a failure depended on whether one was Muslim or Hindu. The "terrible beauty" of the partition of Ireland lay in the eye of the beholder. In early May 1942 Mahasabha, the radical Hindu nationalist group later implicated in the death of Gandhi, organized an "Anti-Pakistan Day" of protest. Renowned radical Veer Savarkar was its president, and he was joined on its Bombay podium by the event's main organizer, Jamnadas Mehta. The large meeting was convened so that Hindus could "raise their voice against any scheme to disintegrate the motherland." Mehta was president of the All India Railway federation in the 1920s. He had studied partition in some detail and had direct contact with Ireland, having visited in 1927 with Subhas Chandra Bose's mentor, V. J. Patel.[16] At the time, Patel and Mehta were on a research trip to the United Kingdom and Ireland in order to study the procedures of the various Houses of Parliament, and although they spent most of their time in London, the two Indians visited the Irish Parliaments in Dublin and Belfast. One report of their visit stands out. While guests of Ulster Unionist Hugh O'Neill, the speaker of the Northern Irish House of Commons, at a luncheon in Belfast, Patel took it upon himself to tell those in attendance that he thought Ireland was simply too small to afford the upkeep of two governments and that he hoped it would not be long before all Ireland would be under one parliament. The press in the Irish Free State took great pleasure in reporting Patel's faux pas, with the *Irish Independent* stating that "it was not, we fear, a function that the host will look back upon with pleasure. For this wise man from the East committed the unpardonable sin of speaking truth and sense to those with whom he broke bread."[17] Mehta, like Patel, had established close contact with Irish nationalists during this time in Europe, and their attitude in relation to Indian independence hardened on their return as a result. Mehta's response to the partition of India once it was mooted was aggressive, and he drew on his Irish experience for his platform speeches. At the Anti-Pakistan Day protests he told his listeners that the experience of partition in Ireland had not been successful and that Irish partition "remained irreconcilable still today." His hardline stance was apparent when he concluded by stating the determination of Hindus to resist Pakistan irrespective of the consequences.[18] Another staunch nationalist and one-time Mahasabha president, B. S. Moonjee, was quick to refer to Ireland in the wake of Stafford Cripps's first failed mission to India in 1942. Moonjee bitterly criticized the rejected proposals, which would have allowed provinces to secede from the proposed postwar Indian federation, and in a statement he declared that "the secession clause would inevitably result in the partition of India on religious grounds and communal lines, resulting in the creation of several Ulsters, constant communal strife, and even civil war."[19] "Ulster" for Hindu nationalists was a dirty word.

In Britain and Ireland during the early 1940s, despite the obvious preoccupation of the press with war coverage, the complicated nature of Britain's India policy was slowly beginning to demand more attention. In Northern Ireland the *Fermanagh Herald* considered the possibility of the partition of the subcontinent. The paper's nationalist bias meant that its commentary was explicitly anti-partitionist, but interestingly it placed the blame for the developing situation squarely with the Muslim community and even expressed a degree of sympathy toward the British government:

It is at such a time, when there is still a faint hope of reconciling Indian separatist ambitions with the obvious needs and difficulties of the British authority in India, that the Muslim section of the Indian people has seen fit to torpedo all hopes of a settlement by demanding Partition as the price of its own acquiescence in any settlement . . . thus again has an "Ulster" managed to thwart Nationalist ambitions and at the same time deny any easement or relief in a difficult situation to a British Government towards which it professes such loyalty.[20]

There were other faint traces of understanding toward the British position from prominent Irish writer and Fabian Society member George Bernard Shaw, who stated in an interview that "India's Ulster was already there." He insisted that there was "no point squabbling about mixed motives and imagining political intrigues, where there was nothing but political bewilderment in the face of a tough problem."[21] The de Valera–controlled *Irish Press* did not offer such expressions of understanding in its coverage. It stated that the British reaction to every demand for Irish independence was to "encourage some minority to offer implacable resistance to the wishes of the majority."[22] It placed the blame for partition equally at the foot of the British government and the Muslim minority community: "Ever since the British withdrawal had been made certain . . . the Muslim League has demanded partition . . . [and] the British Cabinet weakened and temporised. The Muslim league grew bolder and Congress more despondent."[23] In describing the outbreak of violence in India through 1946–1947 the *Irish Press*, quite disingenuously, drew comparisons with events in the wake of Ireland's partition: "Any Irishman could have foretold what it would be. Lurgan and Belfast and many a Six-County village saw those flames and that pogrom prepare the way for partition." Interestingly, it went on to make quite a specific reference to how partition was to be implemented in Bengal: "Irishmen will be immediately reminded of not only Tyrone and Fermanagh but of the block of four counties, Armagh, Derry, Fermanagh and Tyrone, which taken together, would provide that simple majority which, if the British Government's ruling on India were applied to their case, should release them from Orange rule, just as Western Bengal is to escape from the dominion of neighbouring concentrated majorities."[24]

## TECHNICALITIES AND IRISH PRECEDENTS

The series of official British documents relating to the transfer of power in India is littered with references to Ireland, many of them comprising dire warnings of the lessons to be learned from the recent history of British-Irish relations.[25] Many British politicians and administrators had been responsible for policymaking in both countries, including Austen Chamberlain and Lord Birkenhead—both signatories of the Anglo-Irish Treaty of 1921 who also served as secretaries of state for India. Significantly, Leo Amery, who had been secretary of state for Dominion Affairs from 1925 to 1929, served as secretary of state for India during the Second World War and had been a staunch opponent of Irish Home Rule.[26] It was under his stewardship, however, that the first British reevaluation of the Anglo-Irish Treaty of 1921 had taken place, and specifically in relation to the possibility of negotiating a similar treaty with India. He submitted to the British Cabinet in February 1945 a memorandum titled "The Problem of an Anglo-Indian Treaty." Despite the failure of the 1942 Cripps mission, there is evidence in the memo that the India Office was willing to consider partition, or rather "a scheme of settling the relations between His Majesty's Government and the Union (or Unions) of India," or "whether there will be one or more units in India with whom Treaties are to be negotiated."[27] The issue of minorities was given due consideration, and it was acknowledged that this was a particularly tangled problem that had "figured prominently in the 'safeguards' provided in Articles 14 and 15 of the Anglo-Irish Treaty."[28] An interest in the technical aspects of the partition of India was also shown by Irish officials. Irish Taoiseach and minister for External Affairs, Éamon de Valera, had asked his Department of External Affairs secretary, Frederick Boland, to review the 1946 British Cabinet mission's statement on India. De Valera was keen to know more about the dispute that arose between the British government and Congress leaders with regard to the interpretation of particular clauses. Boland drew up a full memorandum, together with a shorter statement summarizing the point at issue. In filling in de Valera about the failure of this Cabinet mission to India, Boland isolated the use of terminology that was recognizable in the Irish context and material that echoed the Irish experience of partition and the withdrawal of British power:

> In their statement of the 6 December, the British Government supported the Muslim view, and declared that they would not force upon "unwilling areas" a Constitution framed without the co-operation of the Muslims. After some hesitation, the All-India Congress Committee accepted the British-Muslim interpretation [but] added a reservation, however, to the effect that a Province or part of a Province would remain free "to take such action as may be necessary to give effect to the wishes of the people concerned."[29]

Both sides ultimately exploited to great effect a similar vagueness in the Anglo-Irish Treaty in relation to the Boundary Commission.

On the transfer of power in August a few months later, the Irish government hesitated about the manner of recognizing the newly independent India and Pakistan. De Valera was not in Dublin at the time but "was anxious to be rung at 1 p.m. that day so that he might settle the text of the congratulatory messages to be sent to the new Indian states." He wanted the messages to go to India in Irish as well as English and wanted "a really good Irish text as it would probably figure in the permanent records of the two states."[30] In the meantime, the Department of External Affairs' counselor, Con Cremin, and assistant secretary Shelia Murphy had a protracted discussion on the appropriate wording of the English text, with Cremin reflecting that "there was a feeling that it might perhaps be a mistake to speak of 'Free India' in the message to Pakistan, although the use of the plural 'Indian peoples' immediately thereafter would tend to counteract any bad impression created. The Assistant Secretary wondered whether the Moslems really regarded themselves as Indians at all. It was subsequently confirmed that Mr Jinnah in public pronouncements had classified the Pakistan population as among the Indian peoples."[31] Murphy and Cremin were clearly aware of the sensitive approach that was needed, no doubt as a result of Ireland's situation and their own experience in the Irish Department of External Affairs of other countries' confusion around the nomenclature of Ireland.

## THE SPECTER OF BRITISH PARTY
## POLITICS AND INDIA

Handing India its independence had become even more complicated following the events of Direct Action Day and the communal rioting that prevailed throughout the following year. In the early days of 1947 the British foreign secretary, Ernest Bevin, confided to the Irish high commissioner to London, John Dulanty, his grim assessment of the situation. Dulanty had already heard another perspective from Jawaharlal Nehru, who thought the British were repeating history:

> About India he said that at the moment he could not see any light at the end of the tunnel. The difficulty was not here but in India. (When talking to me recently Pandit Nehru made use of the same simile—describing the tunnel as being "very long and very dark" but said the difficulty was not really in India but here because the British were trying to do with them what Lloyd George did with us about the Six Counties). Mr Jinnah, formerly of the Hindoo community had been extremely difficult. "And then," he continued, "as I keep telling my colleagues in the Cabinet, if you shut up a man like Pandit Nehru in prison for sixteen years, how can you expect him to have a balanced view about anything?" The solution, he felt, would be found but it would be reached only after a long and arduous struggle.[32]

In reporting to Dublin, however, Dulanty was keen to press home Bevin's concluding remarks to him as he left his office; he had caught Dulanty off guard by referring to the partition of Ireland in a positive light:

> [Bevin] told me that [French foreign secretary] M. Bidault said "a good thing" to him. . . . When he congratulated M. Bidault on his Government's proposals for Indo-China, the latter said that the French had learned a lesson from the British. "What lesson is that?" asked Mr Bevin, "Oh" replied M. Bidault, "like you, we give and we keep." He told me this as we were walking to the door at the end of the conversation: he was on time and I had, therefore, no opportunity to make from our standpoint the obvious comment on what he had—curiously for him—called a "good thing."[33]

It was quite a perturbing experience for an Irish representative to hear such comments from the lips of a British Labor Party minister; there had been much hope in Ireland that the postwar Labor Government might make efforts in the direction of ending partition. For generations Irish nationalists had endured the bitter experience of having the "Irish Question" played as a mere pawn in British party politics, and the Irish press was apt to identify something similar happening in relation to Indian policy and partition: "There is another disturbing element from the British viewpoint. India has become a party question with Labour for withdrawal and Conservatism for staying on. Mr Churchill had made himself the spokesman of the Indian minority, this giving them an implied promise of support, a promise for which India may pay as dearly as Ireland paid and is still paying for similar interference in Irish domestic affairs by the same British party and for the same selfish purpose."[34] In the Dáil (Irish Houses of Parliament) Irish politicians were urging the government to attempt to reengage the Attlee Government on the issue of partition, especially as there appeared to be glimmers of hope that Clement Attlee and his colleagues were more open to addressing Irish grievances than their Conservative predecessors. The Irish Labor Party leader and Teachta Dála (member of parliament) William Norton asked the Taoiseach:

> In view of the fact that Britain is now shedding her control over Burma and over India, is likely to be compelled to shed her extra-territorial rights in Egypt and has now intimated that she proposes to abandon Palestine, would the Taoiseach not consider the advisability, from an Irish standpoint, of making a formal demand on the British Government, that, just as she thinks it desirable to abandon these territories where she has no moral claim, she might emulate that good example by evacuating the Six Counties of this country which she occupies with as little moral claim as that with which she occupied the other countries she is now evacuating?[35]

The Taoiseach had only a short reply: "The whole question is whether making a formal demand of that sort is going to bring us nearer or make more difficult a solution of the problem. If a formal demand is made, that is but one step. I take it that people have to think of what is the next step."[36] De Valera's pessimistic response gives lie to the common interpretations that the partition of Ireland was by 1947 an established fact, that it was not a hotly contested issue, and that it wouldn't become one again until the Border Campaign of the 1950s. As late as 1964, though, the *Irish Times* stated that only one partition since the First World War had been tacitly accepted, and that was Ireland's. The "two Irelands," it said, accorded each other "begrudging mutual acceptance."[37] Arguably, the partition of Ireland was viewed by the British in 1947 as, if not a total success, then not a complete failure either.

## THE ESTABLISHMENT OF THE DOMINIONS
## OF INDIA AND PAKISTAN

The *Irish Press* covered the announcement of the partition of India (Mountbatten's 3 June Plan)—or "The Establishment of the Dominions of India and Pakistan"[38]—in great detail, both on its front page and in an opinion piece. Gandhi's steadfast opposition to the partition of India was emphasized, and Mountbatten's references to Ireland during the press conference in India were reported. Asked what provisions were in place in order to avoid disruption of vital infrastructure in the weeks to come, he answered that such plans "had been worked out in the division of Ireland and that many agreements were still in effect there."[39] In press coverage of the announcement there was evidence on both continents of the "language of abhorrence" from nationalists, outraged at the "vivisection of mother India," to use Gandhian phraseology. Here we touch on a theme common to both Ireland and India; they were like Mazzini's Italy, "endowed by Providence with their own irrefutable boundary marks." Ireland was naturally enveloped by the sea, an island nation, not two; and Gandhi told the Round Table Conference in 1931 that he represented "the whole of India from the Himalayas to Cape Comorin."[40] The *Irish Press* front-page coverage on 5 June 1947 told its readers how "the painful history of Ireland [was] recalled" in the Indian press, which was at that crucial moment in its country's history telling readers of the "nefarious role Britain has played in Ireland. Ulster should have provided the red signal" to India. The *Irish Press* also reported how the *Bombay Chronicle* said that there was no joy in the hearts of millions of Indians "at the prospect of their country's dismemberment."[41] These were graphic allusions to the destruction of a natural national entity, echoing the words of the *Fermanagh Herald*, which had asked how the British government "with its own somber memories of the troubles it had following the Irish Partition [would] wish to force India to accept such a compromise, which would not be a settlement of any sort but a savage operation lacerating the face of India, causing mutilation beyond all recovery."[42]

One significant similarity that both countries had was that Britain was desperate to keep both in the Commonwealth. There was a hope on the part of British politicians and administrators to transform colonies into free states and the empire into a Commonwealth of free and equal members. The desire to maintain this echo of empire was immensely strong and not based on mere symbolism (though this was important) but on security and geopolitics. From a British perspective the willingness of ex-colonies to retain a special connection in the form of Commonwealth membership could be viewed as a triumph of altruistic purpose as opposed to a loss of British standing in the postwar world. Of particular interest in this regard is British monitoring of the anti-partition world tour that Éamon de Valera undertook in 1948. Free from office for the first time in sixteen years, de Valera embarked on a propaganda world tour in an attempt to garner support for the end of partition in Ireland. He spent most of his time in countries with large Irish populations—the United States, Australia, and New Zealand; but on his return he stopped in the newly independent India, where he and Nehru, two former revolutionaries turned statesmen, had dinner and long talks in the evenings on the lawn of Teen Murti House.

Naturally, the Dominions Office was eager to keep track of de Valera's movements and utterances. Crucially, however, it was much less concerned about the effect his tour would have on public opinion in relation to partition in Ireland or India than on the impact that his visit could have on Indian policy in relation to the Commonwealth, which had yet to be clarified. An India outside the Commonwealth could prove problematic for Britain, and taking advice from de Valera was not exactly at the top of the British preferred list of methods to elucidate matters. The Commonwealth Relations Office warned the British high commissioners in both India and Pakistan in advance of de Valera's visit that it might have the effect of encouraging "yet further examination in India (and perhaps Pakistan) of the possible applicability of solution on lines similar to those adopted in Éire to the problem of the future position of India and Pakistan in the Commonwealth."[43] The effect of his opinion in relation to partition was a secondary concern: "anything which Mr de Valera says about the partition question may also be used to draw an analogy between that and the partition of India into two dominions last August."[44] Sir Terence Shone, high commissioner to India, kept the Dominions Office informed of de Valera's every utterance during his trip. First, he noted how, generally, in the course of "various speeches during his passage through India, Mr de Valera emphasised the interest which the people of Ireland had always had in India and their pleasure in India's recently acquired freedom." He went on to take great care to note de Valera's exact remarks with regard to Ireland's relationship with the Commonwealth, as clearly he was also aware of the implications that de Valera's advice to Nehru might have on India's soon-to-be-decided republican status: "As regards Ireland's position in the Commonwealth, Mr de Valera said that, although Éire was an independent republic, she was externally associated with the states of the British Commonwealth because the Irish people felt that such an association met the sentiments of certain elements in their population and was not inconsistent with Éire's national position and interests as a republic."[45] Here we see de Valera acknowledging how the External Relations Act was primarily created with partition and Ulster unionism in mind. The Dominions Office was clearly concerned that the expression of such sentiments in Delhi could induce Nehru to attempt to create a similar set of circumstances in India in the hope that it too could lead to an end to partition, or worse for the British, an India outside the Commonwealth. Shone noted that it was for India "to decide whether or not the devil she knew was better than the devil she did not know."[46] In such circumstances the British government would have to formally review its stance on whether republican status was compatible with Commonwealth membership.[47] Tellingly, Shone reported to the Dominions Office how "although Mr de Valera emphasised throughout that his pronouncements referred solely to Éire and were not proffered in regard to India's future attitude, it was inevitable that his remarks about Éire's relationship with the Commonwealth should give rise to some deliberation on India's own future relationship with the Commonwealth."[48] It seems that in India in 1948, like Ireland in 1921, London's overriding concern, despite communal tensions, was what the new government's position would be in relation to the British Crown.

CONCLUSION

The history and partition of Ireland were ever present during the debate surrounding the partition of India. As a source of inspiration it sustained both Muslim League activists and Hindu nationalists, while at the same time providing British policymakers with a template, albeit an imperfect one, for dealing with minority community concerns. From an Irish perspective there was a keen sense of déjà vu when the circumstances around India's partition gained press attention. The amount of reportage in newspapers and the efforts made to publish Indian opinion demonstrate that the Irish public had an immense appetite for consuming news on India's partition, and in so doing reliving, or rather reengaging, some twenty-five years later, with their own. In 1956 the Irish Department of External Affairs drew up an internal memorandum titled "Partition in Ireland and Abroad"; this short review was prompted by the Cyprus Emergency and the possibility of partition being implemented there. Its conclusions in relation to Ireland and India are worth quoting, because it is an important and concise comparison of the two partitions some ten years after the violent events that brought with them the birth of a new state, Pakistan:

> India is the state which most resembles Ireland in regard to partition. This came about on the withdrawal of the British and the country was divided into mainly Moslem and Hindu areas. Indian partition differs in as much as . . . the Indian Government, while not regarding partition as a desirable solution for the problems it faced on attaining independence, is not now working to end it. It does have frontier problems with Pakistan such as Kashmir and the waters of the Indus valley but it does not dispute now that Pakistan is an independent state with which it is prepared to negotiate.[49]

The author is unidentified, but there is a note of detachment in relation to Northern Ireland on the part of this official that would not have been out of place in Southern Ireland at that time. Although the Irish government maintained an irredentist policy toward Northern Ireland, it was not until the onset of the civil rights movement in the 1960s that the anti-partition movement regained momentum. Similarly, after an initial reprieve in the wake of transfer of power in India, border issues began to simmer, in particular in Kashmir, demonstrating how partition was the origin of many modern-day conflicts in South Asia. Long after the British departure, both partitions persist in various guises on the geographical landscapes of Ireland and India, peculiar but persistent codas to each country's long and ravaging road to independence.

CHAPTER 5

# "CLOSE PARALLELS"?
*Interrelated Discussions of Partition in South Asia*
*and the Palestine Mandate (1936–1948)*
Lucy Chester

## INTRODUCTION

The theme of "close parallels" appears again and again in discussions of the use of partition, or territorial division by a third party, in British India and the Palestine Mandate. In 1937, a senior British politician referred to Indian precedents as providing a "general parallel [that] is very close" to Palestine.[1] In 1945, the governor of Bengal argued that the Indian case was "closely parallel to the Palestine position."[2] In 1947, Zionist doyen Chaim Weizmann saw "great similarity" between India's and Palestine's problems,[3] while a Zionist legal advisor was more cautious, critiquing the view that the two situations "offer a very close parallel."[4] Perhaps most striking is British prime minister Clement Attlee's September 1947 statement that "there was a close parallel between the position in Palestine and the recent situation in India."[5] The repeated solicitation of officials with Indian experience to serve in Palestine speaks more subtly to the depth of the British conviction that the two cases were analogous.

Most Indian nationalist leaders denied such claims, while Arab observers tended to regard them as dangerous. A 1945 Zionist report noted that the Indian National Congress (INC), a secular political party, regarded partition proposals for Palestine as "a most dangerous example for India (Pakistan)," while adding optimistically, "a partition proposal might even gain us some friends in the Muslim League camp."[6] But in 1947, a senior Pakistani diplomat articulated the official Muslim League view that British India and Palestine were essentially different,[7] while an INC representative assured his Zionist interlocutors that "there are no similarities whatsoever between the Indian and Palestine problems."[8] After the creation of Pakistan, an Egyptian onlooker warned that the campaigns for Pakistan and Israel were "parallel policies."[9]

This chapter deals primarily with the role played by arguments about such parallels, rather than with the extent to which India and Palestine actually were or were not close parallels. (Their major differences included geography, demographics, and the length of British involvement.[10] Another difference, which falls outside the scope of this chapter, was the Government of India's 1905 attempt to partition the province of Bengal. This division, intended in part to undermine nationalist activity in the area, was a failure and ended with Bengal's 1911 reunification.) In both cases, questions of minority rights received much political attention: in Palestine, Britain had backed guarantees to establish a "national home" for Jews in Palestine during World War I and in the early 1920s, while in India the question of Muslim political rights in a Hindu-majority land led eventually, in the 1940s, to calls for a separate state for Muslims. In regard to partition proposals in the two territories, British and to a lesser extent Zionist proponents of partition embraced arguments that presented India and Palestine as analogous. Most Indian nationalists, both secular and Muslim, rejected claims that the two cases were similar; with some notable exceptions, Arab leaders seem to have paid less attention to the question of Indian similarities. I am also interested in arguments that were not made about the two cases and in lessons that were not derived; in particular, British officials understood clearly that partition would be difficult and complex to implement in Palestine but did not apply that knowledge to the Indian case.

Although scholars have done a great deal of valuable work on partition in Palestine and in South Asia, there has been little detailed analysis of connections between the two cases. T. G. Fraser provides parallel studies of the high politics behind the three main British imperial examples of partition but examines them in isolation, an approach that will disappoint those interested in direct connections.[11] That those connections abound is clear from the work of other scholars, notably Wm. Roger Louis. Louis is unusual in touching on India's influence on Palestine-oriented policymakers and the press, and doing so allows him to demonstrate that the South Asian case weighed on British leaders' minds as they considered Palestine.[12] More recently, Priya Satia's work on "official conspiracy theories" shows that British fears of collusion between shadowy anticolonial groups around the world played an important role in British governance of Iraq in the 1920s.[13] This anxiety about the (largely imaginary) danger posed by anticolonial connections sheds important light on British policymaking in the decades that followed. In Chapter 6 of this volume, Penny Sinanoglou shows that analogical thinking about connections between Palestine and other territories, including Egypt, Ireland, and India, shaped partition planning in the mandate and helps explain its persistence. Contributions like Louis's, Satia's, and Sinanoglou's contrast with traditional imperial historiography's neglect of the rich field of direct interactions between India and Palestine.

Whereas imperial history tends to focus on the metropole, transnational and transcolonial history provides a promising framework in which to examine interactions that cross colonial lines. Analyzing the webs that linked colonial holdings provides new insights into the development of anticolonial movements and their postcolonial successors, as seen in the work of Rory Miller on Palestine and Ireland, Kate O'Malley on India and Ireland, and P. R. Kumaraswamy on Israel and India.[14] In keeping with this move toward transnational history, my approach is to treat India and Palestine not as isolated cases but as part of larger structures—including imperial and anticolonial networks—with the goal of analyzing their multilayered relationships.

As this volume shows, actors in British colonies had varied approaches to partition—an example of variation within anticolonial movements more broadly. The study of partition and of decolonization more generally would benefit from a clearer understanding of what anticolonialism meant in a range of cases. By spurring discussion, the preliminary suggestions of this chapter may help move the field toward a more rigorous understanding of anticolonialism and the way its various manifestations contested (or adapted) colonial concepts of partition.

Anticolonialism meant different things to different groups and included a range of methods and goals. First, as the chapters by O'Malley, Sinanoglou, and Gordon suggest, anticolonial activists were well aware of the larger transcolonial context of individual anticolonial movements. Some used that context to forge alliances and to contest partition, while others found it threatening because it provided potential precedents for territorial division. Second, anticolonialism could take both secular and religious forms and often involved complicated relationships between religion, secularism, and partition; Devji, Gordon, and Satia weave this subtheme into their chapters. Third, anticolonialism could involve peaceful protest, outright violence, and nuanced approaches in between (as seen in the work of Golani, O'Malley, Beinin, and Satia). This spectrum of approaches to violence accompanied a spectrum of views on partition.

Fourth, Devji, Gordon, Beinin, and Satia show that anticolonialism had varied relationships to nationalism. Some Indian nationalist groups contested colonial control, while others warily collaborated with British rulers. Related to this point is the fifth and perhaps most important aspect of anticolonialism. Anticolonial forms of protest could coexist with more ambiguous relationships to colonialism; here, Gordon's chapter on binational Zionism is particularly illuminating. Many Zionist leaders opposed certain colonial policies but simultaneously saw British rule as providing key benefits to minority groups, especially religious minorities fearful of majority rule. These relationships were dynamic and changed over time. By the 1940s, many Zionists were eager for Britain to leave Palestine.

This overview suggests two conclusions. In terms of methodology, a comparative and transnational foundation is crucial to efforts to define anticolonialism, because it manifested differently in different contexts. Second, a typology of anticolonialism would help scholars understand when, where, and under what circumstances partition, religion, violence, and other factors played key roles in the end of empire. This typology would necessarily combine a broad definition, acknowledging that anticolonialism encompasses many approaches, organizations, and goals, with a specific framework, analyzing variation within anticolonial groups in terms of goals, methods, relationship to other anticolonial groups, and so on.

Examining the cross-fertilization of diverse anticolonial movements is exciting, but it is not easy. Working in multiple archives, in multiple languages, and in multiple historiographies makes the research itself challenging. There are also analytical difficulties in gauging the precise impact these movements had on each other. Activists' communications sometimes expressed ambitions that were never or only partially realized. Where different groups employed similar tactics, it is not always easy to discern whether these methods developed independently or whether one influenced another. And it can be difficult to tease out anxious imperial predictions from actual effect, not least because British fears sometimes became self-fulfilling prophecies. Many anticolonial leaders were well aware of these imperial concerns; this knowledge, combined with a genuine interest in working with fellow activists, further motivated their outreach.

In order to gauge the role that India played in Palestine's development and vice versa, this chapter deals with three distinct phases of partition discussions in the two locales. I selected these cases because of the light they shed on the relationship between policy in India and in Palestine; the longer history of the idea of partition in both regions is beyond the scope of this chapter. The first episode centered on the proposal put forward by the Palestine Royal Commission, better known as the Peel Commission, to create separate Arab and Jewish states. Critical Indian response helped doom this proposal. The idea of partitioning Palestine seemed to have died until Prime Minister Winston Churchill returned to it during the Second World War; although these proposals remained internal, governmental concern about potential Indian reaction was one of several factors that delayed a final decision until events overtook the proposals. During the third period of discussion, Britain moved toward a rushed last-minute partition of India while resisting United Nations plans to divide Palestine. This period saw some of the most intriguing comparisons of the two cases and of their mutual significance.

## THE PEEL COMMISSION

In late 1936, the British government sent a Royal Commission of Inquiry to Palestine to investigate the causes of Arab discontent with the mandate. The commission was headed by Lord William Robert Peel, a former secretary of state for India, and became known as the Peel Commission. Of the commission's five other members, two had Indian expertise: Sir Laurie Hammond, a former governor of Assam, and Reginald Coupland, a colonial historian. The presence of India experts on such a body was not unusual; commissions devoted to colonial issues, in Palestine as elsewhere, typically consisted of men with expertise in other parts of the empire, and India was the biggest source of imperial experience.[15]

The Peel Commission's primary conclusion—and the one that garnered the most international attention—was its recommendation that Palestine be partitioned into a Jewish state and an Arab state, as well as a British-controlled enclave.[16] The notion of partitioning Palestine had originated earlier,[17] but the Peel plan brought the idea to a wider international audience. The reaction of Indians in particular alarmed British officials, who were primed by what Priya Satia calls "conspiracy thinking" to fear a transcolonial uprising sparked by anger over Britain's Palestine policy.[18]

The Government of India, which was already closely monitoring Indian Muslim sentiment in regard to Palestine, reported, "Interest in the matter is widespread, especially in Muhammadan circles," as was "condemnation of the proposed partition of Palestine."[19] The INC, a leading secular nationalist party, also played a role, although British intelligence suggested that INC attention had more to do with politics than with genuine conviction: "There are signs of influential Congress leaders taking up the Arab cause as an occasion for attacking British Imperialism and cultivating Muslim goodwill."[20] In British eyes, the INC's interest in Palestine was opportunistic and therefore presumably insincere. But there was no denying that the Peel proposal was having a widespread negative effect on Indian opinion.

Mohandas Gandhi and Jawaharlal Nehru, two of the INC's most prominent leaders, were both genuinely concerned about the Palestine problem. Gandhi contemplated taking an active role in mediating a Palestine settlement, motivated in large part by his disapproval of the Peel partition plan. Immediately after the Peel report's publication, Gandhi wrote to a Zionist friend, Hermann Kallenbach: "I have read the

Palestine Report. It makes sad reading but the Commission could not do anything more. It almost admits the critical blunder [of] a promise to the Arabs and a contrary one to the Jews."[21] In August 1937, one of Gandhi's close associates, Charlie Andrews, wrote that he and Gandhi saw an opportunity for a peaceful settlement in which India itself could be central: "*Here*, in an extraordinary way, is the key to the whole question."[22] Similarly, Gandhi told Kallenbach, "much of the work lies in India as I visualise the development of the settlement talks."[23] These letters demonstrate that, from Gandhi's perspective, India's potential influence on the partition issue in Palestine lay not only in the wishes of its Muslim population, but also in its potential to facilitate Jewish-Arab accord. In correspondence with another Zionist contact, Nehru wrote: "It seems to me clear that the proposed partition is utterly bad and is bound to create more trouble in the future. It is certainly not a solution of the problem."[24] Elsewhere, Nehru wrote, "enforced partitions are equally doomed to failure. The British Government must also remember the terrible crop of bitterness and ill will that they are sowing, not only in the entire Muslim world but also in large parts of Asia and Africa."[25] Nehru's interpretation of the problems and possibilities in Palestine rested on his conviction that British imperialism worked to divide Jews and Arabs just as it worked to divide Hindus and Muslims in India.

Indian Muslims were well aware of Britain's concern about the possible effect of South Asian protests, and they now began to leverage that political power with the Muslim League, a political party that sought to speak for India's Muslims, making a number of important statements about Palestine. Like the INC, the League roundly condemned the notion of partitioning the mandate. It did so in part out of genuine anger at the idea and in part because its leaders recognized that the Palestine issue represented a valuable rallying point with which to raise the League's profile. The nationalist poet and politician Muhammad Iqbal wrote to party president Muhammad Ali Jinnah recommending that the League pass a "strong resolution" on Palestine, because doing so "will at once popularise the League and may help the Palestine Arabs."[26] Iqbal recognized the potential political advantage that the League, still struggling to establish itself as a major political force, could reap from engaging with the Palestine issue. This awareness of the political benefits of speaking out in favor of Palestinian Arabs was not cynical; it went hand in hand with authentic anger at Zionist inroads in Palestine.

Jinnah addressed the Palestine problem at length in his October 1937 presidential address to the League, saying, "It has moved the Mussalmans all over India most deeply." Claiming to speak not only for Indian Muslims but for Muslims worldwide, he asserted that Britain would be "digging its grave" if it failed to honor earlier promises to the Arabs and pledged Indian Muslim support to "help the Arabs in every way they can."[27] The League membership's response proclaimed that unless Britain abandoned partition in Palestine, Indian Muslims "will look upon Britain as the enemy of Islam and shall be forced to adopt all necessary measures according to the dictates of their faith."[28] Given the history of British fears of Indian Muslims' "inherent" tendency to violence, fears that dated back to the 1857 uprising, such statements would have been understood by British officials as raising the specter of revolt and jihad.[29]

Indian opinion was one factor among many that shaped British policymaking in Palestine, and we should not overstate its impact. As Chaim Weizmann complained in a letter to the Colonial Office, "I am told that under the pressure of Indian Moslems, Arab Kings, Italian intrigue and, last not least, anti-Zionist Jews, the notion is gaining ground in high quarters that partition is impracticable, that the Report of the Royal [Peel] Commission should be given a decent burial."[30] Weizmann's report helps us gauge the relative weight of Indian views, as one important factor in British policymaking for Palestine but not the decisive one. The Arab element was particularly important, as increasing European unrest heightened British concerns about the need for Arab support in case of war. The weight of Indian opinion reinforced the Arab factor but would not have been enough in and of itself to reverse British thinking.

In late 1937, the British government began to move away from the Peel plan in large part because it was alienating increasingly crucial Arab allies. The Foreign and India Offices both worked to overturn the Colonial Office's partition plan for Palestine. In late 1937, the British government began to form a technical commission, ostensibly in order to investigate the feasibility of partitioning Palestine. In practice, the

Foreign Office saw it as a means of escaping the Peel plan, which it feared would irreparably damage Anglo-Arab relations. Headed by John Woodhead (fresh from a term as governor of Bengal), the technical commission became known as the Woodhead Commission—and informally as the "Re-Peel" Commission.[31]

When a Palestinian Arab uprising threatened British control from within the mandate, Britain responded brutally (using techniques adapted from India).[32] In mid-August 1938, Gandhi, who had apparently lost hope of mediating peace, wrote: "What a tragedy going on in Palestine! It is heart-breaking. If there is peace, ultimately, it will be the peace of the grave. However, we must endure what we cannot cure."[33] In November 1938, the British government released the Woodhead report, which amounted to a rejection of the Peel plan. Shortly thereafter, the government announced that the Woodhead report demonstrated that "the political, administrative and financial difficulties involved in the proposal to create independent Arab and Jewish States inside Palestine are so great that this solution of the problem is impracticable."[34] In short, the Woodhead Commission report gave Britain the excuse it now craved to renounce any plan to partition Palestine.

The British renunciation of plans to partition Palestine seemed to calm Indian Muslim opinion, at least initially. The viceroy informed the secretary of state that Indian statements since the announcement were favorable or suggested that Indian Muslims need not concern themselves with Palestine.[35] Another (unsigned) report stressed the need to maintain this positive Muslim reaction, given the unsettled international environment. If war could be averted, this observer wrote, "then I feel certain that the world Muslim opinion can be ignored," but if war did break out, "our enemies may use the discontented Arabs and other world Muslim opinion against us."[36] British paranoia aside, it is true that Indian nationalist organizations, both Muslim and secular, recognized the broad appeal of the Palestine issue in India. Palestine touched not just on Muslim sympathies for Palestinian Arabs, but also on broader Indian resentment of British colonial control. The British government's retreat from the Peel plan temporarily reduced Indian pressure, but Palestine remained a live issue in Indian politics.

This episode establishes that Indian interest in Palestine stemmed both from genuine concern and from, as Iqbal candidly admitted, a realization that Indian politicians had much to gain from publicizing their protests against Britain's Palestine policy. A range of Indians, from religious nationalists to secular politicians, protested British actions in the mandate. This episode also demonstrates that a variety of considerations accounted for the fact that India and Palestine were linked in the minds of British officials. Some officials, especially those in India, were sincerely concerned that Palestine policy might provoke Indian unrest. Others, chiefly Foreign Office officials, seem to have seen what we might call the "India card" as a convenient tool to back anti-partition arguments they championed for other reasons. Finally, it seems likely that British authorities found it more palatable to stress their desire to accommodate the wishes of their Muslim subjects than to admit publicly that imperial weakness compelled them to mollify their Arab allies. In these circumstances, Indian opinion did not compel Britain's move away from partition so much as provide cover for that move.

## WORLD WAR II AND THE CABINET COMMITTEE ON PALESTINE

Despite Britain's public retreat from the Peel partition plan, five years later Winston Churchill directed his cabinet to revisit the question of dividing Palestine. This wartime exploration remained an internal British government matter, so there was no response from Indians, Arabs, or Jews in the areas concerned. Indian anger—and perhaps more importantly the British fantasy of Indian Muslim fury—continued to play an important role, as India Office and Foreign Office objections cited the likelihood of Indian Muslim protests if Britain proposed partition in Palestine again.

In July 1943, Churchill formed a cabinet-level Committee on Palestine and named Leo Amery, secretary of state for India, to it. Amery supported Zionist aims in Palestine (and was a drafter of the 1917 Balfour Declaration). His Zionism was, by his own account, "strategical," based on his conviction that Britain would benefit from a prosperous Jewish state whose leaders felt a debt to Britain, but some scholars argue that Amery's hidden Jewish ancestry played a role.[37] Certainly Amery had close ties to many key decision makers in Britain and in Palestine, and he devoted much attention to the Palestine issue while grappling with India's wartime problems.

The December 1943 Palestine Committee report, which proposed dividing Palestine into a Jewish state, a Jerusalem Territory, Lebanon, and Greater Syria, is notable for its engagement with the small-scale implications of partition.[38] It criticized the Peel Commission's earlier suggestion of separating the cities of Tel Aviv and Jaffa, arguing that for practical reasons the two had to be kept together in the Jewish state, despite Jaffa's large Arab population. Allotting the neighboring towns to separate states would pose almost ludicrous challenges, the committee wrote: "the boundary between the States would have to be drawn down the centre of a road. The [Woodhead] Partition Commission found itself forced to envisage such a road with a high iron railing, forming the actual boundary, along the middle of it; it is unnecessary for us to dilate on the fantastic nature of or on the administrative inconvenience inherent in such an expedient."[39] Two points are worth highlighting here: time and detail. The prolonged discussions of partition within the British government highlighted the problems inherent in dividing even a very small country, with particular attention to local difficulties. British officials had a clear understanding of just how difficult it would be to implement partition in Palestine. These insights did not carry over to British thinking about South Asia.

The Palestine Committee recognized that the solution it suggested was risky but argued that it could be successful if it were implemented quickly. The committee concluded: "There is much to be said for a King Solomon's judgment when there is reasonable hope of each half of the baby surviving and leading a lusty life of its own. But it can only do so if the cut is swift and clean."[40] This metaphor, authored by Amery, implied that the division could resemble a surgical procedure, in which speed and precision would improve the patient's chances for survival. It is also noteworthy that it placed the British in the position of the wise biblical king, with no mention of local input.

Meanwhile, India was descending into crisis. The 1943 Bengal famine caused widespread starvation, and the apathetic British response increased Indian resistance to colonial rule. The anti-British Indian National Army was popular with many Indians. And the Muslim League had since 1940 advocated the formation of a "separate state" for Indian Muslims. In 1944, Reginald Coupland, the noted historian who had served on the Peel Commission, issued a report on India's "constitutional problem." (Amery had helped elect Coupland to the prestigious Beit Chair of Colonial History in 1920, and Coupland was an important influence on Amery's thinking about both Palestine and India.)[41] He drew on an analogy from Palestine to demonstrate his conviction that Indian Muslims were unlikely to give up their demand for a separate state: noting that Palestinian Arabs were unmoved by claims that Zionist settlement had benefited them economically, he argued that Indian Muslims too were likely to prefer independent poverty to wealth under Hindu rule. "The moral for India," he concluded, "is plain. If the calculations made in this chapter are sound, Partition means that the Moslem State or States would be relatively weak and poor. But it cannot be taken for granted that its Moslem champions will abandon it on that account." On the contrary, material considerations would likely be subsumed by nationalist feeling: "Will not Moslem patriots say what those Arabs said: 'What does it matter how weak and poor our homelands are if only we are masters in them?'"[42] Coupland himself did not advocate partition, as Arie Dubnov stresses elsewhere in this volume, but he believed that lessons from Palestine provided insight into likely Indian Muslim reaction.

As the partition committee report circulated among British diplomats abroad, strong objections came in. The British ambassador in Baghdad urged attention to partition's effect on the Muslim world as a whole: "In particular I hope that the probable reaction of the Moslems in India will be examined."[43] He warned that announcing a partition before the defeat of Germany and Japan would be a grave error, providing the enemy with useful propaganda material with which to stir up Indian Muslim resentment.[44] This perspective had its roots in fears of a "grand scheme to undermine the British Empire," fears that arose in the nineteenth century but grew through the 1920s.[45] The Foreign Office's allusion to Indian Muslim feeling in support of its anti-partition campaign was an approach with decades-old imperial underpinnings.

As the former head of Middle East Command, Indian viceroy Archibald Wavell might have been well placed to advise on the intersection of Britain's concerns in India and Palestine, but his frosty relations with Churchill limited his influence. Churchill resisted Amery's repeated efforts to involve Indian officials in the deliberations over Palestine, in part because, as he said, "You know perfectly well how they will reply."[46] Churchill's point was valid; the India Office and the viceroy, concerned primarily with maintaining control and stability in South Asia, were never going to condone a policy deplored by Indian Muslims. Amery's persistence in arguing that the viceroy ought "not to have a decision sprung on him which might seriously affect the whole position in India" is all the more striking given that it was clear that Wavell would oppose Amery's own partition plan.[47]

In October 1944, the Cabinet Committee on Palestine issued another report, in which it acknowledged partition's "unquestionably great" inherent difficulties but again urged partition. Such difficulties became more obvious the longer the subject was discussed, for "the closer the question is examined the more clearly do they stand out. Indeed, any scheme of partition might almost be said to invite destructive criticism."[48] This proposal, like the 1943 version, is notable for its attention to logistical problems. It highlighted the need for joint administration of common services and infrastructure, transfer of administrative records, and allocation of assets. But it also urged haste: "when the time comes, His Majesty's Government should act with unhesitating decision." Yet again, Amery argued for a "swift and clean cut" to enable each of the infant Palestinian and Jewish states to survive.[49]

The viceroy (like so many other British officials) invoked the specter of Indian unrest in opposing partition in Palestine, but this argument was not the deciding factor. Forwarding reports from provincial governors, Wavell asserted that Indian Muslim interest in Palestine was "genuine, and any settlement of the problem unacceptable to Muslim opinion might have very serious results in India."[50] But in the end, Amery's squalling infants, Wavell's concerns, and the Foreign Office's protests had less impact than a single act of terrorism: the assassination of Lord Moyne, Britain's resident minister in the Middle East, on 6 November

1944. Moyne, a political ally and personal friend of Churchill's, was shot by a Zionist terrorist group. In a bitter statement to the House of Commons (and intended for an international audience as well), an outraged Churchill warned, "If our dreams for Zionism are to end in the smoke of an assassin's pistol, and the labours for its future produce a new set of gangsters worthy of Nazi Germany, then many like myself will have to reconsider the position we have maintained so consistently and so long in the past."[51] Moyne's death seems to have brought an end to any serious British consideration of partition in Palestine.[52]

The 1943–1944 discussion of partition did not significantly affect Britain's Palestine policy, but the reasons so little changed during this period help us understand what did occur later in the decade, and why. Not surprisingly, events in the Middle East and in the metropole— such as Moyne's assassination and Churchill's reaction to it—were the decisive factors. India was not in itself central to British policy for Palestine. Amery and Wavell raised the likelihood of Indian protests out of real concern for the Palestine issue's possible impact on Britain's ability to control India at a time of increasing unrest. But the Foreign Office, which led the anti-partition campaign within the government, cited Indian agitation primarily as a means of persuading its colleagues to accept a more pro-Arab policy, not as the true motivation for that policy.

## POSTWAR DISCUSSIONS OF PARTITION

The third chapter of interrelated partition discussions in India and Palestine opened after the war. During this period, Muslim nationalists pushed for autonomy for India's Muslim-majority areas, and beginning in 1947 British officials belatedly but rapidly moved toward a partition of Muslim-majority from Hindu-majority areas. In Palestine, Britain maintained its anti-partition stance, particularly when the United Nations proposed a new partition plan of its own. For the first time, there was simultaneous discussion of partition for India and for Palestine. Some Zionist and British actors embraced the idea that the two cases were analogous, while many Arab and Indian representatives resisted the notion that there were significant similarities.

In early 1945, the governor of Bengal, Richard Casey, drew on Palestine to argue that Britain should establish a deadline for its withdrawal
from India. Because nationalists were, in his opinion, "most unlikely to
reach an agreed solution on their own," he envisioned a set of clear time
limits, which would curb nationalist bickering by serving as "a large-scale
guillotine."[53] Casey (who had extensive experience in the Middle East)
maintained that such defined deadlines were required to facilitate Britain's departure from both India and Palestine. In contrast to Amery's view
of partition as giving new life to infant states in Palestine, Casey's suggested outcome functioned as a death threat; left unspecified was whose
neck would go into the guillotine.

Zionist thinkers recognized that parallels between India and Palestine
could be potentially dangerous. In 1945, F. W. Pollack, a German Jew
who moved to India from Palestine in 1940 (and later served as Israeli
consul in Bombay),[54] reported to the Jewish Agency in Palestine:

> The [Indian National] Congress fears that partition might be proposed in
> Palestine—which would be a most dangerous example for India (Pakistan).
> In this case all Congress circles will fight violently against partition—while
> a partition proposal might even gain us some friends in the Muslim League
> camp. But if, for instance, a Bi National State should be proposed with guar-
> anteed equal rights for Jews and Arabs, we might find many friends amongst
> the Congress Leaders—while Muslim League would fight against such a
> proposal more violently than ever.[55]

Like earlier British observers, Pollack asserted that Indian interest in
Palestine stemmed largely from political concerns. His correspondence
shows that some Zionists continued to hold out hope that even Muslim
Indians could be persuaded to support a Jewish state, on the grounds
that a partition in Palestine would improve the chances of the creation
of Pakistan. To this end, Pollack urged the Zionist leadership to devote
greater attention to Indian popular feeling. He maintained, "Whether the
constant argument that Britain has to consider public opinion in India—
which is [one] hundred per cent against a Jewish Palestine—is justified or
just an excuse, we, in any case, have to do more than we have done hith-
erto to try to influence this hostile public opinion in India."[56] Whether

Indian opinion genuinely altered British policymaking or merely, as Pollack suggested, provided an excuse for British officials to move away from partition, it required a Zionist response.

Jewish advocates of a binational future for Palestine were also attentive to analogies between India and Palestine, which they tended to regard as strained and even dangerous. Judah Magnes, founder of the Ihud (Unity) party, which favored a binational Palestine, believed there were "fundamental differences between Palestine and the Jews on the one hand and Ireland and India on the other hand. I think they are radically different and the analogy is basically a false analogy."[57] Other statements critiqued specific aspects of the analogy with British India, such as the notion that a binational state could be based on separate electorates for Jews and for Arabs, as in South Asia. A pamphlet promoting binationalism described separate electorates as "one of the banes of India's political life."[58] From this perspective, the analogy with South Asia was not only misguided but could exacerbate political divisions in Palestine.

In July 1946, an Anglo-American Committee of Inquiry concluded that one hundred thousand European Jewish refugees should be admitted to Palestine. The preceding months saw widespread rumors of this impending recommendation, just as India was in the thick of its own inquiry: three British cabinet members had arrived in March as part of an effort to craft a political solution that would keep independent India united. In an April 25 meeting with this "Cabinet Mission," Viceroy Wavell reported that the Anglo-American Committee's likely proposal would anger Indian Muslims, adding that he thought the Palestine report "was likely to harden Jinnah [of the Muslim League] in his adherence to Pakistan."[59] In a cable to London, Wavell went further, predicting that "Muslims in India will sympathise [with Arab reaction to the report] and there will be hard words used. Attitude on Pakistan will harden and make negotiations more difficult. Jinnah will certainly use it to emphasise necessity for sovereign Muslim state. Whether more serious results will follow here probably depends on outcome of Cabinet Mission's deliberations. If Muslims decided to resist any proposed constitutional scheme the resentment about Palestine would naturally add fuel to the fire."[60] In June, however, the Muslim League accepted the Cabinet Mission's plan for a federated India; Wavell's fears as to the influence of Palestine policy on events in India seem to have been overstated. In this instance, Palestine's impact on India loomed larger in the imperial imagination than it did in reality, although certainly there was a great deal of Indian interest in and sympathy for Palestinian Arab affairs.

Back in Britain, former India Secretary Leo Amery retained a keen interest in Palestine policy. Following parliamentary discussion of the Anglo-American Committee's report, he wrote to his friend Weizmann to complain of the British leadership's unwillingness to contemplate partition: "They inherited a perfectly good plan for a clear surgical operation the wou[n]d of which might have been largely healed long before this. Instead of that they have been fumbling about probing the sore undecidedly and asking everybody else to come along and probe it with them."[61] Whereas in 1943–1944 Amery had pictured Britain as a Solomonic figure, now he described British leaders as hesitant and incompetent surgeons.

Arabs in Palestine paid less attention to India than Indians paid to the Middle East. Arabic-language newspapers such as *Falastin* and *al-Jami'ah al-'Arabiyah* provided periodic updates on the anti-British struggle in India.[62] Their coverage tended to focus on Gandhi and his secular anticolonial campaign rather than on Jinnah's Muslim political party.[63] As a result, newspaper consumers in Palestine were familiar with Gandhi. Jinnah, however, was so unfamiliar to Arabic-reading audiences in the region that even after he visited Cairo in 1946, a headline in the Egyptian newspaper *Akhbar al-Yaum* referred to him not by name but as "the adversary of Gandhi."[64] This striking example demonstrates the reluctance of Arab newspapers in Palestine and Egypt to engage with Jinnah or the Muslim League's partition platform, let alone to discuss any possible parallels. *Akhbar al-Yaum*'s reporter raised this issue in an interview with Jinnah, explaining "the difficulties for the Arabs if they approved Indian Muslims' stand on the partition because their approval of this principle would provide justification for the Zionist for partitioning Palestine." He recorded that Jinnah dismissed this comparison, saying, "The case is very different."[65] Both Arabs and Indian Muslims viewed the idea of parallels between the demands for Pakistan and for a Jewish state as dangerous and misguided.

When Arab representatives mined the Indian case for evidence to support their demands, they looked for arguments against partition. An anxious Colonial Office official reported to an India Office colleague that Arab delegates in talks with the British planned to argue that it was inconsistent for Britain to allow South Asia's Muslim minority to be ruled by the majority but not to allow Palestine's Jewish minority to be ruled by the majority. He requested help in composing a response, but an India Office official dismissed the parallel between India's Muslim minority and Palestine's Jewish minority entirely, noting, "I do not think that this analogy is a real one."[66]

The significance of this incident lies in the Colonial Office's sense that it needed to examine the India-Palestine analogy precisely because nationalist leaders were likely to use it against Britain. Dealing with communal tensions in multiple holdings left the British Empire vulnerable to accusations of inconsistency from its nationalist opponents. Like Zionist leaders, Arab nationalists saw the value of analogies that used Britain's own colonial holdings against it. Whereas Governor Casey had labeled India and Palestine "closely parallel" for the purpose of deriving lessons helpful in maintaining British control (at least temporarily), the India Office dismissed the same analogy out of hand when Arab diplomats sought to use it to challenge that control.

The year 1947 marked a watershed in the development of partition plans for both India and Palestine. After long avoiding any discussion of an Indian partition (in part because of the failed 1905 partition of Bengal), British leaders announced in June 1947 that they would divide the subcontinent in August of the same year. Although Britain now opposed plans for a division of Palestine, the United Nations began exploring its own partition plan for the mandate. Britain's resistance was based largely on strategic considerations, but in February, Colonial Secretary Arthur Creech Jones also acknowledged that "the longer he had examined the detailed implications of Partition [for Palestine], the more he was impressed by its practical difficulties."[67] The more time British officials devoted to crafting a workable partition plan, the more clearly they saw just how unworkable any division would be. This insight in regard to Palestine contrasts sharply with the attitudes displayed during the rush to implement a South Asian partition.

In Indian minds, Britain remained closely linked with the idea of partitioning Palestine. Pro-INC newspapers viewed the situation in Palestine "as one more example of Britain's imperialist policy of 'divide and rule.'"[68] The Muslim League mouthpiece, *Dawn*, denounced Britain's "simple betrayal of the Arabs" and urged it to adopt "an emphatic repudiation of Zionist aspirations."[69] This position implied League rejection of the notion that there was any significant resemblance between those Zionist aspirations and its own. Jinnah had paid a disappointing visit to Cairo in 1946, which likely drove home the fact that many in the Middle East feared that Pakistan could establish a dangerous precedent for the region.[70]

During the crucial final months of British control over India and Palestine, Zionists stepped up their efforts to use the Pakistan campaign as leverage to gain a Jewish state. On June 3, when Mountbatten announced a plan to partition India,[71] Chaim Weizmann promptly requested the viceroy's assistance in crafting a similar scheme for Palestine: "There is great similarity, as you may have gathered, between the Indian problem and our problem here [in Palestine]. In comparison with India the Palestine problem may seem as a storm in a tea-cup, but I venture to say that the repercussions of the Palestine problem are, and are likely to continue to be, very serious indeed. . . . I believe that a Palestinian Pakistan would be a rational way-out."[72] Weizmann did not specify the similarities he saw between the two cases, apparently assuming that they would be evident to Mountbatten. He acknowledged that Palestine might look small and insignificant compared with India but argued that it was equally important in terms of its potential ramifications. His use of the phrase "Palestinian Pakistan" is particularly intriguing, suggesting that in his mind a Jewish state would have many similarities to the new Muslim state. However, Mountbatten did not accept this invitation.

Mountbatten's partition announcement prompted another Zionist, Jacob Robinson, legal advisor to the Jewish Agency, to take a more rigorous look at comparisons between India and Palestine. In a report titled "Partition of India: Implications for Palestine," Robinson noted that some Zionists hoped that the British decision to create a Muslim state in South Asia might augur an increased willingness to support a

Jewish state in Palestine.[73] He quoted one columnist who, reasoning that "the method of solving the problem in both lands offers a very close parallel," predicted that Pakistan would have "the most far-reaching effect."[74] Robinson was more skeptical. He argued that Britain was unlikely to partition Palestine, concluding that the South Asian partition "only demonstrates once more the tremendous ingenuity of Britain's political thinking, its elasticity in detail as compared with its rigidity in the main objectives."[75] Although the details of Britain's withdrawal were subject to change from case to case, the primary goals, particularly the focus on preserving British interests, remained the same.

Despite Robinson's cautionary analysis, leading Zionists continued to seek Indian support for a Jewish state in Palestine. Eliahu Epstein, head of the Jewish Agency's US political office, met with Asaf Ali, India's UN representative, and tried to persuade him that Mountbatten's plan to divide India and Pakistan could serve as a guide for Palestine. Asaf Ali recoiled. As Epstein reported, "Asaf Ali was rather taken aback for the moment, but then went on to try to explain to me that there are no similarities whatsoever between the Indian and Palestine problems."[76] Asaf Ali argued that while Muslims were indigenous to India, a Jewish state would be "an alien body," a position in keeping with the INC's consistent anti-partition and pro-Arab stance.

Some Arab opinion-makers feared the use of the Pakistan claim as a precedent for the creation of a Jewish state. In a June 1947 interview with Jinnah, for example, an Egyptian newspaper reporter emphasized "the difficulties for the Arabs if they approved Indian Muslims' stand on the partition because their approval of this principle would provide justification to the Zionist for partitioning Palestine."[77] Despite their sympathy for a Muslim quest for a sovereign state, Arabs were concerned that supporting the creation of a state for South Asia's Muslim minority could impede their work against the creation of a state for Palestine's Jewish minority (although as the Pakistan campaign came closer to fruition, Arab leaders hailed it as a model for Muslim liberation.)[78]

Meanwhile, the British were just beginning to grapple with the logistics of partition in South Asia. As recently as early 1947, negotiations had centered on the possibility of creating some form of unified independent

India. Not until March of 1947 did the notion of partitioning South Asia come to the fore. Whereas public and private consideration of partition in Palestine lasted decades,[79] Indian negotiations about implementing partition were compressed into a matter of months. The boundary commission that divided British India into India and Pakistan did not even take shape until the summer of 1947 and was compelled to complete its work in less than two months.[80]

As the boundary commission took shape, Indian Muslims considered what factors might affect the commission's decision—and how to influence those factors. One Muslim official in India wrote to Jinnah to urge that territory desirable for the future Pakistan should immediately be settled by Muslims. "Like the Jews of Palestine," he wrote, "we should concentrate on purely Muslim cities and places and thus swell our population ratio."[81] Consistent with Jinnah's unwillingness to compare Palestine's Jews with India's Muslims, his published papers contain no record of a reply.

The haste of the South Asian division stands in marked contrast to the lengthy, detailed, and often agonized debate over partition possibilities in Palestine.[82] The last of the many commissions sent to Palestine to consider problems there, the United Nations Special Committee on Palestine (UNSCOP), was formed in May 1947. It included a representative from India, as well as from ten other UN member states. UNSCOP's mandate was to consider the future of Palestine, and when it issued its report in September, an eight-member majority called for partition with economic union, while a three-member minority (including the Indian representative) preferred a federal solution.

During testimony before UNSCOP, Chaim Weizmann referred to India's partition in arguing for the division of Palestine, saying, "partition is *à la mode*. It is not only in small Palestine; it is in big India."[83] In a summary of his comments, he more directly framed India's partition as a model for Palestine: "the arguments which speak for partition in India, speak for it also in Palestine. It is true that our problem is much smaller in size, but it would be fallacious to conclude that its repercussions are less serious."[84] This version implies that, because Britain had agreed to grant a minority a state of its own in Pakistan, the UN should do the same for

Jews in Palestine. Leo Amery supported this view, writing to Weizmann: "As you know I have ever since 1937 been a convinced believer in partition, and the Indian outcome, added to the Irish, has only strengthened the case. I do believe that once par[t]ition is decided mutual animos[it]y between Arabs and Jews will subside and working arrangements become possible."[85] Amery seems to have expected that the South Asia partition would reduce Hindu-Muslim tension; he was writing in late July, when some British officials still hoped for a peaceful decolonization in India.

Even in late summer 1947, as the South Asian partition unfolded in extraordinarily bloody fashion, the British leadership viewed it as a model that might guide policy in Palestine. Accurate casualty numbers for the violence that accompanied the creation of India and Pakistan are difficult to come by, but some five hundred thousand people died, while another ten to twelve million or more fled into exile.[86] In addition, tens of thousands of girls and women were raped, abducted, or both.[87] And yet in September, as the slaughter continued, Prime Minister Attlee told the cabinet that "in his view there was a close parallel between the position in Palestine and the recent situation in India" and that "he hoped that salutary results would be produced by a clear announcement that His Majesty's Government intended to relinquish the Mandate and, failing a peaceful settlement, to withdraw the British administration and British forces."[88] In other words, the South Asian division had passed off successfully enough that Attlee felt a similar approach should be used in Palestine. The key similarity was the need for Britain to signal that it meant to withdraw no matter what (a position reminiscent of Richard Casey's 1945 call for "a large-scale guillotine" of a deadline). With this India-Palestine comparison in mind, the British cabinet decided on an "early withdrawal" from Palestine.[89]

Weeks later, another British official used the India-Palestine analogy to make a very different point about violence. On 2 October 1947, Alan Cunningham, Britain's high commissioner in Palestine, met with Husayn al-Khalidi of the Arab Higher Committee and David Ben-Gurion of the Jewish Agency (future prime ministers, albeit briefly in Khalidi's case, of Jordan and Israel, respectively) to discuss the grave situation they faced. He drew their attention to events in India in order to warn of large-scale violence if Britain departed without any agreement between Arabs and Jews: "I suggested to them that they should take note of what was happening in India and . . . wondered whether they had thought out to the full the possible implications and whether by their actions they wished to bring chaos and bloodshed on the ordinary inhabitants of the country."[90] While Attlee used the Indo-Pakistani divide as an example of British withdrawal having gone relatively well, Cunningham held it up as an example of a worst-case outcome. It is conceivable that Cunningham in early October 1947 had better information about the scale of violence in South Asia than Attlee did some two weeks earlier. But Attlee was certainly aware that migration on a massive scale was under way by mid-September.

Arab leaders, too, watched the mass killing in South Asia and invoked it in efforts to warn of impending disaster. In early October 1947, the Lebanese prime minister, Riad Al Solh, argued that if the British withdrew from Palestine, either Jews there would become more open to concessions, "or more likely there would be [a] serious clash as in India."[91] From Solh's perspective, the violent crescendo of Hindu-Muslim conflict in South Asia provided a strong argument against a similar approach in Palestine. But Arab opinion was not monolithic. In December, the Coptic Christian leader and ardent secularist Salama Musa criticized Egyptians who supported the South Asian partition while opposing the division of Palestine, writing, "The Moslems of India and the Jews of Palestine have adopted parallel policies."[92] For Musa, Pakistan remained a dangerous precedent.

In the aftermath of their own division, both India and Pakistan fought against UN proposals for Palestine's partition. As an UNSCOP member, India had championed a federal solution. Pakistan's UN representative, Zafrullah Khan (who had argued the Muslim League case for partition before the boundary commission that divided northwestern India), specifically rejected Weizmann's reference to "the division of India into Moslem and non-Moslem areas as a precedent for the partition of Palestine," because in India "the partition was not artificial and furthermore had the consent of both the Moslems and non Moslems."[93] Expanding on this view later, he also emphasized differences in size and the basic principle, observed in South Asia, "of ceding to the minority a number of areas in which they were in the majority"; unlike in India, where Muslims were "an integral part of the population, in Palestine a minority had been artificially created by settling Jews against the express will of the people."[94] (In private, Zafrullah seems to have held more nuanced views, advising Arab leaders to accede to partition and then boycott the Jewish state.)[95] But Zafrullah's arguments were unsuccessful, and on 29 November 1947, the UN voted to confirm the UNSCOP partition plan, which would divide Palestine into a Jewish state, an Arab state, and an international zone around Jerusalem.

By early 1948, British policymakers recognized the long-term problems caused by the forced migration that had occurred in India and Pakistan. A Foreign Office report titled "The Future of Arab Palestine" predicted that Jews would seek to establish a Jewish state that was economically viable and had defensible boundaries, which would differ from those in the UN proposal. It noted that such boundaries would cause large-scale migration "on the lines of recent events in India."[96] From a Foreign Office perspective, the Indian case was not a positive analogy but a warning—because what had happened in South Asia, with minorities fleeing into exile, could happen in Palestine.

In the end, Britain's refusal to cooperate with the UN partition plan helped seal its doom. This final attempt to partition the Palestine mandate was overtaken by a civil war between Arabs and Jews in Palestine and then by the Arab-Israeli war of 1948. The planned partition boundaries never materialized, being superseded by the 1949 armistice lines and then by ongoing conflict between Israel and its neighbors. The long-discussed Palestine partition faded into smoke, while the last-minute, poorly planned division of India and Pakistan created lasting territorial realities.[97]

CONCLUSIONS

The Peel Commission's 1937 partition plan drew increased Indian attention to Palestine. Indian nationalist leaders had sympathized with Arab concerns about Jewish immigration to Palestine from the 1920s onward, but with the Peel proposal the issue became more prominent in Indian politics. Nationalists recognized an opportunity to exert influence over British policymakers, and although it is difficult to measure the precise impact of Indian views on Britain's Palestine policy, the Muslim League in particular raised the specter of a Palestine-fueled Indian Muslim uprising in its attempts to pressure Britain to adopt a more pro-Arab policy in the mandate.

Although Indian attention to Palestine never rose to the level of sustained unrest, British opponents of the Peel plan frequently cited the threat of such disorder. Indian opinion was not the deciding factor in Britain's 1937–1938 shift away from the Peel plan—Middle Eastern strategic considerations were more important—but it provided valuable cover for imperial leaders who preferred to present themselves as respecting their imperial subjects' desires than giving in to increasing imperial weakness. This successful use of the Indian bogey in the 1930s, overlying persistent conspiracy thinking from earlier decades, revealed a key vulnerability within the British government. Nationalist leaders eager to bolster their Muslim support were already aware that Palestine provided a useful rallying point for this constituency. Their keen observation of imperial anxiety and internal disagreement showed them additional advantages to be reaped from emphasizing their opposition to a division of Palestine.

Both imperial and anticolonial groups used the India-Palestine analogy in their hard-fought campaigns to win public opinion, international support, and much-needed assistance, both material and intangible. Some groups, particularly the Muslim League and Arab observers outside Palestine, found that the analogy between the call for Pakistan and the call for a Jewish state had awkward implications for their own political projects. As these comparisons accrued greater power, they sometimes took unexpected turns, threatening to undermine what might otherwise have seemed like natural alliances.

In short, the partition debates of the late 1930s and early 1940s laid the groundwork for a variety of imperial and anticolonial actors to invoke Indian opinion as a factor that should help shape Palestine policy in the 1940s. The precise meaning of the comparison between potential new homelands shifted depending on who was deploying it, with actors like Weizmann using it to argue for a Jewish state and others like Solh

using it to argue against such a division. As the India-Palestine analogy accumulated more weight in political discussions, those discussions
also featured increasingly grim imagery. Amery initially saw the India-
Palestine comparison as a hopeful one, linked to the image of vigorous
infant states, but for other spectators—and eventually for Amery too—it
conjured darker visions. Casey called for a "guillotine," Weizmann anticipated a "burial," and Gandhi foresaw the "peace of the grave," while
Zafrullah lamented what he saw as Palestine's "bleeding body upon a
cross forever."[98] These metaphoric references to life and death remind us
of partition's central paradox: its tendency to trigger very real dislocation
and even death just as it ushers in new political life.

## CHAPTER 6

# ANALOGICAL THINKING AND PARTITION
# IN BRITISH MANDATE PALESTINE

Penny Sinanoglou

SPEAKING BEFORE THE PERMANENT Mandates Commission of the League of Nations in 1937, British colonial secretary William Ormsby-Gore urged that Britain be allowed to explore the possibility of partitioning Palestine. As justification for this unusual request, he argued: "Palestine was unlike any other country with which the British empire had to deal. . . . The task of the mandatory Power in Palestine was unique. The country was unique: the difficulties were unique."[1] To some extent, indeed, Ormsby-Gore was right. Both the requirements of the mandates system generally and the specific obligations incumbent upon Britain in the Palestine mandate represented significant divergences from prior imperial experience and practice. In addition, the Jewish settler population in Palestine was not altogether typical of the white settler population in the empire as a whole.

The League of Nations' mandates system was established to provide international oversight for the former Ottoman provinces and German colonies seized as a result of World War I.[2] Palestinians were among the many "peoples not yet able to stand by themselves under the strenuous conditions of the modern world" whose "well-being and development" formed "a sacred trust of civilization" that Britain as mandatory power would discharge.[3] Britain thus undertook the obligation not only to protect the civil and religious rights of the people of Palestine, but also, critically, to bring them to self-government. As a former Ottoman territory, Palestine was an "A" class mandate, that is, one whose inhabitants enjoyed the most developed civilizations and were thus closest to full political independence. Britain's support for the establishment of a "Jewish national home" in Palestine was professed in the 1917 Balfour Declaration, which was later both enshrined and developed in the text of the mandate with Britain's full cooperation.[4] It therefore seems fair to say that the textual conundrums of the Palestine mandate, if not the events and circumstances that were later to make them so explosive, were largely of Britain's own making and thus unusual in the history of the empire.

The inclusion of the Balfour Declaration into the mandate for Palestine left Britain in the position of encouraging the immigration of non-Palestinian Jews into the country and overseeing their "close settlement" on the land. Although white settlers populated many areas of the empire, Jewish immigrants to Palestine were distinct from Britain's white settler population in Africa, Australia, and North America in several important ways: their presence in Palestine was due to an explicit scheme to build a "national home," and they constituted not only a nonnative, but also a non-British and nonimperial group. Jewish immigrants to Palestine were largely East European, and, by the mid-1930s, German. Few were British or from other parts of the empire, and though many of the highest-ranking Zionist leaders spoke English, increasingly the Jewish population in Palestine spoke Hebrew. On many counts, then, the Jewish settlers in Palestine could not be included in the imagined imperial community. In sum, the creation, form, and a critical function of the mandate set Palestine apart from all other parts of the British Empire. Palestine stood in a category of its own even in comparison to Iraq and Transjordan, the other Middle Eastern mandated areas assigned to Britain, neither of which included the obligation to establish a Jewish national home, and both of which, not coincidentally, moved rapidly toward some form of self-government.[5] Not surprisingly, historians of both the British Empire and Palestine tend to read the Palestine mandate as a case apart.[6]

And yet, as this chapter will demonstrate, there is much to be gained from recognizing and analyzing the threads that connected Palestine to the early-twentieth-century British Empire. Palestine may have been unique, as Ormsby-Gore asserted, but by 1948 it ended up partitioned, as had Ireland and India before it. The division of a territory into two or more areas under newly independent authority or sovereignty was a striking characteristic of British decolonization during the first half of the twentieth century, and inasmuch as Palestine experienced British planning for partition (the attempted implementation of which was ultimately left to the United Nations), it appears to have been far from unique in the British imperial world. Many others in this volume, especially Faisal Devji, Arie Dubnov, Kate O'Malley, and Lucy Chester, have traced some of the ways in which British, South Asian, and Irish thinkers, politicians, and bureaucrats connected Palestine to other parts of the empire, and Adi Gordon unpacks this theme in reverse, showing how anti-partitionists in Palestine supported their arguments with reference to other, particularly colonial, cases. The current chapter focuses on British policymaking in Palestine and argues that for all its singular structures and strictures, Palestine offers us an important example of partition planning as a process that was both intensely local and fundamentally transnational. Partition as a British policy and practice, this chapter aims to demonstrate, was born of imperial secondment and transfer and was developed by officials who drew both on their own experience on the ground in multiple territories and on prior British imperial partitions. Legions of administrators, both in Palestine and in London, thought through the Palestine problem by placing it side by side with other imperial situations that seemed to them similar in critical ways. The broad concept and details of partition in Palestine owe much of their genesis to these men thinking across but also, crucially, working across the empire.

Partition existed as a set of concepts and practices to which administrators in Palestine and London could refer because they had already been tried in different forms in the British empire during the first two decades of the twentieth century. When faced with a particular set of political problems in Palestine that appeared to fall into a familiar pattern of ethno-religious conflict, British politicians and administrators instinctively turned to what seemed, at least on the surface, to be their analogues in Ireland and India. In the case of Bengal, partition had been implemented, unsuccessfully and therefore temporarily, in order to weaken political agitation and assert imperial control. In Ireland, Britain sought to permanently align religion, political sovereignty, and territory through partition. By the time it became clear that Palestine was going to be a serious political, moral, and economic problem for Britain, partition had found its place within the range of possibilities to which administrators might turn.

The partition idea in Palestine also developed out of a very different set of analogizing impulses, however, as administrators, particularly in Palestine itself, saw the conflict between the Arabs and Jews in terms of that between native Africans and white settlers. Drawing on Lugardian notions of trusteeship, these officials set out to protect Arab cultivators from Jewish settlers by setting up land reserves or cantons and ensuring that Jews would not achieve political dominance in any kind of joint legislature. This impulse to frame what was essentially a political problem in terms of its impact on small agriculturalists dovetailed with the already existing solution of partition by suggesting a territorial answer to the conundrum of Palestine. As Palestinian Arab nationalism asserted itself in Palestine through the mid- to late-1930s, British officials turned away from comparisons to Africa, whose natives were assumed to have no nationalist impulses, and made stronger connections to Ireland and India, where policies had been developed to cut off or contain nationalist blocs.

## EARLY PARTITIONS

The partition of Bengal between 1905 and 1911 may seem an odd place to start since it was not implemented with the intention or effect of creating at least one new independent state. It was ostensibly undertaken in order to rationalize and simplify the administration of a province that covered a large area, contained a population of approximately forty-two million people in 1901, and was, by many accounts, undergoverned.[7] And yet, although British officials had discussed rearranging the provincial boundaries of Bengal for more than a decade, it was the political advantage of such a move that finally tipped the balance toward partition. As the Indian viceroy, Lord Curzon, argued, partition was a measure that would "divide the Bengali-speaking population; that would permit independent centres of activity and influence to grow up; that would dethrone Calcutta from its place as a centre of successful intrigue" and would damage the power of the Indian National Congress.[8] In other words, the partition's aim was to splinter political resistance to British power. Bengal was divided, its eastern portion combined with Assam to form one province, and its western part combined with Bihar and Orissa to form another. Muslims formed a majority in the new eastern province, while non-Bengali Hindus numerically dominated the western province. Curzon's partition thus fragmented the political unity and power of educated middle- and upper-class Bengalis in the Congress party, who correctly read partition as an attempt to weaken the possibility of an all-India political resistance.

From the vantage point of later events in Palestine, the partition of Bengal is significant because it manifested the concept of dividing territory and political representation along religious lines.[9] Although the partition of Bengal was eventually reversed in 1911 in response to massive protests, the principle of representation by confession became entrenched in Indian politics and law. The Muslim League was founded a year after Bengal's partition, and in 1909 the Indian Councils Act (commonly known as the Morley-Minto Reforms) created exclusively Muslim electorates in provincial and central legislative elections and reserved seats for Muslim representatives on these legislative councils. The provisions, coded as protections for religious minorities, were developed and entrenched in the Indian political system through both the Montagu-Chelmsford Reforms of 1919 and the new constitutional framework developed in the 1935 Government of India Act.

Shortly after the passage of the Montagu-Chelmsford Reforms, the Government of Ireland Act (1920) made official the partition of Ireland and the independence of part of the United Kingdom. The act was the immediate descendant of the Home Rule Bill of 1914, though its roots went back well into the late nineteenth century and the Home Rule movement started by Isaac Butts in the 1870s and championed by Charles Stewart Parnell from 1880.[10] It provided for two devolved parliaments, one to sit in Belfast and represent six counties of Ulster, and the other to sit in Dublin and represent the remaining twenty-six counties of Ireland. After the Irish Dáil passed the Treaty with Britain in 1922, six counties of Ulster remained part of the newly renamed United Kingdom of Great Britain and Northern Ireland, while the rest of the Irish counties became the Irish Free State and were given Dominion status. Partition, in this particular case, was given its final legal stamp of approval many months after it had started to become a reality on the ground, and many years after it had first been discussed by British lawmakers. British administrators had been laying the groundwork for a separate administration in Belfast during 1920, while the idea of partitioning four counties had been floated as early as 1911.[11] Again, the logic of religious and political affiliation underlay the territorial division, with the Protestant majority in Ulster refusing to become a minority in Ireland as a whole under Catholic majority rule.

From the British perspective, Ireland's partition, unlike Bengal's, was remarkably successful, despite a civil war in the new Irish Free State and lingering popular irredentism. Ireland was peaceful relative to its earlier state, and most importantly, it no longer represented a drag on British economic and military resources and a persistent thorn in the side of British politics. Through the late 1930s, "partition seemed to have provided a relatively painless way out of the Irish problem."[12] In Ireland, as eventually in India, partition was used to decolonize, and most importantly, to disentangle the Irish question from domestic British politics. As a method of imperial control, partition had proved to be a blunt instrument in Bengal that aroused more opposition than it defeated. The principle of dividing political representation, and therefore indigenous political power, along religious lines, however, was a more subtle tool that survived the reversal of Bengal's partition in 1911, thrived in Government of India Acts through the mid-1930s, and eventually came to full fruition in the partition of India in 1947.

In linking the partitions of Bengal and Ireland, my point is not to suggest that they were identical, or resulted from some uniform tendency to fragment along religious lines. On the contrary, each case developed from a complex set of internal political circumstances, aims, and maneuvers. But from the vantage point of Palestine's administrators, India and Ireland appeared as parallels to Palestine, and thus the partitions and constitutional divisions undertaken in each place provided a potential model to follow.

IMPERIAL PATHWAYS

If the British Empire is thought of as a web created by the movement of peoples, goods, and ideas, then in relation to the Palestine mandate the Colonial Office constituted a critical node. With slightly fewer than fifty administrative officers by 1939, the Colonial Office was responsible for some two million square miles, with a population of approximately fifty million.[13] Not surprisingly, given these numbers, the empire was both administratively and fiscally decentralized. The colonies, including mandates such as Palestine, were expected to be self-financing and the "men on the spot" to take initiative and maintain control without constant reference back to London. The Colonial Office did not administer the colonies; it oversaw them. Governing was left to each colonial administration, in the case of Palestine to the high commissioner and the Palestine government.

For all the empire's decentralization, however, the Colonial Office lent coherence to the colonies in two ways. First, it centrally controlled the (fairly homogeneous) makeup and movement of personnel. Imperial services recruited from a relatively small, and coherent, segment of the British population. Most Colonial Service (and, for that matter Indian Civil Service) recruits were middle-class young men educated at public schools and Oxbridge.[14] They often came from families with a long tradition of service in the empire and frequently married into such families.[15] Sir Ralph Furse single-handedly undertook and managed recruitment for the Colonial Office between 1931 and 1948, relying on personal recommendations to find his candidates and on gut instinct (largely, it appears, based on the quality of the young man's handshake) to accept them into the civil service.[16] Second, and this was increasingly the case in the 1930s, the Colonial Office sought to develop overarching policies for an empire that "gradually became to be seen more as a whole, and as a stage upon which more interventionist and generally applicable policies might be evolved."[17] In addition to working in geographically defined departments, such as the Middle East Department that oversaw Palestine, officials in the Colonial Office began to think thematically across regions with the establishment in the mid-1930s of Economic, Development, and International Relations Departments, the latter designed to coordinate policy across the League of Nations mandates.

The Colonial Office acted as both recruiting base and, as one historian aptly put it, "a large international labour exchange."[18] Officers were routinely seconded to new parts of the empire, and sometimes these temporary assignments became permanent. Awareness of the particular talents or knowledge of a given official flowed not only through the centralized system of the Colonial Office, therefore, but also through his personal contacts in both his home and temporary administrations or governments. Similarly, techniques of administration, management, and development moved through the empire, sometimes directed by the higher officials at the Colonial Office, and other times traveling along peripheral networks.

The movements described above relate only to colonial administrators, but similar networks and paths existed for lawyers, judges, and other law officers.[19] There are also two other important groups whose experiences, though not in country-specific administration, helped to connect disparate parts of the empire. Military men moved around the empire and frequently transitioned into civil administration at all levels, from the lowest district officer to the position of governor or high commissioner. As a result, techniques of counterinsurgency, surveillance, and defense developed in one area often found their way to another. Finally, British politicians and intellectuals roamed the empire, if not in actuality, then in theory. They were the most likely to make facile comparisons between, for example, Ireland and Palestine, but also the most prone to thinking through the philosophical underpinnings of governance at opposite ends of the globe.

## INTELLECTUAL, ADMINISTRATIVE, AND MILITARY CONNECTIONS

Before turning to an examination of the role imperial analogies played in the development of the partition idea in Palestine, it is worth noting the much broader context of cross-imperial learning and borrowing in which these analogies were made. Elements of governance in British Palestine appeared to take their inspiration from Frederick Lugard's principle of indirect rule as elaborated in his influential work on British rule in Africa, published the same year that the League endorsed the Palestine mandate.

The mandate for Palestine, and indeed the entire mandates system, formalized the Lugardian notion that Britain was to be a trustee "to civilization for the development of resources, to the natives for their welfare."[20] The British invention and establishment of the Supreme Muslim Council and the office of the Grand Mufti of Jerusalem seemed designed to enable a Lugardian form of indirect rule by creating a chief, in this case the Mufti, Hajj Amin al-Husayni, and a ruling council in whose hands authority over the Muslim community could be placed.[21] Unlike the Jewish Agency, which increasingly played the role of a shadow government, the Supreme Muslim Council was, as Ronald Hyam describes indirect rule, "not concerned with nation-building. It was designed to facilitate control rather than constructive change, law and order rather than effective modernisation."[22]

The British persistence in classifying the inhabitants of Palestine by religious affiliation, and the related refusal, evident in the text of the mandate, to see the Arabs as a national group, owed much to the dominant British view of Egyptian society as described in Lord Cromer's authoritative work *Modern Egypt*. In great detail, Cromer offered his "evaluation of Egypt as a mélange of different religious and racial communities" that could function economically, politically, and socially only under British rule.[23] The power of religious and racial divisions was such, Cromer believed, that only the British could be counted on to rule impartially and justly. This type of thinking allowed for a convenient slippage from denying nationalism to claiming that even if nationalist sentiments were present, no Egyptian could rule justly over such a diverse population. A similar process worked in British thinking about Palestine: for a time, Arab nationalism seemed not to exist for most British observers, and then when its existence could not possibly be ignored, it was labeled an immature racial nationalism that if given full expression would violate minority rights.[24] The similarities between British ways of seeing Egypt and Palestine were no doubt due to pervasive imperial notions of race, religion, and nation, but they also traveled with the movements of imperial administrators. Gilbert Clayton, Wyndham Deedes, and Ronald Storrs were among those members of the Palestine administration who had spent formative years in Egypt.

Imperial ways of thinking about the role of religion and race as they related to self-government and nationalism formed the intellectual framework in which Palestine's administrators thought through the issues they faced. Palestine was also steeped in imperial knowledge in an even more direct way. Commissioners sent to Palestine over the decades to investigate the causes of violent unrest, the amount of land available for settlement, or the possibility of partition were largely men with a great deal of imperial, and even wider international, experience. They implicitly, and frequently explicitly, placed Palestine in a broad context, suggesting parallels to other cases and drawing upon their experiences elsewhere to suggest solutions for Palestine.

The investigatory commissions created a substantial literature on Palestine that both reflected and shaped thinking and policy. As the last chief secretary of the Palestine government noted in exasperation, "If all the books of statistics prepared for the nineteen commissions that have had a shot at the problem were placed on top of one another they would reach as high as the King David Hotel."[25] The major commissions of the 1920s and 1930s were those investigating the 1921 and 1929 violent disturbances (the Haycraft and Shaw Commissions); the 1930 Hope-Simpson Commission on questions of immigration, land settlement, and development; and the Peel and Woodhead Commissions of 1936/1937 and 1938, respectively. The changing composition of these commissions is instructive, as is the ever-increasing length of their reports. The Haycraft Commission consisted of three members, all from within the Palestine government, who produced a 64-page report on the causes of the 1921 Jaffa riots. The 1930 commission, in contrast, was chaired by Walter Shaw, a retired chief justice of the Straits Settlements, and produced a report that ran to 211 pages. The commissioners included the Liberal member of Parliament R. Hopkin Morris, who had visited Tanganyika in 1928 as part of a delegation sent by the Empire Parliamentary Association, and the Labor member of Parliament Henry Snell, who later went on to serve as parliamentary undersecretary at the India Office in 1931 and the joint committee on Indian constitutional reform in 1933–1934.

The choice of John Hope-Simpson to undertake a deep investigation into questions connected to land meant that a whole range of imperial and international experiences was used to frame the case of Palestine in ways that linked race/religion and land. Hope-Simpson had been a member of the Indian Civil Service for twenty-seven years and chaired the 1924 Indian colonies committee on Indian immigrants in the empire, which acted as an advocate for Indians, particularly those trying to acquire land in the "white highlands" of Kenya. From 1926 to 1930, Hope-Simpson held the position of vice president of the League's Refugee Settlement Commission in Athens, where he dealt with the Greek refugees of the 1920–1922 war and population exchanges with Turkey. Hope-Simpson's expertise on questions of land use and yield, developed through his experience with the settlement of refugees in Greece, was critical to his evaluation of the situation in Palestine. His report argued that virtually no surplus land was available for new immigrants, and he urged the restriction of Jewish immigration and areas of settlement and intensive agricultural development of the entire country. Reflecting his involvement in the Greco-Turkish exchanges and prefiguring the population movement recommended by the Peel Commission, Hope-Simpson noted that agricultural development would require relocating Arab cultivators in order to increase the size of their landholdings.[26] Hope-Simpson's work in the empire and for the League revolved around questions of land and development with a crucial admixture of racial and religious politics.

Officials in the Palestine government also turned to the empire for practical elements of daily governance and mandatory policy. Cross-imperial examples were useful not only when it came time to think through a thorny political problem such as the one apparent in Palestine by the late 1920s, but also, and more frequently, for identifying a series of "best practices" in agricultural development; land management; and laws, development, and security. Land laws developed in India at the turn of the twentieth century set out to protect agricultural smallholders from debt, foreclosure, and general victimization at the hands of moneylenders and landlords. These laws, which were themselves often based on Irish precedent, established a concept that was then transferred to Palestine in a series of land laws designed to protect so-called cultivators.[27] The secondment of Indian irrigation specialists to Palestine's newly formed

Department of Development in 1931 brought imperial expertise to bear on this critical issue.[28] In the important area of land surveys, the Palestine government also benefited from cross-imperial experience. Ernest Dowson, former director of the Egyptian topographical survey, was appointed commissioner of lands for Palestine in 1926, and his reports on land settlement formed the basis for a series of new land laws promulgated in the late 1920s. Dowson was an exemplar of transimperial expert: he advised British administrations in Transjordan, Iraq, and Zanzibar in addition to his work in Egypt and Palestine.[29]

The Palestine government also drew on imperial military and police resources. During the first years of the mandate, the new civilian government had to contend with sporadic Arab attacks on mostly isolated Jewish settlements throughout the country and with the first large-scale riots at Jaffa in May 1921. The military turned to Ireland for techniques and personnel. Nearly eight hundred ex-members of the infamous paramilitary Black and Tans, who had helped suppress the uprising in Ireland in 1920–1921, went on to serve in a newly formed Palestine gendarmerie under their old leader, Henry Tudor.[30] The ex–Black and Tans brought with them experience in managing low-level urban guerrilla warfare, and although they never exhibited the brutality for which they had become notorious in Ireland, their presence apparently intimidated the Arabs.[31] Uprisings of varying shapes, sizes, and types, it seemed, could be suppressed in similar fashions throughout the empire. The use in Palestine of a paramilitary force fresh from the war in Ireland raises the interesting possibility that despite all outward protestations to the contrary, the British authorities saw expressions of nationalism in the Arab disturbances. At the very least, they drew a connection between the types of violence used by each guerilla group.

In the late 1930s, after the resurgence of the Arab Revolt, and particularly after the assassination of District Commissioner for Galilee Lewis Andrews, the Palestine government again turned to the empire for assistance. Charles Tegart, formerly police commissioner in Calcutta, and David Petrie, formerly director of the Indian Intelligence Bureau, arrived in Palestine to research the police force and draw up a plan for its reorganization. Tegart, best known by the public for his ability to disguise himself as a Pathan, had more than thirty years of experience in counter-terrorism and police work in Bengal, during which time he had achieved a record of disrupting terrorist networks and had survived multiple as-sassination attempts.[32] Petrie had served in criminal intelligence in India and later been instrumental in organizing and developing an Indian over-seas intelligence network that he ran, undercover, from Shanghai.[33]

The Colonial Office asked Tegart to take over as inspector general of the Palestine police, and although he refused this request, he spent long periods of time between December 1937 and May 1939 in Palestine in an advisory capacity. Tegart and Petrie worked quickly upon their arrival in Palestine, and by the end of January 1938 they had drawn up a report recommending a major reorganization of the police force including vastly improved training, particularly in the area of languages, infrastructural upgrades, and better pay and benefits.[34] In making these recommenda-tions, Tegart and Petrie referred to their Indian experiences as proof that such measures raised police morale and effectiveness.

Tegart remained in Palestine after Petrie's departure and created a Public Security Committee, which he headed until he left in May 1939. This committee met almost daily, and Tegart undertook a strenuous schedule of meetings with officials, private individuals, and police. In ad-dition, he planned and oversaw the construction of a barbed wire fence along Palestine's northern border, punctuated with small police forts whose design derived from the small fortifications of the North-West Frontier Provinces.[35] This fence was designed to keep out fighters and arms thought to be coming into Palestine over the Syrian border. More than fifty "Tegart forts"—large fortified police stations—were also built in Palestine's interior following Tegart's recommendations. Over the course of his time coordinating internal security measures, the incidence of urban terrorist acts fell; by the time he left Palestine, the army had suc-cessfully put down the Arab Revolt.

## IMPERIAL ANALOGY-MAKING AND PARTITION

Early cantonization and partition plans in Palestine were in part the result of the trends outlined above. Within easy mental reach, British officials in Palestine and London had recent examples of land sale restrictions based on race (Kenya), forced population transfer (Greece-Turkey), and territorial divisions implemented to create particular political outcomes, either by establishing more homogenous constituencies (Bengal) or by creating new states altogether (Ireland). They were also operating in a professional context in which experience gained in one territory was deemed applicable to another, and in which transterritorial movement and thinking were actively encouraged. It is therefore unsurprising that, in thinking about a way out of the Palestine problem, British officials turned for inspiration and direction to analogous situations and solutions outside Palestine.

Archer Cust, Douglas Harris, and Reginald Coupland, the three men instrumental in the process of developing partition plans for Palestine and presenting partition in the 1937 Peel Report, all drew on imperial examples and experience when crafting their plans.[36] As Arie Dubnov demonstrates in this volume, as an academic Coupland had a particularly well-developed tendency to make connections across national and imperial boundaries and to develop theories that could be applied to multiple cases. Despite a struggle within the Peel Commission over partition, Coupland's fellow commissioners were sympathetic to his way of thinking and may indeed have been swayed because the parallel to Ireland seemed so apt.[37] In comparison to the earlier commissions discussed above, the Peel Commission's members covered the widest geographical range. William Peel had served as secretary of state for India from 1922 to 1924 and again for seven months during 1928–1929; as chairman of the Burma round-table conference; and as a member of the joint select committee on Indian constitutional reforms. Sir Horace Rumbold had held diplomatic posts in Europe, Asia, and the Middle East; served as a chief delegate at the second Lausanne peace conference; and acted as chairman of the international commission on the Greco-Bulgarian frontier in 1925. Under the leadership of these two men sat four others with a wide range of imperial, legal, and academic experience. Sir Laurie Hammond was governor of Assam from 1927 to 1929 and a member of the Joint Committee on Indian Constitutional Reform that resulted in the 1935 Government of India Act, which among other things ended the practice of diarchy and proposed a federated system for India. Sir Morris Carter served as the chief of Tanganyika Territory from 1920 to 1924 and was chairman of the Kenya Land Commission of 1932–1933. Carter's experience on this commission is significant since its aim was to evaluate the status of land ownership and tenure by native Africans in Kenya and to assess claims by Africans to alienated land held by nonnative inhabitants.

In a January 1935 memorandum on Palestine, Cust wrote at length about the problems of landless Arabs in Palestine and found a possible solution when he drew a parallel between Palestine and Africa:

> It is legitimate also to seek direction among the varied administrations that govern the destinies of the component parts of the British empire and to enquire whether a problem such as that which confronts the British Administration in Palestine exists in some form elsewhere and, if so, how it is being treated. The East African dependencies, for instance, notably Kenya and Nyasaland, are faced with circumstances that are not dissimilar. There also is the problem of a white immigration, for whose welfare the state must be responsible, that belongs to a far higher plane of civilisation than the indigenous communities into whose territories they have penetrated. The protection of these native communities from exploitation and dispossession by the wealthier and more enterprising immigrants is recognised as a cardinal duty of the Government. It has therefore been established by statute that only in certain areas may land be alienated from the indigenous cultivators, due regard being given in determining those areas to the suitability of the climatic and economic conditions for white colonisation as well as to the material needs of the previous occupants.[38]

By construing Jewish immigration as analogous to white settlement in Africa, and Arabs as parallel to African natives, Cust revealed a particular interpretation of the mandate. Despite the fact that Palestine was an "A" class mandate, meaning that its native inhabitants were civilizationally advanced and would need only a short time of tutelage before being able to govern themselves, Cust's analogy implied that the Arabs of Palestine were in fact at the level of inhabitants in "B" class African mandates. His language mirrored Lugard's quite closely and helped bolster his argument for cantonization; if Jewish and Arab civilizations were so far removed from each other, it would only be natural for them to inhabit separate physical spheres, so that the one group could develop and thrive and the other could be protected. From the point of view of British trusteeship, cantonization would provide clear boundaries for the application of protective land legislation, which would prevent the continued drain of land away from the Arabs.

The move to partition from cantonization between 1935 and 1936 reflected the fact that Cust's analogy was already slightly outdated in 1935 and by late 1936 looked absurd. Especially by the mid-1930s, after the massive influx of immigrants fleeing Germany, Jews were more often characterized by British officials as urban refugees than as white settler colonists. With the Arab Revolt raging by the summer of 1936, most officials would have been unable to ignore the fact that Palestine's Arabs were politically charged and would not accept being treated as if they were African natives in a class "B" mandate, especially when their compatriots in the other "A" mandates had achieved or were rapidly moving toward self-government.

Douglas Harris helped to align Cust's cantonization idea with the political realities of Palestine, though even he was initially intrigued by the possibility of Swiss-style cantons and never really advocated a complete "clean cut." The plans Harris developed, first in collaboration with fellow development officer Lewis Andrews and later over the course of correspondence and conversation with Coupland, owed much to his experience of the complex systems of provincial autonomy in India. This allowed him to think around one of the inherent problems of partition—the great disparity in projected wealth and resources between the Jewish and the Arab states.

Harris thought across the empire because he had lived and worked across it. Before his appointment in 1935 as Palestine's irrigation advisor, Harris had been a consulting engineer and chief irrigation advisor to both the Government of India and provincial Indian governments. While in India, he had been involved in the arrangements for the separation of Sind from the Bombay Presidency in 1931, a separation fraught with tension between Muslim and Hindu political and cultural interests. He had served on the committee charged with working out the financial arrangements between Sind and Bombay and was coauthor of the

resulting report. In a letter to Coupland discussing the details of a potential partition plan, Harris made constant reference to precedents in India.
He suggested that, as with the Montagu-Chelmsford Report, the general
principle of partition and the broad outline of the proposed boundaries should be announced in the Peel Commission Report but that the
specifics should be left to a Boundary Committee and a Financial Committee.[39] Unintentionally echoing documents leaked by the Revisionist
Zionists in 1932, Harris looked to India's constitution as a model for
Palestine, where a system somewhat analogous to diarchy would be
established, with only the partial financial separation of the Arab and
mandated states from the disproportionately wealthy Jewish state. It was
Harris's experience in India that evidently gave him the idea of the Jewish state providing a subvention to the Arab state and mandated enclaves.

Coupland came to the commission having written extensively on the
imperial relationship between Britain and its dominions, the British Empire in East Africa, and the disintegration of the Habsburg and Ottoman
empires in the face of emergent nationalism. From Coupland's perspective, Britain had successfully forged a unit out of its own three nations
(England, Scotland, and Wales) and had then effectively navigated the
pitfalls of national separatism in Canada and South Africa.[40] In a 1933
speech, Coupland sounded remarkably confident in Britain's ability to
continue its unifying streak in the Middle East, boasting, "It is British
policy and British influence alone that prevents the Middle East from
being like the Balkans."[41]

Several years later, Coupland seemed less certain. In a section of the
Peel Report undoubtedly written by Coupland, the theory is presented
that "where the conflict of nationalities has been overcome and unity
achieved—in Britain itself, in Canada, in South Africa—one of the parties concerned was English or British, and that, where that has not been
so, as in the schism between the Northern and Southern Irish or between
Hindus and Moslems in India, the quarrel, though it is centuries old, has
not yet been composed."[42] When the director of education in Palestine,
H. E. Bowman, explained the structure and limitation of government-
funded education in his evidence before the commission, Coupland was
struck by the fact that the Palestine government was unable to educate

Jews and Arabs in the same classroom, or even to insist that they be educated in English in separate classrooms.[43]

In addition to his academic writing on the empire, Coupland had
served as a member of the 1924 royal commission on the superior services in India, which recommended the increased Indianization of the
Indian civil services, and had been an advisor to the Burma round-table
conference of 1931, also under Lord Peel's direction. Not surprisingly,
he was quick to see connections between India and Palestine and requested material from the India office, including Harris's report on the
Sind-Bombay separation. Harris and Coupland evidently saw eye-to-eye
on the applicability of the Indian examples, and in the final report of the
Peel Commission, they were used to support the call for a Jewish subvention to be paid to the new Arab state.[44] India additionally served as
a broad imperial benchmark in the report, which noted that as far as the
Jewish national home was concerned, "Crown Colony government is not
a suitable form of government for a numerous, self-reliant, progressive
people, European for the most part in outlook and equipment, if not in
race. The European communities in the British empire overseas have long
outgrown it. The evolution of self-government in India left that stage
behind in 1909."[45] The only way to give Europeans in Palestine the same
degree of self-government as Indians in India was to partition.

Coupland also saw the similarity with Ireland, which Britain had partitioned in 1922. In a secret interview that the Peel Commission held
with Winston Churchill, Coupland said that in his opinion, "[Palestine]
is very like Ireland in the nineteenth century. The majority of people were
refused Home Rule because the minority were in the way. . . . Presumably Arab nationalism sees it cannot get the self-government which Iraq,
Syria, Trans-Jordan and Egypt have all got, for one reason only, because
the Jewish National Home is there."[46] He declared himself "one of those
who thought that the partition of Ireland was a good thing under the
circumstances and for all time" and presented partition as "a compromise" that would allow the British to keep their promise to the Jews
without having to put down violent Arab uprisings and deny Palestine
self-government.[47] Between Coupland's conviction that the conflict was
intractable and his belief that something could be done about it that had

been done before in other parts of the empire, he became a firm proponent of partition, building on both his own and others' earlier experiences.

Placing Palestine back in the context of the British Empire reveals
a mandate whose unusual requirement to build a Jewish national home
did little to sever it from the networks of British imperial thought,
movement, and policymaking. Irrigation engineers, police officers, and
professors from Calcutta to Dublin borrowed techniques of rule and surveillance, systems of law and regulation, and spatial and political practices
from one part of the empire and adapted them to another. The imperial
threads of analogy were, it turns out, remarkably strong. But they were
also quite pliable, allowing administrators to change tack from Kenyan-
style plans to restrict land sales or to set up native land reserves to a more
Bengali- or Irish-style partition. In the world of late 1930s British imperial planning, partition was seen as a way to reduce the costs associated
with policing restive populations while simultaneously retaining critical
imperial assets such as ports, airfields, and in the case of Palestine, sym-
bolically loaded religious sites. Taken together, the resilience and flexibil-
ity of imperial analogies go some way toward explaining the persistence
of partition across multiple, and very different, cases.

*Part III*
ACCEPTANCE, RESISTANCE,
AND ACCOMMODATION

## CHAPTER 7

# REJECTING PARTITION

*The Imported Lessons of Palestine's Binational Zionists*

Adi Gordon

And as always also now: politics in Palestine is
nothing but the shadow of events in India.
—"Haknesia Hakol'islamit" [The World Islamic
Congress], Brit Shalom editorial[1]

## BINATIONALISM VERSUS PARTITION

"We have no belief in partition for many reasons—religious, historical, political, economic," stated Judah L. Magnes, presenting his oral evidence on behalf of the binational Zionist Ihud association to the United Nations Special Committee on Palestine (UNSCOP) on July 14, 1947. "We regard partition as not only impracticable," he continued, "but, should it be carried through, as a great misfortune for both Jews and Arabs."[2] After more than a quarter century of British mandate, UNSCOP considered competing proposals for Palestine's political future: while the representatives of the Arab states proposed the establishment of a unitary state (with an Arab majority), the Jewish organizations advocated the partition of Palestine into two independent states, one Arab and one Jewish. Magnes, a Zionist leader and the Hebrew University's first chancellor, opposed the path of partition in no uncertain terms and supported a third proposal: speaking of the ideal of "political parity," and acknowledging unqualified "Arab natural rights in Palestine," he advocated the establishment of a binational Arab-Jewish state.[3] Although his positions were very well known in the Yishuv (the Zionist society in Palestine), many Zionists, quite understandably, saw Magnes's evidence at that crucial moment and international forum as illegitimate, inexcusable, indeed traitorous, jeopardizing the looming historical breakthrough of the Zionist movement.

While conceptualizing the oral statement as a case *for* a binational Palestine, Magnes and the binationalists also presented UNSCOP with their case *against* partition, as an additional memorandum. In a short text—consisting of eleven enumerated points—the binationalists effectively pushed back against the assertion that partition was inevitable, or even practical, and that a binational state was a utopian endeavor. The opposite, they claimed, was true. Segregation is "undesirable and unnecessary," it was stated on point three, "but we also believe genuine segregation to be impossible. No matter where you draw the boundaries of the Jewish state, there will always be a very large Arab minority." Point six addressed partitions in general—not only in Palestine—insisting that "wherever you draw these boundaries, you create irredentas on either side of the border. Irredentas almost invariably lead to war." Another point, accordingly, refuted the claim that partition "at least, gives finality. To us it seems to be but the beginning of real warfare." And Palestine's partition, they predicted correctly, would lead not only to warfare: "partition is dependent upon the transfer either forcibly or voluntarily of Arab lands and of Arab population."[4] In the wake of the 1948 Arab-Israeli war, the binational Zionists may have been more clear-eyed than most.

Partition, minoritization, and population transfer are perpetrated in the creation of nation-states in multiethnic regions. At least one of the three would be necessary for the making of any such states. Hence the partition and anti-partition discourses in Palestine of the 1920s, 1930s, and 1940s are essentially a discussion of the merits and demerits, applicability or inapplicability, of nation-states, and ultimately, those are all but part of an even greater transnational struggle on the nature and tenets of the postimperial world order. In that struggle, as we shall see, many local actors came to realize their participation in the reproduction of an imperial situation.[5]

Magnes and the Ihud (Unity) association (founded in 1942) were not the first or only Zionists to reject the vision of a Jewish nation-state and to envision a Zionism politically realized through the creation of a binational Palestine. Though largely forgotten, such calls were made by a considerable number of Zionists already in the wake of the Great War.[6] The first and probably most memorable organization of binational Zionists was the Brit Shalom (Peace Association, or Covenant of Peace), created in Jerusalem in the wake of the Fourteenth Zionist Congress in late 1925. The association's chairman, Arthur Ruppin, was one of the leading Zionists of the day (a member of the Zionist Commission and Zionist Executive Committee), and most tellingly, was known as "the father of Jewish settlement."[7] Indeed, all binational Zionists embodied a certain contradiction—somehow continuing to participate in the very policy they condemned. The founding members of Ihud and Brit Shalom included leading intellectuals in the Yishuv, such as publicist Rabbi Benjamin (Yehoshua Radler-Feldmann), philosopher Hugo Bergmann, future scholar of Jewish mysticism Gershom Scholem, and future scholar of nationalism Hans Kohn. Brit Shalom has always defined itself in opposition to fantasies of ethnic segregation:

> Brit Shalom was established out of the fear that the dispute between the peoples of this land will erupt in destructive and wild passions. It is obvious that neither Jews nor Arabs can live in this small land as if on an island, separate from one another. We have always looked for a bridge of understanding and coexistence, and also now, in these days of incitement and destruction, we call upon all the land's inhabitants, and first and foremost upon their leaders and representative institutions, to overcome the understandable emotional hardships of this hour, and to do all they can to cease the combat and to open direct negotiations between the representatives about the conditions for a future of coexistence in the land which is so dear to both nations, and which belongs to both.[8]

Brit Shalom's periodical, *She'ifotenu* (Our Aspirations), spelled out the general vision already in the editorial of its first volume (1927): "Brit Shalom wishes to create here, in the Land of Israel, a state inhabited jointly by the two peoples living in this country under complete equality of rights, as the two elements that jointly and equally determine the destiny of this country."[9] The future Palestinian state, they clarified in a memorandum submitted to the Jewish Agency Executive a few years later, was to be "neither a Jewish State nor an Arab State, but a bi-racial

State in which Jews and Arabs should enjoy equal civil, political and social rights, without distinction between majority and minority. The two peoples should each be free in the administration of their respective domestic affairs but united in their common interests."[10] Brit Shalom hoped and believed that a binational, cantonized, or federal state could satisfy the core needs and aspirations of both Zionism and Palestinian Arab nationalism.[11]

Brit Shalom, it should be noted, did not yet position itself so clearly and specifically as anti-partition. Partition became a more likely scenario, and thus a much larger issue also for binationalists, following the partition recommendation of the British Royal Commission of Inquiry of 1937 (the Peel Commission).[12] In the 1920s and early 1930s, Brit Shalom still focused its binational agenda around a principled rejection of the nation-state model, which it understood as being based upon an unjustifiable hierarchy between a dominant nationality (a state nationality) and "minorities."[13] On one hand, the group found the prospect of Zionism minoritizing Palestine's Arab population abhorrent. On the other, given the overwhelming Arab majority, it saw a binational Palestine as the only path that could spare Zionism a conflict it ultimately could never win.

The advocacy of a binational Palestine clearly changed over time, reflecting the various proponent organizations (Brit Shalom in 1925, the League for Jewish-Arab Rapprochement in 1939, and Ihud in 1942),[14] but even more clearly reflecting the historical watersheds crossed, such as the 1929 Arab Riots, the Arab Revolt in Palestine (1936–1939), the Peel Commission's Partition Plan (1937), and the UN Partition Resolution (1947). Another change over time had to do with the binationalists' mode of political action. Unlike Ihud, with its bold public statements both to the 1947 UNSCOP and to the 1946 Anglo-American Committee of Inquiry, Brit Shalom's mode of political action, for the most part, was more cautious, hesitant, and "disciplined."[15] While some members of the association—the so-called Radical Circle—hoped to transform Brit Shalom from an advisory group into a politically active group, Ruppin envisioned it merely as a research and study association serving the Zionist organization and dutifully bound by its policy decisions, comparable to the Fabian Society.

Brit Shalom—the one binational Zionist organization I focus on in this chapter—remained a tiny, radical opposition group in the Zionist movement, ever accused of defeatism, even "treason." It failed to raise even minimal interest on the Arab side, much less the integration of Arab members or the creation of a parallel Arab association. Following the Arab Riots of 1929, mainstream Zionism marginalized Brit Shalom even more than before, and its standing deteriorated further. Many of its founding members ceased to believe in the feasibility of a binational solution. Ruppin broke from the binational path with a heavy heart and returned to "mainstream" Zionism; Kohn took the other option and broke with the Zionist movement altogether. By late 1933 Brit Shalom had disbanded. The idea of a binational Palestine, however, would reemerge time and again as an alternative to partition, both before and after the establishment of the Jewish state in 1948.

## THE SPECTER OF COMPARISONS:
## CONTEXTUALIZATIONS AND THEIR FUNCTIONS

Binational Zionists have constantly oscillated between emphasizing the uniqueness of the Arab-Zionist conflict and seeing it in universal terms as typical of the relation between nationalities with conflicting claims to the same land. Even if later scholarship presented Brit Shalom's agenda as exemplifying the uniqueness of the conflict, ultimately scholars tended to emphasize the existence of analogous national conflicts and conflict resolution efforts that informed the binationalist platform. For example, Brit Shalom found myriad similarities to Palestine in the Cypriot riots of October 1931. The Cypriot parallel implied to the Zionists a sense of proportion and solvability (or finitude) with regard to the conflict with the Arabs:

> The situation in Cyprus resembles the one here: Here as there the population is divided between an 80 percent majority and a 20 percent minority. Here and there both are under British colonial rule. Cyprus too has three official languages (English, Greeks, and Turkish) and all of the problems pertaining to the life of two nations in a single land. The Greek of Cyprus aspire to liberation and unification with Greece, like Palestinian Arabs wish to be

united with fellow Arabs in an independent Arab federation. The Turks of
Cyprus, however, do not have the same national aspirations Zionists have
for Palestine.[16]

Hans Kohn, a future scholar of nationalism and Brit Shalom's first
secretary, came to view the nationalities' conflict in Palestine and that
conflict's potential "solutions" as typical of multinational states in the
postimperial order. He also had been an important voice in the international pacifist movement during the late 1920s, especially as a member
of War Resisters' International, so he articulated these parallels uniquely
well when addressing fellow pacifists (rather than Zionists) on pacifist
challenges (rather than on Zionist ones).[17] His article "Aktiver Pazifismus" (Active Pacifism), based on his address at an international pacifist
conference in 1928, presented Palestine as a typical case of a multinational state in the wake of the Great War:

> In a state of multiple nationalities, the problem of pacifism in the context of
> domestic policy is presently more urgent and difficult than the problem of
> pacifism in the context of foreign policy.... For the Czechs need an army not
> for war against external enemies but rather to suppress the Germans at home.
> At present such a problem exists in each multinational state.... The quantita-
> tive concept of [a national] majority must cease to be a power and political
> concept bestowing exclusive rights [*Vorrechte*]. A similar problem exists in
> Palestine. I do not regret this. Pacifist convictions are worth something only
> if upheld when one's own interests are at stake. For this offers us not only the
> possibility of espousing theoretical principles, an easy thing, but also the pos-
> sibility of living out these principles.[18]

Writing in the wake of World War II, Ihud's Gabriel Baer, a social historian of the Middle East, saw a need for a struggle against partition all
over "the Orient":

> The same question, *mutatis mutandis*, is manifest in many countries of the
> Orient: Pakistan in India, the complete partition of Sudan from Egypt, a
> Kurdish state in the Kurdish regions of Iraq, Turkey and Iran.... What
> brings us to object to a partition solution to relations between nations, and
> particularly between non-sovereign nations, is that in the current conditions,

in which the great powers still control the fate of subject nations, this "solution" could not support the development and independence of minorities—
and certainly not those of the majority—for if the "minority state" would be
turned into the great powers' proxy against the local majority, it would only
deepen the hostility between the partitioned nations. . . . Further: the policies
of great powers change . . . but the local nations will have to reside together
also in the future.[19]

The advocates of a binational Palestine—just like the advocates of a
Palestinian partition—grounded their case not only in Palestine's local
realities, but also in the efforts of like-minded activists in other places and
the lessons of other historical arenas. This chapter, focusing on Brit Shalom's official publications, looks at three such fields of reference—Jewish
history, European politics, and colonialism—and suggests that, contrary
to the picture presented in scholarship, it was always colonialism that was
crucial for the binational Zionists' rejection of partition. The decisive contextualization that Brit Shalom set forth, then, was its identification—
mutatis mutandis—of the Zionist-Arab relation as being a relation
between colonizer and colonized. It was this understanding, and where
it situated Zionism both historically and geopolitically, that necessitated
a clear and urgent restatement of Zionism's political goals in Palestine.
Only a complete parity of the nations, it followed, would keep Zionism
clear of settler colonialism, and a binational state seemed to offer the
most natural format for the implementation of such a Zionism.[20]

## RECONSTRUCTING JEWISH POLITICAL
## TRADITIONS

Some of the most memorable statements against partition and in favor of
a binational Palestine were anchored in the binationalists' understanding
of Judaism and Jewish history. Especially the Spiritual Zionists among
them saw the policy toward the Arabs as a trial not only for Zionism's
soul, but also for its Jewishness:

> We come to Palestine with no distinctive Arab mission to speak of. It was
> only through Zionism that we encountered the Arab Question. Here, Zi-
> onism had to show its true face and it failed. The devil's voice, tempting it

with imperialist-nationalist promises, was louder than the still small voice emanating from the writings of [Spiritual Zionist] Ahad Ha'am and [Labor Zionist] A. D. Gordon. And we know: the Arab Question is a Jewish question. It is the question of whether the Jewish spirit is still alive within us, or whether it was lost.[21]

Already in 1925 Hans Kohn wrote to fellow binational Zionist friends Hugo Bergmann and Robert Weltsch of the need for "a restatement of Zionist ideology," clearly juxtaposing mainstream political Zionism with their own binational Zionism. Kohn's ten-point letter, written in broken sentences, situated their advocacy of a binational state and their rejection of partition in the context of Jewish history and their own Jewish worldview. The letter defined their Zionism as "modernized Ahad-Ha'amism linked to that concept we have reached of the essence of nationalism." Kohn's first point was that "Judaism is not a nation like other nations." It has, after all, undergone "2,500 years of spiritualization [*Vergeistigung*], stripping itself of statehood and territoriality." The spiritualized Jewish nationalism "follows its own laws and may even constitute a higher development" compared with other nations. The second point in Kohn's outline offered a more sophisticated understanding of assimilation. Zionism, he stressed, could also become assimilation if, as a national movement, it uncritically betrayed its spiritualized distinctiveness: "Though seen as a turn away from assimilation, Herzl's [political] Zionism is really its continuation. It renounces [Jewish] distinctiveness and leaves nothing of it. . . . Judaism [according to political Zionists] should become like all other nations; should become a political nation and [regain] statehood." With the goals of Jewish majority and statehood rejected, Kohn stated in his seventh point that the only objective of Jewish settlement in Palestine should be a cultural center: Jews are "not aspiring to a Jewish state, no minor new nation-state. Judaism gladly overcame statehood," and that should "also shape its relations to the Arabs."[22]

Bergmann clearly shared this position. In an essay titled "The Question of Relation," which appeared in the first issue of *She'ifotenu*, he stressed that Zionism, rather than being a case for Jewish statehood, can and should be "only the aspiration to realize in our life the spirit of Judaism"; and for that reason, also with regard to the complicated question of Zionism's relation to the Palestinian Arabs, Zionism's compass should be "clinging to Judaism's core essence."[23] In his essay "On the Majority Question" Bergmann expounded further on the distinctively Jewish context of binationalism and on the rejection of all minoritizing policies:

> We know that the Jewish people are the minority nation par excellence. . . . There is a lesson in it: our historical destiny is to fight to change the values in international relations . . . to break the spirit of majority [domination] in international affairs. . . . Our dispersion among the nations bestowed upon us the historical calling to fight for our place among the nations—for our minority existence—while at the same time fight for a new morality in international relations. And the Land of Israel . . . will be a model for the [other] nations in this regard, for in it we will materialize such [just] relations between the two inhabitant nations.[24]

The break with the idea of full political national sovereignty in favor of a binational state, wrote Bergmann, "was no compromise at all, but a historic mission which was bestowed upon us. The Divine has shown the Jewish people His great mercy by [providing us with] a national home which is the homeland of two peoples."[25] Rejecting the path of partition, the binationalists committed their Zionism to coexistence and shared governance. Albert Einstein, a Brit Shalom sympathizer, shared the notion that Jewish history had sensitized, or at least should have sensitized, Jews to the question of minoritization and pointed them to the alternative path of multinational federation. "What saddens me," Einstein told Bergmann, "is less the fact that the Jews are not smart enough to understand this [the need for and viability of a binational Palestine], but rather, that they are not just enough to want it."[26]

The Seventeenth Zionist Congress (in Basel, Switzerland, 1931) seems to have heightened Brit Shalom's awareness of the widening gap between official Zionism and the group's binational vision. On the eve of the congress Robert Weltsch proclaimed that if Zionism kept drifting apart from what he understood as the ethical and humanist spirit of Judaism, "only a single path would remain: to establish next to the existing Zionist Organization . . . a new movement, bound to the glorious legacy of Moses Hess, Ahad Ha'am, A. D. Gordon, Martin Buber and others, and which would aspire to create a suitable format for the realization of Jewish nationalism and of Zionism."[27] Following the congress, binationalist Ernst Simon published a striking essay that he called "A Speech That Was *Not* Delivered at the Congress," alluding to what he saw as the elephant in the room: official Zionism deceives world Jewry in what it promises the Land of Israel can do for them:

> I am relating here primarily to the empty phrase that promises the tormented Jewish people, which have been duped so many times before, the "solution of the Jewish question" through the construction of the Land of Israel. . . . This Zionist Congress could have assumed a historic role and proclaimed that the Jewish Question, by its very essence, has no solutions. Only such acknowledgment would have rendered Zionism possible again. Only such Zionism—purified of any false messianic hopes, of all Sabbateanism and of any empty promises—could maintain that core of the Jewish people which is genuinely interested in Judaism's continued existence, and which will not view that existence as contingent upon political aspirations that, frankly, are nothing but collective assimilation. Zionism . . . was grounded on the false premise that we resemble other nations, and that we should become a nation like all others, [and thus] generated a normalization frenzy.[28]

That, Simon continued, does not make the Zionist construction in Palestine meaningless. Though Zionism cannot solve the "Jewish Question," it does revolutionize the Jewish world, even without establishing a Jewish state, or even without creating a Jewish majority: Palestine offers the only place where the risk of Jewish assimilation virtually does not exist; it is also the only place in which Jews—even as a minority—would be one of the state nationalities.[29]

The awareness that this no longer was how most of the Yishuv saw Zionism's historical role generated among binational Zionists the sense of belonging to a separate, distinctive ideology, on the margins of the movement if not entirely beyond its scope. While Weltsch spoke of "a new movement," Gershom Scholem referred to those few members of the Yishuv "who still think of . . . Palestine's construction as a main means for a national regeneration" as "a minor sect," in theological terms, and as "a cult and not a broad-based national movement."[30] We can see how frequently and emphatically binational Zionists understood their agenda—for a binational Palestine and against a Palestinian partition—as grounded in an understanding of Judaism, of Jewish history, and of Zionism, which set them apart from the rest of the Yishuv and the Zionist movement.

## "PALESTINE SHOULD BECOME AS JEWISH AS SWITZERLAND IS FRENCH": EUROPE'S MULTINATIONAL MODELS

Brit Shalom was made up almost entirely of (former) Europeans, so unsurprisingly the political mechanisms it imagined were inspired by European policies. However, more often than not European politics were discussed by Brit Shalom members as a negative model to be rejected and replaced. Zionism, many of them stressed, had to be something different and better than the ubiquitous mix of nationalizing states and aggressive ethno-nationalism they had witnessed in Europe. In that vein, Bergmann warned fellow Zionists against the type of nationalism that "understands the state as the possession of a single ethnic group" and that "renders the members of other nationalities merely guests." That, he insisted, was foreign to Jewish political tradition and was in fact "an ideology that comes to us from Europe in its decline."[31] With great alarm Bergmann noted:

> Our people no longer have the ambition to create a political regime in *our own* spirit, *our own* tradition, to be a guide to others. But let us break with imitating their [the Europeans'] way. And just as the Italians are hastening to constitute the majority in the South Tyrol so as to ensure their rule over the Germans, just as the Czechs are hastening to ensure their own majority, and the Germans vis-à-vis the Poles, and the Poles vis-à-vis the Ukrainians, and so on and so forth, so too the Jews, long experienced with persecutions [as a minority], demand the same: Let us have a majority in Palestine![32]

The Jews' national movement, he lamented, had fallen prey to the mindless ideological cookie cutter.

Robert Weltsch wrote in a similar vein. Since European Jews stood outside of the dominant state nationality, he insisted that "it would be an interesting irony of history if our [national] liberation would have turned

us into that same type [of national movement] that we previously opposed tooth and nail."[33] Alluding to the alleged dire straits of the successor states of the Habsburg Empire, an editorial in *She'ifotenu* proclaimed
that "the time has indeed come when we [Zionists] and the [Palestinian
Arab] inhabitants of this tiny little land will learn the lesson [from the
ill fate of the successor states] for the sake of Palestine and of the entire
Middle East."[34] Israeli historian Yfaat Weiss has thus commented:

> To the extent that the [binationalist] society's members identified negative
> and threatening models, these were taken from the geographical area that
> stretches from the Ukraine in the East to Germany in the West. But in their
> search for models to copy, the Brit Shalom members did not turn to the
> West, at least not to the generic forms of England and France. They felt that
> those countries could not provide a response to nation-planning in a sphere
> in which two peoples were destined to live side by side.[35]

Yet the binationalists did frequently relate also to several positive European models. In order to better understand the function and motivation behind Brit Shalom's comparison of its agenda for Palestine with
those positive European models, we should bear in mind the develop-
mental rationale upon which British mandatory rule over Palestine—like
all League of Nations mandates—was grounded: the British temporary
administration of Palestine was conceptualized as a benevolent British
service of tutelage and guidance to the local populations toward modern and effective self-government. Thus the second article of "The Palestine Mandate" held Great Britain accountable for "the development of
self-governing institutions."[36] The League of Nations obviously took for
granted that Europe and the West—Britain and France in this case—
modeled the aspired political modernity toward which the local populations were to develop. The tacit assumption that Europe and the West
embodied political modernity was shared by most early Zionists. Political Zionists most evidently sought for the Jews a nation-state akin
to the European ones. This became even more overt in the wake of the
"Wilsonian Moment," when ideas about national self-determination as
key components of the postwar international order captured the world's
imagination. It is precisely against this backdrop that binational Zionists

stressed another very dominant European model that Zionism could follow in Palestine, namely, that of Europe's multinational federations.

And so, when presenting his state mechanism for a binational Palestine, Hans Kohn was inspired by several European examples. Kohn was born and raised in Habsburg Prague, and some of his historical precedents were indeed related to "the former Austrian state," namely, the Moravian Compromise of 1905 and the Bukovinian Compromise of 1910, which Kohn presented as mechanisms that were based on extraterritorial national autonomies (following the Austro-Marxist principle of national personal autonomy).[37] Yet the plans to transform the Habsburg monarchy into "a Vielvölkerreich, a truly multinational state," ultimately remained unrealized, which arguably brought about the empire's demise.[38] Kohn, then, emphasized other examples instead: "The most perfect solution to the issue of two (or more) peoples living together," he stated, "is to be found in Switzerland. . . . In terms of their language policies, something can also be learned from Belgium and Finland."[39] This issue was elaborated upon in Joseph Lurya's essay "National Rights in Switzerland, Finland and Palestine."[40] Brit Shalom's advocacy of a binational Palestine, he accurately reported, "has met with formidable opposition on the part of both Jews and Arabs." Among both parties, many dismissed binationalism offhand as "a visionary dream." But, asked Lurya, "is this idea really utopian? Are there no countries which are governed on this plan? Of course there are!," he responds and explains:

> The laws specifying the rights of the different nationalities in Switzerland and Finland show that there is no dominant and no subject nationality in either country. In both, the majority and the minority enjoy equal rights. Switzerland is neither a German, a French nor an Italian country, but a commonwealth of three nationalities. Similarly, Finland is not a Finnish or a Swedish country, but a binational State. This is the form of government we aim at introducing in Palestine: a country for both nationalities, the Jews and the Arabs.[41]

Brit Shalom's Swiss example was summarized well in *She'ifotenu* in the essay "Zionism and Arab Federation." In response to the famous 1919 proclamation of the Zionist leader Chaim Weizmann that "Palestine should become as Jewish as England is English"—a proclamation that Brit Shalom found nothing short of utopian—the binational formula seemed to promise "that Palestine should become as Jewish as Switzerland is French."[42] The sentence may have been ironic, but it was accurate nonetheless.

Brit Shalom disbanded before the international crisis of the late 1930s and the failure of the minority protection system. Whereas many commentators saw this failure as supporting the case of partition, and of sovereign nation-states of whatever size, the issues of Ihud's *Ba'ayot*—written during World War II and its aftermath—offered a different reading: for Ihud the lesson was that "the current war has greatly shaken the faith in the sovereignty and independence of small, and even of larger, . . . nations and states."[43] Rather than addressing the hard question of enforcement of minority rights and national parity in multinational states, Ihud remained focused on its normative principles when it proclaimed in its memorandum to the Anglo-American Committee of Inquiry in 1946 that

> the failure of the guarantees given to minorities . . . prove that in a binational land the sole guarantee for a minority is a parity with the majority. There is no chance for peace in a land in which one nation rules and another is being ruled. . . . In countries in which there is more than one legally recognized nation—and there are many such countries in Europe and Asia—the minority grows bitter that state bureaucracy, the military, and key positions in the economy and diplomacy are in the hands of the majority nation. In a multinational state, parity is the sole just relation between the nations.[44]

## "THE IMPERIALISM TO WHICH WE ARE WEDDED THROUGH THE BALFOUR DECLARATION"

Brit Shalom's official publications consistently offered a rather damning assessment of the nature of Palestine's mandatory rule as colonial. Discussing Iraq's admission to the League of Nations in Brit Shalom's periodical *She'ifotenu*, Hans Kohn—who in these very years published his pioneering works on the interaction between the Arab nationalists and Western colonial empires—opened with a rhetorical question borrowed from Arnold J. Toynbee: "Are mandates a continuation of old colonial policy, do they aim merely to politically disempower oriental lands, separating them, and repressing their national aspirations in a policy of Divide and Rule?"[45] A response seems to have come in another Kohn article in *She'ifotenu*: "Great Britain rules Palestine as if it were not a mandate territory, but a colony. Its civil code and public law do not even mention the residents' civil rights."[46] This was not only Kohn's position: the following article, Alfred Bonne's analysis of Palestine's economy, made similar insinuations, stating, for example, that "the education and health expenses [of Palestine's government] seem miniscule compared with the police budget."[47]

An editorial stated:

> Most of Palestine's natives [*yelidey ha'aretz*] live in economic conditions that are not capable of modernization without governmental aid. Jews immigrating from the West bring with them both money and organizational power and experience, and these two are sorely lacking among the vast majority of the native population. They . . . need governmental aid to modernize their rural or urban economy. . . . Our [British] government, however, did not do a thing, though it was one of its prime duties as a Mandatory government. It failed to establish any vocational or industrial schools; it established no credit institutions; it did not invest in development of the *fellahin*.

The core problem, the editorial stressed, was that "Palestinian subjects cannot partake in legislation or administration."[48] The editorial cast great doubt on whether Palestine's fiscal policy was truly committed first and foremost to serving the land and its residents.

Brit Shalom, then, saw Arab nationalist opposition to the Western rule, through the League of Nations mandate system, as justified, indeed inevitable. Kohn's article "The New East," for example, presented an unstoppable, fast-paced modernization of "the New East," and particularly of the Arab world, toward the establishment of sovereign states of one sort or another. Zionism, it tacitly follows, needed to prepare for a Middle East with little to no colonial presence in which the local populations exercised complete self-rule.[49] Another *She'ifotenu* article put it more overtly:

It is the fate of the Zionist movement to operate in this atmosphere [of conflict between European colonialism and Arab anticolonialism] and to build up the Jewish National Home in the midst of such [anticolonial] stresses. It makes all Zionist work doubly difficult, but, if we are prepared to see things as they are and to adjust ourselves to the conditions caused by a Middle Eastern Renaissance, we need not despair.

Unfortunately, Zionist activities tend to obstruct this development in Palestine. In the struggle between Europe and Asia, Zionism takes its stand definitely with Europe. We have learned to our cost in the last few years that Zionism is the first to suffer when hostilities break out and is always thrown by Europe as a sop to Cerberus when Asia has to be appeased.

... The lines on which Zionist theory should develop during the coming years are already clear. Our ultimate goal is to build up a strong Jewish center in Palestine. . . . The prerequisite of the success of any such movement is the consent of the Arab peoples; and to secure this consent—to get a new charter, a new Balfour Declaration from the Arabs—must be the goal of a new Zionist advance.[50]

As of the 1920s Brit Shalom came to understand also the Zionist-Arab conflict in (late) colonial and anticolonial terms.[51] Attributing colonialism to the British mandatory administration in Palestine, of course, was easy. The subversive, critical edge of Brit Shalom's binational Zionism, however, was grounded in the understanding of the *Zionist*-Arab interactions (and not only the *British*-Arab interactions) as a relationship between the colonizer and the colonized. Responding to the 1929 Arab Riots, Brit Shalom's Ernst Simon and Escha Scholem wrote the following "regarding the atrocities": "Historical experience shows that colonized peoples . . . channel their national uprisings against the civilian residents of other nationalities in their lands (Ireland, India in the past, the Boxer Rebellion in China, the Herero in South-West Africa, etc.). The violence of such undisciplined and unorganized masses, by necessity, is always manifested in cruel rioting. . . . All these are typical attributes of national liberation wars in colonial lands."[52] The fact that Zionists genuinely did not think of themselves in those terms—as foreigners, conquerors, or colonizers oppressing a colonized native population—and instead saw Zionism as an anticolonial liberation movement, did not make the problem any better. Indeed, it made it much worse.

No member of Brit Shalom articulated this more clearly than Gershom Scholem in an article in *She'ifotenu* in which he tried again to explain the core of the contention between Brit Shalom and all other Zionists.[53] The difference was Brit Shalom's despair about Zionism's "false victory," acquired as Zionism "aligned itself politically to those who ripped the fruits of the World War." Instead of seeking an alliance with Arab nationalism, Zionism chose to align with British imperialism against the political aspirations of the Palestinian Arabs:

> Zionism took its stand, whether involuntarily or, as was more often the case, voluntarily, on the side of the declining rather than of the rising forces. It saw its success in the intrigues of war—Versailles and San Remo and the signing of the Mandate—as a victory. But this victory has now become a handicap and a stumbling block for the entire movement. The force which Zionism joined in those victories was the manifest force, the aggressor. Zionism forgot to link up with the hidden force, the oppressed, which would rise and be revealed soon after. Could a revival movement indeed be on their side, or, more accurately, take shelter under the wings of the victors of the war? Many of the socialists in our [Zionist] camp do not care for such questions, and are enraged when one speaks of the imperialism to which we are wedded through the Balfour Declaration. . . . If Zionism remains with the ruling powers, it will undoubtedly break.

This fraught, late colonial position, Scholem insisted, was denied and repressed by mainstream Zionists. Utterly oblivious of Zionism's predicament, mainstream Zionists appeared to be jubilant over a diplomatic Pyrrhic victory:

> They are not despaired! They seem to believe nothing has happened yet, that no [Zionist] decision was made. They seem to live before Zionism's Original Sin, or pretend to have taken no part in it. As if we did not eat the fruit of Versailles; as if one could easily erase the impact of that feast which is so deeply engrained into our image. And our despair—a despair over a victory in the wrong place and at the wrong time—is what sets us apart from them.

This despair is merely the recognition of our true situation, and it is that which motivates us, and which could potentially generate [in Zionism] new positive forces.

Finally, Scholem also rejected as disingenuous any Zionist claim to neutrality (as if Zionism aligned neither with the Arabs nor with British imperialism, or that it would align itself with both): "Zionism is not in the heavens, and it does not possess the power to unite fire and water. Either it shall be swept away in the waters of imperialism, or else it shall be burnt in the revolutionary conflagration of the wakening East. Mortal dangers beset her on either side and, nevertheless, the Zionist movement cannot avoid a decision."[54]

## A MISALLIANCE

For the binational Zionists the crucial point, before all ethical considerations, was to curb a risky Zionist misalliance with European colonial empires, and especially to encourage an alternative and much needed Zionist alliance with the anticolonial national movements in the East, and particularly with Arab nationalism. It was with much sarcasm that binationalist Rabbi Benjamin commented on how Zionists believed they could put out the fire of Arab hostility with gasoline. He quoted Zionist hardliner Menachem Ussishkin's suggested paths of pacification, based on the wrongheaded Zionist identification with colonial empires: "We [Zionists] shall do as the British and the French," proclaimed Ussishkin. "What they did," Rabbi Benjamin retorted sardonically, "is plainly familiar to us. All we need to do is borrow their air force and fleet."[55] Hugo Bergmann stated similarly that "Zionism's main mistake since the Balfour Declaration was to integrate British bayonets into its political calculus, and to assume that these bayonets could ever replace an actual political plan."[56] That actual political plan had to engage the Arabs directly. The Arabs, after all, would stay in Palestine long after the British had gone. This Zionist misalliance, Robert Weltsch explained in "Our Relation to the [British] Orient Policy," "is based not only on a misunderstanding of Arab politics, but first and foremost on a dangerous misunderstanding of the new nature of British interests and policy: we Zionists are indeed dependent on British support, yet that British support in turn is contingent upon pacification and a political agreement with the Arabs."[57]

The impact of this misalliance was not only diplomatic. It shaped, and in Brit Shalom's view distorted, Zionist ideologies and identities. In a 1929 editorial in *She'ifotenu* Brit Shalom critically discussed the Hebrew press in the Yishuv and quoted Zionist publicists who were, for example, hostile toward the Indian independence movement, or scornful of "Eastern backwardness." Brit Shalom saw this as manifesting how Zionism, or at least many of its prominent spokespeople, unwittingly assumed an old-school colonialist perspective on the East. The editorial identified "a loathing of the east and a disdain of the oppressed" among Zionists and an "awe only of the apparent hegemon." Zionism's problem was not only this siding with the Western empires, but also the very assumption that the rise of the East must, by necessity, mean the decline of the West:

> Does the resurrection of Zion necessitate . . . the continued wretchedness in China, or the foreign rule over India? Reading such things [in the Zionist press] one gets the impression that in order to be a bona fide Zionist one is expected to ridicule the East, its poverty and its struggles to rise and regenerate. . . . Ultimately this question is not a political-economic one, but an inclination of the spirit. We [Zionists] simply appear to hate the oppressed.[58]

An additional ramification of Zionism's misalliance and its accompanying worldview was social: the self-segregation of the Zionist Yishuv from Arab Palestine. In November 1930 Brit Shalom hosted a guest speaker, Muhammad Roshan Akhtar, the Muslim Indian editor of the English-language newspaper *Falastin*. In his talk ("Zionism and Arab Aspirations"), which was later published in *She'ifotenu*, Akhtar compared the Hindu-Muslim conflict in India to the Zionist-Arab one in Palestine and found Palestine's society endlessly more segregated than India's, where one still encountered friendships and professional collaborations and partnerships across communal lines, in a way that seemed entirely absent to him in Palestine:

> Social relations play a very important role as you will find today in studying the Hindu-Moslem problem. I found . . . many who had dropped the old

prejudices and dined and walked together. . . . But [here] you do not find Arabs inviting Jews to a social or other function. I am not speaking of those journalistic stunts. . . . I mean the everyday social, economic and political cooperation, going to each other's places. You have your cafés: the Arabs have theirs. If somebody addresses you in another language than Hebrew, you do not like it. . . . There is neither economic nor political cooperation between Jews and Arabs until social cooperation is started. And it has not been attempted so far.[59]

Increasingly, Brit Shalom envisioned the postimperial future of the Middle East in the shape of an Arab Federation, into which (binational) Zionism would ultimately need to adapt and integrate. This, for example, was the future Akhtar outlined in his talk with Brit Shalom. The binationalists were not enthusiastic—after all, this did significantly complicate the case for a binational Palestine as they envisioned it. Their rejection of the principle of a dominant nationality, for example, seemed at odds with the very premise of an *Arab* Federation. And "yet, as a preliminary search for some common ground for further conversation," this, they felt, "was sufficiently fruitful."[60] As a matter of fact, Bergmann thought along those lines already in the early 1920s.[61]

*She'ifotenu*'s editorial discussed the growing interest by the Arab press in an Arab Federation, which Brit Shalom saw as reaffirming many of its basic stances: "A forward-looking Jewish policy would take this state of affairs into consideration. Currently Jews look only to London and the British Empire. So long as the Zionist Organization discusses land [acquisition] and industrial development only with the London government, our homes are built on sand."[62]

## "OUT OF INDIA, OUT OF THE ORIENT, SHALL GO FORTH THE LAW": BINATIONALISM INSPIRED BY INDIA?

It was no coincidence that Brit Shalom engaged the Muslim Indian Muhammad Roshan Akhtar and publicized that engagement. Binational Zionists, and particularly Brit Shalom members, often looked to India, believing that the lessons of Indian nationalism might be vital for their own national movement in Palestine.[63] After all, Indian nationalists had long struggled with some of the greatest challenges Zionism faced: the colonial setting, the intersection of political nationalism and religion, and the conflicting aspirations of minority and majority populations. Brit Shalom members were overjoyed with the Gandhi-Irwin Pact of 1931, which they defined as "a historic event of boundless significance." Paraphrasing Micah 4:2 they went so far as to proclaim "for out of India, out of the Orient, shall go forth the law."[64] The Indian national movement, they believed, created a model of political development for the whole world, and first and foremost, for Zionism. A few issues of *She'ifotenu* later they also praised Gandhi as "the greatest politician of the Orient."[65]

Yet it still was not clear how exactly Indian experience informed concrete plans for a binational Palestine. An example seemed to be offered by Hans Kohn's outline for a binational Palestine. The outline—included in the first issue (1927) of *She'ifotenu*—was, according to Kohn, inspired by the Commonwealth of India Bill (1925).[66] The unimplemented bill, to be sure, differed greatly from Kohn's outline and was focused on entirely different issues; yet Kohn's proclamation of an Indian inspiration is significant.

Kohn—who seems to have adopted from the Indian setting the Indian terminology of "communal conflict" (rather than the Palestinian *national* conflict)—envisioned two essentially extraterritorial national autonomies in Palestine. Above those two would be a Palestinian government, a central authority "with a minimum of interference and regulation." This authority, however, would be administered by the British on behalf of the League of Nations. For Kohn, though, the true guarantee for the success of this state mechanism lay not above the national autonomies, but beneath them, at the most local levels. This local, communal element, he stressed, was inspired "by the Commonwealth of India Bill, which was outlined in a similar fashion by parts of the Indian national movement":

> The focus of civic political will should occur within the communities, it should develop from the bottom to the top, and any interference from the top should be limited to cases of absolute necessity. There should be a

far-reaching decentralization, the head administration should not constitute
the main pillar in shaping [civic] life, which assigns certain responsibilities
to the communities and regions, but rather communities and regions should
ascertain the matters of immediate concern to the daily life of the citizens,
and should in turn assign parts of their authority to the head administration;
a process that would require a general regulation. Today the communities'
ethnic identity is already largely clarified, almost without exceptions in the
villages, and in part in the cities.[67]

The underlying assumptions of this decentralized political structure, as
historian Yfaat Weiss has noted, are telling.[68] Given that interethnic fusion might prove volatile—as would be manifested a few years later, in
the 1929 riots—Kohn built his binational vision on the more solid small
community or region, whose ethnic identity is overt and hence less contested. Concentrating political life at this communal level would be sure
to keep, and even to increase, the ethnic profile of the smaller community.
At the lowest communal level, this policy would sustain and even inten-
sify ethnic segregation.

In *Muslim Zion: Pakistan as a Political Idea*, Faisal Devji has pointed
to the historical affinities and structural similarities between Zionism
(Israel) and the Muslim League (Pakistan) and contributed greatly to
their compelling analysis: "[B]oth emerged from situations in which
minority populations dispersed across vast subcontinents sought to escape the majorities whose persecution they . . . feared. For it was only
the emergence of national majorities in nineteenth century Europe and
India that turned Jews and Muslims there into minorities, whose apparently irreducible particularity posed a 'problem' or a 'question' for states
newly founded on notions of shared blood and the ancestral ownership
of a homeland."[69] The interest in Muslim Indian nationalism of Brit
Shalom, which sensed some of these similarities, was manifested also in
*She'ifotenu*'s coverage and analysis of the Middle East visits of Maulana
Shaukat Ali (1873–1938), an Indian Muslim nationalist and a leader
of the Khilafat movement. Initially identifying Ali with the politics of
*satyagraha*, Brit Shalom anticipated him to be "an angel of peace" and
thus was profoundly disappointed by "his harsh [anti-Zionist] speeches

in Haifa and elsewhere." Ali advocated the creation of a Muslim university in Jerusalem, which could seem very similar to the spiritual Zionism of many binationalists; however, he had an overly aggressive intent in that regard—to counter the Hebrew University in Jerusalem. "We are saddened," wrote Brit Shalom, "that he gave the [anti-Zionist] speeches he did, and . . . even sadder that the Indian leader bundled the idea of a Muslim university in Jerusalem [as ammunition] in the political strife of the two nations."[70] It should be noted that the Prague-born members of Brit Shalom—Bergmann, Weltsch, and Kohn—were all too familiar with this kind of combative self-segregating nationalist strategy from their hometown. ("In Prague," Kohn wrote in his memoir, "the two national groups lived strictly separated lives. There was little, if any, social or cultural contact between them. Each had its own schools and universities, theatres and concert halls, sport clubs and cabarets, restaurants and cafés—in all fields of life and activity there reigned a voluntary segregation, a kind of tacitly acknowledged 'iron curtain' which separated two worlds living side by side, each one self-contained, scarcely communicating.")[71]

## REGIONAL POTENTIAL PARTNERS: NOT THE
## ONES DEPENDENT ON THE BRITISH EMPIRE

Whereas one Indian Muslim, Muhammad Roshan Akhtar, decried the social segregation between Zionists and Arabs and advocated integration (rather than Zionist reliance on British bayonets), another, Shaukat Ali, seems to have advised Palestinian Arabs to pursue the path of segregation from the Zionists and enhanced ties with the British Empire. It was this latter part that gave pause to Brit Shalom, and it began to view Ali's uncompromising anti-Zionist line as linked to a misalliance with the British. The comparison of Muslim Indian nationalism to Zionism thus persisted, while its significance was inverted. Now it was compared to the Zionist hardliners. The October 1931 issue of *She'ifotenu* noted the second visit of Ali, on the heels of clashes between Palestinian Arabs and the British around Nablus (August 1931): "Such frictions are different from Shaukat Ali's political line, for the power of Muslim Indians, whose representative he is, relies on England." Brit Shalom thus assumed that Ali's words for the Palestinian Arabs would again merge harsh anti-Zionism with a call for an Arab alliance with the British.[72]

This reliance on Great Britain, Brit Shalom claimed, was the source of Ali's unwavering, hopeless anti-Zionism. The group then juxtaposed Shaukat Ali with another important visitor: Makram Ebeid Pasha (1889–1961), secretary-general of the Egyptian Wafd Party. Whereas Ali was a lost cause for any attempted rapprochement, Ebeid—precisely because he and his party were not dependent on British protection—"sees the Zionist question as one which needs to be solved between Jews and Arabs, without a need for a third party." His approach to the Yishuv, thus, was more pragmatic. Though certainly hostile to Zionism, Ebeid was open to negotiation. It was thus with a degree of optimism that Brit Shalom assessed that "so far the Palestinian Arab national movement tended to follow the Egyptian path [of Ebeid] rather than the Indian path [of Ali]."[73]

Brit Shalom was fascinated by the World Islamic Congress that took place in Jerusalem in early December 1931:

> It is interesting to observe the opposition manifested in the congress between the Indian Muslim—the backbone of the Raj—and the Palestinian Arabs, regarding the Mandate. The English-language *Falastin* writes: "the Indian delegates thought an anti-mandate would generate concrete steps for combatting the Mandate, and would overburden the congress. . . . The [Palestinian] Arabs countered that an anti-Mandate statement would be merely a reiteration of the resolution already made by their political representatives. . . . Though both parties rejected the Mandate, the Indians found such a resolution currently impracticable, while in the eyes of the Arabs it merely reaffirmed their known position, leading to no aggressive steps."[74]

But was it true? Were Indian Muslims, as a minority among the Hindus, really more reliant on the British Raj and more integrated in its bureaucracy? Was it, alternatively, a projection either of Jewish political experience as a rather powerless minority in the diaspora or of certain Zionists in the Yishuv whose bond with the British was grounded in an awareness of their frail minority condition? Brit Shalom clearly saw the Indian subcontinent as a crucial arena in the emergence of the postimperial world order, yet ultimately, India, and the colonial context more broadly, failed to offer the binational Zionists any concrete road map beyond the basic notion that Zionism's future could be guaranteed only through a horizontal alliance with the Arab world, and not a vertical one with Western empires.

## CONCLUSION: COLONIAL, EUROPEAN, AND JEWISH PERSPECTIVES ON A BINATIONAL PALESTINE

The three contextualizations of Zionism's "Arab Question"—Brit Shalom's three imported lessons—evidently had different functions in conceptualizing and communicating the rejection of partition, and more broadly the agenda for a binational Palestine. Of the three, only the colonial contextualization necessitated the creation of a binational state and hence categorically rejected Palestine's partition into nation-states. The political future of the Middle East, Brit Shalom regularly stated, would consist of an independent Arab state, or of an Arab Federation, and at any rate, would have little to no colonial presence or control. In such a Middle East, a Jewish nation-state, regardless of its borders, would stand out as a colonial relic. Given Palestine's overwhelming Arab majority, a Jewish nation-state even in a small part of Palestine would be created only against the overt wishes and hopes of a large Arab population within its borders and of the many neighboring Arab states surrounding it. The only political way for Zionism to diffuse colonial affiliation and nature would be by committing itself to complete political parity—a state in which, in the words of Brit Shalom, the two nations would live "under complete equality of rights, as the two elements that jointly and equally determine the destiny of this country." Anything "less" would no longer be Zionism; anything "more" would already be tangled with colonialism and thus, in the long run, could neither thrive nor survive.

However, as we have seen, the colonial context failed to offer the binational Zionists any concrete road maps beyond the basic notion that Zionism's future could be guaranteed only through a horizontal alliance with the Arab world, and not through a vertical alliance with Western empires. Kohn claimed that his binational outline for Palestine was inspired by Indian nationalists, but a closer inspection shows that it more directly resembled Austro-Marxist formulas for a multinational federation consisting of (extraterritorial) national personal autonomies. This, perhaps, should not come as a surprise, as the communal conflict in India differed from the Zionist-Arab conflict at least in one major respect, namely, that both Hindus and Muslims were native; neither was seen as a group of settler colonists, the way Arabs viewed the Zionist Yishuv.

The models presented by Brit Shalom were European, hailing from Switzerland, Belgium, Finland, and the Austro-Hungarian Empire. While the plans to reform the Austro-Hungarian Empire into a multinational state (and especially the Austro-Marxist theory and prescriptions) were part of the political upbringing of several binational Zionists, the motivation behind this reliance on European models was not just personal-biographical. More important, I have argued, was the identification of Europe as a universal model of political modernity. By reminding contemporaries that a great part of European political modernity was in multinational federations, binational Zionists pushed back against the commonplace claim that "binational" means "utopian." Admittedly, these European examples and formulas were better suited to address a national conflict between more or less equal peers. So, for example, while Hans Kohn presented the Moravian Compromise and the Bukovinian Compromise as Habsburg precedents in his outline for a binational Palestine, he also acknowledged that the Czech-German conflict in Bohemia of his upbringing had nothing of "the realities of colonialism," in which "a people try to govern peoples of another race and culture." Such realities, he said, "were unknown in Prague. . . . In Prague there had been a bitter enmity . . . between nationalities that shared a similar racial and cultural background"—not a colonial "clash of two different civilizations, a relationship not of rival peers, but of master and subject, which expressed itself in countless ways." That relationship—between a colonizer of sorts and a colonized of sorts—rendered the Zionist-Arab conflict all the thornier.[75]

The European experiences in and of themselves did not rule out a Palestinian partition. They did not necessitate addressing the national conflict in Palestine in the creation of a binational state—many other conflicts were "solved" through territorial compromise, that is, through partition—but they did provide binational Palestine some legitimizing good company. The one European example that remained surprisingly absent from Brit Shalom's discussion was the Soviet nationalities policy. It is a remarkable absence because, though different in so many ways, the Soviet policy shared the binationalists' acknowledgment of the colonized nationhood of the other party. Like the binational Zionists, the Soviets wished to create a polity that would be neither a nation-state nor an empire. More importantly, the Soviets resembled binationalists in their commitment to curbing the political ambitions and taming precisely *their own* nationhood (Zionism and the Great Russians, respectively), while insisting on the political rights of the other nations (Palestine's Arabs and the Soviet Union's non-Russians, respectively).[76] True, the Soviets could entertain such agendas, given the unique conditions following the collapse of the Romanov Empire. That setting was very different from Palestine of the 1920s and 1930s, but still it is baffling why Brit Shalom failed to discuss the relevance and lessons of the Soviet nationalities policy.[77]

As we return to the Jewish context—to the binationalists' analysis of the national conflict in Palestine in light of their understanding of Judaism, Jewish history, and Jewish political tradition—we should note that quite often Jewish context was not divorced from the European one. For historian Yfaat Weiss "it was not the liberal spirit of Central Europe but the liberal *Jewish* criticism of the illiberal turn to ethnonationalist practices in that geopolitical sphere which gave rise to a synthesis in the spirit of conciliatory Zionism."[78] Similarly, historian Dmitry Shumsky traces the origins of the binational idea of Prague Zionists not so much in the Czech-German conflict in Bohemia, but rather specifically in what he dubbed "Czecho-German Jewry," a term related to "the sociocultural location of Jews who did not understand themselves in monocultural terms, and also to the complex of experiences these people had given that location."[79] In a similar vein Steven Aschheim has linked binationalism's rejection of partition to the subculture of Central European Jews and to its core values ("Bildung in Palestine," in his words). For him, too, the Jewish context emerges out of a critical engagement with the non-Jewish European surrounding: "Not hypostatized German culture in itself, but rather, its historically specific Jewish appropriations and emphases played into their binationalist sensibilities."[80]

These historians have rightly noted that binationalists frequently understood the formative Jewish difference as shaped by the (often antagonistic) interaction with the specific European non-Jewish setting. This was often the case, but not always! Binationalists explained their rejection of partition also—indeed, at least as frequently—by relying on a rather ahistorical essentialist understanding of Jews and Judaism and their task in the world. Magnes, Kohn, Bergmann, Simon, and others insisted that Jews are "not a nation like other nations"; they are "the minority nation par excellence." Wherever they are, they live as a minority. Indeed, over the millennia the Jewish people became a nation "spiritualized," "stripping itself of statehood and territoriality." Zionists who wished to remain true to the distinctive Jewish political tradition must reject partition into nation-states. Advocating partition and desiring a Jewish nation-state, it follows, would be a collective assimilation, an unwitting abandonment of the Jewish political tradition, a wrongheaded adaptation to foreign political traditions. But ostensibly there was even more to it: Jewish spiritualized nationhood, they stated, constituted "a higher development" of nationalism, indeed, a Jewish model of political modernity. In Hugo Bergmann's words, Jews, indeed Zionists, had the "historical destiny . . . to break the spirit of majority [domination] in international affairs." The "historical calling" of the Jews was to "fight for a new morality in international relations."[81] That was the "historic mission which was bestowed upon us," Bergmann proclaimed. "The Divine has shown the Jewish people His great mercy by [providing us] a national home which is the homeland of two peoples," so that the Jewish people could exemplify for the nations of the world a new model of nationalism—a nationalism of morality and coexistence.[82] There is some irony in these statements. This celebration of Jewish statelessness as Judaism's universal mission, as "a light unto the nations," was typical of early Reform Judaism and later of philosopher Hermann Cohen. The Central Europeans among the binationalists had previously objected to such "denationalized" notions and saw their Zionism as a sharp "renationalized" antithesis. The challenge of Zionism's "Arab Question" and the objectionable prospect of Palestine's partition seem to have brought them to a unique synthesis of the two.

## CHAPTER 8

# ARAB LIBERAL INTELLECTUALS AND THE PARTITION OF PALESTINE

Joel Beinin

THE JULY 1937 REPORT of the Palestine Royal Commission (the Peel Commission) proposed the first official plan to partition Palestine into Jewish and Arab states, allocating about 19 percent of British Mandate Palestine for a Jewish state. The great majority of Palestinian intellectuals and political figures opposed the Peel partition plan and all subsequent partition proposals to partition Palestine until the 1970s. Among the prominent opponents of partition were personalities associated with the pan-Arab and anti-imperialist Istiqlal (Independence) Party of the early 1930s—'Awni 'Abd al-Hadi, Muhammad 'Izzat Darwaza, and Akram Zu'aytar. But the fiercest and best-known Arab opponent of the partition of Palestine was the Grand Mufti of Jerusalem, al-Hajj Amin al-Husayni.

Palestinian notables opposed to al-Husayni and Transjordan's Amir 'Abd Allah privately indicated they might accept the Peel partition plan.[1] But they feared swimming against the tide of Arab opinion expressed in the unanimous rejection of partition by the September 1937 Bludan Conference. Consequently, in November 1938 the British government accepted the Woodhead Commission's view that partition was unworkable. Nine years later, despite nearly universal Arab opposition, partition became the internationally approved "solution" to the conflict.

Musa al-'Alami understood that there was little chance that Great Britain, the United States, and Western public opinion would seriously consider the views of Amin al-Husayni, who was discredited as a Nazi collaborator, or former Istiqlalist "radicals." Consequently, after World War II, he recruited a group of Western-educated young intellectuals to articulate a liberal case against partition. They became the key staffers of the Arab Offices authorized by the Arab League. The young liberals believed that the Mufti's collaboration with Nazi Germany during the war "grievously harmed the cause of the Palestinians in Western eyes."[2] They sought to elaborate the arguments for a unitary Palestinian state first expounded by al-'Alami and George Antonius in the 1930s.

Leading British officials acknowledged the "reasonableness" and cogency of the liberals' arguments. Nonetheless, they faced a matrix of insurmountable obstacles: persisting British imperial illusions and resistance to abandoning the Palestine Mandate; the ascendancy of Zionism after the advent of the Nazi regime in 1933; and pressure on Britain from the United States, where Zionist influence in media and political circles was far greater.

The Mufti's jealous insistence on his leadership of the national movement also undermined the liberals' efforts. In April 1936, after the Arab Revolt erupted, Amin al-Husayni became the chairman of the Arab Higher Committee (AHC). The notable-led parties and patronage networks comprising the AHC neither initiated the revolt nor led the peasant insurgency that broke out after the publication of the Peel Commission report. Nonetheless, the AHC claimed to be the sole legitimate representative of the Palestinian Arab national movement.

## GEORGE ANTONIUS AND THE ARAB CASE
## FOR PALESTINE

George Antonius's *The Arab Awakening* presented the first cogent Arab case in English against partition. The argument is based on his more fundamental claim that the 1917 Balfour Declaration expressing British support for a "Jewish national home in Palestine" betrayed promises made to the Arabs in the 1915–1916 Husayn-McMahon correspondence and in other British declarations during and after World War I. The last sections of his book address the Peel Commission's partition proposal and prophetically conclude: "no room can be made in Palestine for a second nation except by dislodging or exterminating the nation in possession."[3]

Born in Alexandria, Egypt, to a Lebanese family, Antonius received an elite British education at Victoria College and graduated from the University of Cambridge in 1913. In 1921 he arrived in Palestine to work in the British administration's Department of Education; he became a Palestinian citizen in 1925. In 1930 he resigned from government service, protesting that he was denied a promotion he thought he deserved.

After abandoning the Peel partition proposal, the British government invited representatives of five Arab states in addition to Palestinian Arab and Zionist delegations to a Round Table Conference at St. James Palace in February 1939. The British hoped that their Arab allies (Egypt, Iraq, and Transjordan) would moderate the demands of the Palestinians and facilitate an agreement with Zionist representatives. Publication of *The Arab Awakening* only months before established Antonius as a formidable figure. Consequently, the British invited him to serve as secretary general of the combined Arab delegation. Although Antonius and Musa al-'Alami represented neither governments nor parties, Jamal al-Husayni, the Mufti's cousin and leader of the Palestinian delegation, considered them the main Arab strategists at the conference.[4]

*The Arab Awakening* and Antonius's briefs at the St. James Conference addressed the British in the King's English, arguing that Britain was obligated to keep its promises to the Arabs, that there was an Arab nation in Palestine, and that Palestinian independence should be based on the democratic principle of majority rule. Several Foreign Office officials privately admitted that Antonius's arguments were compelling. Prime Minister Ramsay MacDonald conceded that the Palestinians had "a very good case." A confidential British memorandum of February 21, 1939, acknowledged that the documents Antonius published were "obviously embarrassing" and that "in all its essentials Mr. Antonius's assertion is perfectly correct."[5] That is to say, the British claim, adduced in the 1922 Churchill White Paper, that Palestine was excluded from the territories in which Britain promised to support Arab independence was not sustained by the diplomatic record.

GEORGE ANTONIUS, MUSA AL-'ALAMI, AND
ALBERT HOURANI: A GENEALOGY OF LIBERAL
ACTIVISM ON PALESTINE

Antonius was the model for the methods later adopted by Musa al-
'Alami, Albert Hourani, and the young Arab intellectuals in their circle.
Hourani and Antonius shared many qualities. Both were of Lebanese
Christian origins and Oxbridge educated. They "felt an urgent mission to
bridge the gap between Britain and the Arabs. [Yet neither] . . . regarded
[their] efforts as particularly successful."[6] Hourani's conception of the
desirable relationship between the Arab world and Great Britain (and
the West more broadly) was articulated in his first substantial study of
the region—a report titled "Great Britain and Arab Nationalism" written
for the Foreign Office Research Department in 1943. He clear-sightedly
analyzed the contradictory potential of Arab nationalism:

> [T]wo concepts of [Arab] nationalism, as a movement for construction of a
> modern, westernized state and society and as a movement of violent resis-
> tance to the West, are already in conflict. . . .
>
>    If the Arabs come to believe that the West is friendly to them, then it is
> possible that the first tendency will prevail. If the Arabs continue to believe
> that the West is hostile to them, then Arab nationalism will turn into Pan-
> Islamism or else into a movement like Nazism, a hopeless, purposeless, self-
> destroying gesture of despair and defiance.[7]

Hourani was a loyal British citizen. From 1939 to 1943 he worked
for the Foreign Office Research Department in London. Then from 1943
to 1945 he served in Cairo as an assistant to Brigadier Iltyd Clayton,
the advisor on Arab affairs in the Office of the Minister Resident in the
Middle East. Like T. E. Lawrence and others, he believed his British and
Arab allegiances could be harmonized. British influence properly exerted,
he hoped, would induce the young Arab intelligentsia to choose the path
of liberalism and Western modernity while maintaining the best of the
Arabo-Islamic tradition: "I believe that Great Britain can only obtain
stable and friendly government in the Arab countries if she can persuade
the educated youth to seek and value her help in solving the internal
problems of their nation; if she can mold them into a ruling class, willing

to take responsibility in initiating schemes of far-reaching reform; and if she can prevent the idealism of youth giving way to bitterness."[8]

On his visits to Jerusalem during these years, Hourani's friendship with Antonius and his wife Katy gained him access to the Palestinian intellectual and political elite. After her husband's death in 1942, Katy hosted Hourani in her Jerusalem home, where she held "a political salon in true French style."[9] Hourani deeply regretted that Antonius "died at the moment when he was most needed, the moment for which his whole life had been a preparation."[10] The commitment of non-Palestinians like Antonius and Hourani to the cause of Palestine reflected the persistence of *bilad al-sham* (greater Syria) as a geographical-cultural unit despite its partition by France and Britain after World War I and therefore the importance of Palestine for Arab politics in the region.

Musa al-'Alami was the first Palestinian Arab to attend the University of Cambridge (class of 1922), where he took an honors degree in law.[11] He was admitted to the bar in 1924 and subsequently served as junior Crown counsel in the Palestine Mandate administration. In 1933 he became High Commissioner Sir Arthur Wauchope's private secretary for Arab affairs. A concerted Zionist campaign to remove him from this influential position resulted in his return to the legal department a year later as government advocate.

Arabs in the Mandate civil service were deeply dismayed by British policy toward the Arab Revolt. To allow them to let off steam, Wauchope proposed to al-'Alami that he submit a memorandum expressing their views.[12] The respectful but firm text criticized British policy, arguing that disregard for the grievances of the Palestinian Arabs had driven them "into a state verging on despair." This attempt simultaneously to represent the Arab community and distance themselves from the violence of the revolt exemplifies the dilemma of the British-educated Arab liberals. They rejected violence and the politics of notables, but they could not openly oppose them lest they be dismissed as British agents. The Peel Commission was sufficiently impressed by the document to include it as an annex to its report.[13]

As a government employee, al-'Alami could not testify before the commission. But he openly criticized the AHC for its decision to boycott the proceedings.[14] After the AHC belatedly relented, Antonius did testify.

Jewish witnesses before the Peel Commission alleged that the government advocate's office had been negligent in prosecuting Arabs accused of terrorism during the revolt. The commission exonerated al-'Alami's office. But based on factually incorrect information about his conduct of two cases, it recommended that a Briton be appointed senior government advocate. In October 1937 al-'Alami was abruptly dismissed from government service and told to leave the country.[15] He went into exile in Beirut.

Hourani considered al-'Alami "the best of the younger generation" of Palestinians (though he was then forty-six) and regretted that he was "not at present [1943] inclined to play an active part in politics."[16] In fact, al-'Alami did not think of himself as a political figure. In his obituary, E. C. Hodgkin, a journalist at the *Times* of London, a friend of al-'Alami, and a close follower of Middle East affairs, characterized al-'Alami as "a reluctant politician. . . . He reminded me of Adlai Stevenson—fascinated at politics but not much good at the rough and tumble. Intellectually superior to most he had to deal with, he would back down if he did not get his way."[17]

Like Antonius and Hourani, al-'Alami understood the value of a British education, familiarity with British politics and society, and fluency in English for the Palestinian Arab cause. He always endeavored to keep channels of communication open. Unlike the two other men, al-'Alami was imbedded in the social and political networks of Arab Palestine. His sister was married to the Mufti al-Hajj Amin's cousin, Jamal al-Husayni. But al-'Alami was in disfavor with the Mufti because he had publicly criticized the AHC's decision to boycott the Peel Commission.

After 1936 the British Colonial Office refused to deal with the Mufti in any capacity. Al-'Alami was instrumental in persuading Colonial Secretary Malcolm MacDonald to release interned members of the AHC, including Jamal al-Husayni, and allow them to attend the St. James Conference.[18] Al-'Alami obtained from MacDonald a protocol placing the independence of Palestine on the conference agenda, which convinced the majority of the AHC to participate.

The British government was not, in fact, willing to begin a transition toward an independent Palestine with an Arab majority, which Antonius and al-'Alami regarded as the ultimate reason for the failure of the St. James Conference. Consequently, the British unilaterally issued the 1939 White Paper, which restricted Jewish immigration and land purchases and proposed an independent, majority Arab state in Palestine after ten years. The AHC rejected the White Paper because it allowed further Jewish immigration, which would strengthen the Zionist position, and because it established no mechanisms to advance the goal of independence, unlike the situation in India.

In July 1940, Colonel S. F. Newcombe arrived in Baghdad to meet with al-'Alami and Jamal al-Husayni. In the presence of Iraqi prime minister Nuri al-Sa'id, they endorsed the 1939 White Paper as part of a package deal involving concrete steps toward self-government in Palestine and persuaded the AHC to go along despite the Mufti's objections. Newcombe may have exceeded his terms of reference, and Prime Minister Winston Churchill refused to endorse the agreement. Al-'Alami's biographer considered this "a milestone along the road which led, six months later, to the Rashid Ali revolt in Iraq."[19]

The Mufti supported Rashid 'Ali's pro-German military coup and fled to Berlin when it failed. Al-'Alami and Jamal al-Husayni opposed it; their relations with Amin al-Husayni became even more strained as a result. Al-'Alami's private views about the Mufti were not far from the official British assessment. In 1946 he confided to Ronald Storrs, the former British military and civil governor of Jerusalem, that the British "probably made a mistake not pushing him [al-Husayni] out altogether."[20]

Hourani also had a negative view of the Mufti. In his 1943 report he wrote that even before the outbreak of the 1936 revolt, many Palestinian Arab leaders found it hard to work with al-Hajj Amin.[21] Like Antonius and al-'Alami, Hourani though it was a "tactical blunder" that the AHC rejected the 1939 White Paper.[22] In 1947 Hourani told Storrs that he considered the Mufti a "disaster for the movement and blames no Jew for refusing to join any republic of which Haj A. would be President."[23]

## THE ARAB OFFICES

The Palestinian Arab parties chose Musa al-'Alami as their delegate to the September–October 1944 Preparatory Conference of the Arab League in

Alexandria. He believed that the Arabs could not prevail through armed struggle and that consequently, an extensive public relations effort was necessary to persuade British and world opinion of the justice of the Arab cause.[24] The Alexandria conference accepted al-'Alami's proposal to establish Arab Offices under his directorship in Jerusalem and several Western capitals to present the Palestine question and other Arab issues to the international community in an appropriate language and style.

However, narrow interests of several governments hindered implementation of the project. The Egyptians sought to delay and ultimately contributed nothing because they did not want to jeopardize the impending negotiations over ending the British military occupation. Moreover, from late May 1946 on, Amin al-Husayni was a semiofficial guest in Cairo. King Faruq, Prime Minister Nuqrashi, and the Egyptian secretary general of the Arab League, 'Abd al-Rahman 'Azzam, viewed the Mufti as a counterweight to their Hashemite rivals; therefore, they sought to preserve al-Husayni's position as the preeminent Palestinian Arab leader and undermine al-'Alami's efforts.[25] The Saudis preferred to work through the Arab heads of state, sought to avoid public diplomacy, and abjured any activity that could lead to friction with the United States and United Kingdom.[26] The Syrians and Lebanese were preoccupied with winning independence from France.

The March 1945 founding meeting of the Arab League ratified al-'Alami's proposal, appointed him director of the Arab Offices, and allocated two million pounds to fund the effort. The Iraqi, Syrian, Lebanese, and Saudi Arabian governments paid their initial funding pledges, enabling offices to open in Jerusalem, London, and Washington, DC, in May and June.[27]

Al-'Alami asked Iltyd Clayton to allow Hourani to leave his position in the Office of the Minister Resident in the Middle East and join the Arab Office in Jerusalem as director of research. Clayton and the Foreign Office were enthusiastic about the idea because they knew Hourani, respected his abilities, and hoped that he would promote the Arab cause with a pro-British orientation.[28] The Arab League had already decided that the Arab Offices "should not link [themselves] with any anti-British elements in America or anti-Jewish propaganda anywhere."[29]

Acting as al-'Alami's lieutenants, Albert Hourani and his younger brother Cecil recruited a group of mostly thirtysomething Arabs educated in Anglo-American institutions to staff the Arab Offices. Cecil candidly acknowledged that "[our] Anglo-Saxon education enabled us to judge what kinds of person would be effective spokesmen for the Arab cause, and be socially acceptable and presentable in the capitals where they would work."[30] Albert Hourani (Oxford class of 1936) was the intellectual star of the young Arab Office staffers. Others, in addition to his brother Cecil (Oxford 1939), included Luli Abul Huda (Oxford 1939), Burhan Dajani (American University of Beirut 1940; Government Law School, Jerusalem, 1948), Nejla Abu Izzeddin (Vassar 1930; Ph.D. University of Chicago 1934), Walid Khalidi (University of London 1945; M.Lit. Oxford 1951), Nasr al-Din al-Nashashibi (M.A., American University of Beirut 1943), and Anwar al-Nashashibi (University of Paris and University of London). Charles Issawi (Oxford 1937, M.Phil. 1944), Yusuf Sayigh (American University of Beirut 1938), and Michel Abcarius (an economist in the Palestine Treasury Department) also contributed to the work of the Jerusalem office.

It is impossible to reconstruct with certainty who served in what office and when on the basis of the available documentary record and contradictory personal recollections.[31] Staffing shifted frequently, partly due to factional considerations. Within fewer than six months, Ahmad al-Shuqayri, then a young lawyer from Acre, served as director of the Washington, DC, and then the Jerusalem offices. An unidentified party opposed the nomination of Raja'i al-Husayni and several proposed Washington staffers, protesting against appointing people "on the basis of their families."[32] Khulusi al-Khayri (London School of Economics, ca. 1930), who had briefly opened an Arab Office in Chicago before al-'Alami realized he would not have a budget for it, became director of the Washington, DC, office by early 1946. His appointment also aroused opposition, apparently because when he served as district commissioner in the Galilee, he had been involved in evicting peasants in Marj Ibn 'Amr and transferring the lands they farmed to the Zionists.[33] The other DC staffers included Cecil Hourani, Samir Shamma, Anwar Nashashibi, 'Awni al-Dajani, and Nejla Abu Izzeddin. Abu Izzeddin was the best educated, the most familiar with the United States, and the most articulate; the Jewish Agency noted that she would "bear watching."[34]

Edward Atiyah, a Lebanese educated at Victoria College and Oxford (1925) and a British civil servant in Sudan for twenty years, became director of the London Arab Office.[35] Atiyah was more than a decade older than most of the Arab Office staffers but fully shared their liberal, pro-British outlook and their negative view of Amin al-Husayni.[36] The London Arab Office published the first issue of the *Arab News Bulletin* on November 28, 1945. In May–June 1946 Hourani became director of the London Arab Office.

The Iraqis contributed fifty thousand dinars to the 1946 budget of the Arab Office; no other Arab states continued their contributions.[37] Consequently, in May 1946 al-'Alami notified the office employees that financial constraints required cutting staff.[38] He also scrapped his original plan to open several offices in the United States as well as Paris, Moscow, and the Arab capitals. After the United Nations General Assembly voted to partition Palestine on November 29, 1947, the Iraqis abruptly halted their funding; the Arab Offices survived only a few more months.

The inadequate and inconsistent financing of the Arab Offices was a consequence of the intense political factionalism in Palestine and the Arab world. Nuri al-Sa'id had been a political enemy of Amin al-Husayni since the latter's support for Rashid 'Ali's coup in April 1941. Al-Sa'id delivered the funds for the Arab Office directly to al-'Alami and made him "solely accountable for expenditure in his own personal capacity."[39] This made it appear that al-'Alami was aligned with the Hashemite monarchies of Iraq and Jordan against the Mufti, Egypt, and Saudi Arabia.

## THE ANGLO-AMERICAN COMMITTEE
## OF INQUIRY

The Arab Offices presented the case against partition and for an independent, democratic Palestinian state based on majority rule in a distinctive voice relying on careful research and documentation, closely reasoned argumentation, a willingness to maintain dialogue, and an appeal to the British sense of fair play. Their most substantial effort was to prepare testimony for the Anglo-American Committee of Inquiry (AACI) on Jewish Problems in Palestine and Europe. The decision to appear before the AACI was a rebuke to al-Hajj Amin al-Husayni, who argued that Palestinian Arabs should boycott the AACI, just as they had at first boycotted the Peel Commission.

In August 1945 President Harry S. Truman, following the recommendation of a presidential envoy to investigate the conditions of Jewish survivors of the Nazi mass murder living in displaced persons camps in Europe, created a diplomatic crisis with Britain by announcing that he supported the immediate immigration of one hundred thousand displaced Jews to Palestine. Consequently, on November 13, 1945, British Foreign Minister Ernest Bevin announced the appointment of the AACI. Its mission was:

1. To examine political, economic and social conditions in Palestine as they bear upon the problem of Jewish immigration and settlement....

2. To examine the position of the Jews in those countries in Europe where they have been the victims of Nazi and Fascist persecution ... and to make estimates of those who wish or will be impelled by their conditions to migrate to Palestine or other countries outside Europe.

3. To hear the views of competent witnesses and to consult representative Arabs and Jews on the problems of Palestine ... and to make recommendations to His Majesty's Government and the Government of the United States for ad interim handling of these problems as well as for their permanent solution.

4. To make such other recommendations to His Majesty's Government and the Government of the United States as may be necessary to meet the immediate needs arising from conditions subject to examination under paragraph 2 above....[40]

This was an inauspicious start from an Arab point of view because these terms of reference linked the fate of Jewish survivors of Nazism to the future of Palestine. In fact, most of the roughly 250,000 displaced European Jews would not have chosen to go to Palestine if any other refuge had been available.[41] Ultimately, about 136,000 went to Israel, 80,000 went to the United States, and 20,000 went to Canada, South Africa, and other countries.[42]

On humanitarian grounds, all six American members of the AACI were sympathetic to the Zionist demand that one hundred thousand European Jewish survivors be permitted to immigrate to Palestine immediately. Two American members—Bartley Crum (a San Francisco lawyer) and James McDonald (former high commissioner of refugees for the League of Nations)—were strongly pro-Zionist. The American co-chairman, Judge Joseph Hutcheson, opposed political Zionism but favored the immigration of the one hundred thousand displaced Jews. Frank Buxton (editor of the *Boston Herald*) supported him. The British co-chairman, Sir John Singleton (a High Court judge), was anti-Zionist and also opposed the immediate immigration of the survivors. In supporting the position of the British government, he was joined by two other British members, Reginald Mannigham-Buller (a pro-imperialist Tory member of Parliament) and Wilfred Crick (an economist). Richard Crossman (a former Oxford don, Labor member of Parliament, and assistant editor of the *New Statesman*) was the outstanding intellectual on the committee and was instrumental in negotiating the consensus that allowed it to issue a unanimous report. Crossman had become a Zionist at the beginning of the mission, when the AACI was in Washington, DC.[43] His commitments deepened after his visits to kibbutzim in Palestine during the course of the AACI's investigations; his memoir, *Palestine Mission*, is partially dedicated to Kibbutz Mishmar ha-'Emek.

Albert Hourani, under the supervision of Musa al-'Alami, was the principal drafter of the Arab Office's evidence to the AACI. On November 24, 1945, he submitted a proposal and program of research to prepare the testimony. By December 7, Hourani and a committee of Jerusalem office staffers—Michel Abcarius, 'Abd al-Hamid Yasin, and Fayiz al-Khuri (the future Syrian ambassador to the United States)—developed a detailed list of subjects to be researched along with suggestions for personnel to prepare the more specialized subjects.[44] With typical modesty, Hourani told al-'Alami that he could not write the section titled "Is Zionism the Solution of the Jewish Question?" However, it seems that he eventually did so because a pamphlet with a similar title was submitted as part of the written evidence provided to the AACI and was published under his name two months later.[45] Hourani also felt he could not take on more technical political, economic, and social issues, which were delegated to Charles Issawi, Yusuf Sayigh, and Michel Abcarius.

This research plan resulted in a three-volume typescript submitted to the AACI titled "The Problem of Palestine." Hourani was the principal author, under the supervision of al-'Alami, with Charles Issawi contributing the economic sections. It was subsequently revised and published as *The Future of Palestine*.[46] A précis of the book was also submitted to the AACI.[47]

Jamal al-Husayni, representing the Arab Higher Committee, was the first Palestinian Arab to speak before the AACI and told the committee: "If these pampered children, if these spoilt children of the British Government, the Zionists, know for once that they are no more to be pampered and spoilt, then the whole condition will be turned to what it has been before World War I. We will become friends probably."[48] This most unlikely scenario made it seem that his alternative scenario was more probable: "The people of this world have always cut their difficulties and knots by coming to grips with one another. Let us do it. Why not do it? You have done it in every war of your history . . . why should we not have this war? . . . It is quite natural. This is God's way."[49]

Jamal was then trying to reorganize the AHC on a more democratic basis by cooperating with independents like Sami Taha, the leader of the Palestine Arab Workers Society, and Ahmad al-Shuqayri of the Arab Office. He also favored cooperating with Arab states, including Iraq. His cousin, al-Hajj Amin, opposed these positions, and relations between them were tense.[50] However, although Jamal had not supported the Axis powers during the war, when Crossman and Crum asked him about the Mufti's wartime record, he defended his cousin.

Al-Shuqayri was the first of the two speakers to address the AACI on behalf of the Arab Office. His tone, inexplicably, was bellicose, rhetorically inflated, and unrealistic—completely antithetical to the style cultivated by the Arab Office. He announced that "if it is a question of violence, the Arabs are prepared to break the record."[51] Hourani was not pleased with what he considered this unnecessarily loud, explosive, and threatening performance.[52] His testimony on behalf of the Arab Office on March 25, 1946, calmly and systematically reviewed and refuted the viability of the three "solutions" for Palestine on the table—partition, a binational state, and continuing the status quo. His fundamental argument was that it was unjust to "turn . . . a majority into a minority in its own country" or to "withhold . . . self-government until the Zionists are in a majority." There-fore, "the only just and practicable solution . . . lies in the constitution of Palestine, with the least possible delay, into a self-governing state, with its Arab majority, but with full rights for the Jewish citizens of Palestine."[53]

Hourani's written evidence elaborated this point, invoking the lan-guage of Western democracy and the British constitutional tradition, ar-guing that the Arabs

> claim the democratic right of a majority to make its own decisions in mat-ters of urgent national concern . . . [A]ny solution of the problem created by Zionist aspirations . . . must accept the principal that the only way the will of the population can be expressed is through the establishment of responsible representative government . . . a democratic government representative of all sections of the population on a level of absolute equality. . . . Those Jews who have already legally entered Palestine, and who have obtained or shall obtain Palestinian citizenship by due legal process will be full citizens of the Palestinian state, enjoying full civil and political rights and a fair share in government and administration.[54]

The Arab objection to partition was therefore "one of principle. If they object to a Jewish State on the grounds of principle in the whole of Pal-estine, they cannot object to it [in part] and they cannot accept it in part. If they accept it in principle in part, they cannot oppose it in principle in the whole. The size and the extent of the Jewish State is irrelevant to the question of principle."[55]

Hourani understood that for the AACI and the British and US gov-ernments, the practicalities of partition were more important than the principle, especially as partition was already an acceptable idea in British imperial discourse and an obvious "compromise" solution. He argued:

> there are grave practical difficulties in the way of partition (difficulties which were dealt with finally in the report of the Woodhead Commission) . . . in regard to administration, to finance, to trade . . . of having an Arab State

which would be confined mainly to the hill country, which is poor and where there is already a problem of rural overpopulation. And above all ... whatever frontiers you attempt to draw for a Jewish State, there would still be a very considerable Arab minority in there, and this Arab minority could not be transferred forcibly because you can't transfer peasants forcibly. And equally, it [the minority] could not be exchanged, because there would not be a similar Jewish minority in the Arab State for which it could be exchanged.

The Peel Commission, as you will recollect, admitted the practical difficulties of partition and said that the more they were examined, the greater they appeared. . . .

[Moreover,] even if [the Zionists] accepted partition in the first place, there are factors at work which would draw them, sooner or later (and probably sooner) into inevitable conflict with the surrounding Arab world. There is a dynamic force in Zionism which, unless it is checked now, will lead them on to destruction. They will be forced into conflict with the Arab world by various factors—by the need to deal with their own Arab minority, which would not consent willingly to become the subjects of a Jewish State and which would rise and protest, and whose protest would be aided actively by surrounding Arab countries.

So that for reasons of internal security and in order to deal with their minority, the Jewish State would be brought into conflict with the surrounding countries.[56]

Hourani concluded his arguments against partition by contending that a Jewish State would be prone to expansionism. However, the demographic and economic reasons he adduced were ultimately less potent than Zionist claims asserting the Jewish right over all of Palestine, real or contrived military-security concerns, and after 1967, messianic religio-nationalism.

Judah Magnes, the president of the Hebrew University, who called for a binational state, was the only Zionist speaker to break ranks with the Jewish Agency's public position calling for a Jewish state in all of Palestine (although privately most Zionist leaders were willing to accept partition). Hourani countered, "the basic Arab objection to Doctor Magnes's proposal is one of principle, which again I needn't elaborate, and objection to the principle of further immigration which would be involved." On the practicalities of binationalism, he pointed out:

> Doctor Magnes, in cross-examination, admitted that force might be necessary in order to bring in the hundred thousand immigrants whom he asked to be brought in immediately. This, it seems to me, destroys the moral basis of his proposals. The great advantage, as he has always urged in his proposals, is that they would make the dream possible and force unnecessary, but now he is willing to show, or, as it appears, to contemplate the use of force in the very beginning of the process, and two consequences immediately follow.
>
> The first: It will be impossible to establish an agreement if force is used at the beginning of a proposal.
>
> Secondly, if force is to be used at all, perhaps it should better be used in support of the policy which has more intrinsically to recommend it. . . .
>
> Moreover, the parity which Doctor Magnes suggests is not so complete as it appears. As we understand his proposals, the Arabs ought to make an immediate concession of a number of immigrants, in return for the granting of self-government some time in the future. Again, self-government is . . . to be granted . . . conditionally upon the Jews and Arabs having already found a way of peace. And again, when and if this self-government is established, it will be incomplete. The veto, as we understand Doctor Magnes's plan, is to lie in the hands of the head of state, and the constitution is not to be drafted by representatives of the people, but by the United Nations organization. . . .
>
> There is one final objection to Doctor Magnes's plan, which is perhaps the most serious of all. Doctor Magnes is a person whose integrity and sincerity none of us doubt, but it is clear to me [that] he only represents a very small section of the Jewish community in Palestine. If his scheme were carried out, it would satisfy Doctor Magnes and his supporters, perhaps, but it would not satisfy the vast majority of Zionists. Perhaps, if a binational state were established, Doctor Magnes and his group would be swept aside and the majority of Zionists would use what Doctor Magnes had obtained for them in order to press their next demands. Doctor Magnes, in other words, might be the first victim of political Zionism.[57]

Hourani concluded his oral presentation with the theme that he had first articulated in his 1943 Chatham House report:

[T]he main task of the Arabs today is to come to terms with Western civilization. . . . Arabs are faced today with a choice between two paths: either
they can go out towards the West and towards the world in openness and
receptiveness, trying to take from the West what is of most value and greatest
depth in its tradition and blend it with their own. . . . Or else they can turn
away from the West and from the world.

I believe the first path is the path that Arabs must follow. . . . Nevertheless, the attitude which the Arabs will take up towards the West . . . depends
very largely upon the attitude which the West takes up towards them. . . .
Zionism for the Arabs has become a test of Western intentions, and so long
as the grievance, the intolerable grievance of Zionism exists, it will be impossible for the Arabs to establish that relationship of tolerance and respect, of
trust and cooperation, with the world and to live at peace with themselves
and their neighbors.[58]

Hourani did not dismiss the possibility of violence, but he made it clear
that he did not advocate it. When Bartley Crum asked him, "Is it part
of your case that in the establishment of an Arab state force might have
to be used?," Hourani replied, "Yes, if you do not broaden that with the
conclusion that I welcome it."[59]

Hourani's presentation made a strong positive impression. His brother
Cecil's judgment that his was "the ablest, the most convincing and the best
presented of all the statements made from the Arab point of view" might
be dismissed as parti pris.[60] However, AACI members and several leading
Zionists acknowledged Hourani's masterful intellect and personal charm.
David Horowitz, director of the Economic Department of the Jewish
Agency, wrote that "his testimony was ably and brilliantly presented. He
analyzed the problem with merciless logic and consistency and tried by
precept and example to show that any solution was liable to provoke a conflict."[61] Arthur Lourie, director of the Jewish Agency's UN Affairs Office
in New York, reported to Nahum Goldman that "Hourani . . . made a most
able and intelligent analysis (from the Arab point of view but with an air of
detachment) of the possible solutions. . . . Hourani is apparently the natural
successor of the late George Antonius; and friend and enemy alike were
loud in their praises of his charm and the distinction of his presentation."[62]

The usually judicious and circumspect Wm. Roger Louis considers Bartley Crum's memoir of his participation in the AACI, *Behind the Silken Curtain*, "a biased, dishonest, and indeed ghost-written account ... an unabashed piece of Zionist propaganda."[63] Nonetheless, Crum acknowledged that "Hourani made an extremely competent summation of the Arab case."[64]

CONCLUSION

The report of the AACI submitted in late April 1946 recommended immediate admission of one hundred thousand Jewish displaced persons to Palestine, as "countries other than Palestine gave no hope of substantial assistance in finding homes for Jews wishing or impelled to leave Europe." It proposed the principle "that Jew shall not dominate Arab and Arab shall not dominate Jew. . . . Palestine shall be neither a Jewish state nor an Arab state." This formulation appeared to endorse a binational state. In fact, it represented the American view that as "the Holy Land" Palestine should not belong solely to its inhabitants. Moreover, the committee recommended that "the Government of Palestine be continued as at present under mandate pending the execution of a trusteeship agreement under the United Nations," unrealistically hoping that the hostility between Jews and Arabs could be attenuated under continued British rule. It also recommended abrogation of the 1940 Land Transfers Regulations limiting the sale of Arab lands to Jews.[65]

Thus the AACI effectively recommended the abrogation of the 1939 White Paper and the indefinite continuation of British rule—a partial victory for the Zionists and a defeat for the principle of independence and self-determination by the majority of the population. The AACI report was ultimately unimportant. Both the Zionists and the Palestinians rejected it, and the British government did not implement it despite its commitment to do so if its recommendations were unanimous.

Rory Miller argues against "the conventional wisdom that there was little organized Arab propaganda of a serious or consequential nature" after World War II, maintaining that the Arab Office in London and its allied Committee for Arab Affairs posed a significant propaganda threat to the Zionist effort.[66] This is based on a serious misreading of both the British political scene and the global balance of power. Winston Churchill, Ramsay MacDonald, Malcolm MacDonald, Arthur Creech Jones, the platform of the Labor Party, the *Manchester Guardian*, and a host of other individuals and institutions from Balfour on were pro-Zionist. Sympathizers with the Palestinian cause—the Arabists in the Foreign Office; several prominent retired imperial proconsuls and diplomats with knowledge of the Middle East, such as Ronald Storrs and Sir Edward Spears; and a few prominent intellectuals, such as H. A. R. Gibb and Arnold Toynbee—were no match for the Zionists and their allies.

More importantly, after World War II London was no longer the primary arena where the future of Palestine was decided. In support of his view of the importance of Arab propaganda activities in London, Miller cites Cecil Hourani's statement that even after the UN partition resolution was adopted in November 1947, the Arab Office considered its London operation "nearer to the centre of decision making [than Washington]" and concentrated its efforts there.[67] The fact that Palestinian Arabs misunderstood the global balance of power cannot justify Miller's doing so. As Walid Khalidi argues, by the formation of the AACI, "Britain transformed its mandate into a condominium with the United States as the senior partner."[68]

In Washington, the Zionists were even stronger than they were in London, beginning with President Truman's support for moderate Zionism. Crossman perceptively noted that "America sympathizes with the National Home because [it] is something very American. . . . Americans, therefore, are liable in their estimate of the Arabs' side to think of them as Red Indians."[69]

The US Democratic and Republican parties had both adopted pro-Zionist planks in their 1944 election platforms. New York, Philadelphia, and other cities critical to Democratic electoral success were bastions of Zionist sentiment, and not only among their large Jewish communities. The British ambassador to the United States noted that the Arab Office's advertisement in the *New York Times* presenting the Palestinian Arab case on Palestine was "the first of its kind to appear in the United States press which habitually features lengthy explanations and statements concerning the Jewish case."[70] The British members of the AACI suspected that the American members' insistence that the committee begin its work in Washington, DC, was meant "to lure us into a hostile atmosphere and submit us to the full blast of Zionist propaganda."[71]

The divergent political sensibilities in London and Washington are captured by the fact that all six British AACI members had read *The Arab Awakening* before beginning their work. Crossman, despite his Zionist sympathies, considered the book "a brilliant survey of Arab history, far superior as a piece of writing to any Zionist publication I had read."[72] The US State Department did not possess a copy, and it is uncertain which, if any, American AACI members read it.

Arab Americans were utterly ineffective. Their testimony before the AACI in Washington made a poor impression. Philip Hitti, the founding father of modern Arab history in American academia, spoke about biblical history, joked about his Hittite and Phoenician ancestors, and addressed other largely irrelevant topics. Moreover, his assertion that Palestine did not exist—"It is only a myth, the mischievous product of Sunday Schools; Palestine is the southern portion of Syria"—was damaging and demonstrated complete ignorance of what was at stake.[73]

The fragile status of the Washington Arab Office was demonstrated in March 1947. At the behest of Representative Adolph Sabath (Democrat from Illinois), the FBI raided its premises in the Wardman Park Hotel, ostensibly to determine whether it cooperated with antisemitic organizations.[74] The US consul-general in Jerusalem responded to Arab complaints saying that this was a routine activity in accord with the Foreign Agents Registration Act. The Jewish Agency office in Washington was, of course, not raided.

Factionalism among the Palestinian Arab leadership and the Arab states undermined the effectiveness of the Arab Offices and weakened the Palestinian position more generally. But the combination of American support for Zionism; the enormous guilt (properly) felt in the West for having stood by as Jews were murdered by the Nazis and, consequently, the desire to compensate Jews by giving them a state (rather than welcoming them in Western Europe or North America); the effectiveness of the Zionist propaganda effort; and, above all, the well-organized Jewish Yishuv in Palestine, including its militias, which had been anticipating for a decade that the fate of Palestine would be determined by force of arms—all made it likely that the Zionists would prevail whatever the Arab Offices might have accomplished. British military intelligence noted, "it was clear that [Albert Hourani] won the hearts of the [Anglo-American] Committee, even if he may not have won their minds. His evidence was a well-reasoned work of art."[75] Despite the intellectual power of Hourani's arguments and the educational credentials, intellectual stature, and commitment to liberal values of his colleagues, they were never likely to prevail politically.

Amikam Nachmani regards Hourani's testimony before the AACI as "a rare instance of his adopting a political pose."[76] Hourani also addressed the Arab-Israeli conflict directly after the 1967 war.[77] Moreover, I would suggest that the views on the relationship between the Arabs and the West expressed in Hourani's 1943 Foreign Office report "Great Britain and Arab Nationalism" and in his testimony before the AACI are entirely consistent with the conceptual frame of his first major scholarly book, *Arabic Thought in the Liberal Age, 1789–1939*. George Antonius's *The Arab Awakening* is an important text in the intellectual genealogy Hourani surveyed in that book. Its omission might be justified only on the grounds that it was not written in Arabic. But Hourani acknowledged that his heart was "forever marked by what happened in Palestine."[78] Perhaps his disappointment over the failure of Antonius and the Arab Offices remained too recent and bitter a memory for him to dispassionately discuss Antonius in *Arabic Thought in the Liberal Age*, although he subsequently did so.[79]

Hourani's more overtly political writing ought not to be viewed as an exception to his scholarship. Both express the outlook of a generation of Anglo-American–educated Arabs who saw their advocacy of the Arab cause in Palestine as consistent with universal, liberal values. As Hourani predicted, they, and more importantly their societies, perceived their failure as a rebuff to Arab liberalism.

## CHAPTER 9

POETS OF PARTITION
*The Recovery of Lost Causes*
Priya Satia

THE STORY of the 1947 Partition of British India is typically rehearsed through the negotiations among political elites—what Muhammad Ali Jinnah wanted, what Mohandas Gandhi wanted, what Lord Mountbatten wanted, and so on. To be sure, we have recently begun to hear a great deal more about how ordinary people experienced and *made* Partition.[1] The transnationally framed essays in this volume further expand our grasp of the event's political and intellectual history. Still, the *meaning* of partition emerges from a very different intellectual genealogy—one also made up of elites in transnational conversations, overlapping with those of Gandhi, Jawaharlal Nehru, and Jinnah. These were Urdu poets, whose voices have been oddly marginalized in the historiography on Partition despite the centrality of literary movements to interwar political culture (not to mention the literary proclivities of Gandhi, Nehru, and Jinnah themselves). This essay puts poets front and center in its quest to understand the meaning of Partition.[2] After all, insofar as Partition was about remaking identity as much as establishing borders, it took shape in the realm of cultural history, molded by particular imaginaries of community, land, nation, progress, freedom, history, loyalty, unity, and so on that we can most readily access in literature. As influential as Nehru's or Jinnah's own imaginaries of nation, minority, and state were, they did not anticipate the way Partition unfolded—as the violent displacement of millions—or the way it was later understood.

The poets I focus on participated in cosmopolitan networks of anti-colonial thought and action—another transnational dimension of India's Partition experience. Their long inconspicuousness in histories of Partition may stem partly from the way their transnational lives and thoughts tend to disturb the comfortable certainties of nationalist narratives. They also destabilize assumptions about Partition's effectiveness in actually creating the unitary, authentic national identities it was supposed to forge from more complex forms of belonging. Indeed, they reveal the at times accidental, at times willful, lived subversion of Partition—in which this volume also participates. Traditional narratives of Partition are often preoccupied with causes—largely, as Gyanendra Pandey observes, because of Indian historians' commitments to particular visions of a unified India. Poets focused more on consequences, as Rakhshanda Jalil notes.[3] But perhaps the distinction can be put another way: by demonstrating its contingent nature, its possible evitability, historians seek, in a way, to transcend the monumental historical divide of Partition, perhaps because it violated some notion of India but also perhaps because it violated lives and commitments that went beyond the national. And poets expressed the possibility of such transcendence in the moment itself. My purpose in writing them back into the story of Partition is to recuperate that mode of transcendence and at once remind us of the compact between poetry and history-writing that these poets helped produce.

I

I learned of that compact through the work of E. P. Thompson, the celebrated historian of the English working class who was also a poet and political activist. Thompson insisted on the poet's centrality to history and leftist politics. He read the history of the English working class with one eye on the Romantic poets of their time. His favorite was the mystical, prophetic, and anti-imperialist William Blake; he disapproved of William Wordsworth's betrayal of the revolutionary spirit. For Thompson, poetry stood for "deeply inspired action. . . . The poet was crucial to revolutionary politics, for he could articulate the longings that, along with practical programs, inspired men to act." Blake "embodied the possibility of poetry and politics, romantic yearning and rational resistance in a single movement."[4] As a historian Thompson set out to recover the creative—poetic—radical capacity of eighteenth-century English workers, in explicit contrast to the rigid "scientific" materialism of the British Communist Party in his own time. His discovery of the imaginative play in earlier British socialist movements gave him some hope for endurance of those values in his time.[5] Thompson's expectations of poets were partly shaped by his boyhood contact with Indian nationalism. His father was the poet and historian Edward John Thompson, whose friendship with Indian nationalists and support for Indian nationalism earned him the moniker "India's prisoner." He, too, loved the Romantics and was particularly inspired by Lord Byron, who died fighting for Greek liberation from the Turks in 1824. Indeed, his own heroism in ministering to the wounded under fire during the British conquest of Iraq in World War I was recognized. After the war, he devoted his life to using the historian's craft to atone for Britain's sins in India. Among his heroically nationalist Indian friends were the poets Rabindranath Tagore and Muhammad Iqbal, both deeply knowledgeable about Western Romantic poetry. E. P. Thompson recalled cadging stamps from the Indian "poets and political agitators" who visited his family's Oxford home in the 1930s and his knowledge that these were the "most important visitors" to their home.[6] One senses that for both father and son it was as much the life that such poets lived on the frontlines of history as the poetry they wrote that made them so admirable. Largely because of his father's influence, the younger Thompson, whatever his preference for Blake, took on a Byronic role in his efforts to guide the British working classes out of the darkness of his own time.[7] In short, anticolonial Indian poets of the 1930s helped produce our discipline's sense of its ethical obligations.

Like historians obsessing over the causes of Partition today, during the period from World War I to the 1950s, leftist Indian poets imagined alternative futures for the subcontinent. Their diverse visions of social equality, communal harmony, and internationalist nationalism might have been utopian; but their recovery may yet light a way forward in our time of social inequality, communal strife, and chauvinistic nationalism. In writing history, Thompson urged, "Our only criterion for judgment should not be whether or not a man's actions are justified in the light of subsequent evolution. After all, we are not at the end of social evolution ourselves." The "lost causes" of the past might yield "insights into social evils which we have yet to cure."[8] And so, we must focus our historical lens at last on the poets who so crucially shaped that lens.

They left this imprint on the discipline partly because the events of that period demanded poetic expression. Partition, like World War I, fascinates historians because it resonates at an almost visceral level as a moral narrative, a moral tragedy, an event in which all the folly of human history was briefly and tragically on flagrant display. This is why poetry remains a primary recourse in remembering and understanding the war and why Partition is a similar poetic mine. The paths of poets from these two worlds crossed, as the Thompson home shows—their neighbor was the World War I poet Robert Graves.

## II

Partition was forged in the crucible of traumatic twentieth-century attempts to remake the world. But it is poetically irresistible also because of its resonance with much older cultural commitments to the idea of "division" in the region where it occurred. Among Punjabis, it plays on culturally deep, mystical-poetic notions of *birha*, the longing for union with the divine, which morphs over time into the *pardesi*'s nostalgia for an increasingly imaginary *watan* (homeland, country). (Literally, *pardesi* means someone from another land, but poetically, it also indicates someone simply away from home.) Indeed, I have found it difficult to extricate these inherited layers of nostalgias in my own psyche; hence perhaps my dilatory approach to the subject of Partition, which I have in various ways attempted to work on since I was nineteen years old. What I offer here builds on that dawning personal insight and is more speculative and hypothetical than rigorously empirical. It is the fruit of long reflection but short research, a beginning for thought.[9] My excuse is that this exercise in recovery, however uneven and self-indulgent, is useful precisely insofar as it raises the possibility of *countless* alternatives.

I came to poets as historical actors in the drama of Partition as I began to realize the extent to which regional poetic tropes had quietly shaped my understanding of my own family history. The Satias were a solidly Congress family from Muktsar in Ferozepur district (now on the border with Pakistan). My great-grandfather was jailed for nationalist activities. In 1947, no one was sure on which side of the border the town would fall. I heard flattering stories of my family's efforts to protect terrified Muslims. I wondered about the masjid opposite our house—Angooran Wali Maseet (Grape Mosque)—which gave the town its romantic sky-line, a dignified yet ghostlike centerpiece of a town famous for *gurdwaras* (Sikh temples) marking Guru Gobind Singh's 1705 battle against the Mughals, a monument to an absent people. My father left for the United States, like many Indian doctors, in the late 1960s. (His first roommate in Chicago was a Pakistani.) All but one of his brothers also left Muktsar, settling in Rajasthan, New Delhi, and Haryana. Their father distributed them thus because of the partitions of Indian Punjab in 1967, which pro-duced the new states of Haryana and Himachal Pradesh: he knew from experience that partition meant uncertainty and sent his sons abroad to insure against that uncertainty, making them *pardesis* cherishing memo-ries of Muktsar. In 1983, against the backdrop of an increasingly militant Sikh separatist movement stoked by Indira Gandhi, my grandfather died. His sons and brother engaged in a property dispute that turned violent, too. The rent familial bonds added more pathos to the nostalgia of those long since dispatched from Muktsar. The home they longed for grew in-creasingly imaginary, and longing itself became a permanent part of their identity as Punjabis.

My mother's family hailed from Multan in West Punjab. Perfumers dependent on regional supply chains, they determined to stay in Pakistan, but circumstances forced their departure some time in 1948. Those "cir-cumstances" remain cloudy—a kidnapping, a fire, a murder, a disguised escape. They landed in the empty home of departed Muslims, in Old Delhi, eventually moving to New Rajinder Nagar, a residential colony in central Delhi made up almost entirely of Punjabi refugees. More embit-tered than the Satias, they were less nostalgic and gravitated to the Hindu right, blaming Congress for causing Partition. Still, my grandmother let fall nuggets of wistful memories, of her father's fabulous *serais* (caravan-saries) outside Multan where she spent her childhood. Granduncles drew maps of a lost city in which their house once stood and may still stand today. In Darya Ganj, surrounded by the remnants of Muslim Old Delhi, my mother grew up with *"Hai Allah"* on her lips more readily than *"Hey Ram,"* whatever the family's antipathy for Islam.

However different these two sides of my family, they shared a certain understanding of Punjabi identity, grounded in a sense of loss and dis-placement as something inexorably fated and something to struggle to spiritually and culturally transcend. The 1940s, 1960s, 1980s, and 2000s produced countless such stories among Punjabis, not to mention those who left even earlier. Heavy military recruitment into the British Indian Army from the second half of the nineteenth century and emigration to North American farmlands from the early twentieth century to escape British rule and poverty had long fuelled the poetic tradition around the *pardesi* and the cult of nostalgia for the Punjabi homeland. Displacement became central to Punjabi identity as it is to Jewish and Armenian iden-tity, but it is distinct in the Punjabi's awareness of his own role in his tragic severance from his home and repeated division of his homeland. His (and I do mean "his" here) is a self-imposed exile guiltily justified by one or another promise of modernity—personal prosperity, for economic migrants; national prosperity, for partition refugees. He self-consciously martyrs the homeland for the progress of its children, secure that in duti-fully pursuing his worldly ends he nevertheless maintains a timeless bond with it, a bond made more transcendently spiritual at each remove from the geopolitical reality of a place called Punjab.[10]

Of course this is a stereotype. There is too much variety across sub-region, caste, class, nation, and gender for this style of Punjabi identity to be true across the board. And yet the stereotype of the Punjabi-who-transcends-Punjab is instantly recognizable largely because of the Indian film industry. My relatives embodied it not only because of their own experiences, but because they saw it mirrored in a steady stream of films from the 1950s. Take, for instance, the films of Yash Chopra, himself a Partition refugee. In his last, posthumously released film *Jab Tak Hai Jaan* (2012), the broken-hearted Indian Punjabi hero—with the requisite

Pakistani "brother" in London—struggles in war-torn Kashmir with his beloved Meera's decision to put god above her love for him—arguably what many Punjabis did during Partition, putting religious bonds above social ones. The name "Meera" invokes the medieval poetess who abandoned worldly love for spiritual union with Lord Krishna. In the film, the separation of Meera and Samar and their undying mutual longing represents the summit of worldly love made divine.[11] Such films play on the Sufi idiom of centuries-old poetic Punjabi romances of sundered yet mystically united pairs: Heer–Ranjha, Sohni–Mahiwal, Sassi–Punnu, Mirza–Sahiba. There are others—Shirin Farhad, Laila Majnun—inherited from farther northwest. Waris Shah's 1766 narration of Heer Ranjha was based on a true story that transpired some two centuries earlier in Jhang. The tragic ending depicting the two lovers, dead before the chance at union, at once sought to express divine love, in which the most intense experience of union with the divine lies in interminable longing. The mystical-poetic concept of *birha* thus elides romantic or erotic allusion with religious devotion. It is a religiously syncretic cultural heritage collapsing art and the spiritual, even the masculine and feminine.[12] Through such translations of Punjab's poetic inheritance and modern historical experience, Bollywood has long told us that love lies in separation and that the Punjabi is always a *pardesi*, the beloved away from home.

These cinematic tropes were shaped directly by Urdu poets of the Partition era. Before Partition, many were tied to the early film industry through the Progressive Writers' Association, which was closely tied to the Indian People's Theatre Association. Then Partition itself brought an influx of displaced writers to the Bombay industry, including Sahir Ludhianvi, Majrooh Sultanpuri, Ismat Chughtai, Bhisham Sahni, Sajjad Zaheer, and others. One of these, the leftist lyricist Prem Dhawan, immortalized the vision of the northwestern Indian carrying his homeland in his heart wherever he may be in the patriotic anthem "Aye mere pyaare watan" (Oh My Beloved Homeland). The song was picturized on a Pashtun selling fruit in Calcutta in the 1961 film *Kabuliwala*, which was based on a Tagore story.

In short, as much as poetry is an obvious recourse for expressing the loss and grief experienced by the redrawing of borders, as it was in Bengal,

Germany, Palestine, Ireland, and elsewhere, in Punjab, poetry about partition was a preexisting cultural inheritance, long cultivated in mystical traditions and earlier emigrations. Is it coincidence or destiny that a region
that for so long depicted love through partition should have been the site
of violent partition itself? Or is the intense Punjabi preoccupation with
these romances a cultural legacy of 1947? The Punjabi poet Amrita Pritam, who left Lahore for Indian Punjab in 1947, explicitly invoked this
cultural coincidence to express her anguish over Partition, particularly the
violence done to women, in "Ajj Aakhaan Waris Shah Nu" (Ode to Waris
Shah). After a detour through the poetic universe in which Pritam took
part, I will return to the plight of Heer that she invoked.

### III

So many of India's nationalist leaders studied in universities abroad that
the *pardesi* sentiment runs like a red thread through their evocations of
patriotism, despite their varying politics. This is particularly true of the
one poet who is always invoked in the history of Partition: Muhammad
Iqbal. Though credited with authoring the notion of a Muslim India,
Iqbal's early patriotism, expressed in his 1902 poem "Lab Pe Aati Hai
Dua" (A Prayer Comes to the Lips), referred vaguely enough to a *watan*
that it remains singable in schools in both Pakistan and India. His 1904
"Tarana-i-Hind" (Indian Anthem) conjured the Hindustani abroad, carrying his homeland in his heart. He wrote this poem when he was about
to leave for his studies in Europe. These evocations of homeland built
on poetic traditions expressing nostalgia for a lost place, coupled with a
critique of empire, that had shaped Urdu poetry during the nineteenth
century. Nevertheless, Iqbal followed Urdu reformers like the poet and
literary critic Maulana Khawaja Hali and Sir Syed Ahmad Khan, the
founder of Aligarh, in criticizing the Sufi tradition for privileging mystical over worldly experiences and producing political passivity.

In fact, Urdu poets had long engaged such issues *through* that Sufi
vein. Modern Urdu poetry had evolved in the context of the worldly
problem of colonialism and the crises of culture and identity it produced,
and the concept of *birha* had long merged worldly with unworldly concerns.[13] In 1835, the four-year-old Daagh Dehlvi was orphaned when his

father was hanged for ordering the assassination of Sir William Fraser, commissioner of the Delhi Territory under the last Mughal emperor (and poet) Bahadur Shah Zafar in 1835. After the death of Daagh's stepfather (the Mughal prince Fakhroo) in 1856, he lived a life of exile from Delhi, in government service in Rampur and Hyderabad. Iqbal was one of his disciples. Urdu *shayri* was part of courtly Mughal culture, but that culture was intimately shaped by the expanding British presence from the eighteenth century. Poets were central to the rebellion of 1857. Fazl-e-Haq Khairabadi, a close associate of Mirza Ghalib, was one of its leaders and died in prison on the Andaman Islands. Ghalib's and Zafar's brokenhearted response to the British destruction of Delhi after the rebellion fed that melancholic anticolonial strain. The British banned some of these poems; censorship also limited what courtly Urdu poets could say. Ghalib's concern for patronage also limited his capacity for ideological rebellion. Meanwhile, Hali immersed himself in Romantic English works, including Wordsworth and Byron, and he and Syed Ahmad Khan worked to fulfill Thomas Macaulay's task of producing an Indian class in the British image.[14]

By the twentieth century, socially conscious yet worldly Indian poets were more willing and able to openly express radical notions, partly thanks to the impetus from the diaspora colonialism had helped create. The Ghadar Party, founded in 1913 in California, for instance, broke with the moderate stance of the Congress movement; its aim was total independence, and it was willing to use violent tactics. Its publication *Ghadar di Gunj* was full of revolutionary poetry. Indian leaders were aware of and influenced by this Californian movement. The Punjabi diaspora the British helped create shaped what happened *in* Punjab; partition begat partition. Banned literature came into Punjab from around the world. Punjabis in Punjab heard of racism against Punjabis in Vancouver and California. Lala Lajpat Rai met with California Punjabis in 1907 and 1916. Many Ghadar members returned to Punjab early in World War I to start an armed rebellion but were hanged or imprisoned. From prison in the Andaman Islands, they wrote poetry in Punjabi, which also lapsed into love poetry in which the homeland from which they were exiled stood in for the beloved.[15] The movement inspired other challenges to

Congress. In 1915, a young student and Arya Samaji in the United Provinces read with outrage about the death sentence pronounced on a Ghadar leader—Ram Prasad Bismil, the poet who would pen the Punjabi communist freedom fighter Bhagat Singh's favorite poem, "Mera Rang de Basanti Chola" (Color My Clothes in the Color of Spring) (1927?), and "Sarfaroshi Ki Tamanna" (The Desire for Rebellion) (1921). These revolutionary sentiments gained steam with the Russian Revolution of 1917. In 1919, the Khilafat movement was launched, a joint Muslim League–Congress movement to pressure the British to preserve the Ottoman caliphate as the Ottoman Empire was broken up. The parties held a joint meeting in Ahmedabad in 1921. Bismil was there, and Hasrat Mohani, a popular poet and fiercely anticolonial journalist, was presiding chair of the League. Both urged passing of a *Purna Swaraj* (complete self-rule) proposal, but Gandhi opposed it, favoring dominion status within the empire as a goal. Mohani was jailed for two years for his radical speeches. The Khilafat movement failed; the Turkish caliphate was abolished in 1924. Around that time, Mohani called for "separate Muslim states in India, *united* with Hindu states under a *National Federal government*." Lajpat Rai endorsed the idea of partitioning Punjab and forming smaller provinces, given the existence already of separate electorates. He noted that this would mean "a clear partition of India into a Muslim India and a non-Muslim India."[16]

Meanwhile, Lala Har Dayal, a founder of the Ghadar movement, encouraged Bismil and Mohani to found the Hindustan Republican Association, which aimed to create a federated republic of the United States of India through organized armed revolution. Mohani was also involved in founding the Communist Party of India around 1925. Bismil was hanged for his participation in the 1925 Kakori conspiracy, in which a group of men planned to rob a train filled with government money. The British Raj worked hard to crush such revolutionary activity, but these poets continued to address the earthshaking events of their time, from the Rowlatt Act to Partition, through an embattled yet burgeoning network of publishers and presses.[17] The British grew ever-more anxious about Muslims on the left, imagining them as the progenitors of Islamic-Bolshevik conspiracy that would threaten the entire world order.[18] In 1928, the Simon

Commission went to Lahore to study constitutional reform, outraging nationalists with its all-white composition. Nationalist groups came together to demonstrate, greeting the commission with black flags. They were *lathi*-charged. The protestors' leader, Lajpat Rai, died of his wounds. Partly to avenge his death, Bhagat Singh and Shivaram Rajguru, with the help of other Hindustan Republican Association members, assassinated the assistant superintendent of police, J. P. Saunders. This was not a popular action, but the struggle Bhagat Singh and his companions then launched in prison for the rights of political prisoners became popular. When they went on a hunger strike in 1929, five thousand supporters gathered in Amritsar to recite poems comparing their love of country to the *qissas* (romantic epics) of Heer Ranjha and Sohni-Mahiwal. The global stock market crash that year produced high unemployment that fueled radicalism and civil disobedience. Then Singh and Rajguru were sentenced to death. Iqbal made his speech about a Muslim India *within* India at a Muslim League meeting in Allahabad just two months later, during a Punjab-wide campaign to appeal Bhagat Singh's sentence, when Bhagat Singh was as popular as Gandhi. Congress also finally agreed to demand *purna swaraj* in 1930; it too was radicalized in the aftermath of the Simon Commission. A series of Round Table conferences followed. Singh was hanged in 1931 while Gandhi was in London for the second Round Table Conference (as well as visiting the Thompsons). Iqbal was there, too. This backdrop of events in Punjab is a crucial context for understanding Iqbal's thinking about the province's future—as is the appeal of creating a new Medina after the collapse of the Turkish caliphate.[19] In England Iqbal met a Cambridge student, Chaudhri Rahmat Ali, who was taken by the idea of a *separate* Muslim Indian state and circulated this idea of Pakistan in a pamphlet in 1933.

The Punjab backdrop is also crucial to understanding the launching of the Progressive Writers' Movement at precisely the same moment. Gurbaksh Singh was a Michigan-trained engineer working with the Indian Railways. In that capacity he accompanied the Simon Commission to Lahore in 1928, when Lajpat Rai was beaten by police. The events afterwards, culminating in the execution of Bhagat Singh, radicalized Gurbaksh Singh. He quit his job and turned to literature. In 1933, the very year that the word "Pakistan" entered the lexicon, he founded the literary journal *Preet Lari*, which was also popular among California's Punjabis and would publish Amrita Pritam's much loved poem in 1947.[20] He also founded the artist colony Preet Nagar, halfway between Lahore and Amritsar, where many leftist Punjabi writers like Pritam ventured.[21]

Many of these writers were part of the Progressive Writers' Movement launched just then by Indian students in England, precisely when the elder Thompson was mixing with poets dealing with the war and writing voluminously in the cause of Indian freedom. These overlapping poetic worlds were shaped by similar modernist and socialist trends. The Marxist Sajjad Zaheer was in England, like Chaudhri Rahmat Ali. The year before Zaheer and three other writers had published *Angare*, a collection of short stories, in Lucknow. This collection drew inspiration from James Joyce, Virginia Woolf, D. H. Lawrence (whose work was itself shaped by orientalist trends), and Russian authors like Chekhov and Gogol. The book unleashed a storm: many were dismayed by its call for reform in the shape of a new secularism rather than within the existing religious praxis.[22] It touched the same nerve as Macaulayite reformism of the previous century,[23] even though it emerged less from British liberalism than from a mix of cosmopolitan and indigenous currents of socialist thought. In any case, the backlash against its alleged blasphemy was validated by the colonial state: the Government of the United Provinces banned the book. Partly to denounce this gagging of his work, Zaheer met with other Indian students and intellectuals in London, including Mulk Raj Anand and M. D. Taseer, to create a league of Progressive writers.

These steps were also part of a wider global trend, as the crash of 1929 triggered a turn toward fascism and communism in Europe, creating a polarizing context of right versus left that made the 1930s a decade of "commitment" for intellectuals. Writers claimed a central role in political and social action, building on older, Romantic notions of the poet's special role in history. Meetings of committed European writers were held in Paris and Madrid as the Nazis came to power in Germany in 1933. The Soviet Writers' Congress met in 1934. The first International Congress of Writers for the Defence of Culture met in Paris in 1935, and Zaheer attended it. In 1936, British writers he knew went to fight in the Spanish

Civil War, seeing it as an ideological battle between fascism and international communism. Committed intellectuals launched the Left Book Club that year to help shape British public opinion toward the left. Similar aesthetic trends of modernism and social realism shaped these writerly communities as they asserted that they mattered in a new way.

After an initial gathering in Allahabad late in 1935, the Progressive Writers' Association (PWA) held its first formal meeting in Lucknow in 1936. The movement's organizational structure was modeled on the European movement. The All-India PWA was affiliated with the International Congress of World Writers as its Indian branch. I am tabling here, unjustly, the entire matter of linguistic preference, the history of Urdu-Hindi and Punjabi.[24] But it is important to note that Urdu writers took the lead in the formation of the All-India PWA, wielding a disproportionate influence on its affairs at the national level, even beyond 1947; indeed, at times the Urdu branch was conflated with the entire organization. In this sense, Urdu literary culture took an "aggressively 'national' stance."[25] Faiz Ahmed Faiz and Sahir Ludhianvi were part of its network in Punjab, as were Bombay-based writers like Sadat Hasan Manto and Ismat Chughtai. Hasrat Mohani joined too, as did Fazl-e-Haq Khairabadi's great-grandson, the poet Jan Nisar Akhtar. Experiment with form was one part of their modernism; the *nazm* came into its own in their hands during this period. (Faiz, incidentally, admired W. H. Auden, who was then at the peak of his political engagement.) But older Western influences were also at work: Wordsworthian ideas about "natural poetry" had become quaint in Europe but were highly influential among Urdu Progressive poets, with their nationalist and proletarian sympathies. Hali's twentieth-century heirs invoked a South Asian way of being idiosyncratically modern, drawing on this heritage in their immediate context in new ways.

Many Progressives were fiercely anticolonial. Iqbal and Tagore gave the organization their blessing, and Nehru was part of the initial association. But the organization's members also departed from the nationalistic style of the mainstream Indian National Congress and Muslim League movements, often because their internationalist sympathies with communism prohibited such parochial commitments. They sought to infuse the nationalist movement with a social and political project aimed at a broader transformation of social and economic relations in India—to make a truly free India. In 1937, the group joined a Kisan Sabha meeting in Amritsar where the Marxist Faiz, a leading labor activist in Punjab, affirmed that middle-class writers *could* relate to peasants and workers. Perhaps Nehru felt threatened by this ambition. In his address to the second Allahabad conference in 1938, he urged the association to include writers exclusively, not politicians like him.[26] This paternalistic guidance betrays either Nehru's shrewd awareness of the group's disruptive potential or a naïve misreading of the political possibilities of poetry (and other writing). Many in the group also had ties to the Communist Party of India. When the British declared India at war in 1939, the members of the PWA were among those who protested. The elder Edward Thompson was deployed on an official British mission to leverage his friendships with literary nationalists in order to appease various parties in India. Meanwhile, Nehru urged Progressive writers to prioritize the nationalist movement, but not all obliged. These poets did not toe any PWA line any more than they toed a single national line. Take Faiz, who married the British communist, poet, and supporter of Indian nationalism Alys George in 1941. He was arguably the leading Progressive voice in Urdu poetry but never spoke for the group or for the Communist Party. Disagreeing with the Congress Party's "Quit India" strategy, he prioritized the fight against fascism and for the Soviet Union. Seeing it as a revolutionary rather than an imperialistic war, he served in the British Indian Army from 1942 to 1947 in the welfare department in charge of publicity, earning an MBE (Member of the Most Excellent Order of the British Empire).[27]

By 1947, PWA membership had grown to near four thousand, with fifty branches. In our understandable but nevertheless obstructive preoccupation with Gandhi, Nehru, Jinnah, and the Mountbattens, we have neglected the political visions of these poets, who were also political actors, unwittingly obliging Nehru's wish that they stay meekly by the sidelines of political history while he occupied center stage. But in their poignant diversity of thought and style lurks a fascinating intellectual history and a generation of creative ideas about South Asian identity and politics. They nurtured richly distinct ideas of nation, religion, gender, community, language, and genre—though all ultimately constrained those anarchic thoughts within the national frames in which they were forced to act, yielding to the dominant, if not quite irresistible, narrative of the nation-state. Individuals of infinite complexity and diversity, invested in an array of social, political, and cultural causes, subordinated all pursuits to the simple question of being Pakistani or Indian. And yet, this is not what they did *at first*: during the decade after Partition, their (often tormented) movements reveal that both bins of history—Pakistan and India—still held many possibilities. When those movements stopped and alternative visions were foreclosed, historians settled down to a half-century of analyzing the winners—the Nehrus and Jinnahs. Here I momentarily peer beyond the horizon at the other roads imagined but not taken.

Some examples: Sahir Ludhianvi left Ludhiana for Lahore after expulsion from college in 1943. His communist views made him a target of the new government of Pakistan, so in 1949 he left, settling in Bombay, where he fed the film industry's iconography of love and homeland while remaining critical of the nation. In the 1957 film *Pyaasa*, about a disillusioned poet, he simplified a poem from 1944 to ask, with a border-transcending geographical referent, "Jinhe naaz hai hind par wo kahan hai?" (Where are those who have pride in Hind?).[28] The Progressive critique still applied; in 1958, he clung to the hope, "Woh subah kabhi to aayegi" (That morning will come some time). Saghar Siddiqui of Ambala went to Lahore in 1947 but took to a life on the streets. Sadat Hasan Manto was endlessly tormented even after moving (calling his nationalist and secularist commitments into doubt for Chugtai, who did not move).[29] He dramatized the absurdity of the choice before him in his famed story "Toba Tek Singh," which closes with the image of the deranged Bishan Singh refusing to choose and dying in the no-man's-land between the two new countries, their respective lunatics contained within barbed wire borders.[30] Manto struggled with depression and addiction; his family committed him to a mental asylum, but alcoholism killed him in 1955. Would he have stayed in Pakistan if he had lived? Meanwhile, Zaheer formed the Communist Party of Pakistan, of which he was secretary general. He was jailed in the Rawalpindi Conspiracy Case in 1951 but was extradited to India in 1954.[31] Faiz stayed in western Punjab but flew to India in 1948 to attend Gandhi's funeral. His poems were consistently patriotic without specifying the nation-state they attached themselves to. Vocally critical of his government as editor of the *Pakistan Times*, vice president of the Trade Union Congress, and secretary of the Pakistan Peace Committee, he too was jailed in the Rawalpindi Conspiracy Case and again later. State persecution ultimately drove him into temporary exile in Beirut. Part of the problem is that the choices were not real (the limiting case being that of women who "chose" to jump into wells); even elites were given only the "illusion of choice."[32] This forces us to rethink the meaning we ascribe to the choice *to* move. At times, the visible destruction of lives and communities also made some question a partition they *had* supported. In 1947 Nasir Kazmi of Ambala moved to Lahore, joyous at the achievement of the creation of a new country, but he then grew disillusioned. Likewise, Munir Niazi of Khanpur moved to Lahore but pined for his hometown: "Wapas na ja wahan ki tere shehr mein Munir / Jo jis jagah pe tha wo wahan par nahin raha" (Don't go back there, for, in your town, Munir / Whoever was where they were is no longer there). Another couplet read: "Shahr ko barbaad kar ke rakh diya us ne Munir / Shaher par ye zulm mere naam par us ne kiya" (He ruined the town, Munir / He did this wrong to the town in my name). What does it mean that Jagannath Azad of Rawalpindi, poet, Persian scholar, and voice for Hindu-Muslim unity, yielded to the fears of friends and family and migrated to India in September? Was his later devotion to scholarly study of Iqbal a way of at once atoning for departure, superseding Partition, *and* understanding its origins?[33] Josh Malihabadi had gone to Delhi after being banished from Hyderabad. He went back and forth across the new border in endless search of belonging, finally settling on Pakistan in 1958, though he continued to pine for India.

Apart from Josh, several Urdu poets with roots in the United Provinces did not move or moved late. Professor Hamid Kamal Narvi left Allahabad for Lahore in 1952. Jazib Qureshi was seven years old at Partition, but his family stayed in Lucknow until 1950. The communist Jaun Elia left for Karachi in 1957. Shakeb Jalali left for Rawalpindi in 1950 at age sixteen; his father remained in India. For him, Partition seems to have offered an opportunity to evade the father who had inexplicably pushed his mother under a train six years earlier. But even this personal tragedy may not be unconnected to the larger political drama: his father was disturbed by conflict between Hindus and Muslims, and so was Shakeb, who started writing poetry in 1947. Departure proved no balm: at Sargodha in 1966, he threw himself in front of a train. Mohani joined the constituent assembly that drafted the Indian constitution but became so skeptical of the process that he never signed it. He died in Lucknow in 1951; would he have moved if he had lived longer? Jigar Moradabadi steadfastly stayed, but his last volume of poetry criticized Indians' role in the violence of Partition: "Bhaag musafir mere watan se mere chaman se bhaag; oopar oopar phool khile hein bheetar bheetar aag." (Run stranger, run from my country, my garden; on the surface flowers have bloomed, but inside there is fire.) He died in 1960. Why did he not move? Would he have, had he lived longer? Or was his love of country also encapsulated in his lines, "Yeh ishq nahin aasaan bus itna samajh leejay / Ik aag ka dariya hai aur doob ke jaana hai" (This love is not easy, just understand this much / It is a river of fire and one must drown to cross)? Dua Dubaivi stayed in Gwalior but migrated to Pakistan when riots shook the city in the 1960s. His son Nida Fazli left instead for Bombay, where he worked as a poet-lyricist and journalist.[34]

A mix of considerations—personal and public, mundane and principled—figured in these decisions.[35] But these deferrals and confusions also reveal the existence of an intriguing window of possibility, a span of a few years during which the meaning and future of India and Pakistan were as yet unformed. The confusion and hesitation in these poets' movements represent a refusal of Partition, even though poetry's long grasp of *birha* as the path to more meaningful union might have made such poets temperamentally more amenable to the notion. Nor were they alone in their tardy and equivocal acceptance of Partition. Oral histories collected by the Citizens Archive of Pakistan and the Partition Archive testify to many belated and incomplete departures. Many who did move thought their displacement would be only temporary; they buried jewelry in walls and floors to be retrieved later. Indeed, my own family in Multan stayed put until 1948. In the end, twelve to fifteen million people migrated, but for long, it was not obvious that Partition would mean total severance.

Even some political leaders thought displacement would be temporary—
and not unreasonably, since critical government functions remained
shared: Pakistan's currency, for instance, was printed in India. The Reserve Bank of India was state bank for both countries until July 1948.
Until the Indian constitution's citizenship clause was introduced at the
end of 1949 (receiving its final form in 1955), the British Nationality and
Status of Aliens Act remained in force, offering a common British nationality that united Indians, Pakistanis, and others in the subcontinent.[36]
For a time the relationship between Pakistan and India still held many
possibilities—at least until the 1965 war. What broken hopes did belated
departure embody? Were these reluctantly partitioned people "indifferent
to nation" in the manner of the border peoples of eastern and southern
Europe during the same period?[37] As Edith Sheffer asks with respect to
the division of Germany, the question is not only when the border on
the ground was drawn, but when the border in the *mind* was created.[38]
Breaking bonds takes time; the journals of the Pakistani PWA continued
to include works by Hindu and Sikh writers in Urdu, until the group was
declared illegal in 1954 (although descendants of it remain active today).
Is it one of those farces of history that leftist Muslim poets like Jaun
Elia gave up on India and left for Pakistan just when the Pakistani state
began to crack down on the left? What alternative visions of South Asian
modernity did this collection of latecomers, exiles, and destroyed souls
abandon in the 1950s? It is worth recovering those visions for whatever
inspiration they may still yield. As Joan Scott observed of E. P. Thompson's thought, "utopias that permit critical assessment of the present in
terms of some deep moral commitment and unleash imaginative longing
for a particular kind of future are compatible with, indeed necessary for,
practical politics."[39]

IV

The alternative visions took shape in the early twentieth century. Indeed, it is important to revisit the original idea of partition as one among
these utopian futures on the table. Its early adherents sought to enact
Enlightenment notions about the rational ordering of society. Partition
promised to produce order out of a religiously and linguistically mixed

society. It promised a homeland to those out of place in nationalist India. Many who moved did so out of faith in this project, out of conviction, at times against the wishes of their families (most famously, Jinnah himself moved despite his daughter's unwillingness to join him). Indeed, the deliberate sacrifice of home and bonds was the price that made the result—participation in the creation of a new nation-state—all the more sacred.[40]

Iqbal's European education shaped his experimentation with partition as a utopian opportunity. After arriving in Europe in 1905, Iqbal researched Islamic mysticism in Germany and England and became convinced that it had no real foundation in original Islam, that it was alien and perhaps even unhealthy. He became interested in "real" Islam's potential as a social and political organization. His notions of the unity of Islam and "real" Islam were his own but were also shaped by orientalist European notions. He went to Cambridge in the steps of his teacher from Government College, Lahore, the British orientalist Thomas Walker Arnold, a great friend of Syed Ahmad Khan, who was returning to England to work in the India Office, thereafter serving in several notable academic and imperial government appointments.

The First World War fueled Iqbal's interest in Islam's potential as a social and political organization. To him, that destructive war showed that competitive nationalism produced militarism, imperialism, and irreligion. Islam seemed to offer a way of moving beyond nationalism, toward a *post*nationalistic world. It was utopian in this ambition, too. Iqbal hoped Muslim political autonomy would foster in one place a less divided and exploitative society based on an Islamic moral system that would serve Muslims and non-Muslims alike.[41]

In seeking to move beyond nationalism, Iqbal was like many other poet-critics of his time. The war had also horrified Rabindranath Tagore. He delivered lectures in Japan and the United States during 1916–1917 criticizing that kind of nationalism. He, too, articulated a very particular kind of love of homeland with unspecified borders. Gandhi was generally critical of Western civilization. British poets who served in the war were also disillusioned, and we know how entangled these intellectual networks were, in London, Oxford, and Cambridge. All this is to point to the global and anticolonial dimensions of this story from the start.

Partition is not just a South Asian story. Among Iqbal's closest friends in Lahore from 1932 was Muhammad Asad, the Austro-Hungarian Jew who opposed Zionism but supported the creation of a Muslim state in South Asia. He had been an advisor to Abdul Aziz Ibn Saud in the 1920s—one of that world of European "spies in Arabia."[42] Like them, he collapsed the tasks of reinventing the Middle East and himself. He would go on to shape Pakistan's constitution and head the Middle East Division of its Ministry of Foreign Affairs. I invoke Arnold's, Asad's, and Iqbal's European travels to highlight the cosmopolitan intellectual context in which the idea of Pakistan took shape, however much it was also about the local mission of saving Muslims from domination by non-Muslims. Enlightenment and Romantic notions are dialectically related in this intellectual history. As the other essays in this volume attest, partition was also part of British imperial and nationalist toolkits passed from colony to colony, as well as an outgrowth of colonial social engineering long bent on privileging communally defined political structures, partly to thwart formation of the kind of solidarities that had produced massive rebellion in 1857. I am merely skimming the surface here, focusing on the chain of influences and sociological bonds to offer a sense of the global production and payoff of these ideas over time, up to our present, as we shall see. Indeed, although we take Partition as synonymous with the mass migration it entailed, mass migration was not part of the plan, even as late as the early 1940s. The idea was rather to create autonomous Muslim-majority areas in which Hindus and Sikhs would remain, while Muslims would remain in areas in which they were minorities—based on the "hostage thinking" described by A. Dirk Moses in his essay for this volume. Then came the idea of splitting Muslim-majority provinces. The idea of mass eviction and migration came only in March 1947 when riots in Rawalpindi enforced the notion that minorities did not belong in the lands that had now been designated Muslim or non-Muslim.[43] In the 1930s, Iqbal was thinking outside the box of nationalism, whatever the ironic appropriation of his goal for nationalistic purposes.[44]

The India that would result from the creation of Pakistan was also imagined through the lens of modern rationalism. Even Indians today who regret Partition speak approvingly of a purer nation formed through the sacrifice of dismemberment. The journalist Alpana Kishore argues that without Partition, India would have gone on wrestling with an unresolved demand for a Muslim nation-state; it would have been haunted by the specter of partition and the very different vision of national development embraced by Pakistan's founders.[45] This recalls B. R. Ambedkar's views on Pakistan. He, too, was an anticolonial thinker who was simultaneously critical of the nation-state. Yet, he saw Partition as unavoidable once the demand had been raised (and given his own notions of Muslim difference); to refuse it would simply endanger the new republic with the constant threat of civil war.[46] (Arguably, in the end, Partition has haunted India anyway.)

But besides these rationalist-idealist visions of a postcolonial Pakistan and India, other utopian visions were also available, for a time. Some saw an equally postnationalist utopic prospect in the challenge of unifying a subcontinent that, they acknowledged, was divided. The Khilafat leader and poet Mohammad Ali Jauhar was president of the Congress Party in 1923 and said:

> I had long been convinced that here in this Country of hundreds of millions of human beings, intensely attached to religion, and yet infinitely split up into communities, sects and denominations, Providence had created for us the mission of solving a unique problem and working out a new synthesis. . . . For more than twenty years I have dreamed the dream of a federation, grander, nobler and infinitely more spiritual than the United States of America, and today when many a political Cassandra prophesies a return to the bad old days of Hindu-Muslim dissensions I still dream that old dream of "United Faiths of India."[47]

Like Mohani and Bismil at that time, Jauhar became disillusioned with Congress and with Gandhi's leadership. He attended the First Round Table Conference in London in 1930–1932 and died in England. He was buried in Jerusalem, at his request. Would he have remained in India or moved to Pakistan in 1947? Or later? Or would his survival have made his utopic dream a more viable possibility?

Others perceived a different utopia: the idea of an India that possessed an inherent unity even in its diversity, that was a single nation, which Partition violated. Husain Ahmad Madani saw imperialism as the disrupter of religiously plural societies that had their own integrity (Iqbal argued that it severed ethnically distinct Muslims who might otherwise have been united around their shared religion).[48] "Diversity within unity" was of course a slogan of the empire itself, and it is perhaps unsurprising then that nostalgia for the Raj at times filters into nostalgia for intercommunal harmony, at times into nostalgia for joint resistance to the Raj. At times, the Unionist Party's popularity in the 1930s under Sir Sikandar Hayat Khan, a close associate of Sir Syed Ahmad Khan, is recalled as proof of the existence of a culturally and politically unified Punjab betrayed by higher politicians (at other times its social conservatism and loyalty to the Raj are recalled as liabilities), even though the pressure of maintaining that unity against the competing forces of the League, Congress, and the British was probably what killed Sikandar Hyat Khan in 1942. We have no way of gauging the accuracy of memories of untroubled pre-Partition harmony, but as Anam Zakaria and other collectors of oral histories note, "memory and how people choose to remember certain events is as important as historical facts themselves."[49] Indeed, some memories were shaped by dismay at the violent change Partition wrought. Even those who did not move witnessed destruction of their communities and the arrival of new, tormented faces—a transformation that made some see the struggle as a waste. At the same time that the Pakistani state whitewashes Sikh history in Punjab—literally in the case of the frescoes at the entrance of the Dera Sahab complex in Lahore[50]—we hear of Pakistanis who miss Diwali and Eastern Punjabis who miss Eid. It is true that many communities have coexisted in India and that Partition included many acts of intercommunal kindness. But equally true are the facts that in the end, *Congress* wanted partition and that, since 1947, community has again and again been constituted through violence in India—impossible facts for those committed to the notion of an eternally unified India betrayed only by Jinnah and the League.[51]

Apart from nostalgia for a lost utopia, even after Partition, many imagined the possibility for a unique international friendship between the two nations, in which the border would not be a divider but rather a bridge permitting connection and communication. Deferrals or reversals of the decision to stay or move, indicated by late departure or ongoing maintenance of binational existence for business and family reasons, are perhaps most symptomatic of this outlook. They represent a willful and wishful belief in the prerogative to remain locally and privately rather than nationally embedded as long as it was practicable. Many crossed legally without much obstruction until the 1965 war; border communities continued to engage in common celebrations of the festival Baisakhi. Others crossed illegally between bordering villages, like Germans in the early years of the Cold War. Zakaria's oral histories include the poignant case of Muhammad Boota, who repeatedly crossed from his adopted village in Pakistan into his old village in Indian Punjab to search for a Sikh girl he had loved. As in the great *qissas*, he never found her but remained devoted to her.[52] The border became more clearly demarcated and impassable after the wars of 1965 and 1971, but even then, through 1986 no line or wire demarcated the border near Kasur villages, and people crossed accidentally.[53]

Finally, and perhaps most importantly, there was the utopian belief that borders would not change anything, even when they became impassable, that an unseverable regional unity transcends the experience and fact of Partition. Here it is crucial to remember that the Indian and Pakistani dream for nation-statehood was fulfilled in a moment in which the entire system of nation-states was in severe crisis, with displaced minorities emerging in the Middle East and Europe.[54] This context shaped calls to rise above both nationalism *and* borders. The Congress leader Maulana Azad (who tried his hand at poetry too in his younger days) insisted even after Partition on the existence of a "composite culture," shared among all and possessing secular and cosmopolitan dimensions. He was a nationalist, in the sense of believing in the reality of an Indian nation that could stand independently of British rule, but he also grasped the dangers nationalism produced for minorities. His solution was to refuse a politics based on fear—to refuse to fear for the fate of a Muslim minority in independent India and to refuse the very notion of a Muslim "minority." This "leap of faith" marks the "*secularism* of Azad's public life," explains Amir Mufti.[55] He articulated this complex vision in a speech in October 1947 in the Jama Masjid in Delhi, which persuaded many Muslims there to stay, just when nationalism was violently reorganizing the region into new nation-states.

Those who articulated such visions at once perceived their vulnerability, their increasingly outdated utopian nature. They knew that refusing nationalism's disruption of pluralism was its own kind of madness, reminiscent of Bishan Singh's stubborn attachment to the no-man's-land of Toba Tek Singh. But while Manto's story encapsulated that madness in a dark, Chekhovian manner, such madness found a different kind of sanction in the Urdu poetic tradition, where madness is less the breakdown of reason than the hopeless idealism of the poetic subject, the lover. They were the *farzaane* (learned, wise men), who double as *deewane* (mad, inspired men) in Jagannath Azad's *ghazal* titled "15 August 1947": "Na puchho jab bahar aayi to deewanon pe kya guzari / Zara dekho ki is mausam mein farzaanon pe kya guzari" (Don't ask what befell the mad [the lovers] when spring came / Just look at what befell the wise in this season). With the plural *deewane,* the *sher* (verse) embraces the world of Azad's fellow poets, his friends, fellow idealists, the losers of this history. And indeed the friendship among poets was one critical way in which the border *was* rendered meaningless, at least for some, especially those who chose to see it as a temporary inconvenience on the way to a future goal that they knew would transcend all borders. While Faiz continued his political and poetic pursuits in Pakistan, his friend Makhdoom Mohiuddin of Hyderabad pursued poetry, lyric-writing for the film industry, labor activism, leadership in the Communist Party of India, trade union activism, and activities with the PWA and the Indian People's Theatre Association. He was also a primary leader of the Telangana Rebellion of 1946 to 1951, in which Communist Party–led peasants rebelled against Telangana landlords and the Nizam of Hyderabad, who tried to crush the rebellion while also refusing to join the Indian union. Makhdoom also inaugurated the short-lived village republic of Paritala. It was unclear where history was heading; it seemed possible that this rebellion would herald a subcontinental peasant revolt. To be sure, the Indian Army brutally crushed it in September 1948 and restored land to the *zamindars,* but then in 1949 a communist revolution succeeded in China. Against this backdrop, leftist poet-activists hoped Partition was a transient event in a longer struggle for far more radical ends. It was inconclusive; and their agreement on that point across the border, their continued solidarity, was a mutual affirmation. Jailed in 1951, like Faiz in Pakistan, Makhdoom wrote the poem "Qaid" (Imprisonment). On his release, he fought elections and joined parliament as a member of the Communist Party of India. The struggle went on.

When Makhdoom died in 1969, Faiz composed a poetic homage adapting his friend's celebrated *ghazal*, "Aap ki yaad aati rahi raat bhar" (Your memory came to me all the night long). Both versions can be read on multiple levels, as all *ghazals*, but let me offer a suggestive reading of the last verse. Makhdoom's version ends, "Koi deewaana galiyon mein phirta raha / Koi awaaz aati rahi raat bhar" (Some madman [lover] wandered in the streets / Some sound came all the night long), evoking the eternal beckoning of some ideal in the night—the time before freedom dawns. The poet fumbles toward it, perhaps never reaching it. It is at once near yet out of reach. Faiz's version ends, "Ek umeed se dil behelta raha / Ek tamanna sataati rahi raat bhar" (The heart amused itself with a hope / A wish tormented [me] all the night long), evoking the desire for communion with a friend who is now impossibly far away, in classic Sufi fashion, but also perhaps a memory of their shared, incomplete pursuit: the soothingly idealistic yet nevertheless agitating hope for a more humane future, a hope that persists despite our knowledge that it *is* an ideal and thus unachievable. For those entangled in this border-transgressing literary and political community, Partition was not a stopping ground; it could not be allowed to become a stopping ground. As Faiz wrote, reflecting on 1947 in 1951, "Chale chalo ki woh manzil abhi nahi aayi" (Let us keep going, for that destination has not yet come). To be sure, the notion of a long, joint journey ahead, despite borders, was also a mechanism for coping with the actual trauma of Partition, which Faiz genuinely felt; he considered it "too Big" to cope with in poetry, apart from his attempt in that 1951 poem, "Subah-e-Azadi" (Freedom's Dawn) (although in allusive ways he did in other works too, I believe).[56] But however disillusioned, he was not giving up. In the late 1950s he wrote the film *Jago Hua Savera* (Awake, It Is Morning) about Bengali fisherfolk. It was made as an Indo-Pak cross-border Progressive collaboration. Others, including Majaz Lukhnavi, Ali Sardar Jafri, and Jagannath Azad, wrote poems insisting that 1947 was the beginning not the end of the struggle they were engaged in.[57]

One might reasonably interpret this indifference to borders as a form of denial, as fantasy. Arguably, works like "Toba Tek Singh" engaged in precisely such fantasy, as literary form, whatever Manto's commitments to social realism. Fantasy is a "departure from consensus reality," in the words of one literary scholar,[58] and belief in the immateriality of the border was a departure from the consensus reality of Pakistani and Indian nation-statehood. More than fantasy, however, it was romance, as articulated clearly in Faiz's and Makhdoom's couplets above. The unattainable end—utopia itself—was a reworking of *birha* in its own way, as was the experience of Partition itself. The border was the worldly reality, and these poets worked in an idiom that was all about transcending worldly reality to attain some higher, more meaningful experience.

The aloofness of poets from Partition helps explain why post-Partition Urdu poetry continued to invoke an extranational geography: the leftist Pakistani poet Ibn-e-Insha (born in Jalandhar in 1927) composed "Tu Kahan Chali Gayi Thi" (Where Had You Gone) in the 1950s, gesturing with equal ease toward Karachi and Delhi. Nazir Qaiser's poetry is as ecumenical in its geography. Shiv Kumar Batalvi, born in western Punjab (and often dubbed Punjab's Byron), drew on the ancient epic about Puran Bhagat of Sialkot for his epic verse play *Loona* in 1965. Jagannath Azad went to India, but his poetry dwelled on memories of his homeland, his lost *chaman* (garden). While in Pakistan on his first post-Partition visit in 1948, he wrote the celebrated couplet, "Main apne ghar mein aaya hoon magar andaaz to dekho / Ke apne aap ko manind-e-mehman leke aaya hoon" (I have come into my own home, but look in what manner / For I have brought myself like a guest). It remained his home. Alienated as he was, he was still not a guest but guest*like*. He was split into both host and guest, at once at home and not at home, *desi* and *pardesi*. Munir Niazi's poetry similarly expressed this sense of never being quite at home and yet being always at home. Pakistani poets also continued to reach for the non-Islamic *but* (idol) and *puja* (worship, implying idol worship) on which the ironic idiom of Urdu poetry depends, despite the vanishing, ghostlike presence of such things in their midst. Indeed, in a sense the entire Indo-Islamic poetic tradition presumes a world of Muslims co-existing with non-Muslims to dramatize the ironies of worldly and un-worldly faith at its core. (Sikh identity markers similarly presume a mixed social context—else why the need for distinguishing markers?)

This literary transcendence of Partition mirrored sociocultural continuities such as the celebrations of "Indian" festivals among Pakistanis near the border.[59] As Zakaria notes, even those who left out of conviction felt a bond with the "home" they abandoned because of ongoing relationships and memories: "There is no clear line for these people; it is difficult to decipher what they love more, where they belong more. This confusion is the only truth for them."[60] If the goal of Partition was a coherent national self, the result was a population of divided selves. The exile, the refugee, the orphaned, the converted, the abducted-and-reclaimed—all these survivors were in different ways split—in many cases violently split, even shredded selves. Permit me a metaphor from physics: In quantum theory, the uncertain, nondeterministic, smeared nature of electrons helps explain the stability of atoms; similarly, the stability of South Asian identity depends on a kind of indeterminacy. Punjabis in particular seem smeared through space. Nations, like the impossibly rigid atomic structures of classical mechanics, cannot contain such uncertainty: Makhdoom and Faiz were both literally *in captivity* in independent India and Pakistan in 1951.

V

Poets' long preoccupation with Partition's effects, or lack of effect, reveals their sense of its epiphenomenal and possibly transient nature, their preoccupation with *other* utopias—unfinished business that Partition traumatically disrupted. Their writings offer the earliest analysis of what Partition did to subjectivity and consciousness, quite apart from the human destruction it unleashed.

Here again we find intriguing intersections with shifting subjectivities in Europe. Some time in the late eighteenth century, Enlightenment notions of a rational self smothered notions of an internally split self among Europeans. The idea of an individuated, internally coherent modern self

took hold.[61] But from the turn of the twentieth century European oc-
cultists and psychologists began to question this idea of selfhood, ex-
perimenting with more porous and divided notions of selfhood, albeit
locating the "split" internally, in the psychology and neurobiology of the
individual, rather than in social claims on that individual.[62] Most notably for the present context, Annie Besant's explorations of spirituality
and selfhood took her from the milieu of British socialism to the highest
circles of the Indian nationalist movement, where she too was part of the
world of poet-activists, joining Sarojini Naidu in representing in London
the case for Indian women to vote. (A poet, Naidu was a Bengali from
Hyderabad who joined the national movement after the 1905 partition
of Bengal and became the second woman to preside over Congress after
Besant. She was governor of the United Provinces of Agra and Oudh in
1947–1949 when Urdu poets there deliberated staying or going.)

Now, the subject of Urdu poetry had long been understood as split.
This was what Sufi longing for union was about. Momin's much-loved
couplet is exemplary: "Tum mere paas hote ho goya / Jab koi doosra nahin
hota" (You are with me thus / As when no second person is there). In true
mystic union, the self becomes extinct. This idiom seems readymade to
address the post-Partition condition of a partial, parted, or divided self
that can nevertheless transcend its own division. Urdu as a poetic language figured critically in the articulation of this subjectivity. As Mufti
shows in his beautiful analysis of Faiz's poetry, Indianness has come to
encompass the disavowal of Indianness (like the electron that both is and
isn't). Mufti cites, paradigmatically, Faiz's "Marsia" (Elegy) from a 1971
collection:

> Dur ja kar qarib ho jitney
> ham se kab qarib the itne
> Ab na aoge tum na jaoge
> vasl o hijran baham hue kitne

> (The extent to which you are close now that you have gone far
> when were you ever so close to me
> Now you will neither come nor go
> how as one union and separation have become.)

In this four-line poem, Mufti perceives a dialectic of self and other in which the subject and object of desire do not so much become one but simultaneously come near and become distant and are rendered uncertain. It recalls Zakaria's story of a man in a Pakistani village who daily *sees* his old village across the border—it is at once near and far.[63] This is the reality of modern Punjabi subjectivity: contradictory, tense, antagonistic. Faiz's grasp of this dialectically produced self clearly resonated; his work has remained phenomenally popular across the region. As Mufti explains, he articulated an "Indian" experience of the self that took division seriously and yet transcended borders and communal and national divides, much as he tried to do in his own literary and political commitments. After all, he worked within an idiom in which indefinite separation from the beloved was the only ground from which to contemplate union. He subversively renders the abandoned home as the *beloved*, rather than a heathen land virtuously abandoned—inverting the religious interpretation of Partition as *hijrat* (in the sense of the Holy Prophet's flight from Mecca to Medina). Urdu could uniquely convey the reality of this split self, nurtured in Pakistan where it was cut off from its homelands in Delhi, the Deccan, and the region of the United Provinces, where Urdu's status simultaneously declined. Poets' worldly experience of exile and refuge gave *hijr* (separation, departure) a range of new, secular connotations, notes Mufti.[64] Faiz's agonistic embrace of that inheritance *is* a South Asian expression of modernity, at once reminding us of the worldly basis of religious experience itself—what early Punjabi romances expressed as allegory, or, in the language of the Punjabi *tappa* (folk lyric): "Milna taan rab nu hai / Tera pyaar bahaana hai" (It is with God that I seek to unite / Your love is merely the pretext). For long, poets have grasped the instrumental nature of worldly experience for the sake of higher spiritual experience. The persistence of that mystical idiom, and the love successive generations profess for it, reveals the continued intimacy of the secular, modern self with its religious inheritance. In this too, modern South Asian subjectivity senses its incompleteness, its exilic existence.[65] In short, we can't think of post-Partition identity only in the terms of the normalized vocabulary of the new nation-states, presuming autonomous national selves based on the European template. (Progressive writers attached to such requirements of normality were the kind who, Mufti speculates, suddenly turned against Manto, whose work and affect fell beyond that pale.)[66]

The possibility of transcending national identity within oneself is powerful. For E. P. Thompson (in Scott's luminous interpretation, again), poetry's role was to "leaven politics with imagination," to suggest a "middle ground between . . . disenchantment with perfectionist illusions and complete apostasy. That ground is the demanding, yet creative place of continuing aspiration."[67] The work of continuing aspiration is the work of Azad's *deewane*. The split South Asian self is the middle ground poets gave us between disenchantment and apostasy. It is Beckett's "I can't go on, I'll go on," and Gramsci's mantra-like "pessimism of the intellect, optimism of the will." The New Left that Thompson helped form in England after the Soviet invasion of Hungary in 1956 attracted the communist, atheist, and anti-imperialist Pakistani Tariq Ali, grandson of Sikandar Hayat Khan and an important interlocutor of Edward Said, another deep thinker about exile and anticolonialism who met Faiz in Beirut. If the British presided over the transnational use of partition as a tool of decolonization, poets and intellectuals from partitioned places formed their own transnational bonds. Ali's anti-imperialist critiques were as globally sweeping as Faiz's poetry about Chile, Palestine, Namibia, and Julius and Ethel Rosenberg. Talal Asad, son of Muhammad Asad, has emerged as a major thinker about religion and secularism. Javed Akhtar, an important political and cultural critic in Modi's India, is the great-great-grandson of Fazl-e-Haq Khairabadi. The chain of inheritance and restless, continuing aspiration is long. Zaheer's granddaughter Pankhuri Zaheer remains a communist activist in Delhi today. The Taseer name remains at the heart of Pakistani politics—and Indian literature.

Thompson visited India for the first time in 1976, after our poets' alternative visions had long expired. He was warmly welcomed by Indira Gandhi and her government in acknowledgment of the friendship between their fathers. But it was the time of Indira's Emergency. He was horrified by the government's repression of dissent and by the Indian Communist Party's support of it and noted the strange convergence of Western "modernizing theory" with orthodox Moscow-directed socialist theory: Both imagined a modern urban intellectual elite with know-how imposing modernity and progress upon the nation. Both prioritized top-down, capital-intensive technologically driven developments depending on a disciplined workforce for national economic takeoff. Through a vulgar (i.e., unpoetic) economic determinism, Marxism echoed utilitarian and positivist ideas.[68] Politics without poetry is lifeless, and poetry without politics tends to the self-indulgent. It is the same in Pakistan. If modern Urdu poetry evolved as critique—of empire *and* nation—it is no surprise that as the left has crumbled, so has poetry's most powerfully transcendent function. Modi's India is bent on suffocating the left further. India's poets have returned their national awards to protest the government's thuggish attacks on dissent of all kinds, rediscovering their role in history and outside exclusionist mainstream nationalism.[69] As we continue to look to technology to save us, despite the unending disasters that pile up before our eyes, it is time perhaps to revisit and reinvent the possibility and promise of poetic action. Poetry is a social and collective endeavor. Indeed, Urdu poetry's *mushaira* culture particularly depends on incorporation of the audience into performance of the poem; it is always both private and public. The writer alone cannot make poetry or poetic action. In Urdu poetry, the reader identifies entirely with the first-person voice of the poet. The poet's place in history becomes the reader's too.

## VI

This possibility for such total identification, for a kind of subsumption in the poet, is astonishingly universal. I identify with the "*Hum*" of Faiz's poetry, even though (on the face of it) I am a woman, a Hindu, and an Indian Punjabi (where he was a man, a Muslim, and a Pakistani Punjabi). It is "queer" in this sense: a space of nonnormative identity and politics. And yet, it could not attend to the plight of Heer. When Jagannath Azad was leaving Pakistan after a visit to return to India, Muhammad Tufail, editor of the Pakistani Progressive literary journal *Nuqush*, brought him sweets at the station, quipping, "Tumhein to yun rukhsat karte hain jaise beti ko rukhsat kiya jaata hai" (You we send away in the way one sends off a daughter).[70] Instead of separation from an ambiguously gendered beloved, he rendered Azad's departure in the clearly gendered form of a daughter leaving her "mother," the motherland, to join her new family after marriage—a rite common to Hindu, Sikh, and Muslim weddings in the region. The departure becomes a forward-looking rite of passage to adulthood—progress itself. It is irreversible but allows still for the married daughter to return on occasion *as a guest*, that is, without substantive entitlements. Tufail's line also reminds us that however vaguely poets rendered it, Partition's violence was deeply gendered. Amrita Pritam's plea to Waris Shah and Manto's stories, like "Khol Do" (Open It), acknowledged that reality.[71]

Shiv Kumar Batalvi's *Loona*, his celebrated 1965 retelling of the ancient epic of Puran Bhagat, attempted to recuperate Punjabi women's agency and sexuality. Stylistically, he was influenced by the *qissas* and European epic poetry. In the original legend, the Sialkot prince spurns the advances of his young stepmother, Loona, a sinfully lustful seductress, who wreaks bloody revenge: Puran's limbs are amputated and he becomes an exile, an ascetic who forgives and blesses his punishers. But Batalvi tells the story from Loona's point of view: the disgust of a lower-caste girl from Chamba at being forcibly married to an old king, her entirely reasonable desire to be with a young man, Puran's rejection of her out of suspicion of her merely sexual rather than spiritual attraction to him, and her self-sacrificial revenge. For in destroying Puran, she destroys herself: she knows she will live in infamy but hopes that her infamy will prevent the creation of more Loonas forced to marry against their will. Having borne the blame for Puran's death for centuries, Loona finds peace in Batalvi's play. Known for his passionate expression of the agony of separated lovers, here Batalvi redeems worldly love and youthful rebellion.[72] The punishing violence of partition is visited on a male body. In blaming society rather than Loona, Batalvi validates the need and desire of all Punjabi women for revenge. He renders the subject of Punjabi history as female. He published this earthily Punjabi-language work on the eve of the linguistic repartitioning of Indian Punjab, when many Punjabi Hindus claimed Hindi as their mother tongue, a choice made possible by the long-standing elision of Hindi with Urdu.

Loona was the *Patakha Guddi* (Firecracker Kite/Girl) of her time.[73] She is the poet of her own destiny. She lives her contradiction as a means of superseding loss, a way of living as if in exile even when at home, as Maulana Azad felt he did, given his particular background and education and relationship to "Muslim" and nationalist politics in his time.[74] Modern Urdu writing, having displaced the relationship of language and self to place as Mufti tells us, is a vehicle for exilic thinking, an awareness, wherever one happens to be, that modern history has been a history of marginalization and uprooting on a massive scale; that split selfhoods are typical, in South Asia, but also in Germany, the Balkans, Cyprus, Palestine/Israel, Ireland, and elsewhere, as this volume testifies.[75] Indeed, the 2016 "Brexit" vote and the Scottish referendum have forced even Britons to contemplate such experience. Urdu was a language cultivated diasporically from the start; its poets have names like Dehlavi, Moradabadi, Mohani, Ludhianvi and so on because they were far from home. These names identified them by the places they left or moved to, as they became immersed in cosmopolitan and mobile networks that made identification of roots necessary; loss of homeland was intrinsic to their meditations.

What is the poet's role in history? Of course the question is romantic. Byron was Romantic; Thompson was Romantic; Faiz was romantic; Punjabis are romantic; land is romantic. And Romanticism has its dangers: the British were Romantic; Nehru was Romantic; Silicon Valley is a Romance. Dams and drones are romantic. The Hindu right and the Islamic right offer their own romances. There is a marketplace of Romance, but the Romance of the left has too long been out of stock. Bollywood can't do it alone, and it too, after all, is bound up in the worship of profit, god, and nation.

# PARTITIONS, HOSTAGES, TRANSFER

*Retributive Violence and National Security*

A. Dirk Moses

WHEREVER CULTURALLY, religiously, or nationally motivated inter-group violence is thought to be endemic and intractable, partition of territory and populations looms as a possible solution. To use the United Nations (UN) jargon, partition is advanced as an "atrocity prevention" measure.[1] There is talk today of partitioning Syria, Iraq, Yemen, and Ukraine due to civil war and foreign intervention, and even Spain faces partition in part because of state violence against the Catalonian independent movement. Cyprus has been de facto partitioned since 1974, while most recently, Sudan has been officially split into two entities to end armed conflict.[2] We know that the UN decided to partition Palestine in 1947 after the British government gave up brokering an agreement in the wake of contrapuntal Arab and Zionist resistance to various plans, including partition in 1937.[3] Likewise, large-scale communal rioting across India in the second half of 1946 prompted the British to partition the country the next year.

Ethno-religious violence gave rise to partition to prevent further such violence. Paradoxically, ironically, and tragically, partition begat still more violence in the form of genocidal massacres and massive ethnic cleansings whose consequences blight the Middle East and South Asia to this day. What is more, the past seventy years reveal that anxieties about disloyal minorities continue, because partitions are never surgically "clean" and complete: the "wrong" people remain caught on the wrong side of the new border, becoming effectively foreign nationals, aliens in an aspirationally pure state. To compound matters, diasporic life is increasing with migration and refugee flows, dissolving the demographic homogeneity that partition was meant to effect, while globalization enables the imagination of worldwide spectral entities like "the Muslims" and "the Jews."[4]

In this epilogue, I explore the dynamic relationship between partition and modalities of constructing security, whether in producing homogeneity or guaranteeing ethnic dominance over minorities: either population "transfer" or, when this is not an option, "communal hostage taking." Alternatively, where states cannot control crises, sectarian militias and even highly motivated individuals can take matters into their own hands in the form of retributive violence: calculated murders, massacres, and expulsions carried out by nonstate actors—from below—based on cycles of revenge and retaliation.[5] Imagining and realizing partition engages these modalities in messy conjunctures as contending parties prosecute the case for, and try to effect, their imagined security. In view of the terrorism, communal riots, further partitions like that of Pakistan and Bangladesh in 1971, and threats of still more "transfers" of Palestinians, the question of violence and minority protection presses itself upon us. Partition does not so much solve minority issues as deposit them into different containers as minority issues reappear in partitioned units.

I examine these modalities not by reconstructing the local mechanisms of mobilization and interaction but by tracing the intersecting and divergent imaginings of national belonging, state borders, and minority loyalty.[6] Our context is the convergence of decolonization struggles in India and Palestine against the horizon of imperial dissolutions and expansions in Europe from the 1920s to the 1940s: the breakup of the continental land empires after the First World War and foundation of new states, including the Greek-Turkish population exchange of 1923; Nazi Germany's extensive border changes of allied and enemy nation-states; and its defeat, resulting in massive expulsions of ethnic Germans from Central and Eastern Europe. I am less interested in the details of these well-studied events and processes than in the arguments advanced to justify new states, their ethno-religious substances, and the question of minorities.

Sociologists have linked ethno-religious violence since the 1990s to globalization crises in which minorities become scapegoats for displaced frustrations about unrealizable ideals of pure nation-states and uncertainties about otherness.[7] A political history of ideas can show that this sort of violence was inscribed into the foundation of nation-states during decolonization in the 1940s.[8] How to relate the immediate postwar cases? Edward Said theorized a linear notion of mobile theory: "ideas and theories travel—from person to person, from situation to situation, from one period to another"—via the "circulation of ideas," including "acknowledged or unconscious influence, creative borrowing, or wholesale appropriation."[9] Historians of empire have long noted what they call a "competitive politics of comparison that accelerated circuits of knowledge production and imperial exchange," practices of mutual observation and borrowing in relation to governance and security.[10] More recently, a global intellectual history posits circulation, diffusion, and adaptation in the study of ideas and texts "across geographical parameters far larger than usual."[11] Whether a global entanglement or global conjuncture, a ubiquitous practice from the 1920s to the 1940s was the mutual observation, analogizing, comparison, and distinguishing of subject positions not only by imperial elites, but by their subalterns waiting impatiently to found their own states.[12] These mental operations were necessarily global in projection and meta-reflective in practice, as leaders of states-in-waiting not only studied political dramas in other parts of the world, but also scrutinized the lessons that their rivals drew from them.

## PARTITIONS, MINORITIES, EXPULSIONS

Partitions are usually studied in isolation as one side of a simplistic unity-division binary of nation/partition, when in fact they are related to empire, federation, and commonwealth along a disaggregation–aggregation continuum.[13] Imperial governors often advanced federalism as a form of minority protection. Federations could restrain refractory white settlers, as in the case of the (ultimately unsuccessful) "closer union" proposals in the late 1920s to extend the native protection provisions of Britain's

Tanganyikan League of Nations mandate to Kenya and Uganda. If the settlers would not submit to incorporation, they could be subject to "administrative separation," the functional equivalent of partition.[14] For the most part, however, "native" majorities were distrusted to justly govern those less numerous minority population groups on whose collaboration empires had long depended in their divide-and-rule tactics. Such was the aim of the Cabinet Mission option the British presented to the All India Congress and All India Muslim League in 1946: a united India of grouped Hindu- and Muslim-majority provinces with a weak center to ensure that the majority Hindus could not dominate the minority Muslims. Similarly, the Anglo-American Committee of British and American delegates who toured Palestine in the same year concluded diplomatically that any political solution had to be based on three principles: "I. That Jew shall not dominate Arab and Arab shall not dominate Jew in Palestine. II. That Palestine shall be neither a Jewish state nor an Arab state. III. That the form of government ultimately to be established, shall, under international guarantees, fully protect and preserve the interests in the Holy Land of Christendom and of the Moslem and Jewish faiths."[15] Its recommendations led to the Morrison-Grady plan of Arab and Jewish provincial self-rule under federal UN-British trusteeship that bore some resemblance to the Cabinet Mission plan in India. Like the Indian parties, Zionists and Arabs rejected this option—accurately discerning the continuing imperial logic of external enforcement and intervention—as did US president Harry Truman, who inclined toward it but was under electoral pressure to lean to the Zionist viewpoint.[16]

In general, the metropole preferred to bundle territory and societies in empire-lite or postimperial arrangements, like federations and commonwealths, if they could be managed with local elites whom they often created and empowered with new positions and governance structures.[17] Partition made sense if this could not be done, or only with difficulty. Britain's partition of Bengal in 1905 was a divide-and-rule measure to that end, although it was reversed only six years later after vehement protest.[18] It is no accident that federative arrangements were canvassed in the British, French, and Dutch empires after the Second World War: the Malay Federation (predecessor of Malaysia and Singapore) between 1948 and 1963, the Central African Federation of 1953–1963, the West Indies Federation between 1958 and 1962, the Federation of South Arabia (forerunner of South Yemen) of 1962–1967, French West African federative ideas, the United States of Indonesia (preferred by the Netherlands to a unified state), and the Dutch-Indonesian Union.[19] To be sure, federal ideas were also attractive to some African leaders of national movements who saw the political benefit of strength in numbers and economic advantage of continued relationships with a metropole.[20] On the whole, though, the drive for sovereignty in a unitary state predominated as decolonization's political model. The UN's imposed federation of Eritrea and Ethiopia in 1952 lasted only until 1962, when the latter annexed the former, precipitating decades of war and ultimately two nation-states.[21]

The chapters in this book focus on the British imperial partitions of Ireland, Palestine, and India. If the British Empire's motivations in considering partition were to control the outcome of the Irish and later partitions, then the context of continental European imperial breakup after the First World War is relevant, in part because the British codesigned the postwar architecture, in part because Indian leaders in particular studied these developments for possible lessons. Partition and minority protection dramas were not just British questions but affected millions of Europeans. To understand the partitions of the 1940s, we need to explore their various linkages and bundle them as international conjuncture of nation- and people-construction.

The creation of new states in Europe after World War I pressed territorial disputes with partition potential onto the agenda, creating minority "problems" and thereby questions of protection and population transfer. Within Europe, the redrawing of borders to reward the Entente's allies and punish the war's losers resulted in the creation of large national minorities in the new states of Poland and Czechoslovakia. Hungarians decried the partition of their country in the Treaty of Trianon (1920) because of its drastic territorial losses and because ethnic Hungarians became minorities in neighboring states, especially Romania. To ensure stability, the League imposed minority protection treaties on these newcomers, thereby delineating hierarchies of sovereignty that those newcomers found humiliating.[22] Having been created from the territory of previous states, these states then squabbled among themselves. In 1919, Poland and Czechoslovakia fought and negotiated over the Teschen/ Cieszyn province of Silesia, which was eventually split between them without consulting the local population.[23] Next door, the League of Nations insisted on a plebiscite in Upper Silesia in 1920 in the dispute between Poland and Germany. To ensure that the respective minorities were well treated, they signed a convention that included the portentous phrase "equitable reciprocity," based on the League's recommendation: mutual observation of the convention would guarantee the welfare of German and Polish co-nationals across the border.[24] Then, most dramatically, the League condoned the Turkish-Greek population exchange in the Treaty of Lausanne (1923) after the brutal warfare between Turkish and Greek forces following the latter's invasion in 1919, hoping thereby to bring peace on the basis of religious homogeneity.[25]

These interwar settlements, largely conducted at the expense of World War I's losers, were eventually overturned by revisionist powers. Beginning with Germany's annexation of the Czechoslovak Sudeten- land, with its preponderance of irredentist ethnic Germans, Czecho- slovakia was effectively partitioned in 1938 with the reluctant consent of the very Western powers that had confected it after the First World War. Poland took little time in opportunistically swallowing Czecho- slovak Teschen/Cieszyn, thereby recovering what it regarded as previ- ously partitioned Polish territory. A year later, the secret protocols of the Molotov–Ribbentrop Pact between the Soviet Union and Nazi Germany partitioned Poland between them and assigned parts of Romania to the Soviets. During the war, Germany further partitioned Romania by re- turning to its Hungarian and Bulgarian allies those lands they lost in the Trianon palace at Versailles. The German vision was of a minority-free Europe, especially of German ones, which should be (re)patriated *heim ins Reich.*[26]

Given the role of Sudeten Germans in destabilizing Czechoslova- kia, the war's victors thought European minorities should be trans- ferred where possible. Referring to the 1923 Lausanne agreement on the Turkish-Greek population exchange, British prime minister Win- ston Churchill called for a clean sweep of Germans from Poland in late

1944, and the British Foreign Office insisted that all ethnic Germans, not just the "guilty" ones, be expelled from Czechoslovakia. They agreed with Edvard Beneš, the leader of the Czechoslovak government in exile, who wanted to drive out the three million Germans and exchange ethnic Hungarians with Slovaks living in Hungary. All told, about twelve million ethnic Germans were expelled from Eastern and Central Europe. The rump of Germany was divided into the four occupation zones that, after the commencement of the Cold War, congealed into partitioned East and West Germany. In this way, the Nazi ideal of a minority-free Europe underlay the postwar order.[27]

Driving the irredentism and anxiety about minorities was—and remains—the construction of primordial consciousness of emplacement, group belonging, and collective fate. As the anthropologist Liisa Malkki has observed, homeland is invested with ontological significance, as in phrases like "the land rose in rebellion" or in the belief about the sacredness of "national soil," thereby naturalizing the relationship between people and land. Botanical metaphors commonly express the link, suggested by the language of "uprooting" from native lands in which people live. Nationality thus constructs refugees as "displaced" from their indigenous settings.[28] Ubiquitous familial terms also gesture to a tribal imaginary of nationalists. The image of a "family of nations," so central to the liberal nationalism of Giuseppe Mazzini in the nineteenth century, echoes this notion.[29] Together, they posit "divine cartographies" that neatly map peoples as naturally emplaced in their homelands, dangerously effacing the heterogeneity and overlapping borders that obtain in the real world.[30] The drama of the "geo-body" can thus endure for millennia,[31] as this declaration about Nagorno-Karabakh by the Armenian National Committee of Australia indicates:

> Historically Armenian, Nagorno Karabakh constituted a part of larger Armenian political entities as early as the 6th century B.C. until the partition of the Kingdom Armenian by Romans and Sasanid Persians at the beginning of the 5th century A.D. Thereafter Nagorno Karabakh was no longer in political union with the Armenian lands to the west and subsequently fell under the rule of the Persians, the now extinct Caucasian Albanians, Mongols,

> Seljuk and Ottoman Turks, the Persians again before being conquered by the Russian Empire in the 19th century A.D. Throughout this period, Nagorno Karabakh remained a bastion of Christendom where Armenia's culture and civilization resisted the ruling alien pressures.[32]

Consequently, fantasized co-nationals are imagined as "stranded" in historically indigenous territories temporarily occupied by aliens. On the basis of these assumptions, the "occupier" can also imagine them as potential hostages, objects of possible reprisal for perceived mistreatment of their own nationals likewise "stranded" across the border.

The violent potential in such ultranationalist assumptions was elaborated by the anthropologist Peter Loizos: the notion of vicarious punishment is based on a "totalizing doctrine of collective passive solidarity [that] allows the nationalist to treat *all* members of an enemy group as dangerously *active*. If they are fertile women they will reproduce and nurture children who will grow into fighting men, or reproducers in turn. Older men and women are givers of advice and succour, and children are simply potential adults. To the ultra-nationalist there can be neither non-combatants nor innocents."[33]

These assumptions gain popularity during communal crises. Historian Taylor Sherman observes a "moral economy" of retribution in Indian partition violence, whereby a symmetry of suffering was required for communal justice. This economy was based on the assumption of subcontinental, indeed global Muslim homogeneity: Muslims had more in common with Muslims in other parts of India, even the world, than with their non-Muslim neighbors. Because of the confessionalization and nationalization of Indian politics over preceding decades, this balancing was now a subcontinental calculation, meaning that innocent Muslims could be made to atone for violence that Muslim militants had perpetrated against innocent Hindus in, say, Hyderabad.[34]

Fatally, this assumption was also shared by Muslim communalists like the All India Muslim League in its "two-nations theory" that South Asian Muslims constituted a nation in every respect like the Hindu nation, rather than a religious minority submerged within a Hindu-dominated India. In fact, notions of a uniform, essentialized, or even interrelated

"Muslim world" were late-nineteenth-century constructions that effaced immense cultural and political diversity.[35] These posited ontologies, like the notion of "Hindu-ness" (*Hindutva*), are forms of epistemological violence that contain potential for physical violence. Abstractions and analogies can kill.

## INDIA AND INTERWAR EUROPE

European affairs served as a screen for various analogical appropriations as Indians imagined post-British futures. Because of Zionism and Britain's Palestine Mandate, the continent was co-imagined with the Middle East and British Empire, offering still more objects for identification and distinction. The German-Czechoslovak confrontation in 1938 in particular was a rich mine for projection possibilities. On one side, a Hindu journalist could write that the creation of an independent Pakistan in the northwest "would place the rest of India at the mercy of an aggressor even more decisively than the loss of the Sudetenland put Czech territory at the mercy of the Nazis."[36] On the other, two Aligarh Muslim University academics drew a different conclusion: "the Muslims of India are a nation by themselves—they have a distinct national entity wholly different from the Hindus and other non-Muslim groups; indeed, they are more different from the Hindus than the Sudeten Germans were from the Czechs."[37] Given the prominence of the German-Czechoslovak conflict in India, this was a statement about the intensity of feeling there.

Vinayak Damodar Savarkar (1883–1966), leader of the ultranationalist Hindu Mahasabha revivalist movement in the 1930s and 1940s, readily agreed that Muslims were utterly distinct from Indians. His *Hindutva: Who Is a Hindu?* (1923) articulated "Hindu-ness" as the authentically indigenous Indian identity that coded Muslims in South Asia as alien conquerors and cultural usurpers; their mass conversion of Hindus should be reversed as part of the Hindu renaissance. He consequently opposed the secular Indian National Congress, founded in 1885, which comprised Indians of all confessions. His notions of national purity and regeneration intersected with foreign national dramas in rigorously consistent ways. In *Hindutva*, he welcomed "Zionist dreams" in Palestine, observing that only Jews approached Hindus in possessing the "conditions under which a nation can attain perfect solidarity and cohesion," namely "people who inhabit the land they adore, the land of whose forefathers is also the land of their Gods and Angels, of Seers and Prophets"—that is, "if ever the Jews can succeed in founding their state there [in Palestine]."[38]

The intensive identification with Jewish nationalism also came from a perception of virtually simultaneous genocidal Muslim invasions of their respective homelands: "The Arabian Moslems invaded Palestine only a few decades before they invaded our Sindh and just as their fanatical fury exterminated the ancient Egyptians or Persians, they attempted to wipe out with fire and sword the Jewish people too."[39] Savarkar thus applauded the UN's decision in November 1947 to partition Palestine and create a Jewish state: "After centuries of sufferings, sacrifices and struggle the Jews will soon recover their national Home in Palestine which has undoubtedly been their Fatherland and Holyland."[40] Opposed to British partitions of the sacred Indian motherlands until the last minute when it meant saving Hindu-majority areas from Pakistan, he regretted that Jews were not granted the entirety of the Palestine Mandate.[41]

With brutal consistency, Savarkar supported Germany's right to choose National Socialism and to expel Jews. Germans could legitimately choose Nazism because nations were constituted by ethnic homogeneities. After all, Jews and Muslims, he said in 1939, identified more with coreligionists abroad than with fellow citizens of the majority population.[42] Such policies were a model for India in relation to the minority Muslim population. He also supported Nazi Germany's policy toward the German minority in the Sudeten region of neighboring Czechoslovakia on the grounds of ethnic democratic self-determination, an argument Hindu nationalists would later make about princely states ruled by Muslims whose majority population was Hindu:

[A]s far as the Czechoslovakia question was concerned the Hindu Sanghatanists [Mahasabhaits] in India hold that Germany was perfectly justified in uniting the Austrian and Sudeten Germans under the German flag. Democracy itself demanded that the will of the people must prevail in choosing their own government. Germany demanded plebiscite, the Germans under the Czechs wanted to join their kith and kin in Germany. It was the Czechs who were acting against the principle of democracy in holding the Germans under a foreign sway against their will. . . . Now that Germany is strong why should she not strike to unite all Germans and consolidate them into a Pan-German state and realise the political dream which generations of German people cherished.[43]

Identifying now with Germans rather than Jews, Savarkar hoped that India was so strong as to politically unify Hindus spread across multiple polities on the Indian subcontinent.

Ironically, the Muslim League reasoned in similar terms even if with different signs. The Sindh League leader Abdullah Haroon praised Hitler for liberating ethnic Germans from Czechoslovak domination in the same way that League-dominated areas should come to the aid of endangered Muslims if persecuted by Hindus. Muhammad Ali Jinnah even invoked British practices of humanitarian intervention: "if Britain in Gladstone's time could intervene in Armenia in the name of protection of minorities, why should it not be right for us to do so in the case of our minorities in Hindustan—if they are oppressed."[44] In his address to the Sindh Muslim League conference in October 1938, he elaborated the identification:

It was because the Sudeten Germans who were forced under the heel of the majority of Czechoslovakia who oppressed them, suppressed them, maltreated them and showed a brutal and callous disregard for their rights and interests for two decades, hence the inevitable result that the Republic of Czechoslovakia is now broken up and a new map will have to be drawn. Just as the Sudeten Germans were not defenceless and survived the oppression and persecution for two decades, so also the Mussalmans are not defenceless and cannot give you their national entity and aspirations in this great continent.[45]

Like their mortal enemies the Hindu Mahasabha, the Muslim League identified with the Germans, although with opposite intentions: the former regarded Germans as akin to Hindus striving to unite against a despotic ruler (the princely states, the British, and the Czechoslovak state as the villains), while the latter sought partition against a tyrannical majority (with Slavs and Hindus as villains). The Muslim League thereby sided with the British in its infamous Munich Agreement with Hitler to partition Czechoslovakia. If the lessons of new postwar states had taught the League anything, it was that minority status was untenable. Majorities could not be expected to treat them well, and unlike raw power, League of Nations treaties and constitutional protections counted for little.

As might be expected, Indian National Congress leaders rejected these analogies. Rajendra Prasad (1884–1963), a lawyer from Bihar who later became the county's first president, sounded a warning about false humanitarian interventions: "Since the authors [the Aligarh Muslim University academics] have compared Hindus and Muslims to Czechs and Sudeten Germans . . . one can only hope that it is not intended that history should repeat itself and India see a war for the conquest of the Czechs (the Hindus) and of Hindustan (Czecho Slovakia) on the pretext of the Indian Czechs'—the Hindus'—ill-treatment of the Indian Sudetens the Muslims."[46] His colleague, Jawaharlal Nehru (1889–1964), also sympathized with Czechoslovakia as a new, democratic, left-leaning, postimperial, and multinational state, albeit with a fractious, indeed irredentist German minority. With his daughter, he visited the country in 1938 as a mark of solidarity before the Munich conference, declining an official invitation to Nazi Germany. An Indo-Czechoslovak Society in Bombay was founded in 1938 to the same end. The Indian national independence movement attracted great attention and sympathy in Czechoslovakia. Already in 1934, Czechoslovak-Indian commercial and cultural relations were institutionalized in university positions and an Oriental Institute in Prague.[47] After his tour of the country, which was preceded by a visit to Republican forces in Spain's civil war, Nehru wrote a series of articles in the English and Indian press denouncing German aggression and Western acquiescence, which he saw as more sinister than appeasement:

> As events have shown they [the Czechoslovaks] have prepared to go to extraordinary length to satisfy every minority claim and preserve peace but everybody knows that the question at issue is not a minority one. If it was the love of minority rights that moved people why do we not hear of the German minority in Italy or the minority in Poland? The question is one of power

politics and the Nazi desire to break up the Czecho-Soviet alliance, to put an end to the democratic state in central Europe, to reach the Rumanian oil fields and wheat, and thus to dominate Europe. British policy has encouraged this and tried to weaken that democratic state.[48]

Like European leftists and many anticolonial nationalists, he associated fascism and imperialism, placing Nazi Germany and the British Empire in the same camp as disavowed allies opposing the Soviet Union, with which he also sympathized although he himself was not a communist. Unlike Savarkar and the Muslim League, he was dismayed, if not surprised, by the British and French betrayal of Czechoslovakia.

The Congress followed Nehru's line, passing a resolution in March 1939 that condemned British foreign policy toward Germany, Italy, and Spain, including Germany's persecution of its Jewish citizens, again in contrast to Savarkar: "International morality has sunk so low in Central and South-Western Europe that the world has witnessed with horror the organized terrorism of the Nazi Government against people of the Jewish race and the continuous bombing from the air by rebel forces of cities and civilian inhabitants and helpless refugees [in Spain]."[49] How German imperialism and pan-Germanism—a cypher for pan-Islamism in Congress eyes—played out in Czechoslovakia confirmed its fears. Not only did the Sudeten-German leader Konrad Henlein claim parity with the Slav majority, but the Nazis detached Slovakia from the Bohemian lands when they occupied the country. The fragmentary implications of pan-Islamic communalism in India for a united country seemed portended in Central Europe. "The entire course of events was fully reported and closely observed in India," noted Beni Prasad (1895–1945), the inaugural professor of politics at Allahabad University.[50]

The Dalit lawyer, political thinker, and drafter of India's first independent constitution, B. R. Ambedkar (1891–1956), also used the Czechoslovak drama to draw lessons for India in *Thoughts on Pakistan* (1941), which he augmented in *Pakistan or the Partition of India* (1945).[51] Speaking as a member of a low-status minority, he was acutely conscious of the demographic preponderance of Hindus, whose caste hierarchies he wished to "annihilate" in a new social order, as he wrote in 1936. His distrust of majorities—and consequent favoring of national homogeneity—thus had two sources: caste and religion.[52] He noted the Muslim League's enthusiastic identification with Germany's intervention for their Sudeten co-nationals and did not dispute the power of the lesson. It was less the Sudeten Germans that interested him, however, than the Slovak nationalists, who used the Sudeten precedent to win constitutional and administrative autonomy within the state. No sooner had they extracted these concessions then they used the threat of German invasion to secede altogether and form a separate state. On the basis of this experience, and the breakup of the Ottoman Empire, Ambedkar instructed his readers on the power of nationalism: "Really speaking the destruction of Czechoslovakia was brought about by an enemy within her own borders. That enemy was the intransigent nationalism of the Slovaks who were out to break up the unity of the state and secure the independence of Slovakia."[53]

The poisoned fruit of such nationalism was terrible violence. In a remarkable section of *Pakistan or the Partition of India*, Ambedkar graphically detailed communal conflict between 1920 and 1940 based on official reports. They made "most painful and heart-rending reading" and indicated "twenty years of civil war between the Hindus and the Muslims in India, interrupted by brief intervals of armed peace." Violence against women in particular showed "the depth of the antagonism which divided the two communities." What is more, violent acts were not condemned by communal authorities "but were treated as legitimate acts of warfare for which no apology was necessary." In the circumstances, "Hindu-Muslim unity" was less a mirage than "out of sight and also out of mind."[54] The two could not be one nation irrespective of united government administrations. Contemporary European history and local experience also taught him this cold reality. Addressing Hindus, he asked them to ponder the viability of an independent India with such internal national conflict:

> This is a lesson which the Hindus will do well to grasp. They should ask themselves: if the Greek, Balkan and Arab nationalism has blown up the Turkish State and if Slovak nationalism has caused the dismantling of Czechoslovakia, what is there to prevent Muslim nationalism from disrupting the Indian State? If experience of other countries teaches that this is the

inevitable consequence of pent-up nationalism, why not profit by their experience and avoid the catastrophe by agreeing to divide India into Pakistan and Hindustan?[55]

In view of irreconcilable nationality conflicts and consequent violence, Ambedkar concluded that states were left with no alternative but to strive for demographic homogeneity. To that end, he supported partition and an independent Pakistan already in 1941, only a year after the landmark Lahore Resolution of the Muslim League, writing, "It is obvious that if Pakistan has the demerit of cutting away parts of India it has also one merit namely of introducing homogeneity."[56]

## MINORITIES: HOSTAGES OR TRANSFER?

The problem for Indian partitionists was that schemes devised in the 1930s and 1940s left large minorities in the new territories. Should they be protected, kept as hostages, or exchanged? The Muslim League's Lahore Resolution was an exercise in studied ambiguity in order to assuage Muslim-majority provinces that wanted to guard their autonomy from a strong central government. The resolution mentioned neither partition nor Pakistan, instead calling for "areas in which the Muslims are numerically in a majority, as in the North-Western and Eastern Zones of India" to constitute "autonomous and sovereign," indeed "Independent States" within a constitutional framework. It thus implied a decentralized Indian union of extant provinces, in which the issue of sovereignty was deferred.[57] As the resolution also implied that the Muslim-majority provinces of the northwest and Bengal would contain large non-Muslim minorities, they should be protected by "adequate, effective and mandatory safeguards," just as Muslim minorities in India should be similarly protected by constitutional provisions.[58] Commenting later on the resolution, Jinnah was characteristically vague, telling minority Muslims to demand safeguards "known to any civilized government" while reminding them that they would be no better off in a united India in which all Muslims, including the "Muslim homeland," remained minority subjects to the Hindu majority. "The division of India will throw a great responsibility upon the majority in its respective zones to create a real sense of security amongst the minorities and win their complete trust and confidence," he said hopefully.[59]

As Sikh leaders never tired of pointing out, why should Sikh collective security in their Punjab homeland not be guaranteed with *their* local sovereignty in the same way as Muslim security? They were not reassured by Muslim League arguments about effective Sikh influence in Punjab under Pakistan, which bore a striking resemblance to Congress arguments about effective Muslim influence in a united India. When partition finally became a reality in early 1947, Sikhs, the Hindu Mahasabha, and Congress insisted that non-Muslim areas of Punjab and Bengal become part of India in any partition demarcation; they could not become minorities in Pakistan. Ambedkar was also adamant on this point.[60]

This logic was shared by Muslim League leaders even from Muslim-minority areas like Uttar Pradesh: the main priority was self-government of Muslim-majority areas so they could not be intimidated by the national Hindu majority. How, then, could Muslim security in non-Muslim areas be guaranteed? Were Jinnah's and the Lahore Resolution's anodyne references to minority protection sufficient? They could be if backed by power. The well-known breakthrough to the notion of a separate Muslim polity was the speech of the lawyer, poet, and politician Muhammad Iqbal (1877–1938) at a Muslim League meeting in 1930. There he demanded "the formation of a consolidated Muslim State in the best interests of India and Islam." The interests of both parties, he suggested obliquely, were served by a system of mutual deterrence: "For India, it means security and peace resulting from an *internal balance of power.*"[61]

Muslim League figures made explicit what remained implicit in Iqbal's hint, namely, a "hostage theory" guarantee of communal peace based on a simple proposition: if you mistreat our minorities, we'll mistreat yours. For that reason, League politicians from Muslim-minority areas, like Choudhry Khaliquzzaman (1889–1973) of United Provinces, wanted all minorities to remain in situ to guarantee mutual deterrence, as he made clear in a letter to Jinnah in 1942: "one of the basic principles lying behind the Pakistan idea is that of keeping hostages in Muslim Provinces as against the Muslims in the Hindu Provinces. If we allow millions of Hindus to go out of our orbit of influence, the security of the

Muslims in the minority Provinces will greatly be minimised."[62] There could be no equitable reciprocity if Pakistan was homogenous.

British leaders were well aware of the theory. Secretary to the governor of the Punjab, Penderel Moon, recalled hostage theory calculations among League leaders in the late 1930s: "there would be so many Muslims in Hindustan and so many Hindus in Pakistan that both sides would hesitate to harass their minorities for fear of reprisals."[63] Choudhry Khaliquzzaman shared these views with the British Cabinet Mission in April 1946 when asked how Muslims remaining in India would benefit from the establishment of Pakistan. "It was not so much that Muslims in Hindu-majority Provinces would be benefited directly," he was reported as saying, "but that the advantages would be indirect because the Government of Hindustan would not be so ready to ill-treat Muslims if they knew that the Government of Pakistan would retaliate. Some sort of balance of power was essential."[64] Hossain Imam, a Muslim League lawyer from Bihar, where Muslims were also a minority, likewise told the British secretary of state that "if there were a Pakistan in being, the Muslims in the minority Provinces would be assured that the Hindus could not treat them badly with impunity" because of the fear of reprisals, even if they were not enacted.[65]

Whether Imam really believed this scheme would work was indicated by his frank admission that minority Muslims would suffer for a redemptive purpose: they "were in effect prepared to sacrifice the interests of 25 million Muslims in Hindustan for the benefit of the rest of the community in Pakistan." Loyally following Jinnah's line, he continued: "The Muslims in the minority Provinces would rather face whatever was in store for them than allow the whole Muslim population to be maltreated."[66] The few, nonetheless tens of millions of Muslims, would suffer to secure Iqbal and Jinnah's vision of a Muslim homeland—as Jinnah put it, the "opportunity [for Muslims] to development their spiritual, cultural, economic, and political life in accordance with their own genius and shape their own future destiny."[67]

The British listeners were unconvinced by the hostage theory. One of them suggested, presciently, that the retaliatory logic, far from dampening violence, might result in "a crescendo of ill-treatment of minorities on both sides of the border."[68] A memo from a British administrator in United Provinces to the viceroy in January 1946 about a conversation with Choudhry Khaliquzzaman registered the skepticism: "He was very naïve about this [the hostage theory] and almost smacked his lips at the thought of the fun the Pakistan Government(s) would have in protecting—vicariously—the interests of their coreligionists in Hindustan!"[69] Choudhry Khaliquzzaman migrated to Pakistan at partition and succeeded Jinnah as leader of the Muslim League. He also knew that Muslims stranded in India were effectively left high and dry because the establishment of Pakistan would mean the absence of an effective Muslim voice at the center of Indian politics.[70]

Accordingly, Jinnah hoped that the League would inherit an unpartitioned Punjab and Bengal with its large Hindu (and in Punjab, also Sikh) minorities, as he made clear in the Cabinet Mission negotiations in 1946.[71] Until the catastrophic population exchanges from below of 1947 and 1948, Jinnah apparently continued to believe in the hostage theory, telling an English journalist that Muslims in India were "fortunate that there would be a corresponding minority of 25,000,000 Hindus in Pakistan." On partition, he was reported as saying, "The minorities are in effect hostages to the requirement of mutual cooperation and good neighbourliness between the Governments of Pakistan and the Indian Union."[72] However, while a sizable Muslim minority remained in India, very few Hindus, Sikhs, and other non-Muslims were left in Pakistan, leading to considerable hand-wringing there. There were even calls for Hindus to return.[73]

Hindu observers were registering this security logic of Muslim communal leaders already in 1931. Sanat Kumar Roy-Chaudhuri, mayor of Calcutta and senior member the Hindu Mahasabha, predictably derided the hostage theory as yet another Muslim strategy to dominate Hindus because more non-Muslims would be under Muslim control than the reverse. Iqbal's speech the year before, he continued, implied a pan-Muslim federation in the northwest to overawe India, a fear also shared by Ambedkar. On the eve of partition, Savarkar predictably vowed that any Muslim mistreatment of Hindus would be met in kind.[74] By contrast, senior Congress figures were appalled by the hostage theory, which was catching on within their ranks. Maulana Abul Kalam Azad (1888–1958), a Muslim Congress leader, recalls that during the partition decision, members reassured Hindu delegates from Sindh, where Hindus were a minority, by saying "the Hindus in Pakistan need have no fear as there would be 45 millions of Muslims in India and if there was any oppression of Hindus in Pakistan, the Muslims in India would have to bear the consequences." He felt that the notion of "retaliation as a method of assuring the rights of minorities seemed . . . barbarous."[75] Rajendra Prasad agreed: "The very idea of ill-treating people who have done nothing wrong and may for all practical purposes be the best of citizens in their own State, because some other independent Government with which they have no concern has misbehaved, is so repugnant to our sense of natural justice that it is inconceivable that either Pakistan or Hindustan will resort to reprisal against its own subjects for the act of an independent Government."[76]

Ambedkar was also appalled by "a scheme of communal peace through a system of communal hostages."[77] He drew on his broad study of European affairs to come to startling conclusions based on arresting analogies. Hindus stuck in Pakistan would be in the "position of the Armenians under the Turks or of the Jews in Tsarist Russia or in Nazi Germany," in this case "as a helpless prey to the fanaticism of a Muslim National State."[78] What is more, India's sovereignty would be threatened by the theory. After all, were Muslims incorrect to observe that "Hitler's bullying tactics" in the German-Czechoslovakia confrontation were "better able to protect the Sudeten Germans in Czechoslovakia than the Sudetens were able to do themselves?"[79] For these reasons, Ambedkar urged a dramatic and drastic alternative: population exchange. The Balkans provided a precedent, in part because of their dreadful record of minority protection, in part because those states successfully transferred minorities. Anticipating skepticism about logistics, he noted the magnitude of the challenge they faced: "It involved the transfer of some 20 million people from one habitat to another. But undaunted, the three [Turkey, Greece, and Bulgaria] shouldered the task and carried it to a successful end because they felt that the considerations of communal peace must outweigh every other consideration." Sounding like the British Peel Commission's invocation of the Turkish-Greek population exchange, Ambedkar concluded that "there is no reason to suppose that what they did cannot be accomplished by Indians."[80] That was the only way to make Hindustan homogenous, he averred.

Ambedkar was not alone in this line of thinking. Syed Abdul Latif, an English literature university academic in Hyderabad, suggested the same from the Muslim perspective in *The Muslim Problem in India* in 1939. He too was well aware of the difficulties, indeed sacrifices that a population exchange would entail, but better that this generation made them for the peace of subsequent generations. He proposed that the League and Congress collaborate on a mutually agreeable scheme, for which European history gave plenty of precedents, and that should commence with voluntary migration.[81] The idea comes up occasionally in Jinnah's speeches. Population exchange, he declared, "as far as practicable will have to be considered."[82]

While the Muslim League toyed with the hostage theory and population exchange, the Congress rejected them for minority protection, although this commitment was tested by communal violence. Rajendra Prasad criticized population exchange as utterly impractical because it would be too costly, the suffering too immense, and the affected populations in India too intermingled, too far from likely borders, and vastly larger than in the Turkish-Greek case. He was, in any event, against the proposition of homogeneous states; they always had minorities.[83] But by the time he signed off on the third edition of *India Divided* in July 1947, after the failed Cabinet Mission and ensuing communal violence in and after August 1946, he had changed his mind. He amended the addendum that supplemented the second edition, now supporting the idea: "The wisest course might therefore be to bring about an exchange of populations and squares between Muslims and non-Muslims, all the Muslims going over to the districts which may be assigned to the Muslim zone, all non-Muslims from those districts being transferred to a district assigned to the non-Muslim zone."[84] The scheme would have to focus on Punjab, the Sikh homeland, transferring Sikhs into a non-Muslim zone.

In the event, the partition plan agreed to by all parties in June 1947 did not include population exchanges, in contrast to the Peel Commission report in Palestine ten years before. The "Radcliffe Line" sundered Punjab and Bengal to separate Muslims and non-Muslims in those majority-Muslim provinces without demographic transfers. When asked about the matter, Viceroy Louis Mountbatten said it was not a question for All-India deliberations: "There are many physical and practical difficulties involved. Some measure of transfer will come about in a natural way . . . perhaps governments will transfer populations. Once more, this is a matter not so much for the main parties as for the local authorities living in the border areas to decide."[85] He had not given the matter much thought.

Indeed, local forces in the border areas ultimately determined events, but not the authorities Mountbatten invoked. Prasad's concerns about the Sikh factor in Punjab were well placed. Throughout their consultations with the Cabinet Mission, Sikh leaders had issued veiled threats that they would take matters into their own hands if partition sundered their lands and if many of them were to be stranded in Pakistan. In fact, they had called for population exchanges to concentrate Sikhs—and that is what occurred.[86] In large measure, the partition violence in that region was organized by Sikh militias that brutally expelled Muslims from areas that they settled with Sikhs who left—or who were likewise expelled from—the eastern, Pakistan areas.[87] In total, up to 17.9 million people left or were driven from their homes during the next four years, mainly in the Punjab and in Bengal, more than 3 million going missing or dying in the process, and hundreds of thousands of girls and women suffering rape and abduction.[88] This was not the orderly population exchange envisaged by some, and certainly not in the numbers required to homogenize India, although Pakistan came close to the ideal.

Certainly, the hostage theory was disproved by this wrenching process; indeed, it was a mechanism of escalation as the British Cabinet Mission had predicted. No government had been able to protect the welfare of its respective communities despite the existence of hostages. State retaliation, as opposed to communal violence, was politically untenable, despite covert support for, or willful blindness to, their pogroms. Instead, now, "many of the original protagonists of Pakistan found themselves a hated minority in an even more completely Hindu polity," as an American

observer noted at the time.[89] Ultranationalist retributive violence was de-
structively creative by homogenizing national demography and political
culture so that reality would more closely accord to the abstraction of the
imagined collective. Hossain Imam, the Bihar Muslim League representative who told the British that he "would rather face whatever was in
store for them [Muslims] than allow the whole Muslim population to be
maltreated," now complained that he expected to be treated as a citizen of
India and not as a hostage.[90]

MUSLIM ZION?

Were the projections of identity between India, Europe, and the Middle
East so intense as to make Pakistan a "Muslim Zion"?[91] Certainly, the
two movements shared the notions of a cultural homeland and elabora-
tion of a nation that, though posited as an abstraction of imagined homogeneity, did not yet exist, and indeed was supposed to be made in and by
the future state. If British authorities hesitated to equate the partitions of
India and of Palestine, that was because they could not analogize between
largely European Jewish settlers whom they regarded as civilizationally
superior to the indigenous Arabs, and Indian Muslims whom they orien-
talized like Arabs.[92] They would have agreed with Maulana Abul Kalam
Azad, who rejected the "analogy of the Jewish demand for a national
home" in April 1946:

> One can sympathize with the aspiration of the Jews for such a national
> home, as they are scattered all over the world and cannot in any region have
> any effective voice in the administration. The condition of Indian Muslims is
> quite otherwise. Over 90 millions in number they are in quantity and qual-
> ity a sufficiently important element in Indian life to influence decisively all
> questions of administration and policy. Nature has further helped them by
> concentrating them in certain areas.[93]

Like the Muslim League, the Congress decried the Balfour Declaration
and British imperialism in general. Unlike the League, the Congress
perceived Zionism since the 1930s as a secessionist movement like the
Muslim League, both collaborating illegitimately with the British, and so
found it easy to reject Palestine's partition. The League's opposition was

predictable: it supported the majority-Muslim Palestinian Arabs in their quest for self-determination and would not equate itself with Zionists. A League resolution in 1938 went so far as to warn the British that its "pro-Jewish policy in Palestine" would make them appear as an "enemy of Islam."[94] The Congress also identified with an independent and united Palestine. As the Zionist demographer and historian Joseph B. Schechtman lamented, it was Mohandas Gandhi (1869–1948) who set the Congress against Zionism by declaring Palestine an Arab country.[95]

Although both parties agreed to partition in South Asia—Congress most reluctantly—both Pakistan and India opposed it for Palestine. India was a member of the UN Special Committee on Palestine (UNSCOP) and, with Iran and Yugoslavia, submitted the minority report supporting a federalization of Palestine, a solution that the Congress had rejected for India because it wanted a strong central state. Pakistan, which led the UN subcommittee to study the Arab proposal for a united Palestine, joined other Islamic countries in contesting partition and, failing that, seeking to limit Jewish control to the small amount of Jewish-owned land (6 percent). When the Arab unitary state proposal was rejected, both Pakistan and India supported the federal idea, which foresaw a binational state. In his memoirs, Pakistan UN representative Sir Chaudhry Zafarullah Khan—himself a member of the Ahmadi minority—said he had been attracted to the binational idea of Judah Magnus, president of the Hebrew University of Jerusalem, whom he had met in 1945. Magnus had impressed upon him the necessity of securing bipartisan support for any solution.[96]

How was one to avoid the implication of hypocrisy by denying Jews national sovereignty when the Muslim League had argued that Muslims constituted a distinct nationality and therefore deserved their own state? The difference, Khan said at the UN, was that both sides had consented to partition in India whereas in Palestine it was being imposed against the will of the majority; that Muslims were a part of India in a way that could not be said of Jews in Palestine, most of whom had arrived in recent years, thereby artificially creating a nationality conflict; and that Muslims in India claimed only majority population areas whereas in Palestine Jews were a minority in virtually all the land they were to be granted by the UN.[97] Besides, he added, would the Americans take Pakistan refugees just because they wanted to go to the United States?[98] For India, partition violated the sacred principle of self-determination. After the failure of the federal plan, which was also dismissed by the Arab bloc, India supported the latter in opposing partition. From the Indian perspective, partition in South Asia was not a concession to secession but a recognition of its right to self-determination.[99] Distinguished in this way, India and Pakistan could oppose the partition of Palestine but reluctantly support the partitions of the Muslim majority provinces of Punjab and Bengal.[100]

Despite the scattered references to population exchange, there was no Pakistan expectation or commitment to an ingathering of all Muslims from India. The League and Pakistan leadership did not envisage the large-scale immigration of Indian Muslims to a historic homeland in the manner that Zionists hoped and anticipated Jews would eventually settle in Eretz Israel.[101] In fact, amid partition violence in October 1947, Jinnah told Pakistan armed forces offices that the flight of Hindus from Sindh in particular harmed the economy and the state; the exodus "was part of a well-organized plan to cripple Pakistan."[102] These are hardly the sorts of sentiments one would have heard from David Ben-Gurion regarding Palestinian Arabs. Nor, later, did Jinnah think that Indian Muslims had an a priori right to settle in Pakistan; the state had no Law of Return like Israel's. He advised Muslims in India to swear "unflinching loyalty to the State."[103] Treating minorities well was the policy as stated in the Lahore Resolution. There was no talk of hostages.

However, because some in India were "bent upon the eviction and extermination of Muslims in India by brutal and inhuman means," Jinnah placed population exchange on the table: "If the ultimate solution to the minority problem is to be mass exchanges of population, let it be taken up at the Governmental palace" rather than "sorted out by bloodthirsty elements."[104] Such a scheme was never seriously considered; neither state had the capacity to cope with more refugees or the will power to exchange minorities for the reasons Rajendra Prasad had given in *India Divided*. India resisted pressure from the far-right Hindus for population exchange and war for more territory to settle migrants. Talk of population exchange was an expression of desperation and hopelessness in the face of seemingly intractable violence from below. Latif seems to have re-canted his views as impractical already by 1946.[105]

Instead, Jinnah took rhetorical responsibility for Muslims in India, who thereby became what Willem van Schendel calls "proxy citizens."[106] This was not a new idea in South Asian discourse, as the Lahore Reso-lution indicated. If the two-nations theory were to be taken seriously, Indian Muslims were in fact culturally Pakistani. To that extent, parti-tion had sedimented into the new states the minority question that was on the table in the All-India discussions. The practice of dealing with the 197 remnant enclaves in one another's countries exemplified this ap-proach. Both sides behaved as if they were responsible for coreligionists/co-nationals in enclaves across the border. The issue was pressing because majority militias demanded enclave loyalty to the surrounding state, which they attacked when it was not forthcoming.[107] In the interests of stemming further refugee flows—in opposite fashion to the situation in Israel and its neighbors at the same time—the states started meeting at interdominion conferences in January 1948 to manage the situation.

It took until 1950 for the two new states to stabilize the situation. Like the League of Nations minority protection regime, the "Agreement Between the Governments of India and Pakistan Regarding Security and Rights of Minorities" (the Nehru–Liaquat Agreement) provided minor-ity protection as an alternative to population expulsion and/or exchange, though without the supervisory oversight of an international organiza-tion: "The Governments of India and Pakistan solemnly agree that each shall ensure, to the minorities throughout its territory, complete equality of citizenship, irrespective of religion, a full sense of security in respect of life, culture, property and personal honour, freedom of movement within each country and freedom of occupation, speech and worship, subject to law and morality."[108]

Joint minority commissions were established for Assam and East and West Bengal, where Hindus remained, to oversee minority rights. Each state's incentive to act against the egregious persecution of minorities at the local level was to forestall the other state becoming the minority's "protector."[109] Likely without realizing the precedent, the India and Paki-stan agreement partially replicated the 1930 Greek-Turkish treaty that made each country responsible for the compensation of those who arrived as part of the Lausanne agreement, ending the mixed commissions supervised by the League.[110] For all the theorizing about hostages and population exchanges, the parties settled on the minority protection option they had disparaged in the lead-up to partition because of its failure in Europe. The League seemed to share a Zionist sense of proprietary interest in proxy citizens abroad, but as a permanent rather than a transitional arrangement, as Zionists conceived it at the time. Indian Muslims were to stay put; Pakistan was not their home irrespective of what the Hindu Mahasabha thought. And yet, as we will see, the Muslim-Zion connection was apparent in another, more fatal way.

## PALESTINE, ISRAEL, AND MINORITIES

In the British Mandate of Palestine, leaders of the large Arab majority urged the British Mandate authorities to limit, if not cease, Jewish immigration from the outset. For their part, Zionists, who could not foresee an independent Jewish state in the 1920s and 1930s, sought to build up the Jewish national home by having the British enable a Jewish majority over time via immigration. Already in 1937, Jewish leaders reluctantly accepted the Peel Commission's partition recommendation, which included Arab population transfers, because a truncated state with a demographic majority was preferable to long-term struggle with a hostile Arab population with no guarantee of eventual sovereignty.[111] As might be expected, Arab leaders resisted the partition recommendation. Throughout the Mandate, they insisted that Palestine be granted independence according to the strictures of Class A Mandates—like Iraq, for instance—as a democratic polity in which Jewish minority rights were respected. As noted in the introduction, the idea that non-European majorities could not be trusted to protect the rights of a "minority," particularly a white European one, long predated the British Mandate. However, the massacre of Assyrians after Iraqi independence in 1933 and violence between Jews and Arabs in Palestine in 1929 gave the British a convenient pretext not to entrust the state to the Arab majority; that is why they considered partition and transferring Arabs from the Jewish territory.[112] Both parties advocated minority rights in the state they wanted to govern. Unlike

India, there was no official discussion of equitable reciprocity or hostages, although that did not preclude retributive violence at the local level. Even so, as we will see below, hostage and population logics were discernible in regional perspective.

In 1947, UNSCOP determined to partition the British Mandate after the British had referred the matter to the UN. The committee's majority report, which awarded most of the Mandate to the Zionists, who constituted a third of Palestine's population, was supported by the General Assembly after considerable arm-twisting of allies by the United States, and in the face of vehement opposition by the majority Arab population.[113] The generous award was designed for future population growth, whose immediate sources were Jewish displaced persons languishing in camps in Germany, although the aim to demographically prevail in Palestine long preceded the Holocaust and was reflected in the Peel Commission's dramatic redistribution of territory to the Zionists, coupled with population transfer, ten years before. Refugee pressures that Europe, the United States, Canada, or Australia were unwilling to accommodate in their own countries were transferred to the Middle East.

The Arab states supported Palestinian leaders in rejecting both the federal state and partition plans of the minority UNSCOP report and majority reports.[114] They sought the termination of the Mandate and establishment of an independent Palestinian state; Jewish minority rights would be safeguarded "in accordance with international law and the United Nations Charter."[115] This was an enduring Arab demand, made recently by Arab representatives to the Anglo-American Committee of Inquiry of 1946. The most articulate representative was the British-Lebanese civil servant and historian Albert Hourani (1915–1993), then working for the Arab Office in Jerusalem.[116] The question of minorities and violence underlay his presentation. Arabs did not want to be converted into a minority via Jewish immigration; if Jews supported partition to avoid ruling over Arabs, the problem was not solved by a Jewish state because it too would inevitably contain a large Arab minority, an argument advanced by Sikhs in India.

Partition was not a solution, Hourani declared. A Jewish neighbor-state in a partitioned Palestine would lead to instability, because it would seek to expand: "I can imagine [that] the pressures of population in the Jewish State would be so great [that] it would turn the thoughts of the governing body to expansion, either in order to settle Jewish immigrants outside the Jewish State, or else in order to evacuate their Arab minority." Arabs, he reminded the committee, had been listening to the Jewish talk of an "evacuation" of Arabs, although he thought, incorrectly as it turned out, that in practice "this Arab minority could not be transferred forcibly because you can't transfer peasants forcibly."[117] Indeed, an intense Zionist discussion about "transferring" Palestinians had been under way for a decade. Although it did not constitute official policy, the preferences of the Zionist high command were readily apparent by 1947.[118] Golda Myerson (Meir) (1898–1978), as acting head of the Jewish Agency Political Department, declared that "we are interested in less Arabs who will be citizens of the Jewish state." Yitzhak Gruenbaum (1879–1970) of the Jewish Agency Executive said that Arabs remaining in the postpartition Jewish state who were citizens of its Arab neighbor would represent "a permanent irredenta." Irrespective of citizenship status, such Arabs, Ben-Gurion maintained, would become a "Fifth Column" in time of war. He feared Arabs would take citizenship in the Jewish state, meaning that they could not be legally expelled.[119]

Even so, continued Hourani, Arabs were willing to share citizenship with Jews who had arrived legally and wanted to be "full members of the political unity," adding ironically, "to try the dangerous experiment of people of different races and ideals living together." He thought the offer generous.[120] Addressing the minority question in a united state, he struck the pose of Indian Congress leaders:

> ... what the Jews could expect would be full civil and political rights, control of their own communal affairs, municipal autonomy in districts in which they are mainly concentrated, the use of Hebrew as an additional official language in those districts, and an adequate share in the administration. It should be clear from this that there is no question of the Jews being under Arab rule in the bad sense of being thrust into a ghetto, or being cut off from the main stream of life of the community, always shunned and sometimes oppressed. The Arabs are offering not this ghetto status in the bad sense, but member-

ship of the Palestinian community. If that community has an Arab character, if the Palestinian state is to be an Arab state, that is not because of racial prejudice or fanaticism but because of two inescapable facts: the first that Palestine has an Arab indigenous population, and the second that Palestine by geography and history is an essential part of the Arab world.[121]

The question for the Arab leadership, he continued, was between "goodwill and force": Were Jews "to live in Palestine with the goodwill of the Arabs," or were they "to rely on force, their own or [that of] others"?[122]

These are the terms that the Muslim League rejected from the Congress because of the fear that permanent minority status could not guarantee security and national development. Similarly, Jews did not want to live in an Arab country, however defined, nor share equal citizenship with Palestinians—again, long before the Holocaust. They felt they were in Palestine by right, not by Arab sufferance, and the British agreed. Hourani was naïve. He did not understand that Zionists could stand firm for three reasons. First, they understood their overwhelming military superiority to the Palestinians after the revolt between 1936 and 1939 had been brutally quashed and the Palestinian leadership imprisoned or exiled. Second, the British and Zionist leadership shared the belief of the Yishuv's essential civilizational superiority to the Arabs, one also held by the majority of League and UN officials and delegates. Arab leaders failed to recognize that the political rights of liberal internationalism were not meant to apply to them, meaning that they continued to send petitions and deputations despite the fact that they had little chance of a hearing.[123] Tellingly, it was obdurate Palestinian resistance, as in the revolt, that led to policy changes in their favor, like the White Paper of 1939. Third, no nationalist movement like Zionism or the Muslim League would rely on its adversaries' goodwill. Ambedkar had highlighted twenty years of violence to underline the lack of goodwill in India. In the Palestine case, it was similarly difficult to imagine goodwill in light of the violent Palestinian resistance of the 1930s and Zionist terror campaign at the time.[124]

The Anglo-American Committee of Inquiry doubted some of Hourani's propositions as well. Its report struck an artful balance between the sides, including the American pressure to allow in one hundred thousand Jewish refugees. Palestine was neither purely Arab, nor Jewish. Neither side should control the other; minority protection declarations and provisions inevitably would prove inadequate. Consequently, to avoid the inevitable "civil strife" that would ensue from "the determination of each to achieve domination" and to establish an independent state, an international mandate should continue, with local self-government to be worked out.[125] As Arie Dubnov notes in his chapter in this book, the British historian who largely drafted the Peel Commission report, Reginald Coupland, wrote to the *London Times* to criticize the Anglo-American Committee report and to readvocate his partition plan. Jews had been ripe for proper self-government for a long time, he insisted. His intervention was anything but prescient, assuring readers—contra Hourani—that "it was impossible to suppose that the Jewish State . . . would be so mad as to violate it [the frontier] and to seek to occupy Arab land beyond it."[126] Coupland could not know that Zionists would assure UNSCOP that they would accept partition on the condition of future expansion.[127]

Hourani's reply in the *Times* rightly pointed out that Coupland was prepared to consign Arabs to minority status in a Jewish state, but not the reverse. But his vague statement that it was dangerous for minorities to rely on foreign powers for protection for "refusing to accept the duties of citizenship" ignored the fact that Zionists had been able to rely on great power backing for much of the Mandate, even if they had felt betrayed by the 1939 White Paper that rejected partition and restricted Jewish migration. The fact remained that a British military presence enabled the development of the Yishuv whatever the latter felt about the former. Nor did Hourani foresee that Israelis could rely on military hardware and support from European states until 1967 and especially the Americans thereafter.[128] Power, not justice and the avoidance of violence, mattered in the end.

Like the British partition plan in India a few months earlier, the UNSCOP plan did not foresee population exchanges but minority protection. And as in India, force prevailed on the ground. Security concerns about the loyalty of remnant enclaves governed the expulsion (and prevention of the return of) Palestinian Arabs by Israeli forces in 1948 and

1949 and territorial expansion well beyond the borders of the 1947 UN partition plan. Take the case of the expulsion of Palestinians from Lydda in July 1948, which the Israeli historian Anita Shapira describes in terms of Hourani's predictions:

> A brief uprising by the residents of Lydda (Lod) exposed the danger inherent in leaving a large bloc containing a hostile population behind the advancing army, midway between Tel Aviv and Jerusalem. The commanders Allon and Yitzhak Rabin, who were considering a large-scale population evacuation, went to consult with [Prime Minister] Ben-Gurion. Ben-Gurion listened to them and did not react; he had an uncanny ability to keep silent when he needed to. It was only at the end of the discussion, as the commanders were about to leave for the battlefield, that, according to Rabin, Ben-Gurion waved his hand and said: "Expel them." . . . [L]ike most of his ministers, he saw the Arabs' exodus as a great miracle, one of the most important in that year of miracles, since the presence of a hostile population constituting some forty percent of the new state's total populace did not augur well for the future.[129]

This operation, which included a massacre of about 250 townspeople, was the outcome of plans to secure territory by destroying Palestinian Arab militias and the villages from which they operated. The outcome, writes historian Benny Morris, was a "war of conquest," even if it unfolded in piecemeal fashion, with local commanders often taking the initiative to expel Palestinians from towns and villages.[130] There was retaliatory violence on both sides. The massacre of the villagers of Deir Yassin in April 1948 by Irgun auxiliaries was avenged by the murder of Jewish academic and medical personnel in a ten-vehicle convoy in Jerusalem by Arab militias.[131]

After the guns fell silent, approximately 700,000 Palestinians had fled or been expelled, while 160,000 Palestinian Arabs were left behind Israeli lines as internal refugees or, if they were lucky, in their own homes. They were then subject to a military occupation until 1966, during which they suffered extensive land expropriation and mobility restrictions and were generally closely monitored. The possibility of expulsion lay open in the case of further conflict with Arab states.[132] The state appealed to "the Arab inhabitants of the State of Israel . . . on the basis of full and equal citizenship," much like Hourani's offer.[133] The Israeli Proclamation of Independence from May 1948 mentioned "complete equality of social and political rights to all its inhabitants irrespective of religion, race or sex." A minorities ministry headed by the first Israeli government's only Sephardic minister, who had liberal views toward the Arab minority, was quickly shut down by Prime Minister Ben-Gurion in 1949. He was effectively replaced by Yehoshua Palmon (1913–1995), advisor to the prime minister on Arab affairs, to oversee Muslim religious institutions with a ministry of religious affairs, thereby casting Palestinians as a religious rather than a national minority. A security hawk who coordinated the martial law regime of the military government of Palestinians, Palmon did not believe in democratic Arab self-administration and "personified the quest for control of the minority and the suspicion of its inherent disloyalty to the state," as one scholar puts it.[134]

At the same time, Jews from Arab countries began arriving in Israel. Now there was talk of an informal population exchange. Joseph B. Schechtman wrote about the European, Indian, and Middle Eastern cases in real time. Early in the 1940s, he was employed by the Institute for Jewish Affairs in New York to study the German expulsions and colonization in Europe.[135] Subsequently, in 1949, he was engaged by the State of Israel to justify the expulsion of Palestinian Arabs and its refusal to allow their return.[136] Schechtman regretted that Pakistani and Indian leaders did not respond in the same way. Instead, they "stubbornly refused to accept the exchange of population as a bitter but inevitable necessity and to conduct it in a constructive way." For partition by itself was insufficient: "The minority problem, which is a question of life and death for the success of any constructive scheme for Palestine cannot be solved without resorting to what the last President Eduard Beneš of Czechoslovakia called 'the grim necessity of transfer.'"[137] Schechtman was effectively saying that the Arabs were an irredentist majority for their inexplicably stubborn refusal to be reduced to minority status in a majority Jewish Palestine.[138]

Schechtman noted the South Asian hostage theory in his short book *Population Transfers in Asia*, published that year.[139] Unlike Muslim League leaders, however, he came to the opposite conclusion. Because

Jews were treated as hostages in Arab countries, they should be brought to Israel. "As a result of the growing anti-Zionist policy on the part of the Arab and Moslem states," he wrote, "the situation of the Jewish minorities in those countries is unbearable. They are considered and treated as hostages." He quoted Arab leaders linking the establishment of Israel to the fate of Jews in their countries. They now faced a "very real threat of physical extermination," and so their "speedy evacuation" was "a matter of utmost urgency." Reflecting a moral economy of symmetry in the Middle East, "such a scheme," he declared, would represent the "fundamentally essential counterpart to the movement of Arabs from Palestine."[140] The Arab-Jewish migration was part of a grand demographic bargain, the Jews' maltreatment the result of hostage thinking that would impel their evacuation and compensate the flight (as he conceived it) of Palestinian Arabs.

Schechtman was also giving voice to Ben-Gurion's public position that made the expelled Palestinian Arabs extraterritorial hostages, implying that they could not return if Jews in Arab countries were mistreated: "the ultimate position of the 300,000-odd Arab refugees from Palestine," the new state leader was reported as stating, "would depend on the treatment meted out to Jewish populations in the Arab lands."[141] In reality, he had no intention of permitting their return and worked to encourage the immigration of Jews in general.

Such notions of effective reciprocity had been voiced before, notably at the World Jewish Congress meeting in 1937 when "population exchange" was the term to refer to Arab Jews while "transfer" applied to Palestinian Arabs, though the idea gained no traction until the realization dawned that the Holocaust had robbed Zionism of its favored migration source. By 1942, Arab Jews were recognized as necessary to populate a future Jewish state, and by the early 1950s the Israeli state realized that their mass migration to Israel could be used as a diplomatic weight to offset the Palestinian refugee problem. This campaign continues to this day.[142] The terms of this migration are thus fraught and contested. The position of the state and advocacy groups for Jews from Arab countries paints a picture of enduring and intense anti-Semitic discrimination that culminated in riots and other measures that drove Jews from their millennia-long homes to Israel; they do not compare this experience to the military occupation endured by Palestinian Citizens of Israel between 1948 and 1966, which was more severe.[143] Arab ultranationalists, by contrast, paint these communities as economically exploitative and Zionist, disloyally supporting the enemy Israel with whom many Arab states were at war in 1948; this argument evinces a retaliatory logic.

Scholarship on the question depicts an uneven process of push and pull factors that resulted in the punctual departure of Arab Jews to many countries. These factors include intense Zionist activism to induce migration, ranging from competition with communists to win the hearts and minds of Iraqi Jews from the early 1940s—mostly unsuccessfully—to the terrorist plot Operation Susannah in Egypt in 1954.[144] In class term, Jews were associated with cosmopolitan commercial elites who had close ties to colonial powers though few to Zionism. Well integrated into these societies, Jews had little incentive to migrate, even impoverished Yemeni Jews, more than forty thousand of whom were induced to leave for Israel under the auspices of a deal cut between Israeli authorities, Jewish organizations, and the rulers of Aden and Yemen.[145]

At the same time, other geopolitical forces were impinging on these communities from the interwar period onward, with the simultaneous rise of Zionism in Palestine, which was reliant on British power, and Arab nationalism, which was anti-imperial in orientation. The notorious Farhud riot in Baghdad in June 1941, during which between 150 and 180 Jews were murdered and their property destroyed, was the result of collaboration charges with the British who defeated a short-lived pro-Axis, independent Iraqi regime and reoccupied the country. In fact, these communities were loyal and saw their futures in Arab states.[146] Israel's defeat of their armies in 1948 discredited these elitist, pro-Western, and conservative regimes with which Jewish communities were associated. In response, they licensed retaliatory violence against these communities to shore up their crumbling position. As a consequence, some 123,000 Iraqi Jews left for Israel between 1949 and 1950. But even with the replacement of these regimes by nationalist revolutionaries in coups during the 1950s, most Jews remained in Egypt, for example, and those who left did not choose Israel as their destination. It was further military defeat to Israel, in 1956 and 1967, that entrenched ultranationalist conceptions of Arab nationhood and intensified legal and economic pressure on Jews to leave. Upon Algerian independence in 1962, most Algerian Jews, who had held French citizenship since 1870, migrated to France. As Joel Beinin's summary of the Egyptian pattern could be generalized, "Between 1919 and 1956, the entire Egyptian Jewish community . . . was transformed from a national asset to a fifth column."[147] Postcolonial Arab nationalism had no place for Jews in its conception of the Arab polity.

## RETRIBUTIVE VIOLENCE AND SECURITY TODAY?

What can we conclude about the relationship between partitions, minorities, and national security and the logic of communal hostage taking, population transfer, and retributive violence? The history of Central Europe in the first half of the twentieth century has been taken as evidence for the proposition that ethnic or national groups with hardened identities cannot live together in compacted zones of comingled settlement. Because of elite mobilization and the fatal logic of "security dilemmas"— the cycle of violence unleashed when the maintenance of security for one group is interpreted as aggression by the other—they are vulnerable to internecine conflicts.[148] The peaceful history of the Federal Republic of Germany is the poster child: partition worked because the minority problem was solved. In fact, hundreds of thousands of ethnic Germans continued to live in the Soviet Union after the war. The reason for stability was that the Federal Republic did not conduct business with the USSR on the basis of the hostage theory. Even though West Germany regarded itself as an ethnically conceived nation-state and enabled migration in specific circumstances, it no longer understood the state as the global headquarters of "Germandom" (*Deutschtum*).[149]

The modalities of national homogeneity and domination persist where states are conceived in ethnocratic terms, with splinters of their nation in others', and others' in theirs. This logic manifests itself in various modalities today. In one form, the Republic of Armenia supports the self-determination of Nagorno-Karabakh, which it regards as "an integral part of historic Armenia."[150] Because ethnic Armenians control this unrecognized entity within Azerbaijan, Armenian policy is to proceed along diplomatic channels in having Nagorno-Karabakh's self-determination legally realized, with the option of unification with the Armenian homeland as the unstated aspiration. Since Armenia has prevailed militarily, violence is no longer necessary.

Various modalities are observable in the case of Israel's external and internal domains. For sixty years, Jews, including Israelis, have lived outside Israel, where they sometimes experience hostagelike treatment, provoking anxiety in Israel. For example, Israeli immigration officialdom and the Knesset Committee on Immigration are as concerned as they are perplexed by Persian Jews' determination to stay put in Tehran. These foreign citizens are accused of being "wealthy Jewish hostages" to Iran despite their own proclaimed sense of well-being. In turn, the only Jewish Iranian in the national parliament internalizes the Iranian state's hostage logic: "My view is that the actions of Netanyahu and his government, the way they behave towards the Palestinians, cause problems for Jews everywhere."[151]

Without doubt, some Jewish communities outside Israel are treated according to the hostage theory—as local objects for retaliation for the actions of the Israeli state. The *Algemeiner* newspaper reported in 2014 that Turkish leaders declared "Turkish Jews will pay dearly" for the Israeli attack on the Turkish ship *Mavi Marmara*, during which Israeli soldiers killed Turkish citizens. In an open letter to the country's chief rabbi that mixed anti-Semitism with the attribution of vicarious responsibility for Israeli policy, a Turkish newspaper wrote, "You have lived comfortably among us for 500 years and gotten rich at our expense. Is this your gratitude—killing Muslims? Erdoğan, demand that the community leader apologize!"[152] In the subsequent exchange of letters between the US Anti-Defamation League and Turkish president Erdoğan about these matters, the latter diplomatically affirmed the equal rights of Jewish citizens and welcomed the fact that they agreed with him regarding the legitimacy of criticizing Israeli actions in Gaza. One wonders whether they had any choice in the matter.[153] That Erdoğan thinks in terms of hostage logics is not surprising when a major American Jewish organization wrote to him as an advocate of Israeli interests. The American Jewish Congress demanded the return of an award it had bestowed on Erdoğan because of his denunciations of the Israeli bombing of Gaza, which, with characteristic hyperbole, he said "surpassed Hitler in barbarism." The Congress's president lamented that the Turkish leader had become "arguably the most virulent anti-Israel leader in the world."[154]

By coming to terms with the fact that not all Jews will migrate to Israel and by encouraging Israel-diaspora solidarity, the State of Israel has effectively adopted the position of the Muslim League in the 1930s and 1940s: Jewish minorities can be sacrificed to ensure Jewish sovereignty in Israel by having to bear the consequences of its security policies. After all, in the Zionist imaginary, persecution is a logical consequence of living among non-Jews. Until relatively recently, this sacrificial logic existed more by accident than design. The largest attack on Jews abroad was in Argentina in 1994, when the Buenos Aires headquarters of a Jewish organization was blown up by Iranian and Lebanese Hezbollah agents in retaliation for Israel's assassination of Hezbollah secretary general Abbas Musawi and his family in 1992. An Israeli defense ministry official who later worked for the Jewish Agency reported that at the time "nobody thought for a minute to consider that it might affect Jews outside Israel. But it did."[155] In response to such attacks, the Jewish Agency for Israel established a think tank in Jerusalem to seek input into state policy that could affect Jewish communities elsewhere. Now Jewish intelligence agencies well understand that their state's actions reverberate globally.

The moral economy of retributive violence is discernible within Israel itself. When three Israeli settler teenagers were murdered on the West Bank in 2014, three ultra-Orthodox young males kidnapped, tortured, and murdered an East Jerusalem Palestinian boy in retaliation. Two of them were charged with the attempted kidnapping of a seven-year-old boy, assaulting his mother, and setting fire to a Palestinian shop the night before. There was less a casual then a reflective relationship between these crimes and the prime minister's emotive revenge tweets that parsed Hayyim Nahman Bialik's famous poem "On the Slaughter" written after the Kishinev pogrom of 1903: "Vengeance for the blood of a small child, Satan has not yet created. Neither has vengeance for the blood of 3 pure youths who were on their way home to their parents who will not see them anymore." He and the political class instantly distanced themselves from the perpetrators when their "nationalistic" motivations became apparent. So did they: "We're not like the sons of Ishmael [meaning Arabs]. . . . We're Jews. We have a heart. . . . We were wrong. We are merciful Jews. We are human beings."[156]

The retaliatory logic extends to all domains. In response to international pressure and the Israeli Supreme Court's decision that the Jewish West Bank settlement (or "outpost") of Amona is illegal and must be evacuated, Israeli prime minister Benjamin Netanyahu declared that West Bank Palestinians and Arab citizens of Israel who have constructed buildings without permits will also have theirs demolished. Naturally, like Erdoğan, he will not publicly admit to retaliation, but the hostage logic is unmistakably at work—for Palestinians almost never receive building permits, and West Bank Palestinians and Jewish Israelis are subject to different jurisdictions because the former are under military occupation (at least in Areas B and C).[157] The fact that the prime minister can say "The same law that obligates the evacuation of Amona, obligates as well the evacuation of other illegal construction in other parts of the country" indicates his Revisionist-settler conception of the West Bank—as Samaria and Judea, parts of Greater Israel, the historic homeland that he thinks was illegitimately partitioned after the British resolved in 1922 to create Transjordan from 76 percent of the original Palestine Mandate envisaged in the Balfour Declaration and its blessing by the great powers at the San Remo conference.[158] The position of US president Donald Trump to support the settler leaders' annexationist aims suggests that reversing this partition is partisan policy despite what the rest of the world thinks. But what about the Palestinians there, who would increase the Arab minority in Israel? Should they be "transferred" as Hourani predicted, or confined to autonomous zones without Israeli citizenship?[159] Whatever the solution, conferring equal political rights on all Palestinians between the Jordan River and the Mediterranean is inconceivable for the counterpartitionist nation-state that seeks to expand territorially while maintaining the security of ethnic homogeneity.

The modalities of partition violence are all too evident in South Asia as well, whether in the reciprocal violence occasioned by the destruction of the Babri Masjid by Hindu ultranationalists in 1992 or their massacre of Muslims in Gujarat in 2002. In both cases, political capital was to be made by targeting Indian Muslims.[160] Everywhere, ultranationalism is stimulated by globalizations's relentless undermining of national sovereignty; insecurity and uncertainty find their compensation in national homogeneity.[161] In India, the Bharatiya Janata Party (BJP) sounds like the Armenian National Committee of Australia in its positing of essential religious-national culture that endures through the ages: "It weathered the storms of invaders, from the Greeks to the Huns, from the Shakas to the Islamic armies of Turks and Afghans. It fought and resisted external oppression and its essential civilization and culture survived great challenges and attempts at effacement. The glory of Vijayanagara and the heroism of Maharana Pratap, of a Shivaji and of a Guru Govind Singh are testimony to the Indian spirit."[162] Having posited this entity, which many scholars think was invented or at least unified by British orientalists and missionaries in the late nineteenth century, the BJP then attempts to force Indians to live by its fantasy of resilient homogeneity.[163] Faisal Devji's brilliant argument in *Muslim Zion* about the radicalizing consequences of institutionalizing an abstraction like a religious or ethnic definition of a nation can be generalized.[164] The violence of the concept produces the violence on the body. Assimilation into Hebrew culture was not a homecoming for Iraqi Jews, observes Orit Bashkin: "The adoption of Israeli citizenship was a painful, violent and traumatic transformation."[165] The conflict between the Mohajir refugee descendants from India and the people of those places where they settled in Pakistan today belies the notion of the Muslim League's two-nation theory.[166] The homogeneous identity that ultranationalists cultivate must grapple with the hard facts of multiple human differences that their ontologies efface, and the suffering body pays the price.

ACKNOWLEDGMENT

Thanks to Taylor Sherman, Harshan Kumarasingham, Arie Dubnov, Laura Robson, Eric D. Weitz, and the outside readers for helpful comments on earlier drafts. The usual disclaimers apply.

INTRODUCTION

1. For useful overviews of these processes, see Robert Hayden, *From Yugoslavia to the Western Balkans: Studies of a European Disunion, 1991–2011* (Leiden: Brill, 2012); Sabrina Ramet, *Thinking About Yugoslavia: Scholarly Debates About the Yugoslav Breakup and the Wars in Bosnia and Kosovo* (Cambridge: Cambridge University Press, 2005); Mansur Khalid, *The Paradox of Two Sudans: The CPA and the Road to Partition* (Trenton, NJ: Africa World Press, 2015); and John Young, *The Fate of Sudan: The Origins and Consequences of a Flawed Peace Progress* (London: Zed Books, 2012). For a few examples of proposals on dividing Iraq and Syria, see especially Dilip Hiro, "Is Partition a Solution for Syria?," *Yale Global Online*, July 31, 2012, http://yaleglobal.yale.edu/content/partition-solution -syria; Fred Dews, "The Right Way to Partition Iraq (If Necessary)," *Brookings Now*, July 9, 2014, http://www.brookings.edu/blogs/brookings-now/posts/2014/07/the-right-way-to -partition-iraq; Fareed Zakaria, "An Enclave Strategy for Iraq," *Washington Post*, June 19, 2014; Thomas Friedman, "Syria Scorecard," *New York Times*, June 22, 2013; and Nicholas Sambanis and Jonah Schulhofer-Wohl, "Partitions in Practice: The Case Against Dividing Iraq," *Foreign Affairs*, December 1, 2014.

2. See Timothy Mitchell, *Carbon Democracy: Political Power in the Age of Oil* (London: Verso, 2011), for a trenchant summary of the emergence of this new language of "self-determination" and its economic implications for the Western European imperial powers.

3. Susan Pedersen has traced the many ways in which structures of "internationalism" were largely derived from imperial models and imperial ideologies, from the League of Nations onward. See especially her "Empires, States and the League of Nations," in *Internationalisms: A Twentieth-Century History*, ed. Glenda Sluga and Patricia Clavin (Cambridge: Cambridge University Press, 2017), 133–138.

4. On this point and historians' fuzzy understanding of the new political and diplomatic language of the interwar period, see Arie Dubnov, "Notes on the Zionist Passage to India, or: The Analogical Imagination and Its Boundaries," *Journal of Israeli History* 35, no. 3 (2016): 177–214.

5. The emergence of this minority-majority discourse is chronicled in some detail in Eric D. Weitz, "From the Vienna to the Paris System: International Politics and the Entangled Histories of Human Rights, Forced Deportations, and Civilizing Missions," *American Historical Review* 113, no. 5 (2008): 1329–1333, and Mark Mazower, "Minorities and the League of Nations in Interwar Europe," *Daedalus* 126, no. 2 (1997): 47–63. Wilson's revision of "self-determination"—which had emerged as a socialist idea about collectivist political expression within multiethnic states—meant, as Weitz puts

it, "free white men coming together consensually to form a democratic political order." See his "Self-Determination: How a German Enlightenment Idea Became the Slogan of National Liberation and a Human Right," *American Historical Review* 120, no. 2 (2015): 485.

6. With one notable exception—T. G. Fraser's *Partition in Ireland, India, and Palestine: Theory and Practice* (New York: St. Martin's, 1984)—historians of partitions have generally avoided the comparative methods that were (and remain) popular among political scientists. For a "transnational critique" of the comparative approach, see Dubnov, "Notes on the Zionist Passage to India," 8–9.

7. Dictionary definitions of the word "partition"—the infallible *Oxford English Dictionary* provides four different meanings to the verb and a dozen definitions for the noun—provide little help, as they blur the distinctions between division and partition, border and barrier, division and separation. Furthermore, citing etymologies dating back to the fifteenth century, they fail to make clear the novelty of partition as a political idea. See "partition, v." and "partition, n.," OED: Oxford English Dictionary Online, www.oed .com/view/Entry/138297, accessed January 9, 2018.

8. Robert Schaeffer, *Warpaths: The Politics of Partition* (New York: Hill and Wang, 1990), 7.

9. Brendan O'Leary, "Analysing Partition: Definition, Classification and Explanation," *Political Geography* 26 (2007): 886–908, quotation on 888. Like Schaeffer, O'Leary distinguishes between premodern divisions of territory and modern partition, noting that the notion of partition and objections to it "take the nation-state and its national territory for granted," while premodern states "treated lands as real estate. . . . Thus, in feudal and patrimonial regimes, 'partition' had no political meaning outside of estate law; and land divisions were not the subject of debates over their national public legitimacy."

10. This metaphor appeared most notably, though not only, in the Peel Commission report that first proposed the partition of Palestine in 1937. Nationalist opponents of partition often favored organicist imagery as well, rendering it an artificial "cut in the flesh," a violation of the "sacred body" of the "motherland." Before walls or fences were erected, scissors were the leitmotif appearing in cartoons. Emblematically, even when O'Leary attempted to add precision to our discussion, he ended up using metaphorical language to describe partition: "a fresh border cut" through at least one "national homeland," unfastening," "tearing"; see O'Leary, "Analysing Partition," 887.

11. Some scholars have viewed Ulster as the legacy of an early modern settler colonial project that at times rose to the level of genocide; see, for instance, Ben Kiernan, *Blood and Soil: A World History of Genocide and Extermination from Sparta to Darfur* (New Haven, CT: Yale University Press, 2007), 169–212. On the original settlement, see also Nicolas Canny, *Making Ireland British, 1580–1650* (Oxford: Oxford University Press, 2001), and Éamonn Ó Ciardha and Micheál Ó Siochrú, eds., *The Plantation of Ulster: Ideology and Practice* (Manchester: Manchester University Press, 2012). For a useful overview of the Ulster question in the subsequent centuries, see especially Alvin Jackson, *Home Rule: An Irish History, 1800–2000* (New York: Oxford University Press, 2003), and *The Two Unions: Ireland, Scotland, and the Survival of the United Kingdom, 1707–2007* (Oxford: Oxford University Press, 2012).

12. On the 1916 Easter Rising and its wartime context, see Fearghal McGarry, *The Rising: Ireland—Easter 1916* (Oxford: Oxford University Press, 2010); Charles Townshend, *Easter 1916: The Irish Rebellion* (Chicago: Ivan R. Dee, 2006); and Alan Ward, *The Easter Rising: Revolution and Irish Nationalism* (Wheeling, IL: Harlan Davidson, 2003).

13. Robert F. Foster, *Modern Ireland, 1600–1972* (London: Penguin, 2011), 494.

14. This idea is central to much recent literature on violent ethnic conflict in the late Ottoman Empire; see, for instance, Ipek Yosmaoğlu, *Blood Ties: Religion, Violence, and the Politics of Nationhood in Ottoman Macedonia* (Ithaca, NY: Cornell University Press, 2014), and Ryan Gingeras, *Sorrowful Shores: Violence, Ethnicity, and the End of the Ottoman Empire, 1912–1923* (Oxford: Oxford University Press, 2009).

15. Eamon de Valera to David Lloyd George, September 30, 1921, reprinted in *Further Correspondence Relating to the Proposals of His Majesty's Government for an Irish Settlement* (London: His Majesty's Stationery Office, 1921), 11.

16. Quoted in Lee Ward, "Republican Political Theory and Irish Nationalism," *European Legacy* 21, no. 1 (2015): 1–19, quotation on 12.

17. The task was assigned to the Irish Boundary Commission, in charge of interpreting Article XII of the treaty, to come up with such a line, "in accordance with the wishes of the inhabitants, so far as may be compatible with economic and geographical conditions." Quoted in Ged Martin, "The Origins of Partition," in *The Irish Border: History, Politics, Culture*, ed. Malcolm Anderson and Eberhard Bort (Liverpool: Liverpool University Press, 1999), 57–112, quotation on 70. For additional analysis, see K. J. Rankin, "The Role of the Irish Boundary Commission in the Entrenchment of the Irish Border: From Tactical Panacea to Political Liability," *Journal of Historical Geography* 34, no. 3 (2008): 422–447.

18. For more on the Greek-Turkish "population exchange" of 1923, see especially Bruce Clark, *Twice a Stranger: The Mass Expulsions That Forged Modern Greece and Turkey* (Cambridge, MA: Harvard University Press, 2006); Renee Hirshon, *Crossing the Aegean: An Appraisal of the 1923 Compulsory Population Exchange Between Greece and Turkey* (New York: Berghahn Books, 2004); and Onur Yildirim, *Diplomacy and Displacement: Reconsidering the Turco-Greek Exchange of Populations, 1922–1934* (New York: Routledge, 2006).

19. See Laura Robson, *States of Separation: Transfer, Partition, and the Making of the Modern Middle East* (Oakland: University of California Press, 2017); Matthew Frank, "Fantasies of Ethnic Unmixing: Population Transfer and the Collapse of Empire in Europe," in *Refugees and the End of Empire: Imperial Collapse and Forced Migration in the Twentieth Century*, ed. Panikos Panayi and Pippa Virdee (Houndmills, Basingstoke: Palgrave Macmillan, 2011), 81–101; and Umut Özsu, *Formalizing Displacement: International Law and Population Transfers* (Oxford: Oxford University Press, 2015).

20. On this point see Weitz, "From the Vienna to the Paris System"; Aristide R. Zolberg, "The Formation of New States as a Refugee-Generating Process," in *The Global Refugee Problem: U.S. and World Response, Annals of the American Academy of Political and Social Sciences* 467 (1983): 24–38; Nathaniel Berman, *Passion and Ambivalence: Colonialism, Nationalism, and International Law* (Leiden: Brill, 2011); and Robson, *States of Separation*.

21. Quoted in Christopher Sykes, *Crossroads to Israel* (Bloomington: Indiana University Press, 1973), 7.

22. See Laura Robson, *Colonialism and Christianity in Mandate Palestine* (Austin: University of Texas Press, 2011), chap. 2; Bernard Wasserstein, *Herbert Samuel: A Political Life* (Oxford: Clarendon, 1992); and John Strawson, *Partitioning Palestine: Legal Fundamentalism in the Palestinian-Israeli Conflict* (Chicago: University of Chicago Press, 2010), chap. 2.

23. See Barbara J. Smith, *The Roots of Separatism in Palestine: British Economic Policy, 1920–1929* (Syracuse, NY: Syracuse University Press, 1993), and Jacob Metzer, *The Divided Economy of Mandatory Palestine* (Cambridge: Cambridge University Press, 1998).

24. The literature on British policy, Zionist development, and Palestinian nationalism during the mandate years is extensive. On the development of separate political and economic spheres for Arabs and Jews, see particularly Charles Smith, *Palestine and the Arab-Israeli Conflict*, 8th ed. (Boston: Bedford/St. Martin's, 2013); Rashid Khalidi, *The Iron Cage: The Story of the Palestinian Struggle for Statehood* (Boston: Beacon, 2006); and Assaf Likhovski, *Law and Identity in Mandate Palestine* (Chapel Hill: University of North Carolina Press, 2006). On Labor Zionism and its efforts (not always successful) to enforce all-Jewish enclaves in Palestine, see particularly Zachary Lockman, *Comrades and Enemies: Arab and Jewish Workers in Palestine, 1906–1948* (Berkeley: University of California Press, 1996); Gershon Shafir, *Land, Labor, and the Origins of the Israeli-Palestinian Conflict, 1882–1914* (Cambridge: Cambridge University Press, 1989); Zeev Sternhell, *The Founding Myths of Israel: Nationalism, Socialism, and the Making of the Jewish State* (Princeton, NJ: Princeton University Press, 1998); and Mark LeVine, *Overthrowing Geography: Jaffa, Tel Aviv, and the Struggle for Palestine, 1880–1948* (Berkeley: University of California Press, 2001).

25. On the British response and the gradual intensification of the military campaign against the revolt, see particularly Jacob Norris, "Repression and Rebellion: Britain's Response to the Arab Revolt in Palestine of 1936–39," *Journal of Imperial and Commonwealth History* 36, no. 1 (2008): 25–45.

26. John Newsinger, *British Counterinsurgency, from Palestine to Northern Ireland* (London: Palgrave, 2002); Richard Andrew Cahill, "'Going Berserk': 'Black and Tans' in Palestine," *Jerusalem Quarterly* 38 (2009): 59–68; Matthew Hughes, "The Banality of Brutality: British Armed Forces and the Repression of the Arab Revolt in Palestine, 1936–39," *English Historical Review* 124, no. 507 (2009): 313–354. For an intriguing sketch of a transnational history of counterinsurgency, see Laleh Khalili, "The Location of Palestine in Global Counterinsurgencies," *International Journal of Middle East Studies* 42, no. 3 (2010): 413–433.

27. Vladimir (Ze'ev) Jabotinsky, *'Al ha-haluka* [On Partition] (Jerusalem: Berit hatsahar, 1937) (translation ours). It is worth noting that with the outbreak of the Second World War, shortly before his death, Jabotinsky abandoned this view and declared that the Turkish-Greek model was not a failure after all and that the Arab population in Palestine "will have to make room" for the flood of Jewish refugees he expected pouring from Europe. See Vladimir Jabotinsky, "Population Exchanges—Notes in Jabotinsky's Handwriting, in English," Vladimir Ze'ev Jabotinsky Papers, Jabotinsky Institute, Tel-Aviv, Alef-1-2/12, quoted (and discussed) in Gil Rubin, "The Future of the Jews: Planning for the Postwar Jewish World, 1939–1946" (PhD diss., Columbia University, 2017), chap. 2. Notably, Jabotinsky's biographer, Joseph B. Schechtman, gained a reputation as a world-renowned expert on the subject with the publication of his study *European Popula-*

*tion Transfers, 1939–1945* (New York: Oxford University Press, 1946). In 1948 Schecht-man served as an advisor to the Israeli government's Transfer Committee. See also Colin Shindler, "Opposing Partition: The Zionist Predicaments After the Shoah," *Israel Studies* 14, no. 2 (2009): 88–104, and Antonio Ferrara, "Eugene Kulischer, Joseph Schechtman and the Historiography of European Forced Migrations," *Journal of Contemporary History* 46, no. 4 (2011): 715–740.

28. Aaron S. Klieman, "In the Public Domain: The Controversy over Partition for Palestine," *Jewish Social Studies* 42, no. 2 (1980): 147–164; Elad Ben-Dror, "The Success of the Zionist Strategy vis-à-vis UNSCOP," *Israel Affairs* 20, no. 1 (2014): 19–39. On Ihud, see Adi Gordon's contribution to the current volume as well as Paul Mendes-Flohr, *A Land of Two Peoples* (Oxford: Oxford University Press, 1983); Joseph Heller, *Mi-Berit sha-lom le-Ihud: Yehudah Leib Magnes veha-maavak li-medinah du-leumit* [From "Brit Shalom" to "Ihud": Judah L. Magnes and the Struggle for a Binational State] (Jerusalem: Magnes, 2003); and Eric Jacobson, "Why Did Hannah Arendt Reject the Partition of Palestine?," *Journal for Cultural Research* 17, no. 4 (2013), 358–381.

29. Discussed in greater detail in Robson, *States of Separation*, 132ff.

30. The term "civil war" seems to have been introduced three decades ago by the Pal-estinian historian Walid Khalidi but has been absorbed since into the writings of Israeli historians (a rare phenomenon in that contested field of historiography). See Walid Kha-lidi, "A Palestinian Perspective on the Arab-Israeli Conflict," *Journal of Palestine Studies* 14, no. 4 (1985): 35–48; Yoav Gelber, *Palestine, 1948: War, Escape and the Emergence of the Palestinian Refugee Problem* (Brighton: Sussex Academic Press, 2006); Benny Mor-ris, *1948: A History of the First Arab-Israeli War* (New Haven, CT: Yale University Press, 2008); and James L. Gelvin, *The Israel-Palestine Conflict: One Hundred Years of War*, 3rd ed. (Cambridge: Cambridge University Press, 2014), 127.

31. On the 1948 expulsion of the Palestinians, see especially Benny Morris, *The Birth of the Palestinian Refugee Problem, 1947–1949* (Cambridge: Cambridge University Press, 1987), and *The Birth of the Palestinian Refugee Problem Revisited* (Cambridge: Cambridge University Press, 2003); and Avi Shlaim, *Collusion Across the Jordan: King Abdullah, the Zi-onist Movement, and the Partition of Palestine* (New York: Columbia University Press, 1988).

32. As the chapters in this volume show, these parallel trajectories were not hidden from the eyes of the contemporaneous political actors, who assumed that the political futures of the two regions would likely follow a similar pattern. See for example the con-fidential memo composed by Jacob Robinson, "Partition of India: Implications for Pales-tine," June 4 [?], 1948, S25/9029, Central Zionist Archives, Jerusalem. Robinson, director of the Institute for Jewish Affairs in New York and a professor of international law at Columbia University, was appointed legal advisor of the Jewish Agency delegation in New York. In a typical example of transnational "analogical thinking," Robinson prophesied that Palestine would probably follow the same trajectory as India and also made clear references to Home Rule and the Ulster problem in Ireland. A few days later, Chaim Weizmann wrote to Lord Mountbatten, India's last viceroy, stating that creating a "Pal-estinian Pakistan" would be the best solution to the Palestine problem. See Weizmann to Mountbatten, June 10, 1947, 2725, Weizmann Archive, Rehovot, Israel. For further analysis of this parallelism, see Lucy Chester's chapter included in the present collection.

33. In the Bengali case, for instance, this early, local administrative partition was initially considered a welcome move in the eyes of the Hindu leadership, eager to restore an influence that had long been in decline and increasingly anxious, in this era of communalism, about living "under the sway of 'Muslim majority.'" Joya Chatterji, *The Spoils of Partition: Bengal and India, 1947–1967* (Cambridge: Cambridge University Press, 2007), 71. On the making of communalism more generally, see especially Gyanendra Pandey, *The Construction of Communalism in Colonial North India* (Delhi: Oxford University Press, 1994); Suranjan Dass, *Communal Riots in Bengal, 1905–1947* (Delhi: Oxford University Press, 1991); and Partha Chatterjee, *The Nation and Its Fragments: Colonial and Postcolonial Histories* (Princeton, NJ: Princeton University Press, 1993).

34. See, for instance, Nicholas Dirks, *Castes of Mind: Colonialism and the Making of Modern India* (Princeton, NJ: Princeton University Press, 2001); Ayesha Jalal, "Exploding Communalism: The Politics of Muslim Identity," in *Nationalism, Democracy and Development: State and Politics in India,* ed. Ayesha Jalal and Sugata Bose (Delhi: Oxford University Press, 1998), 76–103; and C. A. Bayly, *Indian Society and the Making of the British Empire* (Cambridge: Cambridge University Press, 1988). This practice was subsequently exported to the Middle East, particularly British-controlled Egypt and Palestine; see C. A. Bayly's exploration of parallels between Egypt and India with regard to religious minorities in his "Representing Copts and Muhammadans: Empire, Nation, and Community in Egypt and India, 1880–1914," in *Modernity and Culture: From the Mediterranean to the Indian Ocean,* ed. Leila Fawaz and C. A. Bayly (New York: Columbia University Press, 2002), 158–203; and Robson, *Colonialism and Christianity in Mandate Palestine,* chap. 2.

35. The meaning and origins of the "two-nation" theory are discussed in Stephen P. Cohen, *The Idea of Pakistan* (Washington, DC: Brookings Institution Press, 2004), chap. 1, and Mridu Rai, "Jinnah and the Demise of a Hindu Politician?," *History Workshop Journal* 62 (2006): 232–240.

36. For an assessment of various scholarly positions on this question, see Rai, "Jinnah and the Demise of a Hindu Politician?," and Ayesha Jalal, *The Sole Spokesman: Jinnah, the Muslim League, and the Demand for Pakistan* (Cambridge: Cambridge University Press, 1985).

37. Sugata Bose and Ayesha Jalal note that "the majority of legislators in both provinces rejected partition; the decisive votes in favor of partition were cast by east Punjab and west Bengal legislators acting under Congress whip," the Congress hoping that a partition decision would assure it full control over the Hindu majority provinces. See Sugata Bose and Ayesha Jalal, *Modern South Asia: History, Culture, Political Economy* (London: Routledge, 2011), 152–153. A number of scholars have pointed out that support for partition was strongest in the Muslim-minority provinces and fairly weak in the majority areas where Pakistan was ultimately established; see, for instance, Stephen Cohen, who notes in his 2004 book on the subject: "Support for the Muslim League and a separate Muslim state had been strongest in North India, where Muslims had been in a minority. However, Pakistan was established on the periphery of the subcontinent, where Muslims were in a majority but support for Pakistan was weak" (*The Idea of Pakistan,* 36).

38. Bose and Jalal, *Modern South Asia,* 154.

39. For a detailed look at their political and technological development, see Sumit Ganguly and Devin T. Hagerty, *Fearful Symmetry: India-Pakistan Crises in the Shadow of Nuclear Weapons* (Seattle: University of Washington Press, 2005).

40. See Pedersen, "Empires, States and the League of Nations," 133–138.

41. For a political science argument against ad hoc partitions, see James D. Fearon, "Separatist Wars, Partition, and World Order," *Security Studies* 13, no. 4 (2004): 394–415.

42. Tai Yong Tan and Gyanesh Kudaisya, *The Aftermath of Partition in South Asia* (London: Routledge, 2000).

43. W. H. [Wystan Hugh] Auden, "Partition," *Collected Poems* (New York: Random House, 1976), 604. Auden's poem is dated May 1966.

44. John Boulting and Jeffrey F. Dell (directors), *Carlton-Browne of the F.O.* (London: Charter Film Productions, 1959).

45. Joya Chatterji, *The Spoils of Partition: Bengal and India, 1947–1967* (Cambridge: Cambridge University Press, 2007); Yasmin Khan, *The Great Partition: The Making of India and Pakistan* (New Haven, CT: Yale University Press); Vazira Fazila-Yacoobali Zamindar, *The Long Partition and the Making of Modern South Asia: Refugees, Boundaries, Histories* (New York: Columbia University Press, 2007).

46. Urvashi Butalia, *The Other Side of Silence: Voices from the Partition of India* (Durham, NC: Duke University Press, 2000), 5, 275–276.

47. Gyanesh Kudaisya, "The 'Regional' Turn in the Writing of Modern Indian History: Some Notes on the State of the Field," *South Asia* 39, no. 1 (2016): 277.

48. For some key examples of this outcome- and memory-focused literature, see Gyanendra Pandey, *Remembering Partition: Violence, Nationalism and History in India* (Cambridge: Cambridge University Press, 2001); Zamindar, *The Long Partition*; and Ayesha Jalal, *The Pity of Partition: Manto's Life, Times, and Work Across the India-Pakistan Divide* (Princeton, NJ: Princeton University Press, 2013). It has significant parallels in the literature on the Palestinian *nakba*; see, for instance, Nur Masalha, "Remembering the Palestinian Nakba: Commemoration, Oral History and Narratives of Memory," *Holy Land Studies* 7, no. 2 (2008): 123–156; Ahmad H. Sa'di and Lila Abu-Lughod, eds., *Nakba: Palestine, 1948, and the Claims of Memory* (New York: Columbia University Press, 2007); and in literature on Ireland, for instance, Ian McBride, ed., *History and Memory in Modern Ireland* (Cambridge: Cambridge University Press, 2001).

49. See, for instance, the once-popular though fundamentally erroneous work by Joan Peters, *From Time Immemorial: The Origins of the Arab-Jewish Conflict over Palestine* (New York: Harper and Row, 1984), a work so inaccurate that the London *Spectator* called it "a piece of disinformation roughly the size and weight of a dried cowpat"—one of many scathing reviews unearthed and discussed in Norman Finklestein, *Image and Reality of the Israel-Palestine Conflict* (London: Verso, 2003), 45.

50. See note 33 above as well as Shmuel Dothan, *Pulmus-Ha-Halukah Bi-Tekufat Ha-Mandat* [The Partition Controversy During the British Mandate in Palestine] (Jerusalem: Yad Yitzhak Ben Zvi, 1979); Itzhak Galnoor, *The Partition of Palestine: Decision Crossroads in the Zionist Movement* (Albany: State University of New York Press, 1995); and Joseph Heller, "The Anglo-American Committee of Inquiry on Palestine (1945–1946): The

Zionist Reaction Reconsidered," in *Essential Papers on Zionism*, eds. Jehuda Reinharz and Anita Shapira (New York: New York University Press, 1996), 689–723.

51. See, for instance, Constantine Zurayk, *The Meaning of the Disaster* (Beirut: Khayat's College Book Comparative, 1956); Walid Khalidi, ed., *From Haven to Conquest: Readings in Zionism and the Palestine Problem Until 1948* (Beirut: Institute for Palestine Studies, 1971); Albert Hourani, *A History of the Arab Peoples* (Cambridge, MA: Belknap, 1991); and, before 1948, George Antonius, *The Arab Awakening* (London: Hamilton, 1938).

52. See in particular Morris, *The Birth of the Palestinian Refugee Problem, 1947–1949*; Shlaim, *Collusion Across the Jordan*; and Ilan Pappe, *The Making of the Arab-Israeli Conflict, 1947–1951* (London: Tauris, 1992).

53. Nur Masalha, *Expulsion of the Palestinians: The Concept of "Transfer" in Zionist Political Thought* (Washington, DC: Institute for Palestine Studies, 1992). Some of his subsequent work expands on this theme; see *A Land Without a People: Israel, Transfer and the Palestinians, 1949–96* (London: Faber and Faber, 1997), and *The Politics of Denial: Israel and the Palestinian Refugee Problem* (London: Pluto, 2003).

54. The more recent literature has tended to focus on social history and on political economy; see, for instance, Ted Swedenburg, *Memories of Revolt: The 1936–1939 Rebellion and the Palestinian National Past* (Minneapolis: University of Minnesota Press, 1995); Ellen Fleischmann, *The Nation and Its "New" Women: The Palestinian Women's Movement, 1920–1948* (Berkeley: University of California Press, 2003); Robson, *Colonialism and Christianity in Mandate Palestine*; Jacob Norris, *Land of Progress: Palestine in the Age of Colonial Development, 1905–1948* (Oxford: Oxford University Press, 2013); and Sherene Seikaly, *Men of Capital: Scarcity and Economy in Mandate Palestine* (Stanford, CA: Stanford University Press, 2015).

55. This situation was worsened by the difficulties Palestinian researchers have faced finding relevant archival sources, which are scattered in any number of often-inaccessible archives across the Middle East, within Israel, and in the United Kingdom. Unsurprisingly, much literature on the *nakba* has had to focus on oral sources and questions of memory; see, for instance, Anaheed Al-Hardan, *Palestinians in Syria: Nakba Memories of Shattered Communities* (New York: Columbia University Press, 2016).

56. Musa Alami, "The Lesson of Palestine," *Middle East Journal* 3, no. 4 (1949): 373–405, quotation on 388.

57. Ariella Azoulay and Adi Ophir, *The One-State Condition: Occupation and Democracy in Israel/Palestine* (Palo Alto, CA: Stanford University Press, 2012), 3; Neve Gordon, *Israel's Occupation* (Berkeley: University of California Press, 2008), 26.

58. As Azoulay and Ophir put it: "Half a century is a very long time in modern history. One cannot possibly regard such a long-lasting political situation as a historical 'accident' that happened to the State of Israel. . . . A new conceptual grid is necessary in order to explain *that* and *how* Israelis and Palestinians have been governed since 1967 by the same ruling power, within the bounds of the same regime." See *The One-State Condition*, 11.

59. For a brief overview of this colonial political economy in the occupied territories, see Gelvin, *The Israel-Palestine Conflict*, 183–189; for a more detailed account, see Sara Roy, *The Gaza Strip: The Political Economy of De-Development* (Washington, DC: Institute for Palestine Studies, 1995).

60. Amos Oz, *How to Cure a Fanatic* (Princeton, NJ: Princeton University Press, 2010), 1–36; Amos Oz, *Dear Zealots: Letters from a Divided Land*, trans. Jessica Cohen (Boston: Random House, 2018).

61. This conclusion was eventually shared by other analysts, including Edward Said, who in 2000 described what he saw as "Oslo's malign genius, that even Israel's 'concessions' were so heavily encumbered with conditions and qualifications and entailments that they could not be enjoyed by the Palestinians in any way resembling self-determination." On Arafat's concessions, he continued: "Caught between his own track record of having already signed seven years of peace process agreements with Israel and the prospect of signing what was obviously meant to be the last one, Yasir Arafat balked ... he might have awakened to the enormity of what he had already signed away (I would like to think that his nightmares are made up of unending rides on the bypassing roads in Area C)." See *From Oslo to Iraq and the Road Maps: Essays* (New York: Pantheon, 2004), 12, 23.

62. See, among others, Geoffrey Arenson, "Settlement Monitor," *Journal of Palestine Studies* 42, no. 2 (2013): 143–158.

63. Tony Judt, "What Is to Be Done?," in *When the Facts Change: Essays, 1995–2010* (New York: Penguin, 2015), 165.

64. See, for instance, Michael Laffan, *The Partition of Ireland* (Dublin: Dublin Academic Press, 1983); Stephen Duffy, *The Integrity of Ireland: Home Rule, Nationalism, and Partition, 1912–1922* (Madison, NJ: Fairleigh Dickinson University Press, 2009); and James Anderson and Liam O'Dowd, "Imperialism and Nationalism: The Home Rule Struggle and Border Creation in Ireland, 1885–1925," *Political Geography* 26, no. 8 (2007): 934–950, all of which draw fairly straight lines between the late-nineteenth-century conversations surrounding "Home Rule" and the specifics of the border negotiations of 1921.

65. Nicholas Mansergh, *The Prelude to Partition: Concepts and Aims in Ireland and India* (Cambridge: Cambridge University Press, 1978), and *The Unresolved Question: The Anglo-Irish Settlement and Its Undoing 1912–72* (New Haven, CT: Yale University Press, 1991). The historiography of the partition question in general and Mansergh's specific contributions in particular are dealt with in Antoine Mioche, "India or North America? Reflections on Nicholas Mansergh's Partition Paradigm," *Eire-Ireland* 42, nos. 1–2 (2007): 290–310.

66. Margaret O'Callahan, "Genealogies of Partition: History, History-Writing, and 'The Troubles' in Ireland," *Critical Review of International Social and Political Philosophy* 9, no. 4 (2006): 619–634, quotation on 623.

67. See, for instance, Thomas Hennessey, *Dividing Ireland: World War I and Partition* (London: Routledge, 1998), and Stacie Goddard, *Indivisible Territory and the Politics of Legitimacy: Jerusalem and Northern Ireland* (Cambridge: Cambridge University Press, 2010).

68. For examples of this "new" imperial approach, see David Lambert and Alan Lester, eds., *Colonial Lives Across the British Empire: Imperial Careering in the Long Nineteenth Century* (Cambridge: Cambridge University Press, 2006), which focuses on how "ideas, practices and identities developed trans-imperially as the moved from one imperial site to another" (2); and Nicholas Dirks, who comments similarly that "we need to see colonialism less as 'a process that began in the European metropole and expanded outwards' and more as 'a moment when new encounters within the world facilitated the formation

of categories of metropole and colony in the first space" (*Colonialism and Culture* [Ann Arbor: University of Michigan Press, 2001], 6). These historians offer a useful approach but have not themselves sought to apply it to the comparative study of partition as an imperial tactic.

69. J. G. A. Pocock, "The Limits and Divisions of British History: In Search of the Unknown Subject," *American Historical Review* 87, no. 2 (1982): 311–336, quotation on 313.

70. Chaim Kaufmann, "When All Else Fails: Ethnic Population Transfers and Partitions in the Twentieth Century," *International Security* 23, no. 2 (1998): 120–156, quotation on 154.

71. Thomas Chapman and Philip G. Roeder, "Partition as a Solution to Wars of Nationalism: The Importance of Institutions," *American Political Science Review* 101, no. 4 (2007): 677–691, quotation on 677.

72. Nicholas Sambanis and Jonah Schulhofer-Wohl, "What's in a Line? Is Partition a Solution to Civil War?," *International Security* 34, no. 2 (2009): 82–118, quotation on 83.

73. On the definition of the word "minority" and its emergence as a concept in diplomatic exchange, see Benjamin Thomas White, *The Emergence of Minorities in the Middle East: The Politics of Community in French Mandate Syria* (Edinburgh: Edinburgh University Press, 2011); Seteney Shami, "'Aqalliyya/Minority' in Modern Egyptian Discourse," in *Words in Motion: Towards a Global Lexicon*, ed. Carol Gluck and Anna Lowenhaupt Tsing (Durham, NC: Duke University Press, 2009); and Robson, *States of Separation*, especially chap. 3.

74. A. Dirk Moses, "Partitions and the Sisyphean Making of Peoples," *Refugee Watch* 46 (2015): 36–50, quotation on 39.

75. The centrality of these nineteenth- and twentieth-century British imperial preoccupations to partition helps explain the relative absence of the idea from French imperial circles in the same period; it may also help to explain the concomitant imperial interest in federations being explored at the same time. See, for instance, Jason Parker, "The Failure of the West Indies Federation," in *Ultimate Adventures with Britannia*, ed. Wm. Roger Louis (London: Tauris, 2009), 235–246.

76. Edward Said, *The World, the Text, and the Critic* (Cambridge, MA: Harvard University Press, 1983), 226–227.

77. Geoffrey Wheatcroft, "The Myth of Malicious Partition," in *Penultimate Adventures with Britannia: Personalities, Politics and Culture in Britain*, ed. William Roger Louis (London: I. B. Tauris, 2008), 153–167.

78. Hiro, "Is Partition a Solution for Syria?"

79. For just a few examples of this conversation, see James Stavridis, "It's Time to Seriously Consider Partitioning Syria," *Foreign Policy*, March 9, 2016, and Barak Mendelsohn, "Divide and Conquer in Syria and Iraq: Why the West Should Plan for a Partition," *Foreign Affairs*, November 29, 2015.

CHAPTER 1

1. Aamir R. Mufti has written an important book on this theme, *Enlightenment in the Colony: The Jewish Question and the Crisis of Postcolonial Culture* (Princeton, NJ: Princeton University Press, 2007).

2. Jacqueline Rose, *The Question of Zion* (Princeton, NJ: Princeton University Press, 2005), 83.

3. For a fine discussion of the ambiguity of national belonging in Israel, see Zali Gurevitch, "The Double Site of Israel," in *Grasping Land: Space and Place in Contemporary Israeli Discourse and Experience*, ed. Eyal Ben-Ary and Yoram Bilu (Albany: State University of New York Press, 1997), 203–216.

4. Beni Prasad, *The Hindu-Muslim Questions* (Allahabad: Kitabistan, 1941), 69.

5. Syed Abdul Vahid, ed., *Thoughts and Reflections of Iqbal* (Lahore: Sh. Muhammad Ashraf, 1992), 50–51.

6. Ibid.

7. Muhammad Iqbal, *Stray Reflections* (Lahore: Sh. Ghulam Ali and Sons, 1961), 15.

8. See, for instance, the second chapter of Iqbal's *The Reconstruction of Religious Thought in Islam* (New Delhi: Kitab Bhavan, 1990).

9. Cited in Souleymane Bachir Diagne, *Bergson postcoloniale: l'élan vital dans la pensée de Léopold Sédar Senghor et de Mohamed Iqbal* (Paris: CNRS Éditions, 2011), 65.

10. See his *Reconstruction*, especially chaps. 2 and 5.

11. Vahid, *Thoughts and Reflections of Iqbal*, 75.

12. Ibid., 60.

13. Ibid., 163.

14. Ibid., 162.

15. Ibid., 193.

16. Iqbal, *Stray Reflections*, 29.

17. Muhammad Iqbal, *Kulliyat-e Iqbal Farsi* (Lahore: Iqbal Academy, 1990), 134. Translation by Arthur J. Arberry, in Muhammad Iqbal, *The Mysteries of Selflessness* (London: John Murray, 1953), 40–41.

18. Iqbal, *Kulliyat-e Iqbal Farsi*, 144–145, trans. Arberry, *Mysteries*, 51.

19. Vahid, *Thoughts and Reflections of Iqbal*, 167–168.

20. Ibid., 173.

21. Iqbal, *Kulliyat-e Iqbal Farsi*, 554–555. Translation by Arthur A. Arberry, in Sir Muhammad Iqbal, *Javid-Nama* (London: George Allen and Unwin, 1966), 69–70.

22. Iqbal, *Kulliyat-e Iqbal Farsi*, 551–552. My translation heavily modifies Arberry's in *Javid-Nama*, 67–68.

23. Vahid, *Thoughts and Reflections of Iqbal*, 42.

24. Ibid., 78.

25. Iqbal, *Kulliyat-e Iqbal Farsi*, 489, trans. Arberry, *Javid-Nama*, 26–27.

26. The most sophisticated work on Iqbal now seems to be published in French. For a discussion of Iqbal's theology, see Abdennour Bidar, *L'Islam face à la mort de Dieu* (Paris: François Bourin Editeur, 2010).

27. Muhammad Iqbal, "Jibril-o Iblis," in *Kulliyat-e Iqbal Urdu* (Aligarh: Educational Book House, 1997), 435. My translation.

28. Iqbal, *Kulliyat-e Iqbal Farsi*, 656. My translation is a heavily modified version of Arberry's in *Javid-Nama*, 135.

29. S. Hasan Ahmad, *Iqbal: His Political Ideas at Crossroads* (Aligarh: Printwell, 1979), 80. Iqbal's correspondence with Thompson forms part of the latter's papers in the Bodleian

Library at Oxford University, and facsimiles of it have been published together with a commentary in Ahmad's book.

30. Gabriel Piterberg, *The Returns of Zionism: Myths, Politics and Scholarship in Israel* (London: Verso, 2008), chap. 5.

31. See Naveeda Khan, "The Law and the Ahmadi Question," in *Muslim Becoming: Aspiration and Skepticism in Pakistan* (Durham, NC: Duke University Press, 2012), 91–119.

32. Muhammad Iqbal, *The Development of Metaphysics in Persia: A Contribution to the History of Muslim Philosophy* (Lahore: Bazm-i-Iqbal, 1959), 144.

33. For the changing tradition of being "crazy" with God but "careful" of Muhammad, see C. M. Naim, "Be Crazy with God, . . ." *Outlook*, December 27, 2012, http://www .outlookindia.com/article.aspx?283453#1.

34. Vahid, *Thoughts and Reflections of Iqbal*, 249.

35. Ibid., 250.

36. Ibid., 252.

37. Ibid., 273.

38. Ibid., 259–260.

39. Ibid., 260.


CHAPTER 2

I thank Nir Arielli, Maria Birnbaum, Priya Satia, Penny Sinanoglou, Ran Shauli, Peter Stansky, and Bernard Wasserstein for reading and providing valuable feedback on earlier drafts of this chapter. The research this chapter is based upon was supported in part by the Israel Science Foundation (grant No. 1012/16).

1. For a critique of comparative history, see my "Notes on the Zionist Passage to India, or: The Analogical Imagination and Its Boundaries," *Journal of Israel History* 35, no. 2 (2016): 177–214. For a comparative history of the three partitions, see T. G. Fraser, *Partition in Ireland, India, and Palestine: Theory and Practice* (New York: St. Martin's, 1984).

2. Reginald Coupland, *The Cripps Mission* (London: Oxford University Press, 1942).

3. Alfred E. Zimmern, *The Greek Commonwealth: Politics and Economics in Fifth-Century Athens* (Oxford: Clarendon, 1911), 70, 188, 482, and *passim*.

4. Jeanne Morefield, *Covenants Without Swords: Idealist Liberalism and the Spirit of Empire* (Princeton, NJ: Princeton University Press, 2005), esp. chap. 2; Reba N. Soffer, *Discipline and Power: The University, History, and the Making of an English Elite, 1870–1930* (Stanford, CA: Stanford University Press, 1994); Reba N. Soffer, *History, Historians, and Conservatism in Britain and America from the Great War to Thatcher and Reagan* (Oxford: Oxford University Press, 2009).

5. R. Coupland to Gilbert Murray, September 14, 1912, Papers of Sir Reginald Coupland (1), MSS. Brit. Emp. s. 403, 1904–1948, Bodleian Library of Commonwealth and African Studies at Rhodes House, University of Oxford (hereafter Coupland Papers [1]), Box 1, file 2, item 8. Coupland cherished many of his juvenilia and student lecture notes from that period, including an essay entitled "Carthage, a study in Empire" (circa 1910), miscellaneous "Greek History Chapters" and an unpublished essay on "English mutations of Greek Tragedy," that found their way to Coupland Papers (1), Box 1, file 2, items 1 and 5–9.

6. R. Coupland to Winston S. Churchill, May 26, 1915, Papers of Sir Winston Churchill (Chartwell Papers), CHAR 2/65/64.

7. J. R. [John Robert] Seeley, *The Expansion of England*, ed. John Clive (Chicago: University of Chicago Press, 1971 [1882]), 38. For an expanded historiographical discussion, see Amanda Behm, *Imperial History and the Global Politics of Exclusion: Britain, 1880–1940* (London: Palgrave Macmillan, 2018).

8. See in particular H. E. [Hugh Edward] Egerton, *A Short History of British Colonial Policy* (London: Methuen, 1897). Coupland was the one who wrote the entry on his former mentor for the *Oxford Dictionary of National Biography*. See [Reginald Coupland], "Egerton, Hugh Edward (1855–1927)," in *Oxford Dictionary of National Biography*, ed. J. R. H. Weaver (London: Oxford University Press, H. Milford, 1937), 285–286.

9. Hugh Edward Egerton, *Federations and Unions Within the British Empire* (Oxford: Clarendon, 1911), 8.

10. The origins of this branch of liberal thought were brilliantly recaptured by Duncan Bell and Theodore Koditschek, as well in the constantly growing body of literature dedicated to imperial liberalism. See Duncan Bell, *The Idea of Greater Britain: Empire and the Future of World Order, 1860–1900* (Princeton, NJ: Princeton University Press, 2007); and Theodore Koditschek, *Liberalism, Imperialism and the Historical Imagination: Nineteenth Century Visions of Greater Britain* (Cambridge: Cambridge University Press, 2011). See also Uday Singh Mehta, *Liberalism and Empire: A Study in Nineteenth-Century British Liberal Thought* (Chicago: University of Chicago Press, 1999); Jennifer Pitts, *A Turn to Empire: The Rise of Imperial Liberalism in Britain and France* (Princeton, NJ: Princeton University Press, 2005); and Karuna Mantena, *Alibis of Empire: Henry Maine and the Ends of Liberal Imperialism* (Princeton, NJ: Princeton University Press, 2010).

11. On this point, I follow Alex May, who suggests that Coupland "was always to be found on the more 'democratic' wing of the Round Table." See Alex C. May "The Round Table, 1910–66" (PhD diss., Oxford University, 1995), 61. On Curtis's early work with Milner and Jan Smuts in South Africa, see Walter Nimocks, *Milner's Young Men: The "Kindergarten" in Edwardian Imperial Affairs* (Durham, NC: Duke University Press, 1968).

12. Max Beloff, *Imperial Sunset*, Vol. 2: *Dream of Commonwealth, 1921–42* (Houndmills, Basingstoke: Macmillan, 1987), 6–7; see also Max Beloff, "Dream of Commonwealth," *Round Table* 60, no. 240 (1970): 463–470, and Frederick Madden, "The Commonwealth, Commonwealth History and Oxford, 1905–1971," in *Oxford and the Idea of Commonwealth: Essays Presented to Sir Edgar Williams*, ed. David K. Fieldhouse and Frederick Madden (London: Croom Helm, 1982), 7–29.

13. J. R. M. [James Ramsay Montagu] Butler, *Lord Lothian, Philip Kerr, 1882–1940* (New York: St. Martin's, 1960); David Reynolds, "Lord Lothian and Anglo-American Relations, 1939–1940," *Transactions of the American Philosophical Society* 73, no. 2 (1983): 1–65.

14. "South Africa: Richard Feetham, C.M.G.," *Round Table* 56, no. 222 (1966): 205–208. For additional biographical information, consult the Papers of the Hon. Richard Feetham, MSS. Afr. s. 1793, Bodleian Library of Commonwealth and African Studies at Rhodes House, Oxford University.

15. See Deborah Lavin's introduction to *Friendship and Union: The South African Letters of Patrick Duncan and Maud Selborne, 1907–1943*, ed. Beatrix Maud Cecil Selborne and Deborah Lavin (Cape Town: Van Riebeeck Society, 2010).

16. [R. H. Brand], "John Dove," *Round Table* 24, no. 95 (1934): 463–468. See also John E. Kendle, *The Round Table Movement and Imperial Union* (Toronto: University of Toronto Press, 1975); and Deborah Lavin, *From Empire to International Commonwealth: A Biography of Lionel Curtis* (Oxford: Clarendon, 1995).

17. According to one suggestion, the name "The Moot," which later referred to the editorial committee of the *Round Table* journal, originated in the title Leo Amery gave to these meetings.

18. Ralph Furse, future director of recruitment in the Colonial Service, was Coupland's competitor for the job. See Ralph Furse, *Aucuparius: Recollection of a Recruiting Officer* (London: Oxford University Press, 1962), 35–36. During the 1920s, Furse served as private secretary to successive secretaries of state, including Lord Milner, Churchill, Leo Amery, and Lord Passfield.

19. For example, Coupland to R. H. Brand, February 23, 1918, Papers of the Round Table, 1904–1971, MS. Eng. Hist. c. 847, Bodleian Library, Oxford University, f. 4–7; Coupland to Colclough, June 3, 1918, ibid., f. 127–128.

20. Jeanne Morefield, *Empires Without Imperialism: Anglo-American Decline and the Politics of Deflection* (New York: Oxford University Press, 2014), 101.

21. Coupland Papers (1), Box 3. The box contains a proof version (dated 1920) and table of contents of a book manuscript that was prepared for Clarendon Press. Though unpublished, some of these ideas did make their way into the first articles he published in the *Round Table*.

22. [Reginald Coupland], "The Last Phase," *Round Table* 7, no. 26 (March 1917): 195–217, quotation on 211.

23. [Reginald Coupland], "Freedom and Unity," *Round Table* 8, no. 29 (December 1917): 85–99, quotation on 85.

24. Reginald Coupland, *The Quebec Act: A Study in Statesmanship* (Oxford: Clarendon, 1925), and Reginald Coupland, "Foundation of British Commonwealth," *Times*, March 1, 1929, 9. See also Coupland's introduction to an abridged version of John George Lambton Durham, *Durham Report*, ed. Reginald Coupland (London: Clarendon, 1945), v–lxviii.

25. John McColgan, "Implementing the 1921 Treaty: Lionel Curtis and Constitutional Procedure," *Irish Historical Studies* 20, no. 79 (1977): 312–333; Nicholas Mansergh, *The Unresolved Question: The Anglo-Irish Settlement and Its Undoing, 1912–72* (New Haven, CT: Yale University Press, 1991), chaps. 6–7; Margaret O'Callaghan, "Old Parchment and Water: The Boundary Commission of 1925 and the Copperfastening of the Irish Border," *Bullan; An Irish Studies Journal* 1, no. 5 (2000): 27–55.

26. David Harkness, "Britain and the Independence of the Dominions: The 1921 Cross-Roads," in *Nationality and the Pursuit of National Independence*, ed. Donnchadh Ó Corráin and T. W. Moody (Belfast: Appletree, for the Irish Committee of Historical Sciences, 1978), 141.

27. J. E. [John Edward] Kendle, "The Round Table Movement and 'Home Rule All Round,'" *Historical Journal* 11, no. 2 (1968): 332–353; J. E. Kendle, *Federal Britain: A History*

(London: Routledge, 1997), chaps. 1–4; George Boyce, "Federalism and the Irish Question," in *The Federal Idea*, Vol. 1: *The History of Federalism from Enlightenment to 1945*, ed. Andrea Bosco (London: Lothian Foundation Press, 1991), 119–138; Alvin Jackson, *Home Rule: An Irish History, 1800–2000* (New York: Oxford University Press, 2003), chap. 9.

28. [Coupland], "Freedom and Unity," 93, 97, 96.

29. For biographical details, see "Mr. F. S. Oliver [obituary]," *Times*, June 5, 1934, 19; G. M. Trevelyan, "Mr. F. S. Oliver: An Appreciation," *Times*, June 6, 1934, 9; Richard Davenport-Hines, "Oliver, Frederick Scott (1864–1934)," *Oxford Dictionary of National Biography* (London: Oxford University Press, 2004), online at Oxford DNB, https://doi .org/10.1093/ref:odnb/35305, accessed December 12, 2012.

30. J. E. [John Edward] Kendle, *Ireland and the Federal Solution: The Debate over the United Kingdom Constitution, 1870–1920* (Montreal: McGill–Queen's University Press, 1989), chap. 3.

31. F. S. [Frederick Scott] Oliver, *Alexander Hamilton: An Essay on American Union* (London: A. Constable, 1907). Daniel Gorman went as far as suggesting that Curtis was attracted to Oliver's Hamiltonian model, considering it "the ideal template for a commonwealth." See Daniel Gorman, "Lionel Curtis, Imperial Citizenship, and the Quest for Unity," *Historian* 66, no. 1 (2004): 67–96, quotation on 85.

32. Oliver, *Alexander Hamilton*, 453–454.

33. E.g., see H. E. [Hugh Edward] Egerton to Reginald Coupland, April 27, 1916, in Coupland Papers (1), Box 4, file 1, ff. 1–2.

34. Reginald Coupland, *Welsh and Scottish Nationalism: A Study* (London: Collins, 1954), 240.

35. Reginald Coupland, *The Study of the British Commonwealth: An Inaugural Lecture Delivered Before the University of Oxford on 19 November, 1921* (Oxford: Clarendon, 1921). Coupland resigned from the editorship of the *Round Table* journal in late 1919 in order to secure the Beit Professorship. However, in letters he sent Philip Kerr, he stated explicitly that he saw the Beit Professorship as being "both in my own interests and those of the Round Table," and on another occasion, he went as far as describing himself, probably without any irony, as "not so much . . . a person as a vehicle of Imperial work." See Coupland to P. Kerr, March 13, 1919, and December 15, 1928, quoted in May, "The Round Table," 228, 235.

36. Reginald Coupland, "Reflections on a Visit to Dublin," in *The Empire in These Days: An Interpretation* (London: Macmillan, 1935), 57–78, quotation on 70.

37. Penny Sinanoglou, "British Plans for the Partition of Palestine, 1929–1938," *Historical Journal* 52, no. 1 (2009): 131–152; Penny Sinanoglou, "The Peel Commission and Partition, 1936–1938," in *Britain, Palestine, and Empire: The Mandate Years*, ed. Rory Miller (Burlington: Ashgate, 2010), 118–140, as well as her contribution to the current volume.

38. Matthew Frank, "Fantasies of Ethnic Unmixing: Population Transfer and the Collapse of Empire in Europe," in *Refugees and the End of Empire: Imperial Collapse and Forced Migration in the Twentieth Century*, ed. Panikos Panayi and Pippa Virdee (Houndmills, Basingstoke: Palgrave Macmillan, 2011), 81–101.

39. Arnold J. Toynbee, *The Western Question in Greece and Turkey: A Study in the Contact of Civilizations* (New York: Howard Fertig, 1970 [1923]), 18.

40. [Arnold J. Toynbee], "The Outlook in the Middle East," *Round Table* 10, no. 37 (December 1919): 55–97, quotations on 60, 97.

41. [Reginald Coupland], "Turkey, Russia and Islam," *Round Table* 8, no. 29 (December 1917): 100–138, esp. 107–111.

42. Coupland, *The Study of the British Commonwealth*, 6, 9, 16.

43. Reginald Coupland, "Freedom and Unity [1924]," in *The Empire in These Days: An Interpretation* (London: Macmillan, 1935), 32–49, quotation on 47.

44. Edmund Burke, *Reflections on the Revolution in France* (London: Penguin, 1968 [1790]). Burke applied the idea of trust to colonial rule during the Hastings affair, using it to signify a moral method of governing India. For him, to impose rule upon "backward" peoples for the sake of their advancement was not only a right, but a moral duty; see Edmund Burke, "Speech on Fox's East India Bill [1783]," in *The Writings and Speeches of Edmund Burke*, Vol. 5: *India: Madras and Bengal, 1774–1785*, ed. P. J. Marshall and William B. Todd (Oxford: Clarendon, 1981), 378–404.

45. Peter Lyon, "The Rise and Fall and Possible Revival of International Trusteeship," *Journal of Commonwealth and Comparative Politics* 31, no. 1 (1993): 96–110, quotation on 97.

46. Kevin Grant, *A Civilised Savagery: Britain and the New Slaveries in Africa, 1884–1926* (New York: Routledge, 2005). I thank Abigail Green for calling my attention to this book.

47. Coupland, *The Study of the British Commonwealth*, 28–29. Coupland dedicated much attention to Pitt's doctrine of trusteeship in his 1928 lecture "The After Effects of the American Revolution on British Policy," first delivered at the University of London as the Sir George Watson Lecture in the winter of 1928 and later published as *The American Revolution and the British Empire* (London: Longmans, Green, 1930).

48. [Reginald Coupland], "The Future of Colonial Trusteeship," *Round Table* 24, no. 96 (September 1934): 732–745, quotation on 742.

49. Quoted in Susan Pedersen, "Settler Colonialism at the Bar of the League of Nations," in *Settler Colonialism in the Twentieth Century: Projects, Practices, Legacies*, ed. Caroline Elkins and Susan Pedersen (New York: Routledge, 2005), 125. See also Susan Pedersen, *The Guardians: The League of Nations and the Crisis of Empire* (Oxford: Oxford University Press, 2015).

50. Up to 1936 very few articles dealt with the Middle East in general and virtually none focused entirely on Palestine, with the exception of a single, commissioned essay by T. E. Lawrence ("The Changing East," *Round Table* 10, no. 40 [1920]: 756–772) that was somewhat dismissive of Zionist schemes. One possible explanation for this marginality was that the issue was divisive: while some Round Tablers, such as L. Amery and Philip Kerr, were enthusiastic about Zionism and saw Palestine as a strategic stronghold that would help British penetration of the region, others, including Curtis, were worried that governing this new territory brought with it further responsibility that England could not take upon itself, at least not without American support. For discussion, see William Roger Louis, *In the Name of God, Go!: Leo Amery and the British Empire in the Age of Churchill* (New York: W. W. Norton, 1992).

51. Bernard Wasserstein, "Patterns of Communal Conflict in Palestine," in *Jewish History: Essays in Honour of Chimen Abramsky*, ed. Ada Rapoport-Albert and Steven J. Zipperstein (London: P. Halban, 1988), 611–628. Ussama Makdisi suggests that the notion of "sectarianism," imported from India, became by that time a useful prism for understanding the Middle East. See Ussama Makdisi, "Pensée 4: Moving Beyond Orientalist Fantasy, Sectarian Polemic, and Nationalist Denial," *International Journal of Middle East Studies* 40, no. 4 (2008): 559–660. This proposal was elaborated for Palestine in Laura Robson, *Colonialism and Christianity in Mandate Palestine* (Austin: University of Texas Press, 2011).

52. Josiah Clement Wedgwood, *The Seventh Dominion: On the British Administration in Palestine* (London: Labour Publishing, 1928). On Wedgwood, see Paul Mulvey, *The Political Life of Josiah C. Wedgwood: Land, Liberty and Empire, 1872–1943* (Rochester, NY: Boydell, 2010). For the Seventh Dominion League, see Norman Rose, "The Seventh Dominion," *Historical Journal* 14, no. 2 (1971): 397–416, as well as my article "'Ha-medinah she-ba-derekh' o ha-imperiah makah shainit?: impairi'alizem federativi ve-le'umiut yihudit be-ikbot milḥemet ha-olam ha-rishonah" [Jewish Nationalism in the Wake of World War I: A "State-in-the-Making" or the Empire Strikes Back?], *Israel: Studies in Zionism, and the State of Israel* 23 (2016): 5–35. Jewish supporters of the Seventh Dominion idea included Lewis B. Namier, the prominent historian (and political secretary for the Jewish Agency in Palestine from 1929); Leopold J. Greenberg, the influential editor of the *Jewish Chronicle*; and Vladimir (Ze'ev) Jabotinsky, the leader of the Revisionist Zionists.

53. Josiah C. Wedgwood was one of those who initiated the idea, alongside Wyndham Deeds and Blanche E. C. Dugdale (aka "Baffy"). See announcement by George Mitchell, Secretary of the Society, "The Palestine Mandate," *Times*, March 13, 1928, 12; and "Zionist Movement," *Times*, May 8, 1929, 11. Alex May claims that Kerr joined the Palestine Mandate Society in 1928. See May, "The Round Table," 281. Chaim Weizmann was well aware of these developments as well. He would later write in his autobiography about Robert Cecil: "To him the reestablishment of a Jewish Homeland in Palestine and the organization of the world in a great federation were complementary features of the next step in the management of human affairs." See Chaim Weizmann, *Trial and Error: The Autobiography of Chaim Weizmann* (Westport, CT: Greenwood, 1972 [1949]), 191.

54. Report of the Inter-Imperial Relations Committee, Imperial Conference (1926), Parliamentary Papers, Vol. 11, 1926, Cmd. 2768.

55. Quoted in my book *Isaiah Berlin: The Journey of a Jewish Liberal* (New York: Palgrave Macmillan, 2012), 116.

56. Sinanoglou, "British Plans for the Partition of Palestine," 149.

57. There were, in fact, four different tasks: First, to ascertain the underlying causes of the violent clashes that broke out in Palestine; second, to "inquire into the manner in which the Mandate for Palestine is being implemented in relation to the obligations of the Mandatory towards the Arabs and Jews respectively"; third, to determine, on the basis of testimonies taken from local Jews and Arabs, whether their complaints regarding the way in which the Mandate was implemented are justifiable; and fourth, to recommend what *alternative* measures should be executed in order to prevent the recurrence of such grievances. These wide terms may explain why the commission dedicated so much effort

to collecting testimonies, resulting in eighty-five sittings (conducted between November 16, 1936 and January 18, 1937). The fourth point in particular leaves much room for interpretation and was an open call for the speakers appearing before the committee not only to describe the existing situation, but also to offer their visions of the future. See Palestine: Report of the Royal Commission (Cmd. 5479), PRO CAB 24/270 (London: July 7, 1937), 474, quotation on 2.

58. See Motti Golani's chapter in this volume. Shmuel Dothan had previously argued that the conventional wisdom, assuming that Coupland invented the idea ex nihilo, was a "myth . . . improved by Weizmann ten years afterwards, in the memoirs he was writing at a time when the idea of partition was emerging victorious." See Shmuel Dothan, *A Land in the Balance: The Struggle for Palestine, 1918–1948*, trans. Jeffrey M. Green (Tel Aviv: Israeli Ministry of Defense Press, 1993), chap. 5, esp. 196. Golani follows this suggestion but shows *why* Weizmann had to invent such a myth.

59. Cust's memorandum is included in a folder containing a list of cantonization proposals prepared between February and November 1936: National Archives, Kew; Colonial Office: "Cantonisation of Palestine: Proposals," CO 733/302/9 (formerly CO 733/302/75288); http://discovery.nationalarchives.gov.uk/details/r/C823557.

60. See [Lord] Melchett [aka Alfred Moritz Mond], "Palestine," *Times*, March 1, 1935, 10; followed by a reply by Archer Cust, "Palestine," *Times*, March 5, 1935, 12, and Norman Bentwich, "The Palestine Mandate," *Times*, October 7, 1935, 8; followed by yet another reply by Archer Cust, "The Palestine Mandate," *Times*, September 17, 1935, 10.

61. Minutes dated June 29, 1936, included in "Cantonisation of Palestine: Proposals." For discussion, see also Lauren Banko, *The Invention of Palestinian Citizenship, 1918–1947* (Edinburgh: Edinburgh University Press, 2016), chap. 3, esp. 186–188.

62. "The Palestine Inquiry: Jewish Demands," *Times*, February 12, 1937, 16. For transcripts and notes of Jabotinsky's testimony, see Jabotinsky Papers, Aleph-1/36-4, Jabotinsky Institute, Tel Aviv.

63. [Arnold J. Toynbee], "The Palestine Report and After," *Round Table* 27, no. 108 (1937): 740–754, quotations on 741, 754, 749.

64. Reginald Coupland, "Confidential: The Sequel to the Palestine Royal Commission," in Papers of Sir Reginald Coupland (3), MSS. Medit. s. 36, Bodleian Library, University of Oxford.

65. See, in particular, Coupland to Philip Kerr, December 8, 1938, in ibid., fols. 5–7.

66. Horace Rumbold, William Morris Carter, Harold Morris, and Reginald Coupland, "The Future of Palestine: Jews and the New State, a Federal Solution," *Times*, May 22, 1939, 13.

67. Reginald Coupland, "The Jew and the Arab: Conditions of Settlement in Palestine," *Times*, July 13, 1946, 5. Coupland's piece infuriated Albert Hourani, an otherwise polite gentleman. Coupland, Hourani wrote in reply, has no problem in leaving "a large number of Arabs to the good intentions of a Jewish government" and is "too optimistic when he expresses the hope that the Arab leaders will come to realize that partition is the 'best deal open to them.'" The future development would take the reverse direction: "The Jewish minority would be adequately protected in an Arab State by its own strength and organization." And he added a disquieting warning: "More important still, it should be

emphasized that the Jews are in fact dependent on Arab good intention, whether they like it or not." See Albert Hourani, "Jew and Arab," *Times*, July 30, 1946, 5.

68. Reginald Coupland, "Diary, India: 1941–1942," Papers of Sir Reginald Coupland (2), MSS. Brit. Emp. s. 7–15, 1909–1942, Bodleian Library, University of Oxford (formerly preserved at the Rhodes House, Oxford).

69. Reginald Coupland, "Speech at the Annual Dinner of the Oxford Majlis," February 25, 1931, Coupland Papers (1), Box 5; Reginald Coupland, "Dominion Status: A Definition of Facts [Letter to the Editor]," *Times*, November 26, 1931, 15; in response to Winston S. Churchill, "India and Dominion Status," *Times*, November 25, 1931, 13.

70. Resolution of the Indian National Congress at Ramgarh, March 20, 1940, reproduced in C. H. Philips, Hira Lal Singh, and Bishwa Nath Pandey, eds., *The Evolution of India and Pakistan, 1858–1947: Select Documents* (London: Oxford University Press, 1962), 338–339.

71. Coupland, *The Cripps Mission*, 16–17; Robin James Moore, *Churchill, Cripps, and India, 1939–1945* (Oxford: Clarendon, 1979), 30.

72. Coupland, "Diary, India: 1941–1942," January 15, 1942, 57.

73. Reginald Coupland, "Possibilities of the Final Settlement," in Coupland, "Diary, India: 1941–1942," 274–281. See also his exchanges with Leo Amery, August 10, 1942, to July 27, 1943, in Coupland Papers (1), Box 5, file 2, ff. 28–43, where the prospect of an all-India constitution was still regarded as the correct political scheme for the subcontinent.

74. Reginald Coupland, *The Future of India; the Third Part of a Report on the Constitutional Problem in India* (London: Oxford University Press, 1943), 84–86.

75. Ibid., 90.

76. See, for example, the similarity in the main arguments and proposals of Coupland in his 1941 *Round Table* essay, his wartime trilogy, and his 1945 book. See [Reginald Coupland], "India in the Post-War World," *Round Table* 31, no. 123 (1941): 500–510. Coupland's assessments and much of the demographic data he provided in volume III of his reports were based on census reports provided to him by M. W. M. Yeatts, Census Commissioner for India. See Coupland Papers (1), Box 5, folder 2, ff. 69–99.

77. On this point I follow Yasmin Khan, *The Great Partition: The Making of India and Pakistan* (New Haven, CT: Yale University Press, 2007).

78. Margaret O'Callaghan, "Genealogies of Partition: History, History-Writing and 'the Troubles' in Ireland," *Critical Review of International Social and Political Philosophy* 9, no. 4 (2006): 619–634, quotation on 624.

79. Reginald Coupland, "Nationalism in the British Commonwealth [L. Mond Lecture]," Coupland Papers (1), Box 4, folder 3, ff. 186–187. See also newspaper coverage of the lecture: "Nationalism and Democracy," *Manchester Guardian*, June 22, 1945, 6; "Rule by Numbers," *Manchester Guardian*, June 22, 1945, 4. Coupland planned this to be part of a larger, multi-volume project on Nationalism in the Commonwealth. Due to failing health he was able to complete only the first volume, Welsh and Scottish Nationalism, which he handed to his publisher on November 5, 1952, a day before he died.

80. Brendan O'Leary, "Analysing Partition: Definition, Classification and Explanation," *Political Geography* 26, no. 8 (2007): 886–908. See also Brendan O'Leary, "Debating

Partition: Evaluating the Standard Justifications," in *Routledge Handbook of Ethnic Conflict*, ed. Karl Cordell and Stefan Wolff (New York: Routledge, 2011), 140–157.

## CHAPTER 3

1. David Ben-Gurion, *Letters to Paula and the Children* (in Hebrew) (Tel Aviv: Am Oved, 1968), Letter to Amos, July 27, 1937, 175–185. Ben-Gurion was chairman of the Jewish Agency Executive (1935–1948) and the first prime minister and defense minister of Israel (1948–1953, 1955–1963).

2. This proposition is firmly grounded in Penny Sinanoglou, "British Plans for Partition of Palestine, 1929–1938," *Historical Journal* 52, no. 1 (2009): 131–152.

3. For example, James Rosenberg to Weizmann, December 9, 1929, 12-1339A, Weizmann Archives (hereafter WA), Weizmann Institute of Science, Rehovot, Israel; Sir Michael Sadler, Master of University College, Oxford, to Weizmann, December 9, 1929, WA 12-1332; Moritz Bilsky and Robert Weltsch to Zionist Executive, London, October 15, 1929, WA 15-1313; and Arye Naor, *Greater Israel, Theology and Policy* (Haifa: University of Haifa Press, 2001), 72–74.

4. Chaim Weizmann to James Marshall, January 17, 1930, WA 17-1358; Weizmann to Robert Weltsch, November 25, 1929, in Chaim Weizmann, *The Letters and Papers of Chaim Weizmann*, 25 vols. (London: Oxford University Press, 1968–1984), Vol. 14, no. 110.

5. Dr. Weizmann, "The Zionist Movement Under the Palestine Mandate," *Central Asian Society*, November 12, 1929, WA 7-1323.

6. Lord Passfield (Sidney Webb), the colonial secretary (1929–1931), was behind the new policy document that was approved by the British government.

7. Weizmann to Smuts, November 28, 1929, WA 1-1332, and also to Einstein, November 29, 1929, WA 18-1333.

8. Weizmann to Felix Warburg, January 16, 1930, in Weizmann, *Letters and Papers*, Vol. 14, no. 184.

9. Weizmann to Felix Warburg, London, November 13, 1929, WA 2-1324.

10. Dr. Moritz Bilsky and Dr. Robert Weltsch to Weizmann, October 15, 1929, WA 15-1313; Weizmann to Einstein, November 29, 1929, WA 18-1333.

11. Weizmann to James Marshall, January 17, 1930, in Weizmann, *Letters and Papers*, Vol. 14, no. 187, p. 208.

12. Chaim Weizmann, "Notes on the Attitude of the British Administration in Palestine Towards the Jewish National Home," January 4, 1931, WA 8-1472.

13. Weizmann interview, July 6, 1931, WA 12-1517.

14. Weizmann's testimony to Peel Commission *in camera*, January 8, 1937, WA 9-1954. Until 1937, this phrase bore a dual meaning. It signified not only concern about the situation of the Jews if they were to remain a minority, but also a promise that they would not harm the Arabs if and when the latter were to become a minority—in accordance with the Zionist aspiration of the time. This duality is expressed persistently by Weizmann and in his interlocutors. See, e.g., Weizmann's conversation with the archbishop of Canterbury, March 4, 1937, WA 3-1968.

15. Cust was not considered sympathetic to the Zionist cause; Weizmann pushed for his dismissal after the unrest of 1929.

16. For a concise survey of the different plans, see Nathaniel Katzburg, "The Second Decade of the British Mandate in Palestine, 1931–1939," in *The British Mandate Period, Part One*, ed. Moshe Lissak (Jerusalem: Bialik Institute, 2004), 384–387 (in Hebrew); Itzhak Galnoor, *The Partition of Palestine: Decision Crossroads in the Zionist Movement* (Sde Boker: BG University Press, 1995), 64–67 (Hebrew edition); and Shmuel Dotan, *The Struggle for Eretz Israel* (Tel Aviv: Defiance Ministry, 1981), 119–120 (in Hebrew).

17. In 1933, Jacobson flayed the Brit Shalom group as though they were strangers whose approach he was encountering for the first time. In fact, they were not strangers to him at all. Jacobson's report on his tour of Syria, Lebanon, and Palestine, May 12, 1933, WA 1-1636.

18. Jacobson Plan, January 20, 1932, WA 7-1555, and see also the appended map. Weizmann's eastward tendency, in the event of partition, arises from a discussion of a somewhat hallucinatory plan to establish a "second Jewish national home" in northern Syria under French auspices. It emerges from this discussion that Weizmann wanted territories on the Syria-Palestine border, not in northern Syria. Jacobson to Zelig Brodetsky, "Various Thoughts About the Syrian Project," December 11, 1930, WA 17-1459, emphasized that this was a bad and unrealistic idea. On Weizmann's tendency to forge a link with Syria and his great caution in this regard, see also his testimony to the Peel Commission, January 8, 1937, WA 9-1954.

19. On the plan, see exchanges of personal messages between Jacobson and Weizmann, WA 7-1555.

20. Dotan, *The Struggle for Eretz Israel*, 75.

21. Jacobson wrote Weizmann a heartfelt letter after the latter was deposed as WZO president in the summer of 1931. He was moved, he noted, to an unusual expression of frankness: "And you must always count me among the circle of the most loyal and devoted 'comrades in the struggle'—based on awareness; and among the circle of friends—based on deep affection and feelings of respect"; Jacobson to Weizmann, August 7, 1931, WA 24-1522.

22. Jacobson to Weizmann, August 7, 1931, WA 24-1522, and August 16, 1931, WA 4-1525.

23. Arlosoroff to Weizmann, June 30, 1932, in *Jerusalem Diary* (Tel Aviv: Davar, 1949), 341 (in Hebrew). Arlosoroff was in the grip of despair at this time. In the letter, he praised the plan but thought it was not realistic, as the Jews would remain a minority even in Jacobson's proposed state. Thus, the problem would change quantitatively but not qualitatively. He therefore turned to the idea of a takeover by force. This was not made public at the time.

24. Jacobson to Weizmann, January 20, 1932, WA 7-1555 (in French). Weizmann's surprising reply is implicit from Jacobson's letter. His partition plan was indeed appended to the letter.

25. Jacobson's report on his tour of Syria, Lebanon, and Palestine, May 22, 1933, WA 1-1636. Other than the connection with Jacobson, our knowledge of Weizmann's role

in regard to the first explicit partition plan for Palestine is largely circumstantial. Thus, for example, something of his attitude toward the partition idea may be gleaned from a plan—which apparently did not exist, though rumors of it spread concurrent with Jacobson's formulation in the first half of 1932—of the former Egyptian Khedive, Abbas Hilmi Pasha. This interesting issue overshadowed Jacobson's plan, for good and for ill. Arlosoroff to Zelig Brodetsky, February 8, 1932, WA 16-1559; also Robert Weltsch to Weizmann, February 15, 1932, WA 17-1559; Arlosoroff, too, fell into this Egyptian trap; see *Jerusalem Diary*, 120, 166, 204.

26. The sour atmosphere is reflected in a leaflet disseminated in Jerusalem in early 1932 by Revisionist students: "What we need is not a Chaim Weizmann Peace Chair, but a Jabotinsky Military Academy"; Robert Weltsch to Weizmann, February 15, 1932, WA 17-1559.

27. Doris May (Weizmann's personal assistant in the Zionist Office, London) to Weizmann, March 29, 1932, WA 8-1563.

28. Jacobson's report to Weizmann on his conversation with Theodoli at the League of Nations headquarters, Geneva, November 2, 1933, WA 2-1678A; also November 3, 1933, WA 5-1678B; January 17, 1934, WA 2-1711A; Jacobson to Weizmann, Paris, January 27, 1934, WA 16-1713.

29. Chaim Weizmann to Vera Weizmann, Bern, December 9, 1933, WA 8-1691.

30. Jacobson to Weizmann, Geneva, January 17, 1934, WA 2-1711A; Weizmann to Jacobson, January 19, 1934, in Weizmann, *Letters and Papers*, Vol. 16, no. 209; Jacobson to Weizmann, January 27, 1934, WA 16-1713; Jacobson's report on "A conversation which took place between H. E. Mussolini and Dr. Weizmann in the Palazzo Venezia," February 17, 1934, WA 6-1724A.

31. Weizmann to Lola Hahn-Warburg, Port of Naples, February 22, 1934, in Weizmann, *Letters and Papers*, Vol. 16, no. 249.

32. Ibid.; the British Ambassador to Rome after a conversation with Weizmann, February 19, 1934, FO371/17876, British National Archives, Kew; Jacobson died in 1934, leaving Weizmann without his closest partner on the road to partition.

33. Bialik's remarks at a Tel Aviv reception in honor of Weizmann, March 21, 1934, WA 20-1731. A line just before this quotation was thoroughly erased. Could it have contained an explicit mention of the partition idea?

34. Moshe Smilansky, "Our Cultural Height," *Bustanai* 8, April 18, 1934, 4 (in Hebrew). A reading of the article suggests that Smilansky's opposition to a partitioned state was very similar to that voiced by Arlosoroff two years earlier, namely, that there would be less territory but no fewer problems, as the Jews would still lack a majority even in the partitioned territory. In other words, the issue of a majority, which Weizmann wanted to eliminate, would actually remain—and even more forcefully—in partition. From here the way was short to the idea of a population transfer (a common mechanism at the time).

35. Weizmann to Shertok, London, October 2, 1936, in Weizmann, *Letters and Papers*, Vol. 17, no. 327.

36. Lecture by Cust at the Royal Central Asian Society, March 4, 1936, A173/81/1, Central Zionist Archives, Jerusalem.

37. Weizmann was absent from London at the beginning of June 1936 and did not reply to Cust's ideas—which were sent to him on May 28—until June 9. Weizmann to Cust, June 9, 1936, WA 5-1913; Cust to Weizmann, June 16, 1936, WA 33-1915; Cust report to Colonial Office, June 28, 1936, WA 1-1918A, on his meeting with Weizmann on June 26. Although Cust promised Weizmann that the details of their conversation would remain secret, he transmitted a summation to the Colonial Office, together with his earlier correspondence with Weizmann. Weizmann, who also received a copy, expressed the hope that Cust had not yet forwarded the material, as he wished to make corrections. But it was too late. Cust to Weizmann, June 29, 1936, WA 14791A; Weizmann to Cust, June 30, 1936, WA 21-1918A.

38. Dotan, *The Struggle for Eretz Israel*, 121, according to *Doar Hayom*, June 11, 1936; Weizmann to Cust, June 9, 1936, WA 5-1913; Cust to Weizmann, June 16, 1936, WA 33-1915; Cust to Weizmann, June 29, 1936, WA 14791A; Weizmann to Cust, June 30, 1936, WA 21-1918A.

39. See, for example, Blanche (Baffy) Dugdale's letter to the *Times* on the eve of Weizmann's contacts with Cust, May 1936, WA 2-1004. She objected to Cust's plan on the basis of the assumption that it referred solely to Palestine, not to Transjordan. Indeed, in the early Jacobson-Weizmann formulations, in the event of partition the Jewish state would receive territories in the northern section of Transjordan, on the border with Palestine.

40. Dotan, *The Struggle for Eretz Israel*, 121–122. On Weizmann's tendency toward an association with Iraq, Syria, and Lebanon, see his testimony before the Peel Commission, January 8, 1937, ibid. The middleman between these two Zionist leaders—one on the ascent, the other on the descent—was Leopold Amery, a former colonial secretary, a conservative, a pro-Zionist, and an old friend of Weizmann. Amery had been advocating a separation solution between Jews and Arabs for months and was certainly an appropriate interlocutor for Weizmann on this subject.

41. Meir Hazan, *Moderation: The Moderate Approach in Hapoel Hatza'ir and Mapai, 1905–1945* (Tel Aviv: Am Oved, 2009), 260–262 (in Hebrew).

42. On the report in *Davar*, see ibid., 261.

43. The autobiography was published in Hebrew in Israel (Jerusalem: Schocken) in 1949 and immediately thereafter also in the United States (New York: Harper Brothers, 1949) and Britain (London: Hamish Hamilton, 1949). Not by accident there is confusion in both the British and the American versions regarding Coupland. In some editions he appears in the text but not in the index and sometimes vice versa; in some editions he does not appear at all.

44. Coupland to Weizmann, All Souls College, Oxford, February 18, 1950, WA 14-2911.

45. Also absent from that session was the commission's deputy chairman, Sir Laurie Hammond. Did he perhaps meet with the Arabs to find out their reaction to the partition idea? The question has no clear answer. Hazan, *Moderation*, 260–262.

46. Weizmann chose a relatively convenient forum (the advisory committee to the Zionist Executive, which was composed wholly of his people, and in the presence of Shertok,

who was one of the first to learn of Weizmann's support for partition) to reveal briefly but reliably a few details about the meeting in Nahalal. Meeting of the Advisory Committee, Zionist Office in London, April 14, 1937, WA 22-1975.

47. Weizmann to Coupland, Personal, April 19, 1937, WA 3-1977.

48. Blanche Dugdale, *Baffy: The Diaries of Blanche Dugdale 1936–1947*, ed. N. A. Rose (London: Vallentine Mitchell, 1973), April 10, 1937, 41.

49. Ibid., May 29–31, 1937, 44–45; April 27, 1937, 41–42.

50. Moshe Sharett, *Political Diary* (Tel Aviv: Am Oved, 1971), 178 (in Hebrew).

51. Hazan, *Moderation*, 261–262.

CHAPTER 4

1. For further reading in relation to the partition of Ireland, see Michael Laffin, *The Partition of Ireland: 1911–1925* (Dundalk: Dungalgan, 1983).

2. See Yasmin Khan, *The Great Partition: The Making of India and Pakistan* (New Haven, CT: Yale University Press, 2008), for an excellent and detailed account of the partition of India.

3. Nicholas Mansergh, *Nationalism and Independence: Selected Irish Papers* (Cork: Cork University Press, 1997), 37–38.

4. Ronald Hyam, *Britain's Declining Empire: The Road to Decolonisation, 1918–1968* (Cambridge: Cambridge University Press, 2006), 113.

5. Telegram, Samar Sen to Éamon de Valera, 4 May 1946, 305/41, National Archives of Ireland (hereafter NAI), Department of External Affairs (hereafter DEA). The term "Indian Ulsterisation" was included in this telegram from the Indian economist Samar Sen to de Valera asking for a message of sympathy to be sent in advance of an Indian meeting opposing "Indian Ulsterisation." Sen was studying at the London School of Economics at the time.

6. See Kate O'Malley, *Ireland, India and Empire: Indo-Irish Radical Connections, 1919–64* (Manchester: Manchester University Press, 2008); and Michael Silvestri, *Ireland and India: Ireland, Empire and Memory* (Basingstoke: Palgrave Macmillan, 2009). For a detailed look at British policy in relation to the implementation of partition in both countries, see T. G. Fraser *Partition in Ireland, India and Palestine: Theory and Practice* (New York: Saint Martin's, 1984).

7. C. H. Philips and Mary Doreen Wainright, eds., *The Partition of India: Policies and Perspectives, 1935–47* (London: Allen and Unwin, 1970), 511.

8. Patrick French, *Liberty or Death: India's Journey to Independence and Division* (London: Flamingo, 1997), 123.

9. *Times of India*, 25 March 1940, 6.

10. *Times of India*, 16 January 1945, 5.

11. *Times of India*, 3 September 1945, 8. This statement supports Ayesha Jalal's argument that Jinnah never thought Pakistan would be created and used the threat of Pakistan as a means to merely strengthen the voice of the Indian Muslim minority community in advance of independence. See Ayesha Jalal, *The Sole Spokesman: Jinnah, the Muslim League and the Demand for Pakistan* (Cambridge: Cambridge University Press, 1985).

12. *Sunday Independent*, 8 September 1946, 5.

13. *Times of India*, 12 April 1940, 6.

14. Ibid.

15. *Times of India*, 20 April 1940, 7.

16. O'Malley, *Ireland, India and Empire*, 57. V. J. Patel was a founder of the Indian-Irish Independence League in Dublin in 1932. He was an older brother of Vallabhbhai Sardar Patel.

17. *Irish Independent*, 21 May 1927, 8.

18. *Times of India*, 11 May 1942, 5.

19. *Irish Press*, 8 April 1943, 1. This reference alludes to the often cited "Moth eaten Pakistan" argument, that if pushed to concede to Muslim demands, any geographical truncation in order to establish Pakistan would prove too small and weak to survive. This was an argument also used in the partitioning of Ireland, with the number of counties and the demographics of each one being crucial factors in the viability of the northern state.

20. *Fermanagh Herald*, 5 September 1942, 2.

21. *Irish Press*, 21 August 1946, 5.

22. *Irish Press*, 30 August 1944, 2.

23. *Irish Press*, 5 June 1947, 4.

24. Ibid.

25. Nicholas Mansergh, ed., *India: The Transfer of Power*, 12 vols. (London: HMSO, 1973–1983).

26. Deirdre McMahon, "A Larger and Noisier Southern Ireland: Ireland and the Evolution of Dominion Status in India, Burma and the Commonwealth, 1942–9," in *Irish Foreign Policy 1919–1966: From Independence to Internationalism*, ed. Michael Kennedy and Joseph Skelly (Dublin: Four Courts Press, 2000), 155–156.

27. Mansergh, *Transfer of Power*, 5:503, 509.

28. Ibid., 5:511.

29. Memorandum titled "Summary of Attached Memorandum on the Disputed Clauses in the British Cabinet Mission's Statement on India," by F. H. Boland, 21 January 1947, 305/41, NAI, DEA.

30. Minute by Con Cremin, 14 August 1947, 305/41, NAI, DEA.

31. Ibid.

32. Dulanty to F. H. Boland, 4 January 1947, 417/22, NAI, DEA.

33. Ibid. This comment by Bidaut possibly relates to the Franco-Vietnamese conference at Fontainebleau in the summer of 1946.

34. *Irish Press*, 22 February 1947, 6.

35. *Dáil Debates*, vol. 108 (Dublin: Dublin Stationary Office), 15 October 1947, cols. 350–352; also available online at Houses of the Oireachtas, Dáil Éireann Debate—Wednesday, 15 Oct 1947," https://www.oireachtas.ie/en/debates/debate/dail/1947-10-15/2/.

36. Ibid.

37. *Irish Times*, 12 April 1964, 4.

38. This is the title of the Irish Department of External Affairs' file on India gaining independence; 305/41, NAI, DEA.

39. *Irish Press*, 5 June 1947, 1.

40. Mansergh, *Nationalism and Independence*, 35.

41. *Irish Press*, 5 June 1947, 1.

42. *Fermanagh Herald*, 5 September 1942, 2.

43. Telegram, CRO [Commonwealth Relations Office] to UK HC [high commissioner] in India and UK HC in Pakistan, 2 June 1948, 35/3930, National Archives of the United Kingdom (NAUK), Dominions Office (DO).

44. Ibid.

45. Shone to Dominions Office, 9 July 1948, 35/3930, NAUK, DO. Two months later, de Valera's successor as Taoiseach, John A. Costello, announced his government's intentions to repeal the External Relations Act, a controversial piece of legislation drawn up by de Valera during the abdication crisis of 1936 that maintained a tenuous link between Ireland and the Commonwealth. On making this announcement while on an official trip to Canada, Costello confirmed that after its repeal, Ireland would not be a member (associate or otherwise) of the Commonwealth.

46. Ibid.

47. This is exactly what happened at the Commonwealth Prime Ministers' Conference of April 1949 and resulted in the London Declaration. This kept India, a republic, within the Commonwealth. De Valera told Nicholas Mansergh in 1952 that he would have been "happy to accept [the] Indian solution." Mansergh, *Nationalism and Independence*, 185.

48. Ibid.

49. Unsigned Memorandum, "Partition in Ireland and Abroad," 1956, 305/14/313, NAI, DEA.

## CHAPTER 5

1. Amery to Melchett, 20 July 1937, AMEL 1/5/46, part 1, Leo Amery Papers, Churchill Archives Center (CAC), Churchill College, Cambridge, United Kingdom.

2. Casey to Ismay, 12 March 1945, Ismay Papers 4/6/9a, Liddell Hart Centre for Military Archives, King's College, London.

3. Weizmann to Mountbatten, 10 June 1947, 2752 VI 10–14, Weizmann Archives (WA), Weizmann Institute of Science, Rehovot, Israel.

4. Jacob Robinson, "Partition of India: Implications for Palestine," S25/9029, p. 62, Central Zionist Archives (CZA), Jerusalem.

5. Minutes of 20 September 1947 Cabinet meeting, Cabinet 76 (47) Conclusions, CAB 128/10, p. 19, United Kingdom National Archives (UKNA), Kew.

6. Pollack to Haydt, Jewish Agency, 20 November 1945, CZA S25/3536, p. 21.

7. UN press release, 7 October 1947, GA/PAL/7, p. 5, https://unispal .un.org/DPA/DPR/unispal.nsf/5ba47a5c6cef541b802563e000493b8c/ 55e9b2df2e5cc5d685256929006e1d24/$FILE/gapal07.pdf.

8. Epstein memo, 30 June 1947, CZA L35/126, p. 2.

9. "Arabs Demand Unitary State," *Palestine Post*, 7 December 1947, 1.

10. Lucy Chester, "Boundary Commissions as Tools to Safeguard British Interests at the End of Empire," *Journal of Historical Geography* 34, no. 3 (2008): 495.

11. T. G. Fraser, *Partition in Ireland, India, and Palestine: Theory and Practice* (New York: St. Martin's, 1984).

12. Wm. Roger Louis, *The British Empire in the Middle East* (Oxford: Clarendon, 1984), esp. chaps. 3–7.

13. Priya Satia, *Spies in Arabia: The Great War and the Cultural Foundations of Britain's Covert Empire in the Middle East* (Oxford: Oxford University Press, 2008), chap. 6.

14. Rory Miller, "'An Oriental Ireland': Thinking About Palestine in Terms of the Irish Question During the Mandatory Era," in *Britain, Palestine and Empire: The Mandate Years*, ed. Rory Miller (Farnham: Ashgate, 2010), 157–176; and Rory Miller, *Ireland and the Palestine Question, 1948–2004* (Dublin: Irish Academic Press, 2005); Kate O'Malley, *Ireland, India and Empire: Indo-Irish Radical Connections, 1919–64* (Manchester: Manchester University Press, 2008); P. R. Kumaraswamy, *India's Israel Policy* (New York: Columbia University Press, 2010).

15. Harold F. Gosnell, "British Royal Commissions of Inquiry," *Political Science Quarterly* 49, no. 1 (1934): 84–118.

16. Palestine Royal Commission Report [Peel Report], 1937, Cmd. 5479, pp. 381–386.

17. Penny Sinanoglou, "British Plans for the Partition of Palestine, 1929–1938," *Historical Journal* 52, no. 1 (2009): 131–152.

18. Satia, *Spies in Arabia*, 8–9.

19. Government of India Intelligence Bureau Weekly Report, 24 July 1937, IOR L/PS/12/3347, British Library (BL).

20. Ibid.

21. Gandhi to Kallenbach, 20 July 1937, Gandhi-Kallenbach Correspondence, Vol. 3, S. No. 246, Gandhi Papers, Private Archives Section, National Archives of India, New Delhi (hereafter Gandhi Papers).

22. Andrews to Kallenbach, 20 August 1938, Kallenbach Papers, cited in Gideon Shimoni, *Gandhi, Satyagraha and the Jews: A Formative Factor in India's Policy Towards Israel* (Jerusalem: Hebrew University, 1977), 37; emphasis added.

23. Gandhi to Kallenbach, 28 August 1937, Vol. 3, S. No. 248, Gandhi Papers.

24. Nehru to Shohet, 26 August 1937, CZA S25/6312, p. 471.

25. Letter to the editor, *Time and Tide*, 8 October 1938, Correspondence, Vol. 19, 195–199, Jawaharlal Nehru Papers, Nehru Memorial Museum and Library, New Delhi.

26. Iqbal to Jinnah, 7 October 1937, in G. Allana, ed., *Pakistan Movement: Historic Documents* (Karachi: University of Karachi, 1968), 146–147.

27. Syed Sharifuddin Pirzada, ed., *Foundations of Pakistan*, Vol. 2 (Karachi: National Publishing House, 1970), 272.

28. Ibid., 277–278.

29. For an early example of British concerns about an imagined Indian Muslim duty to rise against the Raj, see the Government of India's commissioning of William W. Hunter's 1876 report on the question. *The Indian Musalmans*, 3rd ed. (Delhi: Indological Book House, 1969).

30. Weizmann to Shuckburgh, Colonial Office, 31 December 1937, PREM 1/352, pp. 203–211, UKNA.

31. Cazalet letter, 13 January 1938, PREM 1/352, UKNA.

32. Tegart II/2/59-124, Tegart Papers, GB165-0281, Middle East Centre, St. Antony's College, Oxford University.

33. Gandhi to Kallenbach, 17 July 1938, Vol. 3, S. No. 257, Gandhi Papers.

34. Palestine: Statement by His Majesty's Government in the United Kingdom, 1938, Cmd. 5893, p. 3.

35. Linlithgow to Zetland, 23 November 1938, IOR L/PO/5/38(ii), p. 229, BL.

36. Letter to Willingdon, 1 December 1938, IOR L/PO/5/38(ii), p. 224, BL.

37. Wm. Roger Louis, *In the Name of God, Go!* (New York: W. W. Norton, 1992), 72–73; William D. Rubinstein, "The Secret of Leopold Amery," *Historical Research* 73, no. 181 (2000): 175–196.

38. Report of Committee on Palestine to the War Cabinet, 20 December 1943, PREM 4/52/1, p. 133, UKNA.

39. Ibid., 140.

40. Ibid., 145.

41. Louis, *In the Name*, 56.

42. Reginald Coupland, *The Indian Problem: Report on the Constitutional Problem in India* (New York: Oxford University Press, 1944), 99.

43. Ambassador to Eden, 24 February 1944, PREM 4/52/1, p. 160, UKNA.

44. Ibid., 161.

45. Satia, *Spies in Arabia*, 205.

46. Churchill to Amery, 21 May 1944, PREM 4/52/1, p. 106, UKNA.

47. Secretary of State for India to Prime Minister, 3 October 1944, PREM 4/52/1, p. 86, UKNA.

48. Committee on Palestine Report, 16 October 1944, PREM 4/52/1, p. 73, UKNA.

49. Ibid., 74.

50. Wavell to Amery, 19 October 1944, IOR/L/PO/5/34, p. 11, BL.

51. House of Commons Debate, 17 November 1944, Hansard, vol. 404, col. 2242.

52. Michael J. Cohen, "The Moyne Assassination, November, 1944: A Political Analysis," *Middle Eastern Studies* 15, no. 3 (1979): 370–371.

53. Casey to Ismay, 12 March 1945.

54. Joan Roland, *The Jewish Communities of India*, 2nd ed. (New Brunswick, NJ: Transaction, 1998), 225, 243.

55. Pollack to Haydt, Jewish Agency, 20 November 1945, CZA S25/3536, p. 21.

56. Ibid.

57. J. L. Magnes, "A Solution Through Force?," in *Towards Union in Palestine: Essays on Zionism and Jewish-Arab Cooperation,* ed. M. Buber, J. Magnes, and E. Simon (Jerusalem: Ihud Association, 1947), 16.

58. [Ihud?], "Federalization and Bi-Nationalism," 8 August 1946, FO 371/61940, p. 155 verso, UKNA.

59. Meeting Record, 25 April 1946, in *The Transfer of Power in India, 1942–7,* vol. 7, ed. Nicholas Mansergh (London: HMSO, 1970–1983), doc. 138.

60. Wavell to Henderson, 25 April 1946, in Mansergh, *Transfer,* vol. 7, doc. 143.

61. Amery to Weizmann, 1 August 1946, AMEL 2/2/28, part 1, CAC.

62. An important if incomplete collection of the Palestine Mandate's Arabic-language periodicals is preserved in the Al-Aqsa Mosque Library, which is available online courtesy

of the British Library's Endangered Archives Project. See EAP119/1, http://hviewer.bl
.uk/IamsHViewer/Default.aspx?mdark=ark:/81055/vdc_100000000035.0x000031, accessed 13 March 2015. As Adi Gordon notes in Chapter 7 of this volume, *Falastin* also
had an English-language edition, edited by an Indian Muslim.

63. See, for example, "Mahatma Gandhi: His View of the Palestine Problem Remains
Unchanged," *Falastin*, 23 June 1939, 1.

64. Taqiuddin al-Solh, "The Adversary of Gandhi Speaks," *Akhbar al-Yaum*, 7 June
1947, in *Quaid-i-Azam Mohammad Ali Jinnah Papers*, vol. 2, ed. Z. H. Zaidi et al. (Islam-
abad: Quaid-i-Azam Papers Project, 2000), doc. 65enc.

65. Ibid.

66. Eastwood to Turnbull, 17 September 1946, IOR L/PJ/10/110, p. 10, BL; Turnbull
to Croft, September 1946, IOR L/PJ/10/110, p. 5, BL.

67. Cabinet 18(47) Conclusions, 7 February 1947, CAB 128/9, p. 119, UKNA.

68. Quoted in Symon to Cabinet, 25 February 1947, CO 733/482/3, p. 4, UKNA.

69. Ibid.

70. H. E. B. Catley, "Indian and Pakistan[i] Relations with the Middle East," *Asian
Review* 50 (1954): 199.

71. Mansergh, *Transfer*, vol. 11, doc. 44.

72. Weizmann to Mountbatten, 10 June 1947, WA 2752 VI 10-14.

73. [June?] 1947, CZA S25/9029, pp. 1–6.

74. Harry S. Cohen, column in *The Day*, 10 June 1947, quoted in Robinson, "Partition
of India," CZA S25/9029, p. 6.

75. CZA S25/9029, p. 6.

76. 30 June 1947, CZA L35/126, p. 2.

77. Taqiuddin al-Solh, "The Adversary of Gandhi Speaks," *Akhbar al-Yaum*, 7 June
1947, in *Jinnah Papers*, vol. 2, 65enc.

78. "'Pakistan Will Show That Islam Carries Seeds for World Peace'—Envoys' Trib-
utes to Qaed-e-Azam," *Dawn*, 11 June 1947, 1.

79. Sinanoglou, "British Plans."

80. Lucy Chester, *Borders and Conflict in South Asia: The Radcliffe Boundary Commission
and the Partition of Punjab* (Manchester: Manchester University Press, 2009).

81. Qureshi to Jinnah, in *Jinnah Papers*, vol. 1, part 1, doc. 125.

82. See, for example, the detailed discussion of the necessary height and other characteristics of the fence that would divide Tel Aviv and Jaffa in the Woodhead report (Palestine Partition Commission Report, 1938, Cmd. 5854, p. 41).

83. UN General Assembly Official Records, Second Session, 8 July 1947, p. 81.

84. "Summary of Statement by Dr. Chaim Weizmann," 8 July 1947, AMEL 2/2/28,
part 2, p. 19, CAC.

85. Amery to Weizmann, 28 July 1947, AMEL 2/2/28, part 1, CAC.

86. Patrick French, *Liberty or Death: India's Journey to Independence and Division* (London: HarperCollins, 1998), 347–349.

87. Ritu Menon and Kamla Bhasin, *Borders and Boundaries: Women in India's Partition*
(New Brunswick, NJ: Rutgers University Press, 1998), 70.

88. Cabinet 76 (47) Conclusions, Cabinet meeting minutes, 20 September 1947, CAB 128/10, p. 19, UKNA.

89. Ibid., 17.

90. 2 October 1947, Cunningham V/1/77, GB165-0072, Cunningham Papers, Middle East Centre, St. Antony's College, Oxford University.

91. Beirut to Foreign Office, 2 October 1947, CO 733/482/7, p. 32, UKNA.

92. "Arabs Demand Unitary State," *Palestine Post*, 7 December 1947. Musa had a long-standing interest in India, having written a book on Gandhi and the "Indian Revolution" in the early 1930s: *Ghāndī wa al-Ḥarakah al-Hindīyah* (Cairo: Salāmah Mūsá lil-Nashr wa al-Tawzī', 1934[?]).

93. UN press release, 7 October 1947, GA/PAL/7.

94. UN General Assembly Official Records, First Committee, 217th Meeting, 30 November 1948, p. 815.

95. Heydt [aka Haydt] to Brodetzky, 1 January 1948, WA 2806; British Embassy Damascus to Foreign Office, 2 December 1947, FO 816/111, doc. 58, UKNA.

96. OCP (48)3, 10 January 1948, CAB 134/527, p. 2, UKNA.

97. In the east, these realities were later significantly modified by the 1971 secession of East Pakistan, which became Bangladesh.

98. Casey to Ismay, 12 March 1945; Weizmann to Shuckburgh, 31 December 1937; Gandhi to Kallenbach, 17 July 1938; UN General Assembly Official Records, 126th Plenary Meeting, 28 November 1947, p. 1370.

CHAPTER 6

1. Permanent Mandates Commission, Minutes of the Thirty-Second [Extraordinary] Session Devoted to Palestine (C.330.M.222.1937.VI), 83.

2. Susan Pedersen, *The Guardians: The League of Nations and the Crisis of Empire* (Oxford: Oxford University Press, 2015).

3. Covenant of the League of Nations, Article 22 (4), (1).

4. For more on the negotiations that resulted in the main elements of the Balfour Declaration being written into the mandate, see John J. McTague Jr., "Zionist-British Negotiations over the Draft Mandate for Palestine, 1920," *Jewish Social Studies* 42 (1980): 281–292, and James Renton, "Flawed Foundations: The Balfour Declaration and the Palestine Mandate," in *Britain, Palestine, and Empire: The Mandate Years*, ed. Rory Miller (London: Ashgate, 2010), 15–37.

5. Transjordan, which was administered as part of the Palestine mandate, though without the Jewish national home stipulations, became nominally independent in 1928, while Iraq gained its independence and joined the League of Nations in 1932, the first formerly mandated territory to do so.

6. See, for instance, Ronald Hyam, *Britain's Declining Empire: The Road to Decolonisation, 1918–1968* (Cambridge: Cambridge University Press, 2006), and Bernard Wasserstein, *The British in Palestine: The Mandatory Government and the Arab-Jewish Conflict, 1917–1929*, 2nd ed. (Oxford: Oxford University Press, 1991).

7. Gordon Johnson, "Partition, Agitation and Congress: Bengal, 1904 to 1908," *Modern Asian Studies* 7 (1973): 533.

8. Curzon to Brodrick, February 2, 1905, MSS Eur F 111/168, Curzon Papers, Oriental and India Office Collections, British Library, quoted in ibid., 550.

9. On the immediate late-nineteenth-century antecedents of the Bengal partition, see V. P. Menon, *The Transfer of Power in India* (Bombay: Orient Longman, 1957), 9.

10. The evolutions of ideas and movements rarely have neatly defined boundaries. Thus, it could be argued that the seeds of the Home Rule movement began germinating in the 1840s. See, for example, David Harkness, "Ireland," in *Oxford History of the British Empire*, vol. 5 (Oxford: Oxford University Press, 1999), 118.

11. R. F. Foster, *Modern Ireland, 1600–1972* (London: Viking Penguin, 1988), 466.

12. T. G. Fraser, "Ireland and India," in *An Irish Empire?: Aspects of Ireland and the British Empire*, ed. Keith Jeffery (Manchester: Manchester University Press, 1996), 77–93, quotation on 92.

13. A. H. M. Kirk-Greene, *Britain's Imperial Administrators, 1858–1966* (Basingstoke: Macmillan, 2000), 23. The India Office oversaw a population of some four hundred million people.

14. Many authors have noted the preponderance of Irish officers in the Indian civil service in the nineteenth and early twentieth centuries. See, for example, S. B. Cook, *Imperial Affinities: Nineteenth Century Analogies and Exchanges Between India and Ireland* (New Delhi: Sage, 1993), and David Gilmour, *The Ruling Caste: Imperial Lives in the Victorian Raj* (London: John Murray, 2005).

15. For more on the class background of recruits, their training, and their service, see Gilmour, *The Ruling Caste*, and Bernard Porter, *The Absent-Minded Imperialists: Empire, Society, and Culture in Britain* (Oxford: Oxford University Press, 2004), 39–63. On the familial aspect of imperial, in this case Indian, service, see Elizabeth Buettner, *Empire Families: Britons and Late Imperial India* (Oxford: Oxford University Press, 2004).

16. On Furse, see Robert Heussler, *Yesterday's Rulers: The Making of the British Colonial Service* (Syracuse, NY: Syracuse University Press, 1963); on the handshake, see Ralph Furse, *Aucuparius: Recollections of a Recruiting Officer* (Oxford: Oxford University Press, 1962), 230.

17. Ronald Hyam, "Bureaucracy and 'Trusteeship' in the Colonial Empire," in *The Oxford History of the British Empire: The Twentieth Century*, ed. William Roger Louis (Oxford: Oxford University Press, 1998), 257.

18. Roza El-Eini, *Mandated Landscape: British Imperial Rule in Palestine, 1929–1948* (London: Routledge, 2006), 7.

19. Shaunnagh Dorsett and John McLaren, eds., *Legal Histories of the British Empire: Laws, Engagements and Legacies* (London: Routledge, 2014).

20. Frederick Lugard, *The Dual Mandate in British Tropical Africa* (London: William Blackwood and Sons, 1922), 391.

21. Rashid Khalidi, *The Iron Cage: The Story of the Palestinian Struggle for Statehood* (Boston: Beacon, 2006), 55–64. Similarly invented traditions were used in the British mandate of Iraq, on which, see Toby Dodge, *Inventing Iraq: The Failure of Nation Building and a History Denied* (New York: Columbia University Press, 2003).

22. Hyam, *Britain's Declining Empire*, 15.

23. Roger Owen, *Lord Cromer: Victorian Imperialist, Edwardian Proconsul* (Oxford: Oxford University Press, 2004), 357.

24. The attacks on Assyrians in Iraq after that mandate's independence were undoubtedly on the minds of British and Permanent Mandates Commission officials when pondering the situation in Palestine. The Peel Commission tried hard to find out how exactly the Palestinian Arabs proposed to deal with the nearly four hundred thousand Jews already in Palestine in the event of a unitary independent state being established. The results were not encouraging; Arab representatives claimed that the Jews could not be assimilated or accommodated but refused to say how they would deal with this problem. See Palestine Royal Commission, Minutes of Evidence Heard at Public Sessions (with Index), Colonial no. 134 (London: HMSO, 1937), 298, 314.

25. Henry Gurney, "Palestine Postscript," 21, GUR 1/2, Middle East Centre, St. Antony's College, Oxford, quoted in Tom Segev, *One Palestine, Complete: Jews and Arabs Under the British Mandate* (New York: Henry Holt), 9.

26. Palestine: Report on Immigration, Land Settlement and Development, 1930, Cmd. 3686, 146. Indeed, some Zionists hoped that Hope-Simpson would recommend the transfer of some Arabs to Transjordan or Iraq in order to make room for Jewish colonists. Kenneth W. Stein, *The Land Question in Palestine, 1917–1939* (Chapel Hill: University of North Carolina Press, 1984), 91.

27. John W. Cell, *Hailey: A Study in British Imperialism, 1872–1969* (Cambridge: Cambridge University Press, 1992), 278–280. On the Protection of Cultivators Ordinances, see El-Eini, *Mandated Landscape*, 417–418.

28. On the movement of irrigation techniques within the twentieth-century British Empire, see Daniel R. Headrick, *The Tentacles of Progress: Technology Transfer in the Age of Imperialism, 1850–1940* (New York: Oxford University Press, 1988), 190–208. One of the seconded specialists, who later played a critical role in developing partition plans, authored a comprehensive volume on Indian irrigation: D. G. Harris, *Irrigation in India* (London: Oxford University Press, 1923).

29. On Dowson's work in land settlement, and for a compelling argument on the importance of the empire and imperial experience in shaping British land practices in Palestine, see Martin P. Bunton, *Colonial Land Policies in Palestine, 1917–1936* (Oxford: Oxford University Press, 2007). On Dowson and Sheppard, see Dov Gavish, *A Survey of Palestine Under the British Mandate, 1920–1948* (London: RoutledgeCurzon, 2005), 153–155.

30. Tudor's transimperial career is what ultimately brought the Black and Tans to Palestine. Churchill (whom he had first met while a member of the Royal Horse Artillery in Bangalore, India) appointed Tudor as police advisor to the Dublin Castle administration and later suggested him for the position of director of public safety in Palestine. See Tudor's autobiographical account, Misc. 175 (2658), Imperial War Museum, London.

31. Neil Caplan, *Palestine Jewry and the Arab Question, 1917–1925* (London: Frank Cass, 1978), 122. The time the Black and Tans spent in Palestine is alluded to in the lyrics of a Dublin ballad from the 1930s, "Come Out Ye Black and Tans." One verse begins: "Come tell us how you slew / Them ol' Arabs two by two."

32. K. F. Tegart, "Charles Tegart: Memoir of an Indian Policeman," undated manuscript, MSS Eur C235/1, p. 97, Oriental and India Office Collection, British Library,

London. On the mythology around disguise in the Indian police, see Michael Silvestri, "The Thrill of 'Simply Dressing Up': The Indian Police, Disguise, and Intelligence Work in Colonial India," *Journal of Colonialism and Colonial History* 2 (2001): doi: 10.1353/cch.2001.0024. On Tegart's career, see John Curry, *Tegart of the Indian Police* (Tunbridge Wells: Courier, 1960); and Michael Silvestri, "'An Irishman Is Specially Suited to Be a Policeman': Sir Charles Tegart and Revolutionary Terrorism in Bengal," *History-Ireland* (Winter 2000): 40–44.

33. Richard J. Popplewell, *Intelligence and Imperial Defence: British Intelligence and the Defence of the Indian Empire, 1904–1924* (London: Frank Cass, 1995), 269–272. Petrie later went on to become the head of Britain's Security Service (MI5).

34. Papers, correspondence, and memoranda relating to this project are in Box 2/2, Tegart Papers, Middle East Centre, St. Antony's College, Oxford University.

35. Charles Townshend, "The Defense of Palestine: Insurrection and Public Security," *English Historical Review* 103, no. 409 (1988): 943.

36. On the plans, see Penny Sinanoglou, "British Plans for the Partition of Palestine, 1929–1938," *Historical Journal* 52, no. 1 (2009): 131–152.

37. Penny Sinanoglou, "The Peel Commission and Partition," in *Britain, Palestine, and Empire: The Mandate Years*, ed. Rory Miller (London: Ashgate, 2010), 119–140.

38. L. G. Archer Cust, "The Future of Palestine," January 18, 1935, CO 733/283/12, National Archives, Kew.

39. D. G. Harris to R. Coupland, April 15, 1937, CO 733/351/2, National Archives, Kew.

40. For a greater discussion of Coupland's work and philosophy, see T. G. Fraser, "Sir Reginald Coupland, the Round Table and the Problem of Divided Societies," in *The Round Table, the Empire/Commonwealth and British Foreign Policy*, ed. Andrew Bosco and Alex May (London: Lothian Foundation, 1997), 407–422.

41. R. Coupland, "The British Empire and the World Crisis," in *The Empire Club of Canada Speeches, 1933–1934* (Toronto: Empire Club of Canada, 1934), 166–175, quotation on 166.

42. Palestine Royal Commission Report [Peel Report], 1937, Cmd. 5479, 375.

43. Palestine Royal Commission, Minutes, 48–51.

44. Peel Report, 386.

45. Ibid., 122.

46. Martin Gilbert, *Winston S. Churchill*, Companion Volume 5, part 3 (London: Heinemann, 1982), 608–609.

47. Ibid., 612.

CHAPTER 7

1. *She'ifotenu* 2, no. 10 (1932): 326.

2. [Judah L. Magnes], "Oral Evidence Before the United Nations Special Committee on Palestine at the Public Meeting Held in Jerusalem on Monday, 14 July 1947," in Judah L. Magnes, M. Reiner, Lord Samuel, E. Simon, and M. Smilansky, *Palestine: Divided or United? A Case for a Bi-National Palestine Before the United Nations* (Jerusalem: Achva Cooperative, 1947), 40.

3. Ibid., 32, 46.

4. "The Case Against Partition: Additional Memorandum Presented to UNSCOP," in ibid., 75–76.

5. To be sure, both nation-states and their alternatives were capable of such reproduction (or better put: both nation-states and their alternatives were incapable of transcending and overcoming the imperial situation). See "From the Editors: Experiencing the Imperial Situation Without Empire," *Ab Imperio* 2 (2016): 9–17.

6. An early example, perhaps the earliest overt one, is Hans Kohn's 1919 essay "On the Arab Question," in which Kohn proclaimed that the future "Palestinian state . . . will not be a national state for an indefinite period, but a multinational one (*Nationalitätenstaat*)." Hans Kohn, "Zur Araberfrage," *Der Jude* 4, no. 12 (1919): 567–569. This translation is based on Wilma Abeles Iggers, ed., *The Jews of Bohemia and Moravia: A Historical Reader* (Detroit: Wayne State University Press, 1992), 239–242.

7. Members of Brit Shalom decried the systematic injustice caused by Zionist settlement in Palestine. As functionaries of Zionist organizations, however, they can be seen as the architects of that policy. This was much more than ironic; in fact, it represented an existential contradiction. On some level the members of Brit Shalom were torn.

8. Brit Shalom, [Untitled excerpt from the leaflet "Our Estimation"], *She'ifotenu* 1, no. 4 (1930): 3.

9. Quoted in Aharon Kedar, "Brith Shalom," *Jerusalem Quarterly* 18 (Winter 1981): 68.

10. "The Brit-Shalom Society's Programme for Co-operation Between Jews and Arabs," in *Jewish-Arab Affairs: Occasional Papers Published by the Brit Shalom* (Jerusalem: [Brit Shalom], 1931), 47.

11. Different binational Zionists envisioned different political mechanisms at different times, and many of them focused on the general anti-partition principle first, leaving the question of detailed mechanisms to a later stage. The 1926 platform of Brit Shalom's Hans Kohn, for example, was based on the Austro-Marxist concept of a federation of extraterritorial national autonomies. Shlomo Kaplanski (who was not a member of Ihud but was featured in its periodical *Ba'ayot*) labeled his 1944 platform "Paritative Federation" and already envisioned a gradual transition from an extraterritorial federation to a regional (cantonal) one. Ihud's 1946 statement before the Anglo-American Committee of Inquiry detailed a cantonal federation. Hans Kohn, "Zur künftigen Gestaltung Palästinas," in *Zionistische Politik: Eine Aufsatzreihe*, ed. Hans Kohn and Robert Weltsch (Mährisch-Ostrau: Farber, 1927), 275; [Shlomo Kaplanski], "Bemaagal Baayoteinu" (In Our Circle of Problems), *Ba'ayot* 1, no. 3 (Sivan 5704/May 1944), 137; "Tazkir Agutad Ihud el Vaadat Hachakira" (Ihud's Memorandum to the Committee of Inquiry), *Ba'ayot* 2, no. 4 (Nissan 5706/April 1946), 28.

12. Penny Sinanoglou, "The Peel Commission and Partition, 1936–1938," in *Britain, Palestine and Empire: The Mandate Years*, ed. Rory Miller (Farnham: Ashgate, 2010), 119–140.

13. Minorities and majorities, Brit Shalom cofounder Hans Kohn insisted, are "primarily political and not numerical concepts." Hans Kohn, "Minorities," in *Encyclopaedia Britannica*, 15th ed., vol. 15 (Chicago, 1947), 564–576, quotation on 564.

14. The various binationalist organizations are introduced in the pioneering work of Susan Lee Hattis, *The Bi-National Idea in Palestine During Mandatory Times* (Haifa: Shikmona, 1970).

15. Even before the formation of Ihud, Magnes testified already before the Woodhead Commission (1938), probing the feasibility of the Peel Commission's partition plan.

16. "Dvar Hama'arechet" (Editorial), *She'ifotenu* 2, no. 9 (1931): 291.

17. Kohn was a member of the International Council of War Resisters' International from 1926 to 1928 and again from 1931 to 1934. On his pacifist career, see Dieter Riesenberger, "Hans Kohn (1891–1971): Zionist und Pazifist," *Zeitschrift für Religions u. Geistesgeschichte* 4, nos. 1–2 (1989): 166–174. See also Adi Gordon, "The Ideological Convert and the 'Mythology of Coherence': The Contradictory Hans Kohn and His Multiple Metamorphoses," *Leo Baeck Institute Yearbook* 55 (2010): 273–293. On War Resisters' International in general and Kohn's role in it, see Devi Prasad, *War Is a Crime Against Humanity: The Story of "War Resisters' International"* (London: War Resisters' International, 2005), especially 118–132.

18. Hans Kohn, "Aktiver Pazifismus," *Neue Wege: Blätter für religiose Arbeit* 23, no. 2 (1929): 84.

19. Gabriel Baer, "Lekach Ha Tragedia Ha Kurdit" (The Lesson from the Kurdish Tragedy), *Ba'ayot* 2, no. 5 (Elul 5706/September 1946): 225–237, quotation on 236.

20. The scholar who most effectively discussed that dimension of binational Zionism is Amnon Raz-Krakotzkin. See Amnon Raz-Krakotzkin, "A National Colonial Theology: Religion, Orientalism and the Construction of the Secular in Zionist Discourse," *Tel Aviver Jahrbuch für Deutsche Geschichte* 30 (2002): 304–318; and Amnon Raz-Krakotzkin, "On the Right Side of the Barricades: Walter Benjamin, Gershom Scholem, and Zionism," *Comparative Literature* 65, no. 3 (2013): 363–381.

21. "Dvar Hama'arechet" (Editorial), *She'ifotenu* 3, no. 1 (1932): 1–2.

22. Hans Kohn to Robert Weltsch, December 21, 1925, AR 7185, box 7, folder 18, Robert Weltsch Collection, Leo Baeck Institute Archives, New York.

23. Hugo Bergmann, "She'elat Hayachas" (The Question of Relation), *She'ifotenu* 1, no. 1 (1927): 19–20.

24. Hugo Bergmann, "Lish'elat Harov" (On the Majority Question), *She'ifotenu* 1, no. 3 (1929): 25.

25. Ibid., 38.

26. "Chalifat Michtavim im Professor A. Einstein" (Correspondence Professor A. Einstein) [Albert Einstein's letter of June 19, 1930, to Hugo Bergmann], *She'ifotenu* 1, no. 5 (1930): 17.

27. Robert Weltsch, "Likrat Hakongress Hayudzayin" (Problems of the XVII Zionist Congress), *She'ifotenu* 2, no. 4 (1931): 132.

28. Ernst Simon, "Ne'um Shelo Ne'emar Bakongress" (A Speech Which Was Not Delivered at the Congress), *She'ifotenu* 2, no. 5 (1931): 166.

29. Ibid., 167–168.

30. Gershom Scholem, "Bemai Ka'Mipalgi" (What's the Trouble About?), *She'ifotenu* 2, no. 6 (1931): 196–197, 199, 200–201.

31. Bergmann, "Lish'elat Harov" (On the Majority Question), 24.

32. Ibid., 26 (emphasis added).

33. Robert Weltsch, "Hasochnut Vehale'umiut," (The Agency and the Nationality), *She'ifotenu* 1, no. 3 (1929): 9.

34. "Dvar Hama'arechet" (Editorial), *She'ifotenu* 3, no. 2 (1932): 35.

35. Yfaat Weiss, "Central European Ethonationalism and Zionist Binationalism," *Jewish Social Studies* 11, no. 1 (2004): 112–113.

36. Article 2 of "The Palestine Mandate," Avalon Project, Yale Law School, July 24, 1922, http://avalon.law.yale.edu/20th_century/palmanda.asp.

37. Indeed, historian Dmitry Shumsky even claimed that the entire binationalist agenda of the Prague-born (or Bohemia-born) binationalists was founded on their formative late-Habsburg experience and their early identification with autonomist-federative reform plans. Dmitry Shumsky, *Zweisprachigkeit und binationale Idee: Der Prager Zionismus 1900–1930*, trans. Dafna Mach (Göttingen: Vandenhoeck & Ruprecht, 2012).

38. Hans Kohn, *Living in a World Revolution: My Encounters with History* (New York: Trident, 1964), 18.

39. Hans Kohn, "Lidmuta Hapolitit Shel Eretz Israel" (The Political Formation of Palestine), *She'ifotenu* 1, no. 1 (1927): 29, see also 31.

40. Joseph Lurya, "Hazchuyot Hale'umiot Bishvaytz Befinland Uve'eretz Israel" (National Rights in Switzerland, Finland, and Palestine), *She'ifotenu* 1, no. 3 (1929): 10.

41. Ibid., 19. Brit Shalom's claim regarding Finland was reiterated also in "Dvar Hama'arechet" (Editorial), *She'ifotenu* 2, no. 1 (1931): 4.

42. Mordekhai Ben Ephraim, "Tzionut Vefederatzia Aravit" (Zionism and Arab Federation), *She'ifotenu* 2, no. 4 (1931): 138.

43. [Kaplanski], "Bemaagal Baayoteinu" (In Our Circle of Problems), 141.

44. "Tazkir Agutad Ihud el Vaadat Hachakira" (Ihud's Memorandum to the Committee of Inquiry), 27–28.

45. Hans Kohn, "Knisat Iraq El Chever Hale'umim" (The Admission of Iraq to the League of Nation), *She'ifotenu* 3, no. 4 (1932): 117.

46. Hans Kohn, "He'arot Achadot Al She'elot Konstitutzioniyot Shel Hamandat Ha'eretz Yisra'eli. Sof" (Several Comments on Constitutional Questions of the Palestine Mandate. Part II), *She'ifotenu* 2, no. 2 (1931): 49–50.

47. A. Bonne, "Problemot Hameshek Hakaspi Be'eretz Israel" (Monetary Problems in Palestine), ibid., 63.

48. "Dvar Hama'arechet" (Editorial), *She'ifotenu* 3, no. 4 (1932): 99–100.

49. Hans Kohn, "Hamizrach Hechadash" (The New East), *She'ifotenu* 1, no. 2 (1928): 14–17.

50. "Notes and Comments," Editorial, in *Jewish-Arab Affairs: Occasional Papers*, 2–3. See also "Dvar Hama'arechet" (Editorial), *She'ifotenu* 3, no. 2 (1931): 81–82.

51. For a thought-provoking historiographic introductory discussion of the relationship between Zionism and colonialism, see Derek J. Penslar, "Zionism, Colonialism and Postcolonialism," *Journal of Israeli History* 20, nos. 2–3 (2001): 84–98.

52. E[rnst] Simon and E[scha] Simon, "Ba'aspaklarya Shelanu" (From Our Perspective), *She'ifotenu* 1, no. 4 (1930): 37. Fellow binational Zionist Rabbi Binyamin (Yehoshua Radler-Feldmann, 1880–1957) objected: "The atrocities of Hebron and Safed cannot be

clarified by technical comparison to that which happened in other countries. There are singular traits here, and precisely as a pan-Semite I do not intend to overlook the gaping rift." R.B., "Mimgliton Hashigyon" (The Annals of Folly), ibid., 44.

53. Scholem, "Bemai Ka'Mipalgi" (What's the Trouble About?), 201–203.

54. Translation based on Amnon Raz-Krakotzkin, "'On the Right Side of the Barricades': Walter Benjamin, Gershom Scholem, and Zionism," *Comparative Literature* 65, no. 3 (2013): 363–381.

55. Rabbi Benjamin, "Hamizracha" (Eastward Ho! III), *She'ifotenu* 2, no. 3 (1931): 142.

56. Hugo Bergmann, "Anachnu ushcheneinu" (We and Our Neighbors), *She'ifotenu* 2, no. 6 (1931): 209.

57. Robert Weltsch, "Yachasenu Limdiniyut Hamizrach" (Our Relation to the [British] Orient Policy), *She'ifotenu* 1, no. 1 (1927): 40. The Hebrew text was based on his earlier German-language articles in the *Jüdische Rundschau* from 1922 and 1925.

58. "Tzlalim" (Silhouettes), Editorial, *She'ifotenu* 1, no. 5 (1929): 13–14.

59. M. R. Akhtar, "Tzionut Vetikvat Hamizrach" (Zionism and Arab Aspiration), *She'ifotenu* 2, no. 1 (1931): 19. The Hebrew translated title speaks of "Orient's Aspirations," and not only Arab ones.

60. "Dvar Hama'arechet" (Editorial), *She'ifotenu* 2, no. 1 (1931): 2.

61. Hugo Bergmann, "Die arabische Föderation" (The Arab Federation), *Wiener Morgenzeitung*, June 21, 1923, 1–2.

62. "Dvar Hama'arechet" (Editorial), *She'ifotenu* 2, no. 2 (1931): 43–44.

63. For a recent thought-provoking overview of the mutual gazes of Indian nationalists on one hand and Zionists on the other, see Arie M. Dubnov, "Notes on the Zionist Passage to India, or: The Analogical Imagination and Its Boundaries," *Journal of Israeli History* 35, no. 2 (2016): 177–214. Another personal connection between binational Zionist "partition objectors" and Muslim Indians can be seen in the person of Sir Abdur Rahman, representative of India at the 1947 United Nations Special Committee on Palestine. The representatives of India—alongside those of Iran and Yugoslavia—held the minority position at UNSCOP in favoring a federal state plan and objecting to the partition plan.

64. "Dvar Hama'arechet" (Editorial), *She'ifotenu* 2, no. 1 (1931): 8. The biblical quotation is "For from Zion will go forth the law / Even the word of the Lord from Jerusalem."

65. "Dvar Hama'arechet" (Editorial), *She'ifotenu* 2, no. 10 (1932): 326.

66. Kohn, "Lidmuta Hapolitit Shel Eretz Israel," 31. The German original ("Zur politischen Gestaltung Palästinas") was originally published in German in *Jüdische Rundschau* on June 25, 1926. It was later reprinted in Hans Kohn and Robert Weltsch, *Zionistische Politik: Eine Aufsatzreihe* (Mährisch-Ostrau: Farber, 1927), 268–291.

67. Kohn, "Lidmuta Hapolitit Shel Eretz Israel," 31.

68. Weiss, "Central European Ethonationalism and Zionist Binationalism," 93–117.

69. Faisal Devji, *Muslim Zion: Pakistan as a Political Idea* (Cambridge, MA: Harvard University Press, 2013), 3.

70. "Dvar Hama'arechet" (Editorial), *She'ifotenu* 2, no. 1 (1931): 6–7.

71. Kohn, *Living in a World Revolution*, 9–10.

72. "Dvar Hama'arechet" (Editorial), *She'ifotenu* 3, no. 7 (1931): 221.

73. Ibid., 221–222, 224.

74. "Dvar Hama'arechet" (Editorial), *She'ifotenu* 2, no. 10 (1932): 326.

75. Kohn, *Living in a World Revolution*, 94–95, 130. See also Hans Kohn, War Diary, October 14 and 17, 1915, AR 259, box 23, folder 2, Hans Kohn Collection, Leo Baeck Institute Archives, New York.

76. Terry Martin, "Affirmative Action Empire: The Soviet Union as the Highest Form of Imperialism," in *A State of Nations: Empire and Nation-Making in the Age of Lenin and Stalin*, ed. Ronald Grigor Suny and Terry Martin (New York: Oxford University Press, 2001), 67–90. Ihud was already more interested in the Soviet Union "as a multinational State." See, for example, "Tazkir Agutad Ihud el Vaadat Hachakira" (Ihud's Memorandum to the Committee of Inquiry), 28.

77. Hans Kohn, for one, was intrigued and inspired by the Soviet nationalities policy and published two books on the matter: *Sinn und Schicksal der Revolution* (Vienna: E. P. Tal, 1923); and *Der Nationalismus in der Sowjetunion* (Frankfurt am Main: Societäts-Verlag, 1932). See also Adi Gordon, *Toward Nationalism's End: An Intellectual Biography of Hans Kohn* (Waltham, MA: Brandeis University Press, 2017), chap. 2.

78. Weiss, "Central European Ethonationalism and Zionist Binationalism," 98 (emphasis added).

79. Dmitry Shumsky, "Historiography, Nationalism and Bi-nationalism: Czech-German Jewry, the Prague Zionists, and the Origins of the Bi-national Approach of Hugo Bergmann" [in Hebrew], *Zion* 69, no. 1 (2004): 61; Schumsky, *Zweisprachigkeit und binationale Idee*, 72.

80. Steven E. Aschheim, *Beyond the Border: The German-Jewish Legacy Abroad* (Princeton, NJ: Princeton University Press, 2007), 14.

81. Bergmann, "Lish'elat Harov" (On the Majority Question), 25.

82. Ibid., 38.

CHAPTER 8

1. Philip Mattar, ed., *Encyclopedia of the Palestinians* (New York: Facts on File, 2000), 336; Benny Morris, *One State, Two States: Resolving the Israel/Palestine Conflict* (New Haven, CT: Yale University Press, 2009), 102.

2. Cecil Hourani, *An Unfinished Odyssey: Lebanon and Beyond* (London: Weidenfeld and Nicolson, 1984), 65.

3. George Antonius, *The Arab Awakening: The Story of the Arab National Movement* (Philadelphia: J. B. Lippincott, 1939), 412.

4. Susan Silsby Boyle, *Betrayal of Palestine: The Story of George Antonius* (Boulder, CO: Westview, 2001), 18 n. 2; Walid Khalidi, "On Albert Hourani, the Arab Office, and the Anglo-American Committee of 1946," *Journal of Palestine Studies* 35, no. 1 (2005): 64.

5. Boyle, *Betrayal of Palestine*, 3–4, 10, 15.

6. Donald Reid, "Arabic Thought in the Liberal Age Twenty Years After," *International Journal of Middle East Studies* 14, no. 4 (1982): 553–554.

7. Albert Hourani, "Great Britain and Arab Nationalism, 1943," 4–5, Box 2, File 4, Clayton Papers, St. Antony's Middle East Centre Archives (henceforth SAMEA). Copy in British National Archives, Foreign Office 141/1206 (henceforth BNA, FO).

8. Ibid., 6.

9. Richard Crossman, *Palestine Mission: A Personal Record* (New York: Arno, 1977), 123.

10. Hourani, "Great Britain and Arab Nationalism," 60.

11. Khalidi, "On Albert Hourani," 63; Geoffrey Warren Furlonge, *Palestine Is My Country: The Story of Musa Alami* (London: Murray, 1969), 81, 100–102.

12. Furlonge, *Palestine Is My Country*, 109–110; according to Khalidi, "On Albert Hourani," 64, Antonius also participated in drafting the memorandum.

13. Great Britain Palestine Royal Commission, "Palestine Royal Commission Report" (London: His Majesty's Stationary Office, 1937), 401–403.

14. Furlonge, *Palestine Is My Country*, 117.

15. Ibid., 111–112.

16. Hourani, "Great Britain and Arab Nationalism," 60.

17. E. C. Hodgkin, *Spectator*, June 30, 1984.

18. Furlonge, *Palestine Is My Country*, 117–122.

19. Al-'Alami's address to the Preparatory Conference of the Arab League, December 22, 1944, BNA, FO 371/45235, 67; quotation from ibid., 127–128.

20. Ronald Storrs Diary, July 6, 1946, Box 6/7, Storrs Papers, Pembroke College, Cambridge.

21. Hourani, "Great Britain and Arab Nationalism," 60. This judgment is supported by "Manifesto by Arab Leaders Now in Syria," July 10, 1939, BNA, FO 371/23238, 197–211, in which political and military leaders of the revolt denounce al-Hajj Amin al-Husayni and the AHC's rejection of the White Paper.

22. Hourani, "Great Britain and Arab Nationalism," 58.

23. Storrs Diary, October 24, 1947.

24. Furlonge, *Palestine Is My Country*, 130–135.

25. "Protocol of Preparatory Committee for Arab Congress," December 22, 1944, BNA, FO 371/45235, 64; Farquhar to Churchill, July 4, 1945, BNA, FO 371/45239, 91–92; H. Stonehewer-Bird, "Visit of Musa Alami to Bagdad," May 4, 1945, BNA, FO 371/45238, 143–145; Furlonge, *Palestine Is My Country*, 138–139, 150.

26. "Protocol of Preparatory Committee for Arab Congress," 39–72. Al-'Alami thought the Saudis were also concerned that they did not have adequate resources or suitable personnel to contribute to the effort. Jordan to Foreign Office, January 6 and 22, 1945, BNA, FO 371/45235, 80–82, 87.

27. "Irgun ha-misradim ha-'araviyim—shonot," 332/28 peh, Israel State Archive (Archion ha-Medina, henceforth ISA).

28. Clayton to Baxter, November 28, 1945, BNA, FO 371/45241, 111.

29. Colonel de Gaury, "Material for a History of the Arab Union, 1939–1945," BNA, FO 371/45241, 11.

30. C. Hourani, *An Unfinished Odyssey*, 57.

31. The relevant memoirs include Khalidi, "On Albert Hourani," 76; C. Hourani, *An Unfinished Odyssey*, 57–58; and Izzat Tannous, *The Palestinians: A Detailed Documented Eyewitness History of Palestine Under British Mandate* (New York: I.G.T., 1988), 369–371.

See also the Jewish Agency, Washington Office report by Eliahu Epstein and Moshe Perlman to Arthur Lourie, August 24, 1945, Central Zionist Archive (henceforth CZA) L/70. The Israeli Army seized the archive of the Jerusalem Arab Office when it closed Orient House in 2001. After review by the Foreign Ministry Research Department, the papers were designated "abandoned documents" (*te'udot netushot*), declassified, and deposited in the Israel State Archive. They provide only a fragmentary and unsystematically arranged record. It is unclear whether all the documents have been preserved.

32. Tanzimat al-maktab al-'arabi fi amrika li-sanat 1946–1947, Jerusalem, February 6, 1946, "Hora'ot le-mar hourani be-noge'a le-ptichat ha-misrad ha-'aravi be-washington," ISA 338/7 peh; Khadim al-qadiyya to Musa al-'Alami, n.d., "Michtavim le-Musa 'Alami—tazkirim ve-hitkatvut," ISA 338/1 peh.

33. Letters to Musa al-'Alami, April 22 and May 1, 1945, ISA 345/15 peh.

34. Musa al-'Alami, Instructions to C. A. Hourani, April 2, 1946, "Hora'ot le-mar Hourani be-noge'a le-ftichat ha-misrad ha-'aravi be-washington," ISA 338/7 peh; Eliahu Epstein and Moshe Perlman to Arthur Lourie, August 24, 1945, CZA L/70.

35. Tannous, a partisan of the Mufti, claims he was the first director, but no other source mentions this.

36. Rory Miller, "The Other Side of the Coin: Arab Propaganda and the Battle Against Zionism in London, 1937–48," *Israel Affairs* 5, no. 4 (1999): 218.

37. "Irgun ha-misradim ha-'araviyim—shonot," ISA 332/28 peh.

38. Letter from Musa Alami to employees of the Arab Office, May 15, 1946, "Hora'ot le-mar Hourani," ISA 338/7 peh.

39. Khalidi, "On Albert Hourani," 66.

40. Anglo-American Committee of Inquiry, "Preface," in *Report to the United States Government and His Majesty's Government in the United Kingdom*, Pub. 2536 (Washington, DC: GPO, 1946), Avalon Project, Yale Law School, http://avalon.law.yale.edu/20th_century/angpre.asp.

41. Yosef Grodzinsky, *In the Shadow of the Holocaust: The Struggle Between Jews and Zionists in the Aftermath of World War II* (Monroe, ME: Common Courage Press, 2004).

42. "Displaced Persons," *Holocaust Encyclopedia*, United States Holocaust Memorial Museum, http://www.ushmm.org/wlc/en/article.php?ModuleId=10005462.

43. Wm. Roger Louis, *The British Empire in the Middle East, 1945–1951* (Oxford: Oxford University Press, 1984), 397–407.

44. A. H. Hourani to Musa Eff. Alami, December 7, 1945, "ha-Va'ada ha-anglo-amerika'it le-vdikat sugiyot eretz yisra'el," ISA 338/15 peh.

45. A. H. Hourani, "Is Zionism the Answer to the Jewish Problem?," Pamphlets on Arab Affairs, no. 2 (London: Arab Office, June 1946).

46. Arab Office, London, *The Future of Palestine* (Geneva: Imprimerie Centrale, 1947).

47. Arab Office, Jerusalem, *The Problem of Palestine: Evidence Submitted by the Arab Office, Jerusalem, to the Anglo-American Committee of Inquiry, March 1946* (Washington, DC: Arab Office, 1946).

48. Jamal al-Husayni, Anglo-American Commission of Inquiry, "Jerusalem Public Hearings," March 12, 1946, 22.

49. Ibid., 19.

50. Issa Khalaf, *Politics in Palestine: Arab Factionalism and Social Disintegration, 1939–1948* (Albany: State University of New York Press, 1991), 122.

51. Anglo-American Commission of Enquiry, "Jerusalem Public Hearings," March 25, 1946, 169.

52. Abdulaziz A. Al-Sudairi, *A Vision of the Middle East: An Intellectual Biography of Albert Hourani* (London: Centre for Lebanese Studies, in association with I. B. Tauris, 1999), 117.

53. "The Case Against a Jewish State in Palestine: Albert Hourani's Statement to the Anglo-American Committee of Enquiry of 1946," Jerusalem Public Hearings, March 25, 1946, *Journal of Palestine Studies* 35, no. 1 (2005): 80–81.

54. Arab Office, Jerusalem, *The Problem of Palestine*, 1, 8, 9.

55. "The Case Against a Jewish State in Palestine," 81.

56. Ibid., 82.

57. Ibid., 83–84.

58. Ibid., 90.

59. Bartley C. Crum, *Behind the Silken Curtain: A Personal Account of Anglo-American Diplomacy in Palestine and the Middle East* (New York: Simon and Schuster, 1947), 255.

60. C. Hourani, *An Unfinished Odyssey*, 67–68.

61. David Horowitz, *State in the Making* (New York: Knopf, 1953), 67.

62. Letter from A.L., March 30, 1946, Z6/287-19, Nahum Goldman Papers, CZA.

63. Louis, *The British Empire in the Middle East*, 411.

64. Crum, *Behind the Silken Curtain*, 254.

65. Anglo-American Committee of Inquiry, "Chapter 1: Recommendations and Comments," in *Report to the United States Government and His Majesty's Government in the United Kingdom*, Avalon Project, Yale Law School, http://avalon.law.yale.edu/20th_century/angch01.asp.

66. Miller, "The Other Side of the Coin," 220.

67. Rory Miller, *Divided Against Zion: Anti-Zionist Opposition in Britain to a Jewish State in Palestine, 1945–1948* (Portland, OR: Frank Cass, 2000), 15; C. Hourani, *An Unfinished Odyssey*, 71.

68. Khalidi, "On Albert Hourani," 70.

69. Richard Crossman, "Lecture to the RIIA," June 13, 1946, Crossman Papers, SAMEA.

70. Earl of Halifax to the Foreign Office, November 8, 1945, BNA, FO 371/45394.

71. Crossman, *Palestine Mission*, 14.

72. Ibid., 41, 123; Louis, *The British Empire in the Middle East*, 401.

73. "Testimony Before the Anglo-American Committee on Palestine by Professor Philip K. Hitti," [Washington Public Hearings, January 11, 1946] (Washington DC: Arab Office, 1946), GB165-0504, Palestine Pamphlets, SAMEA.

74. Jewish Telegraphic Agency, "F.B.I. Agents Raid Arab Office in Washington; State Department Investigating," March 11, 1947; Shotef shonot, 3/1947–5/1947, ISA 329/21 peh.

75. H.Q. British Troops in Palestine and Transjordan, "Fortnightly Intelligence Newsletter," no. 11, March 17–30, 1946, BNA, War Office 169/23021 Part 1.

76. Amikam Nachmani, "A Rare Testimony: Albert Hourani and the Anglo-American Committee, 1946," in *Middle Eastern Politics and Ideas: A History from Within*, ed. Ilan Pappé and Moshe Ma'oz (London: Tauris Academic Studies, 1997), 91.

77. Albert Hourani and Jacob Talmon, *Israel and the Arabs* (London: J. B. Wolter Groningen, 1967).

78. Quoted in Al-Sudairi, *A Vision of the Middle East*, 106.

79. Albert Hourani, "The Arab Awakening Forty Years Later," in *The Emergence of the Modern Middle East* (London: Macmillan, 1981), 193–215.

CHAPTER 9

This essay has benefited from conversations with countless individuals over time, but I particularly thank here Guneeta Singh Bhalla, Hamida Chopra, Arie Dubnov, Sadaf Jaffer, Sunil Khanna, Aishwary Kumar, Aprajit Mahajan, Ana Minian, Ishmeet Narula, Nazir Qaiser, Jazib Qureshi, Jagat and Indira Satia, Sudipta Sen, Nishita Sharma, Bikramjit Singh, Pashaura Singh, Poonam Singh, Tashie and Naheed Zaheer, and Anam Zakaria. An earlier version of this essay was published by *Tanqeed: A Magazine of Politics and Culture*, at Tanqeed.org.

1. See the work of the Berkeley-based Partition Archive and the Citizens Archive of Pakistan (CAP).

2. In 2001 Gyanendra Pandey called on historians to explore the meaning of Partition in terms of what it produced—the social arrangements, the forms of consciousness, and the subjectivities it created—rather than focus obsessively on causes. See his *Remembering Partition: Violence, Nationalism and History in India* (Cambridge: Cambridge University Press, 2001), 50.

3. Pandey, *Remembering Partition*, 50; Rakhshanda Jalil, *Liking Progress, Loving Change* (Delhi: Oxford University Press, 2014), 334.

4. Joan Scott, "Women in *The Making of the English Working Class*," in *Gender and the Politics of History* (New York: Columbia University Press, 1999 [1988]), 80–81, citing Henry Abelove. See also, generally, E. P. Thompson, "Commitment and Poetry" *Stand* 20 (1979): 53–57, and "Outside the Whale," in *The Poverty of Theory and Other Essays* (London: Merlin, 1978 [1959]).

5. In 1960, as he wrote *The Making of the English Working Class*, he criticized the poet W. H. Auden for retreating from the political engagement that had once taken him as far as risking his life in the Spanish Civil War—Auden repeating Wordsworth's fall. A few years later, Auden ventured into political terrain just enough to pen "Partition," a satirical poem about Sir Cyril Radcliffe's role in partitioning India "Between two peoples fanatically at odds / With their different diets and incompatible gods."

6. E. P. Thompson, "The Nehru Tradition," in *Writing by Candlelight* (London: Merlin, 1980), 138.

7. I have written about this at length in "Byron, Gandhi, and the Thompsons: The Making of British Social History and Unmaking of Indian History," *History Workshop Journal* 81 (2016): 135–170.

8. E. P. Thompson, *The Making of the English Working Class* (New York: Vintage, 1966 [1963]), 13.

9. I leave out major figures, do not distinguish between Urdu and Punjabi, and neglect Bengal entirely. I am painfully aware that I write cursorily here about subjects that others have researched at great length. See, for instance, the work of Veena Das, Ashis Nandy, Ravinder Kaur, Bhaskar Sarkar, Gyanendra Pandey, Mushirul Hasan, Yasmin Khan, Neeti Nair, Jisha Menon, Faisal Devji, Lucy Chester, David Gilmartin, and Vazira Zamindar.

10. Alpana Kishore told Anam Zakaria that certain Punjabi cultural traits, like irreverence, help explain why they do not take Partition "seriously" and instead push it aside. Their grandparents had moved abruptly beyond it, and a long history of invasions through the region also desensitized them. Anam Zakaria, *The Footprints of Partition: Narratives of Four Generations of Pakistanis and Indians* (New Delhi: HarperCollins, 2015), 165. But the sensitivity captured in volumes of oral histories that Zakaria and the Partition Archive have collected belie this suggestion. The cavalierness toward Partition is more complex; it is certainly rooted in the sense of a long history of displacement, but there is "baggage" aplenty. On Afghans as "imperial cosmopolitans" too, see Robert Crews, *Afghan Modern: A Global History of a Nation* (Cambridge, MA: Harvard University Press, 2015).

11. On Partition in Indian cinema, see Bhaskar Sarkar, *Mourning the Nation: Indian Cinema in the Wake of Partition* (Durham, NC: Duke University Press, 2009). Yash and his brother B. R. Chopra did not see any connection between Partition and their film *Waqt* (1965), in which a family is separated by an earthquake—a natural cracking of the land that might easily be read as an allegory for Partition. Yash did think that many Hindi films dealt with Partition but could name only a few. His brother, on the other hand, felt the industry avoided the topic; both discounted allegorical interpretations of popular films. Sarkar concludes that Yash's impression that Partition *had* been an explicit subject of Hindi films was based on the many oblique depictions of it and diagnoses the industry as simultaneously repressing and representing Partition (119–124). Most well known among films addressing Partition directly are those of Ritwik Ghatak; the TV film *Tamas* (1988), based on Bhisham Sahni's 1974 novel of that name; and the film *Garam Hawa* (1973), based on a story by Ismat Chughtai. Deepa Mehta's *Earth*, based on Bapsi Sidhwa's novel *Cracking India*, is also in this category, as is *Train to Pakistan* (1998), based on Khushwant Singh's 1956 novel of the same name. The close bond between literature and these films is notable. Of course, there has been a spate of more recent films on the Indo-Pak border, such as *Gadar, Veer Zara*, and *Bajrangi Bhaijaan*, besides the more military-focused ones like *Border, LOC*, and so on. The "split self" described later in this essay finds its echo in the double roles that have been so popular in Hindi films.

12. This poetic universe is highly gendered, in those erotic connotations, but also ungendered in its often ambiguously gendered first-person subject. The historian Joan Scott noted that E. P. Thompson included poetry in "the masculine, in opposition to a set of unacceptable excluded terms—the domestic, the spiritual, the expressive, the religious, the undisciplined, and the irrational—all of which are coded as feminine" (Scott, "Women in *The Making*," 83). The gender politics of poetry in Punjab may not be dramatically different, but the layering of social and political content on often highly gendered motifs

of spiritual and worldly love suggests a more complex gender story. Themes of love and society were more separate in most Romantic English poetry.

13. See also Jalil, *Liking Progress*, chap. 1. Some of the information on poets in the next pages is derived from the Urdu Academy of the Bay Area (organized by Tashie Zaheer) and the Bay Area mushairas organized by Hamida Chopra.

14. Frances Pritchett, *Nets of Awareness: Urdu Poetry and Its Critics* (Berkeley: University of California Press, 1994), 146–147, 154, 167. The historian and parliamentarian Thomas Macaulay served in the supreme council of the East India Company from 1834 to 1838, overseeing major educational and legal reforms. His 1835 "Minute on Indian Education" was a rebuttal to council members who believed that Indian students should continue to be educated in Sanskrit and Arabic as well as English; his view won.

15. Akshaya Kumar, *Poetry, Politics and Culture: Essays on Indian Texts and Contexts* (Delhi: Routledge, 2009), 214–218; Jalil, *Liking Progress*, 75. The Ghadar Party split between communist and anticommunist factions after the war. I thank Bikramjit Singh for his personal memories on this subject. *Preet Lari* remains in print today, with its headquarters still at Preet Nagar. Note that farther northwest, too, the left offered an alternative vision: in 1930, the Red Shirt Movement began in the North-West Frontier Province, joining forces with Congress's nonviolence.

16. Neeti Nair, *Changing Homelands: Hindu Politics and the Partition of India* (Cambridge, MA: Harvard University Press, 2011), 77.

17. Jalil, *Liking Progress*, chap. 2.

18. Priya Satia, *Spies in Arabia: The Great War and the Cultural Foundations of Britain's Covert Empire in the Middle East* (Oxford: Oxford University Press, 2008), chap. 6. Jalil notes the British surveillance of the PWA in *Liking Progress*, chap. 5.

19. See Venkat Dhulipala, *Creating a New Medina: State Power, Islam, and the Quest for Pakistan in Late Colonial North India* (New York: Cambridge University Press, 2015).

20. Gurbaksh Singh had visited California while studying in the United States and was watched by British intelligence, but he showed few signs of his later radicalism at that time. Personal communication from Pashaura Singh, October 30, 2015.

21. Poonam Singh, editor of *Preet Lari*, personal communication, October 27, 2015.

22. Geeta Patel, *Lyrical Movements, Historical Hauntings: On Gender, Colonialism, and Desire in Miraji's Urdu Poetry* (Stanford, CA: Stanford University Press, 2002), 98; Jalil, *Liking Progress*, chap. 4; Shabana Mahmud, "Angare and the Founding of the Progressive Writers' Association," *Modern Asian Studies* 30, no. 2 (1996): 447–467. Only five copies of the book survived, two making their way to the Oriental Library in London. In 2014 Penguin India and Rupa Publications brought out an English translation. For more on the way their time in Europe shaped Zaheer, see Jalil, *Liking Progress*, 109–112.

23. See note 14 above.

24. On Urdu-Hindi, see Alok Rai, *Hindi Nationalism* (New Delhi: Orient Longman, 2001); Amrit Rai, *A House Divided: The Origin and Development of Hindi/Hindavi* (Delhi: Oxford University Press, 1985); Christopher King, *One Language, Two Scripts: The Hindi Movement in Nineteenth Century North India* (New Delhi: Oxford University Press, 1994); Kavita Datla, *The Language of Secular Islam: Urdu Nationalism and Colonial India* (Honolulu: University of Hawaii Press, 2013); Amir Mufti, *Enlightenment in the Colony: The*

*Jewish Question and the Crisis of Postcolonial Culture* (Princeton, NJ: Princeton University Press, 2007), 140–153; Shamsur Rahman Faruqi, *Early Urdu Literary Culture and History* (New Delhi: Oxford University Press, 2001); and Ajmal Kamal, "A Critique of Language Snobs: Urdu and the Politics of Identity," *Tanqeed*, February 2015, http://www.tanqeed.org/2015/02/the-uses-and-abuses-of-language-snobs-urdu-and-the-politics-of-identity/. The abandonment of Punjabi among Hindus in India and Muslims in Pakistan is an enormous question bound up with partitions of the twentieth century. On the related matter of the languages lost as a result of Partition, see "Partition Impacted on Several Languages," *Business Standard*, April 26, 2014, http://www.business-standard.com/article/news-ians/partition-impacted-on-several-languages-114042600817_1.html.

25. Mufti, *Enlightenment in the Colony*, 180; Patel, *Lyrical Movements*, 89.

26. Jalil, *Liking Progress*, 247.

27. See Hafeez Malik, "The Marxist Literary Movement in India and Pakistan," *Association for Asian Studies* 26 (1967): 655. Kaifi Azmi and Makhdoom Mohiuddin felt similarly about the war.

28. All translations in this essay are my own. For poetry, I have tried to give literal translations preserving the syntax rather than literary translations conveying deeper meanings.

29. I thank Sadaf Jaffer for this observation.

30. Mufti, *Enlightenment in the Colony*, 201–202.

31. Zaheer and Faiz went to Rawalpindi to meet some disaffected army officers who proposed a coup against the government. The group decided *against* the plan; nevertheless, a case was built, and they were jailed after a special tribunal without jury.

32. Pandey, *Remembering Partition*, 170. There are also nonwriterly examples of artistic wavering on nation: Ustad Bade Ghulam Ali Khan moved to Pakistan but then returned to India. I will leave for another essay an analysis of Indian Punjabi musicians of this era, from Madan Mohan to Jagjit Singh to Ayushmann Khurrana and how their particular paths shaped their articulation of *Punjabiyat*.

33. Azad did not meet Iqbal himself. His father, the poet Tilok Chand Mehroom, was a friend of Iqbal. When the latter returned to India from Europe in 1918, Mehroom wrote him a letter including a poem, "Aana tera mubarak Europe se aane waale," that incorporated references to "Tarana-i-Hind." Hamida Chopra, lecture, *mushaira*, August 23, 2015, Indian Community Center, Milpitas, California.

34. This backdrop may shed light on his famous couplet "Kabhi kissiko mukammal jahan nahin milta / Kahin zameen to kahin aasman nahi milta" (No one ever gets a complete world / In some places one doesn't get the ground, in some, the sky).

35. I am not presenting here the narrative of the actual unfolding of Partition—how it became the plan and how it came to take the shape it did. The material fact here is that those decisions—about separation versus federation, which bits of land and which infrastructure went to which side, whether people should move—were hasty and late, and there was much confusion as the process unfolded. Up to the last minute, alternative schemes emerged—plans to make Calcutta, Lahore, Karachi, and Delhi autonomous city-states; to create a united independent Bengal; and so on. Some people moved out of fear, some

for mundane reasons, some by accident, others out of conviction, many because they were systematically hounded out.

36. Sunil Amrith, *Crossing the Bay of Bengal: The Furies of Nature and the Fortunes of Migrants* (Cambridge, MA: Harvard University Press, 2015), 222. Many Muslims who moved temporarily, in search of safety, were prevented from returning to their homes in India by new laws commandeering "evacuee property"; ibid., 224.

37. Peter Judson, *Guardians of the Nation: Activists on the Language Frontiers of Imperial Austria* (Cambridge, MA: Harvard University Press, 2007); Pamela Ballinger, *History in Exile: Memory and Identity at the Borders of the Balkans* (Princeton, NJ: Princeton University Press, 2002).

38. Edith Sheffer, *Burned Bridge: How East and West Germans Made the Iron Curtain* (New York: Oxford University Press, 2011). Vazira Fazila-Yacoobali Zamindar has analyzed the making of the western Indo-Pak border in response to the refugee crisis and the way national difference was constructed there, in that space of most blurred identity, over time. Zamindar, *The Long Partition and the Making of Modern South Asia: Refugees, Boundaries, Histories* (New York: Columbia University Press, 2007).

39. Scott, "Women in *The Making*," 80.

40. See oral histories in Zakaria, *Footprints of Partition*, 81, 118. On Pakistan as a utopian ideal, see also Pandey, *Remembering Partition*, 27–30.

41. Barbara Metcalf, *Husain Ahmad Madani: The Jihad for Islam and India's Freedom* (Oxford: Oneworld, 2009), 114.

42. Satia, *Spies in Arabia*.

43. Pandey, *Remembering Partition*, 26–32.

44. On Iqbal's political imagination, see also Faisal Devji's essay in this volume.

45. Zakaria, *Footprints of Partition*, 169.

46. B. R. Ambedkar, *Thoughts on Pakistan* (Bombay: Thacker, 1941); B. R. Ambedkar, *Pakistan, or the Partition of India* (Bombay: Thacker, 1944); Aishwary Kumar, *Radical Equality: Ambedkar, Gandhi, and the Risk of Democracy* (Stanford, CA: Stanford University Press, 2015), 242–247.

47. Mohammad Ali Jauhar, 1923, reproduced in *Sources of Indian Tradition: Modern India, Pakistan, and Bangladesh*, vol. 2, eds. Rachel Fell McDermott et al. (New York: Columbia University Press, 2013), 409.

48. Mufti, *Enlightenment in the Colony*, 164, 175–176; Metcalf, *Husain Ahmad Madani*, 114, 118. Much Indian historical writing is in this vein and has found it difficult to escape the obligation to demonstrate that oneness. This is partly because, apart from the Ambedkar approach, it was difficult for Indians to read Partition as anything but loss; Pakistanis, however nostalgic, could at least pin hope on the strength of having created something new. To some Pakistanis, India is a dreamlike homeland, an origin story more than a land from which they are exiled. Still, many survivors of Partition on both sides recall untroubled pre-Partition times marked by intercommunal harmony. Zakaria, *Footprints of Partition*, 95, 105, 124.

49. Zakaria, *Footprints of Partition*, 79.

50. Nadhra Khan, "Lahore Revisited: The City and Its Nineteenth Century Guidebook," lecture, August 30, 2015, Indian Community Center, Milpitas, California.

51. As Pandey notes, violence did not "accompany" Partition; it was constitutive of it. Pandey, *Remembering Partition*, 3–4, 48, 52, 64. See also Mufti, *Enlightenment in the Colony*, 175.

52. Zakaria, *Footprints of Partition*, 18. See also the story of Ghulam Ali in Zamindar, *Long Partition*, 1–2.

53. Zakaria, *Footprints of Partition*, 27–28.

54. Mufti notes that nationalism has historically been "a great *disrupter* of social and cultural relations," setting forth "an entire dynamic of inclusion and exclusion within the very social formation that it claims as uniquely its own and with which it declares itself identical." By rendering some part of that formation as "minority," it renders that group potentially movable. Thus, it has historically been a force for violent displacement. Mufti, *Enlightenment in the Colony*, 13.

55. Mufti, *Enlightenment in the Colony*, 165.

56. Jalil, *Liking Progress*, 276 n. 74. Faiz did not think he wrote about Partition beyond this 1951 poem. On the Indian Communist Party's shifting views of Partition, see ibid., 348–350.

57. For instance, Majaz wrote, "Yeh aftab ka partav hai aftab nahin. . . . Yeh intiha nahin aghaz-e-kaar-e-mardaa(n) hai" (This is the reflection of the sun, not the sun. . . . This is not the end but the beginning of the work of men). Many poets on both sides of the border criticized the dawn of independence (Nadeem Qasmi, Jan Nisar Akhtar, Kaifi Azmi, Majrooh Sultanpuri, Naresh Kumar Shad, and Qateel Shifai).

58. Kathryn Hume, *Fantasy and Mimesis: Responses to Reality in Western Literature* (New York: Methuen, 1984), 21, quoted in Karline McLain, "The Fantastic as Frontier: Realism, the Fantastic, and Transgression in Mid-Twentieth Century Urdu Fiction," *Annual of Urdu Studies* 16 (2001): 139–165.

59. Riyaz Wani, interview with Anam Zakaria, Tehelka.com, September 5, 2015, available at http://www.tehelka.com/2015/08/i-hope-my-stories-can-challenge-the -perception-of-india-pakistan-relations-anam-zakaria/.

60. Zakaria, *Footprints of Partition*, 84.

61. See Dror Wahrman, *The Making of the Modern Self: Identity and Culture in Eighteenth-Century England* (New Haven, CT: Yale University Press, 2006).

62. See, for instance, Judith Walkowitz, *City of Dreadful Delight: Narratives of Sexual Danger in Late-Victorian London* (Chicago: University of Chicago Press, 1992), 70.

63. Zakaria, *Footprints of Partition*, 29. A similar phenomenon transpires on the German border towns Sheffer describes in *Burned Bridge*.

64. Mufti, *Enlightenment in the Colony*, 211–212, 216, 221–224, 239, 243.

65. On this, see also Mufti, *Enlightenment in the Colony*, 222, 238–239. This is not a uniquely South Asian quality, of course. See, for instance, Thomas Laqueur, *The Work of the Dead: A Cultural History of Mortal Remains* (Princeton, NJ: Princeton University Press, 2015).

66. Mufti, *Enlightenment in the Colony*, 208. Manto was disowned by the Pakistani Marxist-leaning literary set. Charged with obscenity, he avoided his prison sentence with hard labor on appeal.

67. Scott, "Women in *The Making*," 81–82.

68. Scott Hamilton, *The Crisis of Theory: E. P. Thompson, the New Left, and Postwar British Politics* (Manchester: Manchester University Press, 2011), 159–162; Hamilton's 2007 talk at the History Department of the University of Auckland, "'An Appetite for the Archives': New Light on EP Thompson," *Reading the Maps* (blog), March 29, 2007, http://readingthemaps.blogspot.co.nz/2007/03/appetite-for-archives-new-light-on-ep.html.

69. See David Barstow and Suhasini Raj, "Indian Writers Spurn Awards as Violence Flares," *New York Times*, October 18, 2015, 1, 4.

70. I thank Hamida Chopra for sharing this story.

71. Much scholarly work on Partition likewise diagnoses the two new states' complicity in appropriating Partition violence against women within an ideology of community and nation. See the work of Urvashi Butalia, Ritu Menon, Kamla Bhasin, and Veena Das.

72. For more on Loona, see Sa Soza, *Shiv Kumar Batalvi* (New Delhi: Sahitya Akademi, 2001), 58–90.

73. This phrase is the title of a song recently penned by Irshad Kamil, a Muslim poet from Malerkotla in Indian Punjab, sung by Jyoti and Sultana Nooran (Punjabi Muslims from Jalander) and composed by A. R. Rahman for Imtiaz Ali's film *Highway* (2014).

74. On Azad, see Mufti, *Enlightenment in the Colony*, 179. Certainly, it is also a luxury of class.

75. Mufti, *Enlightenment in the Colony*, 243–244, 257. In Pakistan today the Punjabi language movement has ties to the Mazdoor Kissan Party and claims Marxist commitments.

EPILOGUE

1. United Nations Office on Genocide Prevention and the Responsibility to Protect, Atrocity Crimes, "Prevention," http://www.un.org/en/genocideprevention/prevention.html.

2. The partitions of Korea and Vietnam were not occasioned by internal ethnic conflict but to end international wars. Robert Schaeffer, "How to Break Up a Country Without Causing Havoc," *New Republic*, October 16, 2017; Robert Schaeffer, *Severed States: Dilemmas of Democracy in a Divided World* (Lanham, MD: Rowman and Littlefield, 1999); Bruce Riedel, "Is Yemen Headed for Partition?," *Al-Monitor*, October 31, 2016; Jean Aziz, "Is Syria Moving Towards Partition?," *Al-Monitor*, April 16, 2013; Tim Arango, "With Iraq Mired in Turmoil, Some Call for Partitioning the Country," *New York Times*, April 28, 2016; Mario Silva, "After Partition: The Perils of South Sudan," *University of Baltimore Journal of International Law* 3, no. 1 (2014): 63–90.

3. Bruce Hoffman, *Anonymous Soldiers: The Struggle for Israel, 1917–1947* (New York: Alfred A. Knopf, 2015).

4. Special Issue, "Global Spaces/Local Places: Transnationalism, Diaspora, and the Meaning of Home," *Identities: Global Studies in Culture and Power* 13, no. 3 (2006).

5. Cf. Allen D. Grimshaw, "Genocide and Democide," in *Encyclopedia of Violence, Peace, and Conflict*, 3 vols. (San Diego: Academic Press, 1999), 2:58; Paul R. Brass, "The Partition of India and Retributive Genocide in the Punjab, 1946–47: Means, Methods and Purposes," *Journal of Genocide Research* 5 (2003): 71–101.

6. Recent local studies include Subhasish Ray, "Intra-Group Interactions and Inter-Group Violence: Sikh Mobilization During the Partition of India in a Comparative Perspective," *Journal of Genocide Research* 19, no. 3 (2017): 382–403; Ranabir Samaddar, "Policing a Riot-Torn City: Kolkata, 16–18 August 1946," *Journal of Genocide Research* 19, no. 1 (2017): 39–60; Samir Kumar Das, ed., *Minorities in South Asia and in Europe: A New Agenda* (Kolkota: Samya, 2010).

7. Arjun Appadurai, "Dead Certainty: Ethnic Violence in the Era of Globalization," *Public Culture* 10, no. 2 (1998): 225–247; Arjun Appadurai, *Fear of Small Numbers: An Essay on the Geography of Anger* (Durham, NC: Duke University Press, 2006).

8. It is understood that constructing the formally equivalent citizen who comprised these nation-states generated minoritization processes in heterogeneous imperial societies and that these nation-states were indirect products of homogenization processes driven by the market's imperative for functionally equivalent units. Partha Chatterjee, *Nationalist Thought and the Colonial World: A Derivative Discourse* (Minneapolis: University of Minnesota Press, 1993); David Lloyd, "Ethnic Cultures, Minority Discourse, and the State," in *Colonial Discourse/Postcolonial* Theory, ed. Francis Barker, Peter Hulme, and Margaret Iversen (Manchester: Manchester University Press, 1994), 221–238.

9. Edward Said, "Traveling Theory," in Edward Said, *The World, the Text, and the Critic* (Cambridge, MA: Harvard University Press, 1983), 226; first published in *Raritan* 1, no. 3 (1982): 41–67. See also the introduction to this volume by Arie Dubnov and Laura Robson.

10. Ann Laura Stoler and Carole McGranahan, "Imperial Formations," in *Imperial Formations*, ed. Ann Laura Stoler, Carole McGranahan, and Peter C. Perdue (Santa Fe, NM: SAR, 2007), 4.

11. Samuel Moyn and Andrew Sartori, "Approaches to Global Intellectual History," in *Global Intellectual History*, ed. Samuel Moyn and Andrew Sartori (New York: Columbia University Press, 2013), 4.

12. Arie M. Dubnov, "Notes on the Zionist Passage to India, or: The Analogical Imagination and Its Boundaries," *Journal of Israeli History* 35, no. 2 (2016): 177–214.

13. A notable exception is Laura Robson, *States of Separation: Transfer, Partition, and the Making of the Modern Middle East* (Oakland: University of California Press, 2017).

14. Michael D. Callahan, "The Failure of 'Closer Union' in British East Africa, 1929–31," *Journal of Imperial and Commonwealth History* 25, no. 2 (1997): 267–293.

15. Anglo-American Committee of Inquiry, Chapter I, Avalon Project: Documents in Law, History, and Diplomacy, Yale Law School, http://avalon.law.yale.edu/20th_century /angch01.asp.

16. H. Levenberg, "Bevin's Disillusionment: The London Conference, Autumn 1946," *Middle Eastern Studies* 27, no. 4 (1991): 615–630; John B. Jurdis, "Seeds of Doubt: Harry Truman's Concerns About Israel and Palestine Were Prescient—and Forgotten," *New Republic*, January 15, 2014.

17. Mahmood Mamdani, *Citizen and Subject: Contemporary Africa and the Legacy of Late Colonialism* (Princeton, NJ: Princeton University Press, 1996).

18. See Penny Sinanoglou's chapter in this volume.

19. Michael Collins, "Decolonization and the 'Federal Moment,'" *Diplomacy and State-craft* 24, no. 1 (2013): 21–40; Jennifer Foray, "A Unified Empire of Equal Parts: The Dutch Commonwealth Schemes of the 1920s–40s," *Journal of Imperial and Commonwealth History* 41, no. 2 (2013): 259–284; Spencer Mawby, *Ordering Independence: The End of Empire in the Anglophone Caribbean, 1947–69* (Houndmills: Palgrave Macmillan, 2012); James C. Parker, *Brother's Keeper: The United States, Race, and Empire in the British Caribbean, 1937–1962* (Oxford: Oxford University Press, 2008).

20. Frederick Cooper, *Citizenship Between Empire and Nation: Remaking France and French Africa, 1945–1960* (Princeton, NJ: Princeton University Press, 2014); Gary Wilder, *Freedom Time: Negritude, Decolonization, and the Future of the World* (Durham, NC: Duke University Press, 2015).

21. Tekeste Negash, *Eritrea and Ethiopia: The Federal Experience* (Uppsala: Nordiska Afrikainstitutet, 1997).

22. Carol Fink, *Defending the Rights of Others: The Great Powers, the Jews, and International Minority Protection, 1878–1938* (Cambridge: Cambridge University Press, 2006); Eric D. Weitz, "From the Vienna to the Paris System: International Politics and the Entangled Histories of Human Rights, Forced Deportations, and Civilizing Missions," *American Historical Review* 113, no. 5 (2008): 1313–1343.

23. Kevin Hannan, *Borders of Language and Identity in Teschen Silesia* (New York: Peter Lang, 1996).

24. Geneva Convention Concerning Upper Silesia, Signed May 15, 1922, Annex 1, Part 3, Rights of Minorities in Upper Silesia (Minority Schools) (in French), http://www .icj-cij.org/files/permanent-court-of-international-justice/serie_A/A_15/52_Droits_de _minorites_en_Haute_Silesie_Ecoles_minoritaires_Annexe_1.pdf; Julius Stone, *Regional Guarantees of Minority Rights: A Study of Minorities Procedure in Upper Silesia* (New York: Macmillan, 1933), 3, 6, 223. Thanks to Natasha Wheatley for drawing my attention to this convention and Stone's book. Generally, see Brendan J. Karch, "Nationalism on the Margins: Silesians Between Germany and Poland, 1848–1945" (PhD diss., Harvard University, 2010).

25. Volker Prott, *The Politics of Self-Determination: Remaking Territories and National Identities in Europe, 1917–1923* (Oxford: Oxford University Press, 2016).

26. Roger Moorhouse, *The Devil's Alliance* (New York: Basic Books, 2014); Anthony Read and David Fisher, *The Deadly Embrace: Hitler, Stalin and the Nazi-Soviet Pact, 1939–1941* (New York: W. W. Norton, 1989).

27. R. M. Douglas, *Orderly and Humane: The Expulsion of the Germans After the Second World War* (New Haven, CT: Yale University Press, 2013). Ethnic Hungarians were to be expelled from Czechoslovakia for the same reason, but the Hungarian state would not accept them. Josef Kalvoda, "National Minorities Under Communism: The Case of Czechoslovakia," *Nationalities Papers* 16, no. 1 (1988): 1–21.

28. Liisa Malkki, "National Geographic: The Rooting of Peoples and the Territorialization of National Identity," *Current Anthropology* 7, no. 1 (1992): 24–44.

29. Malkki calls this mode of thinking the heroization or romanticization of the indigenous, which she regards suspiciously as a sedantarism that "directly enables a vision of territorial displacement as pathological." Malkki, "National Geographic," 31.

30. Sankaran Krishna, *Postcolonial Insecurities: India, Sri Lanka and the Question of Nationalism* (Minneapolis: University of Minnesota Press, 1999).

31. Thongchai Winichakul, *Siam Mapped: A History of the Geo-Body of a Nation* (Honolulu: University of Hawaii Press, 1994).

32. Armenian National Committee of Australia, "Nagorno Karabakh," http://www .anc.org.au/nagorno-karabakh.

33. Peter Loizos, "Intercommunal Killings in Cyprus," *Man* 23, no. 4 (1988): 650. Emphasis in original.

34. Taylor C. Sherman, *Muslim Belonging in Secular India: Negotiating Citizenship in Postcolonial Hyderabad* (Cambridge: Cambridge University Press, 2015), 21–22, 35–36.

35. Cemil Aydin, *The Idea of the Muslim World: A Global Intellectual History* (Cambridge, MA: Harvard University Press, 2017); Reece Jones, "The False Premise of Partition," *Space and Polity* 18, no. 3 (2014): 285–300. On South Asian Islam, see Ayesha Jalal, *Self and Sovereignty: Individual and Community in South Asian Islam Since 1850* (London: Routledge, 2000).

36. B. Shiva Rao, "A Vicious Circle in India," *Foreign Affairs* 19 (July 1941): 846.

37. Syed Zafarul Hasan and Mohamad Afzal Husain Qadri, "The Problem of Indian Muslims and Its Solutions," February 2, 1939, in *The Paradoxes of Partition, 1937–1947*, ed. S. A. I. Tirmizi (New Delhi: Manak, 1998), 612.

38. Vinayak Damodar Savarkar, *Hindutva: Who Is a Hindu?*, 5th ed. (Bombay: S. S. Savarkar, 1969), 136–137. For analysis of this foundational text of the Hindu right, see Jyotirmaya Sharma, *Hindutva: Exploring the Idea of Hindu Nationalism* (New Delhi: Penguin Viking, 2003).

39. Marzia Casolari, "Hindutva's Foreign Tie-up in the 1930s: Archival Evidence," *Economic and Political Weekly*, January 22, 2000, 224.

40. V. D. Savarkar, "Glad to Note That Independent Jewish State Is Established," December 19, 1947, *Historic Statements by Savarkar*, ed. S. S. Savarkar (Bombay: G. P. Parchure, 1967), 135.

41. I cannot determine whether Savarkar was aware of the European Enlightenment debates about Jewish assimilation and citizenship that resulted in the Jews' construction as a minority and that Aamir R. Mufti argues provided the paradigm for minoritization processes in the imperial possessions like India; Aamir R. Mufti, *Enlightenment in the Colony: The Jewish Question and the Crisis of Postcolonial Culture* (Princeton, NJ: Princeton University Press, 2007).

42. Casolari, "Hindutva's Foreign Tie-up," 224.

43. Ibid., 223.

44. Venkat Dhulipala, *Creating a New Medina: State Power, Islam, and the Quest for Pakistan in Late Colonial North India* (Delhi: Cambridge University Press, 2015), 19.

45. Hector Bolitho, *Jinnah: Creator of Pakistan* (Karachi: Oxford University Press, 1954), 109.

46. Rajendra Prasad, *India Divided*, 3rd ed. (Bombay: Hind Kitabs, 1947), 183.

47. Stanislava Vavroušková, "Ways to Understand India: The Czech Experience," *Acta Orientalia Vilnensia* 9, no. 2 (2008): 125–132.

48. Jawaharlal Nehru, "The Betrayal of Czecho-Slovakia," *Manchester Guardian*, September 8, 1938, in *Unity of India: Collected Writings, 1937–1940* (New York: John Day, 1942), 286; Miloslav Krasa, "Jawaharlal Nehru and Czechoslovakia at the Time of the 1938 European Crisis," *India Quarterly* 45, no. 4 (1989): 359.

49. Maulana Abul Kalam Azad, *India Wins Freedom: An Autobiographical Narrative* (Hyderabad: Orient Longman, 1988), 26.

50. Beni Prasad, *The Hindu-Muslim Questions* (Allahabad: Kitabistan, 1941), 67–72.

51. B. R. Ambedkar, *Thoughts on Pakistan* (Bombay: Thacker, 1941); B. R. Ambedkar, *Pakistan or the Partition of India* (Bombay: Thacker, 1945). The second book contains long passages taken verbatim from the first, including the material on Czechoslovakia. A recent study is Aishwary Kumar, *Radical Equality: Ambedkar, Gandhi, and the Risk of Democracy* (Stanford, CA: Stanford University Press, 2015).

52. B. R. Ambedkar, *Annihilation of Caste*, ed. S. Anand (London: Verso, 2014).

53. Ambedkar, *Pakistan or the Partition of India*, 203.

54. Ibid., 175–178.

55. Ibid., 209.

56. Ambedkar, *Thoughts on Pakistan*, 217.

57. See the discussion in Ayesha Jalal, *The Sole Spokesman: Jinnah, the Muslim League, and the Demand for Pakistan* (Cambridge: Cambridge University Press, 1994), 54–58; Harshan Kumarasingham, *A Political Legacy of the British Empire: Power and the Parliamentary System in Post-Colonial India and Pakistan* (London: I. B. Tauris, 2013), chap. 4.

58. Ibid., 241–242; Lahore Resolution (1940), HistoryPak.com, http://historypak.com/lahore-resolution-1940.

59. Muhammad Ali Jinnah, "Statement on the Lahore Resolution," in *Some Recent Speeches and Writings of Mr. Jinnah*, ed. Jamil-ud-din Ahmad (Lahore: Sh. Muhammad Ashraf, 1942), 159.

60. Sugata Bose, "A Doubtful Inheritance: The Partition of Bengal in 1947," in *The Political Inheritance of Pakistan*, ed. D. A. Low (London: Palgrave Macmillan, 1991), 130–143; Ambedkar, *Pakistan or the Partition of India*, 104.

61. Muhammad Iqbal, "Presidential Address to the 25th Session of the All-India Muslim League Allahabad, 29 December 1930," in *Speeches, Writings, and Statements of Iqbal*, ed. Latif Ahmed Sherwani, 2nd rev. ed. (Lahore: Iqbal Academy, 1977), 15. Emphasis added. Amar Sohal, "Ideas of Parity: Muslims, Sikhs and the 1946 Cabinet Mission Plan," *South Asia* 40, no. 4 (2017): 709–710. See Faisal Devji's chapter in this volume.

62. Quoted in Jalal, *The Sole Spokesman*, 59 n. 54, 182.

63. Penderel Moon, *Divide and Quit* (London: Chatto and Windus, 1961), 20.

64. *The Transfer of Power, 1942–7. The Cabinet Mission, 23 March—29 June 1946*, vol. 7, ed. Nicholas Mansergh (London: Her Majesty's Stationary Office, 1977), 166.

65. Ibid., 246.

66. Ibid., 245–246; Dhulipala, *Creating a New Medina*, 172.

67. Jinnah, "Statement on the Lahore Resolution," 158.

68. *The Transfer of Power*, vol. 7, 166–167. Affirming this view is S. R. Sen, "Communal Riots: Anticipation, Containment and Prevention," *Economic and Political Weekly* 28, no. 15 (1993): 628.

69. *The Transfer of Power, 1942–7. The Post-War Phase: New Moves by the Labour Government, 1 August 1945—22 March 1946*, vol. 6, ed. Nicholas Mansergh (London: Her Majesty's Stationary Office, 1976), 727.

70. Choudhry Khaliquzzaman, *Pathway to Pakistan* (Lahore: Longmans, 1961).

71. Hamsa Alavi, "Ethnicity, Muslim Society, and the Pakistan Ideology," in *Islamic Reassertion in Pakistan: The Application of Islamic Laws in a Modern State*, ed. Anita M. Weiss (New York: Syracuse University Press, 1986), 23.

72. A. G. Noorani, "Jinnah & Muslims of India," *Criterion Quarterly* 3, no. 4, November 20, 2012, http://www.criterion-quarterly.com/jinnah-muslims-of-india; Weldon James interview with Jinnah, *Collier's*, August 25, 1947.

73. Vazira Fazila-Yacoobali Zamindar, *The Long Partition and the Making of Modern South Asia: Refugees, Boundaries, Histories* (New York: Columbia University Press, 2007), 71–76.

74. Sanat Kumar Roy-Chaudhuri, "The Hostage Theory and Its Dangers in Constitution Framing," *Modern Review*, September 1931, 303–306; Ambedkar, *Pakistan or the Partition of India*, 374; Dhanajay Keer, *Veer Savarkar*, 2nd ed. (Bombay: Popular Prakashan, 1966), 381.

75. Maulana Abul Kalam, *India Wins Freedom*, complete ed. (Madras: Orient Longman, 1988), 151, 216.

76. Prasad, *India Divided*, 232, 328.

77. Ambedkar, *Pakistan or the Partition of India*, 96.

78. Ibid., 98.

79. Ibid., 103.

80. Ibid., 102.

81. Syed Abdul Latif, *Muslim Problem in India Together with an Alternative Constitution for India*, foreword by Sir Abdulla Haroon (Bombay: Times of India Press, 1939), 35–38.

82. Jinnah, "Statement on the Lahore Resolution," 158. More quotations in *Jinnah on World Affairs: Select Documents, 1908–1948*, ed. Mehrunnisa Ali (Karachi: Pakistan Study Centre, University of Karachi, 2007).

83. Prasad, *India Divided*, 27, 188–193, 324–327.

84. Ibid., 400.

85. Yasmin Khan, *The Great Partition: The Making of India and Pakistan*, new ed. (New Haven, CT: Yale University Press, 2017), 100.

86. Ibid., 122.

87. Ray, "Intra-Group Interactions and Inter-Group Violence"; Brass, "The Partition of India"; Swarna Aiyar, "August Anarchy: The Partition Massacres in Punjab, 1947," *South Asia* 18 (1995): 13–36.

88. Prashant Bharadwaj, Asim Khwaja, and Atif Mian, "The Big March: Migratory Flows After the Partition of India," *Economic and Political Weekly* 43, no. 35 (2008): 39–49; Prashant Bharadwaj, Asim Khwaja, and Atif Mian, "Population Exchange and Its Impact on Literacy, Occupation and Gender—Evidence from the Partition of India," *International Migration* 53, no. 4 (2014): 90–106.

89. Phillips Talbot, "The Rise of Pakistan," *Middle East Journal* 2, no. 4 (1948): 387.

90. Papiya Ghosh, "Writing Ganga-Jamni: In the 1940s and After," *Social Scientist* 34, nos. 11–12 (2006): xi–xii.

91. Faisal Devji, *Muslim Zion: Pakistan as a Political Idea* (London: Hurst, 2013).

92. See Lucy Chester's chapter in this volume.

93. Azad, *India Wins Freedom*, 150.

94. Presidential Address of Mr MA Jinnah Read on 8th October 1938, 5–6, Internet Archive, https://archive.org/stream/SpeechesOfPoliticalReligious LeadersOfSindhGulhayatInstitute/PresidentialAddressOfMrMaJinnahOctober 1938ResolutionsAndDonations_djvu.txt; Fareed Ali Shamsi, "India and the Problem of Palestine" (master's thesis, Aligarh Muslim University, 1968), chap. 1.

95. Joseph B. Schechtman, "India and Israel," *Midstream* (August–September 1966): 48–61.

96. Muhammad Zafrullah Khan, *The Forgotten Years: Memoirs of Sir Muhammad Zafrullah Khan*, ed. A. H. Batalvi (Lahore: Vanguard, 1991), 184–185.See Adi Gordon's chapter in this volume.

97. S. M. Burke, *Pakistan's Foreign Policy: An Historical Analysis* (London: Oxford University Press, 1973), 138; T. G. Fraser, *Partition in Ireland, India and Palestine: Theory and Practice* (London: Palgrave Macmillan, 1984), 176; P. R. Kumaraswamy, "Beyond the Veil: Israel-Pakistan Relations," Memorandum no. 55 (Tel Aviv: Jaffee Center for Strategic Studies, Tel Aviv University, March 2000), http://institutobrasilisrael .org/cms/assets/uploads/_BIBLIOTECA/_PDF/democracia-e-sociedade-israelense /4766c3f1ea0a333fdf43b17de01ade0f.pdf

98. Ad Hoc Committee on the Palestinian Question: Report of Sub-Committee 2, A/ AC.14/32, November 11, 1947, http://unispal.un.org/pdfs/AAC1432.pdf.

99. Leonard A. Gordon, "Indian Nationalist Ideas About Palestine and Israel," *Jewish Social Studies* 37 nos. 3–4 (1975): 221–234.

100. Umbreen Javaid and Malik Tauqir Ahmad Khan, "Pakistan and the Question of Recognising Israel: Historical Issues and Future Prospects," *South Asian Studies* 29, no. 2 (2014): 61–71.

101. Tahir Hasnain Naqvi, "The Politics of Commensuration: The Violence of Partition and the Making of the Pakistani State," in *Beyond Crisis: Re-Evaluating Pakistan*, ed. Naveeda Khan (New Delhi: Routledge, 2010), 77–78.

102. Muhammad Ali Jinnah, "Address to Civil, Naval, Military & Air Force Offices of the Pakistan Government at Khaliqdina Hall, Karachi, October 11, 1947," in *Speeches and Writings of Mr. Jinnah*, ed. Jamil-ud-din Ahmad, Vol. 2 (Lahore: Sh. Muhammad Ashraf, 1947), 418.

103. Ibid., 420.

104. Ibid.

105. Khan, *The Great Partition*, 122.

106. Willem van Schendel, "Stateless in South Asia: The Making of the India-Bangladesh Enclaves," *Journal of Asian Studies* 61, no. 1 (2002): 127.

107. Ibid., 123, 131.

108. Agreement Between the Governments of India and Pakistan Regarding Security and Rights of Minorities (Nehru–Liaquat Agreement), April 8, 1950, LII of India, Indian Treaty Series, http://www.commonlii.org/in/other/treaties/INTSer/1950/9.html.

109. Pallavi Raghavan, "The Making of South Asia's Minorities: A Diplomatic History, 1947–52," *Economic and Politics Weekly*, May 21, 2016, 45–52. Thanks to Taylor Sherman for alerting me to this article.

110. Nicolas Doumanis, *Before the Nation: Muslim-Christian Coexistence and Its Destruction in Late-Ottoman Anatolia* (Oxford: Oxford University Press, 2013), 170. Thanks to Eric D. Weitz for pointing out this parallel.

111. See Arie Dubnov's and Penny Sinanoglou's chapters in this volume.

112. Benny Morris does not probe the British pretext: Morris, "Explaining Transfer: Zionist Thinking and the Creation of the Palestinian Refugee Problem," in *Removing Peoples: Forced Removal in the Modern World*, ed. Richard Bessell and Claudia B. Haake (Oxford: Oxford University Press, 2009), 349–360.

113. Benny Morris, *1948: A History of the First Arab-Israeli War* (New Haven, CT: Yale University Press, 2008), 52–60. For details of the internal and external pressures on the US position, see John B. Jurdis, *Genesis: Truman, American Jews, and the Origins of the Arab/Israeli Conflict* (New York: Farrar, Straus and Giroux, 2014).

114. UNSCOP Minority Report of 1947: A Federated State, http://www.pa-il.com/2011/09/unscop-minority-report-of-1947.html.

115. Nabil Elaraby, "Some Legal Implications of the 1947 Partition Resolution and the 1949 Armistice Agreements," *Law and Contemporary Problems* 33, no. 1 (1968): 99. Elaraby was an Egyptian diplomat and First Secretary, Mission of the United Arab Republic to the United Nations.

116. Walid Khalidi, "On Albert Hourani, the Arab Office, and the Anglo-American Committee of 1946," *Journal of Palestine Studies* 35, no. 1 (2005): 60–79.

117. Albert Hourani, "The Case Against a Jewish State in Palestine: Albert Hourani's Statement to the Anglo-American Committee of Enquiry of 1946," *Journal of Palestine Studies* 35, no. 1 (2005): 82, 86.

118. Nur Masalha, *Expulsion of the Palestinians: The Concept of "Transfer" in Zionist Political Thought* (Washington, DC: Institute for Palestine Studies, 1992); Nur Masalha, *A Land Without a People: Israel, Transfer and the Palestinians, 1949–96* (London: Faber and Faber, 1997).

119. Morris, *1948*, 52.

120. Hourani, "The Case Against a Jewish State in Palestine," 82.

121. Ibid., 87.

122. Ibid.

123. Natasha Wheatley, "Mandatory Interpretation: Legal Hermeneutics and the New International Order in Arab and Jewish Petitions to the League of Nations," *Past and Present* 227 (2015): 205–248. Thanks to Laura Robson for input here.

124. Ami Pedahzur and Arie Perliger, *Jewish Terrorism in Israel* (New York: Columbia University Press, 2011).

125. Anglo-American Committee of Inquiry Report.

126. Reginald Coupland, "The Jew and the Arab. Conditions of Settlement in Palestine: The Case for Partition Restated," *Times* (London), July 13, 1946, 5.

127. Eldad Ben-Dror, "The Success of the Zionist Strategy vis-à-vis UNSCOP," *Israel Affairs* 20, no. 1 (2014): 19–39. Thanks to Arie Dubnov for alerting me to this article.

128. Albert Hourani, "Jew and Arab," letter to the *Times* (London), July 30, 1946.

129. Anita Shapira, *Ben-Gurion: Father of Modern Israel*, trans. Anthony Berris (New Haven, CT: Yale University Press, 2014), 170–171.

130. Morris, *1948*, 290, 119.

131. Ibid., 125–128.

132. Arnon Degani, "The Decline and Fall of the Israeli Military Government, 1948–1966: A Case of Settler-Colonial Consolidation?," *Settler Colonial Studies* 5, no. 1 (2014): 84–99; Shira Robinson, *Citizen Strangers: Palestinians and the Birth of Israel's Liberal Settler State* (Stanford, CA: Stanford University Press, 2013).

133. Provisional Government of Israel, "Proclamation of Independence," The Knesset, http://www.knesset.gov.il/docs/eng/megilat_eng.htm; Michael M. Karayanni, "The Separate Nature of the Religious Accommodations for the Palestinian-Arab Minority in Israel," *Northwestern Journal of International Human Rights* 5, no. 1 (2006): 41–71; Amal Jamal, *Arab Minority Nationalism in Israel: The Politics of Indigeneity* (Abingdon: Routledge, 2011).

134. Alisa Rubin Peled, *Debating Islam in the Jewish State: The Development of Policy Toward Islamic Institutions in Israel* (Albany: State University of New York Press, 2001), 150–151 Don Peretz, "Early State Policy Towards the Arab Population," in *New Perspectives on Israeli History: The Early Years of the State*, ed. Laurence J. Silberstein (New York: New York University Press, 1991), 98.

135. Antonio Ferrara, "Eugene Kulischer, Joseph Schechtman, and the Historiography of European Forced Migrations," *Journal of Contemporary History* 46, no. 4 (2011): 715–740; Mark Mazower, *No Enchanted Palace: The End of Empire and the Ideological Origins of the United Nations* (Princeton, NJ: Princeton University Press, 2009), 117–123.

136. Rafael Medoff, *Militant Zionism in America: The Rise and Impact of the Jabotinsky Movement in the United States, 1926–1948* (Tuscaloosa: University of Alabama Press, 2002), 214–215.

137. Joseph B. Schechtman, *Population Transfers in Asia* (New York: Hallsby, 1949), 86. There is no footnote for this quotation, but we know he was quoting Beneš, "Speech at the Foreign Press Association, London, 28 April 1942," in *War and Peace Aims of the United Nations*, ed. Louise W. Holborn (Boston: World Peace Foundation, 1943), 427–428. Cf. Nur Masalha, "From Propaganda to Scholarship: Dr. Joseph Schechtman and the Origins of the Israeli Polemics on the Palestinian Refugees," *Holy Land Studies* 2 (2002): 188–197; Ferrara, "Eugene Kulischer, Joseph Schechtman."

138. Morris makes the point that in the 1930s Zionist leaders had adjudged a future Palestinian minority to be irredentist: Benny Morris, "Explaining Transfer: Zionist Thinking and the Creation of the Palestinian Refugee Problem," in *Removing Peoples: Forced Removal in the Modern World*, ed. Richard Bessell and Claudia B. Haake (Oxford: Oxford University Press, 2009), 349–360.

139. Schechtman, *Population Transfers*, 10.

140. Ibid., 115.

141. C. L. Sulzberger, "Ben Gurion Bans Immigration Curb," *New York Times*, July 22, 1948, 16; Schechtman, *Population Transfers in Asia*, 130.

142. Yehouda Shenhav, "Arab Jews, Population Exchange, and the Palestinian Right of Return," in *Exile and Return: Predicaments of Palestinians and Jews*, ed. Ann M. Lesch and Ian S. Lustick (Philadelphia: University of Pennsylvania, 2005), 225–245.

143. Justice for Jews from Arab Countries, http://www.justiceforjews.com/narrative .html. A useful corrective in the press is David Cesarani, "A Different Kind of Catastrophe: The Suffering of Jewish Communities in Arab Countries Shouldn't Be Played Off Against the Plight of the Palestinians," *Guardian*, June 23, 2008.

144. Esther Meir-Glitzstein, *Zionism in an Arab Country: Jews in Iraq in the 1940s* (London: Routledge, 2004); Joel Beinin, *The Dispersion of Egyptian Jewry: Culture, Politics, and the Formation of a Modern Diaspora* (Berkeley: University of California Press, 1998), 19–20.

145. Esther Meir-Glitzstein, *The Magic Carpet Exodus of Yemenite Jewry: An Israeli Formative Myth* (Eastbourne: Sussex Academic Press, 2014). The Imam of Yemen apparently profited from the Jewish property, and more than eight hundred of them died en route because of logistical bungling.

146. Orit Bashkin, *New Babylonians: A History of Jews in Modern Iraq* (Stanford, CA: Stanford University Press, 2012); Aline Schlaepfer, "When Anticolonialism Meets Antifascism: Modern Jewish Intellectuals in Baghdad," in *Minorities and the Modern Arab World*, ed. Laura Robson (Syracuse, NY: Syracuse University Press, 2016), 93–106.

147. Beinin, *The Dispersion of Egyptian Jewry*, 22; Norman Stillman, "Frenchmen, Jews, or Arabs? The Jews of the Arab World Between European Colonialism, Zionism, and Arab Nationalism" in *Judaism and Islam: Boundaries, Communication, and Interaction*, ed. Benjamin H. Hary, John L. Hayes, and Fred Astren (Leiden: Brill, 2000), 123–138; Rachel Simon, "Zionism," in *The Jews of the Middle East and North Africa in Modern Times*, ed. Reeva Spector Simon, Michael Menachem Laskier, and Sara Reguer (New York: Columbia University Press, 2002), 176–178; Abdelwahab Meddeb and Benjamin Stora, eds., *A History of Jewish-Muslim Relations: From the Origins to the Present Day*, trans. Jane Marie Todd and Michael B. Smith (Princeton, NJ: Princeton University Press, 2013).

148. Shiping Tang, "The Onset of Ethnic War: A General Theory," *Sociological Theory* 33, no. 3 (2015): 256–279; Stuart J. Kaufman, "Symbolic Politics or Rational Choice? Testing Theories of Extreme Ethnic Violence," *International Security* 30, no. 4 (2006): 45–86; Jerry Z. Muller, "Us and Them," *Foreign Affairs*, March–April 2008; Chaim Kaufman, "When All Else Fails: Ethnic Population Transfers and Partitions in the Twentieth Century," *International Security* 23, no. 2 (1998): 120–156; Nicholas Sambanis, "Partition as a Solution to Ethnic War: An Empirical Critique of the Theoretical Literature," *World Politics* 52, no. 4 (2000): 437–483; Nicholas Sambanis and Jonah Schulhofer-Wohl, "What's In a Line? Is Partition a Solution to Civil War?," *International Security* 34, no. 2 (2009): 82–118. A useful compilation is Roy Licklider and Mia Bloom, eds., *Living Together After Ethnic Killing: Exploring the Chaim Kaufman Argument* (Abingdon: Routledge, 2007).

149. Jannis Panagiotidis, "Germanizing Germans: Co-ethnic Immigration and Name Change in West Germany, 1953–93," *Journal of Contemporary History* 50, no. 4 (2015): 854–874; Jannis Panagiotidis, "What Is the German's Fatherland? The GDR and the Resettlement of Ethnic Germans from Socialist Countries (1949–1989)," *East European Politics & Societies and Cultures* 29, no. 1 (2015): 120–146.

150. Ministry of Foreign Affairs of the Republic of Armenia, Nagorno-Karabakh Issue, Historical Data, http://www.mfa.am/en/artsakh-issue/.

151. Tzvi Ben Gedalyahu, "New Efforts to Bring Iran's 'Wealthy Jewish Hostages' to Israel," *Arutz Sheva: Israel National News*, December 14, 2010, http://www.israelnationalnews.com/Generic/Generic/SendPrint?print=1&type=0&item=141144; Kate Sengupta, "Iran's Jews on Life Inside Israel's 'Enemy State': 'We Feel Secure and Happy,'" *Independent*, March 16, 2016.

152. "Violent Riot Targets Israel Embassy in Turkey; IHH Head Says 'Turkish Jews Will Pay Dearly,'" *Algemeiner*, July 17, 2014, https://www.algemeiner.com/2014/07/17/violent-riots-target-israel-embassy-in-turkey-ihh-head-says-turkish-jews-will-pay-dearly-photos.

153. "Exchange of Letters with Turkish President Erdoğan Regarding Hostility Towards Jews in Turkey," ADL, September 5, 2014, http://www.adl.org/israel-international/israel-middle-east/content/l/letters-adl-erdogan.html. Thanks to Deborah Lipstadt for drawing my attention to this general issue in Turkey.

154. "Erdoğan Returning Jewish American Award," *Ynetnews*, July 29, 2014, http://www.ynetnews.com/articles/0,7340,L-4551831,00.html. Cf. Nathan Glazer, "American Jews and Israel: The Last Support," *Interchange*, November 1976.

155. J. J. Goldberg, "Hatreds Ancient and New," *Democracy: A Journal of Ideas* 30 (Fall 2013), http://democracyjournal.org/magazine/30/hatreds-ancient-and-new.

156. Gal Beckerman, "Did Bibi's 'Vengeance' Tweets Provoke Violence?," *Forward*, July 3, 2014, https://forward.com/opinion/201352/did-bibis-vengeance-tweets-provoke-violence; Itmar Sharon, "Abu Khdeir Murder Suspect Gives Chilling Account of Killing," *Times of Israel*, August 12, 2014, http://www.timesofisrael.com/we-said-they-took-three-of-ours-lets-take-one-of-theirs; Stephen J. Zipperstein, "Benjamin Netanyahu's Favorite Poet—and Ours," *Forward*, July 7, 2014, https://forward.com/opinion/israel/201553/benjamin-netanyahus-favorite-poet-and-ours.

157. Yotam Berger, "Israel Wrecks 18 Palestinian Structures for Every One It Licenses in West Bank Area C," *Haaretz*, December 27, 2016, http://www.haaretz.com/israel-news/.premium-1.761306.

158. Herb Keinon, "Netanyahu Gives Directive to Expedite Demolition of Illegal Homes in Arab Sector," *Jerusalem Post*, December 17, 2016; Gideon Biger, *The Boundaries of Modern Palestine, 1840–1947* (London: Routledge Curzon, 2004). The Jewish Virtual Library refers to the 1922 British White Paper decision as the "first partition of Palestine": "Palestine, Partitions, and Partition Plans," http://www.jewishvirtuallibrary.org/jsource/judaica/ejud_0002_0015_0_15344.html.

159. Ben Sales, "Most Religious Zionists Want Arabs Out of Israel, Study Finds," *Times of Israel*, October 23, 2015, http://www.timesofisrael.com/most-religious-zionists-want-arabs-out-of-israel-study-finds; Pieter Beaumont, "Plan to Transfer Arab-Israelis to New Palestinian State Seeks Legal Approval," *Guardian*, March 26, 2014; Naftali Bennett, "For Israel, Two-State Is No Solution," *New York Times*, November 5, 2015.

160. Ornit Shani, *Communalism, Caste, and Hindu Nationalism: The Violence in Gujarat* (Cambridge: Cambridge University Press, 2007); Paul Brass, "The Gujarat Pogrom of 2002," Social Science Research Council, Contemporary Conflicts, March 26, 2004, http://conconflicts.ssrc.org/archives/gujarat/brass.

161. Shruti Kapila, "Once Again, Sedition Is at the Heart of Defining the Nation," *The Wire*, February 28, 2016, https://thewire.in/22763/once-again-sedition-is-at-the-heart-of -defining-the-nation/.

162. Bharatiya Janata Party, About the Party, http://www.bjp.org/about-the-party#.

163. Andrew J. Nicholson, *Unifying Hinduism: Philosophy and Identity in Indian Intellectual History* (New York: Columbia University Press, 2010); Geoffrey Oddie, *Imagined Hinduism: British Protestant Missionary Constructions of Hinduism, 1793–1900* (New Delhi: Sage, 2006). Criticism of this view is found in Brian K. Pennington, *Was Hinduism Invented? Britons, Indians, and the Colonial Construction of Religion* (Oxford: Oxford University Press, 2005).

164. Devji, *Muslim Zion.*

165. Orit Bashkin, *Impossible Exodus: Iraqi Jews in Israel* (Stanford, CA: Stanford University Press, 2017), 4.

166. Farhan Hanif Siddiqi, *The Politics of Ethnicity in Pakistan: The Baloch, Sindhi and Mohajir Ethnic Movements* (Abingdon: Routledge, 2012).

# SUGGESTIONS FOR FURTHER READING

Anderson, Malcolm, and Eberhard Bort, eds. *The Irish Border: History, Politics, Culture.* Liverpool: Liverpool University Press, 1999.

Azoulay, Ariella, and Adi Ophir. *The One-State Condition: Occupation and Democracy in Israel/Palestine.* Palo Alto, CA: Stanford University Press, 2012.

Bayly, C. A. *Indian Society and the Making of the British Empire.* Cambridge: Cambridge University Press, 1988.

Berman, Nathaniel. *Passion and Ambivalence: Colonialism, Nationalism, and International Law.* Leiden: Brill, 2011.

Butalia, Urvashi. *The Other Side of Silence: Voices from the Partition of India.* Durham, NC: Duke University Press, 2000.

Canny, Nicolas. *Making Ireland British, 1580–1650.* Oxford: Oxford University Press, 2001.

Chatterjee, Partha. *The Nation and Its Fragments: Colonial and Postcolonial Histories.* Princeton, NJ: Princeton University Press, 1993.

Chatterji, Joya. *The Spoils of Partition: Bengal and India, 1947–1967.* Cambridge: Cambridge University Press, 2007.

Clark, Bruce. *Twice a Stranger: The Mass Expulsions That Forged Modern Greece and Turkey.* Cambridge, MA: Harvard University Press, 2006.

Dass, Suranjan. *Communal Riots in Bengal, 1905–1947.* Delhi: Oxford University Press, 1991.

Dirks, Nicholas. *Castes of Mind: Colonialism and the Making of Modern India.* Princeton, NJ: Princeton University Press, 2001.

Dubnov, Arie. "Notes on the Zionist Passage to India, or: The Analogical Imagination and Its Boundaries." *Journal of Israeli History* 35, no. 3 (2016): 177–214.

Fraser, T. G. *Partition in Ireland, India, and Palestine: Theory and Practice.* New York: St. Martin's Press, 1984.

Gelvin, James L. *The Israel-Palestine Conflict: One Hundred Years of War,* 3rd ed. Cambridge: Cambridge University Press, 2014.

Goddard, Stacie. *Indivisible Territory and the Politics of Legitimacy: Jerusalem and Northern Ireland.* Cambridge: Cambridge University Press, 2010.

Hayden, Robert. *From Yugoslavia to the Western Balkans: Studies of a European Disunion, 1991–2011.* Leiden: Brill, 2012.

Hennessey, Thomas. *Dividing Ireland: World War I and Partition.* London: Routledge, 1998.

Hirshon, Renee. *Crossing the Aegean: An Appraisal of the 1923 Compulsory Population Exchange Between Greece and Turkey*. New York: Berghahn, 2004.

Jackson, Alvin. *Home Rule: An Irish History, 1800–2000*. New York: Oxford University Press, 2003.

Jacobson, Eric. "Why Did Hannah Arendt Reject the Partition of Palestine?" *Journal for Cultural Research* 17, no. 4 (2013): 358–381.

Jalal, Ayesha. *The Pity of Partition: Manto's Life, Times, and Work Across the India-Pakistan Divide*. Princeton, NJ: Princeton University Press, 2013.

———. *The Sole Spokesman: Jinnah, the Muslim League, and the Demand for Pakistan*. Cambridge: Cambridge University Press, 1985.

Jalal, Ayesha, and Sugata Bose, eds. *Nationalism, Democracy and Development: State and Politics in India*. Delhi: Oxford University Press, 1998.

Khalidi, Rashid. *The Iron Cage: The Story of the Palestinian Struggle for Statehood*. Boston: Beacon, 2006.

Khalidi, Walid. "A Palestinian Perspective on the Arab-Israeli Conflict." *Journal of Palestine Studies* 14, no. 4 (1985): 35–48.

Khalili, Laleh. "The Location of Palestine in Global Counterinsurgencies." *International Journal of Middle East Studies* 42, no. 3 (2010): 413–433.

Khan, Yasmin. *The Great Partition: The Making of India and Pakistan*. New Haven, CT: Yale University Press, 2008.

Kiernan, Ben. *Blood and Soil: A World History of Genocide and Extermination from Sparta to Darfur*. New Haven, CT: Yale University Press, 2007.

Kumar, Radha. "The Troubled History of Partition." *Foreign Affairs* 76, no. 1 (1997): 22–34.

LeVine, Mark. *Overthrowing Geography: Jaffa, Tel Aviv, and the Struggle for Palestine, 1880–1948*. Berkeley: University of California Press, 2001.

Lockman, Zachary. *Comrades and Enemies: Arab and Jewish Workers in Palestine, 1906–1948*. Berkeley: University of California Press, 1996.

Mansergh, Nicholas. *The Prelude to Partition: Concepts and Aims in Ireland and India*. Cambridge: Cambridge University Press, 1987.

Masalha, Nur. *Expulsion of the Palestinians: The Concept of "Transfer" in Zionist Political Thought*. Washington, DC: Institute for Palestine Studies, 1992.

———. *A Land Without a People: Israel, Transfer and the Palestinians, 1949–96*. London: Faber and Faber, 1997.

Mazower, Mark. "Minorities and the League of Nations in Interwar Europe." *Daedalus* 126, no. 2 (1997): 47–63.

Mendes-Flohr, Paul. *A Land of Two Peoples*. Oxford: Oxford University Press, 1983.

Mitchell, Timothy. *Carbon Democracy: Political Power in the Age of Oil*. London: Verso, 2011.

Morris, Benny. *The Birth of the Palestinian Refugee Problem, 1947–1949*. Cambridge: Cambridge University Press, 1987.

———. *1948: A History of the First Arab-Israeli War*. New Haven, CT: Yale University Press, 2008.

Moses, A. Dirk, ed. *Empire, Colony, Genocide: Conquest, Occupation, and Subaltern Resistance in World History.* New York: Berghahn, 2008.

———. "Partitions and the Sisyphean Making of Peoples." *Refugee Watch* 46 (2015): 36–50.

Norris, Jacob. "Repression and Rebellion: Britain's Response to the Arab Revolt in Palestine of 1936–39." *Journal of Imperial and Commonwealth History* 36, no. 1 (2008): 25–45.

O'Callaghan, Margaret. "Genealogies of Partition: History, History-Writing, and 'The Troubles' in Ireland." *Critical Review of International Social and Political Philosophy* 9, no. 4 (2006): 619–634.

O'Leary, Brendan. "Analysing Partition: Definition, Classification and Explanation." *Political Geography* 26 (2007): 886–908.

Özsu, Umut. *Formalizing Displacement: International Law and Population Transfers.* Oxford: Oxford University Press, 2015.

Panayi, Panikos, and Pippa Virdee, eds. *Refugees and the End of Empire: Imperial Collapse and Forced Migration in the Twentieth Century.* Houndmills, Basingstoke: Palgrave Macmillan, 2011.

Pandey, Gyanendra. *The Construction of Communalism in Colonial North India.* Delhi: Oxford University Press, 1994.

———. *Remembering Partition: Violence, Nationalism and History in India.* Cambridge: Cambridge University Press, 2001.

Pedersen, Susan. "Empires, States and the League of Nations." In *Internationalisms: A Twentieth-Century History*, edited by Glenda Sluga and Patricia Clavin, 133–138. Cambridge: Cambridge University Press, 2017.

———. *The Guardians: The League of Nations and the Crisis of Empire.* Oxford: Oxford University Press, 2015.

Robson, Laura. *Colonialism and Christianity in Mandate Palestine.* Austin: University of Texas Press, 2011.

———. *States of Separation: Transfer, Partition, and the Making of the Modern Middle East.* Oakland: University of California Press, 2017.

Sa'di, Ahmad H., and Lila Abu-Lughod, eds. *Nakba: Palestine, 1948, and the Claims of Memory.* New York: Columbia University Press, 2007.

Said, Edward. *The World, the Text, and the Critic.* Cambridge, MA: Harvard University Press, 1983.

Schaeffer, Robert. *Warpaths: The Politics of Partition.* New York: Hill and Wang, 1990.

Schechtman, Joseph B. *European Population Transfers, 1939–1945.* New York: Oxford University Press, 1946.

Shafir, Gershon. *Land, Labor, and the Origins of the Israeli-Palestinian Conflict, 1882–1914.* Cambridge: Cambridge University Press, 1989.

Shindler, Colin. "Opposing Partition: The Zionist Predicaments After the Shoah." *Israel Studies* 14, no. 2 (2009): 88–104.

Shlaim, Avi. *Collusion Across the Jordan: King Abdullah, the Zionist Movement, and the Partition of Palestine.* New York: Columbia University Press, 1988.

Smith, Charles. *Palestine and the Arab-Israeli Conflict,* 8th ed. Boston: Bedford/St. Martin's, 2013.

Sternhell, Zeev. *The Founding Myths of Israel: Nationalism, Socialism, and the Making of the Jewish State.* Princeton, NJ: Princeton University Press, 1998.

Strawson, John. *Partitioning Palestine: Legal Fundamentalism in the Palestinian-Israeli Conflict.* Chicago: Chicago University Press, 2010.

Tan, Tai Yong, and Gyanesh Kudaisya. *The Aftermath of Partition in South Asia.* London: Routledge, 2000.

Weitz, Eric D. "From the Vienna to the Paris System: International Politics and the Entangled Histories of Human Rights, Forced Deportations, and Civilizing Missions." *American Historical Review* 113, no. 5 (2008): 1329–1333.

———. "Self-Determination: How a German Enlightenment Idea Became the Slogan of National Liberation and a Human Right." *American Historical Review* 120, no. 2 (2015): 462–496.

White, Benjamin Thomas. *The Emergence of Minorities in the Middle East: The Politics of Community in French Mandate Syria.* Edinburgh: Edinburgh University Press, 2011.

Young, John. *The Fate of Sudan: The Origins and Consequences of a Flawed Peace Process.* London: Zed Books, 2012.

Zamindar, Vazira Fazila-Yacoobali. *The Long Partition and the Making of Modern South Asia: Refugees, Boundaries, Histories.* New York: Columbia University Press, 2007.

Zolberg, Aristide R. "The Formation of New States as a Refugee-Generating Process." *Annals of the American Academy of Political and Social Sciences* 467 (1983): 24–38.

# CONTRIBUTORS

**Joel Beinin** is the Donald J. McLachlan Professor of History and professor of Middle East history at Stanford University. He received his PhD from the University of Michigan in 1982 before going to Stanford in 1983. From 2006 to 2008 he served as the director of Middle East studies and professor of history at the American University in Cairo. In 2001–2002 he served as president of the Middle East Studies Association of North America. Beinin has written or edited nine books, most recently *Social Movements, Mobilization, and Contestation in the Middle East and North Africa*, co-edited with Frédéric Vairel (2011), and *The Struggle for Worker Rights in Egypt* (2010). His articles have been published in leading scholarly journals as well as *The Nation, Middle East Report*, the *Los Angeles Times*, the *San Francisco Chronicle, Le Monde Diplomatique*, and others.

**Lucy Chester** is associate professor of history and international affairs at the University of Colorado at Boulder. The author of *Borders and Conflict in South Asia: The Radcliffe Boundary Commission and the Partition of Punjab* (2009), she is currently at work on a book-length study of connections between British India and the Palestine mandate in the decades leading up to Britain's withdrawal. Articles related to this project include "Factors Impeding the Effectiveness of Partition in South Asia and the Palestine Mandate," published in an edited volume (*Order, Conflict, and Violence*; 2008); "Boundary Commissions as Tools to Safeguard British Interests at the End of Empire" (*Journal of Historical Geography*, 2008); and a research note, "On Creating a Palestinian Pakistan" (*Sh'ma: A Journal of Jewish Responsibility*, 2011). Her work has been supported by a number of fellowships and grants, including awards from the American Institute of Indian Studies, the American Institute of Pakistan Studies, and the Smith Richardson Foundation.

**Faisal Devji** is Reader in Indian History at the University of Oxford and Fellow of St. Antony's College. He has held faculty positions at the New School in New York, Yale University, and the University of Chicago, where he also received his PhD in intellectual history. Devji is the author of *Landscapes of the Jihad: Militancy, Morality, Modernity* (2005); *The Terrorist in Search of Humanity: Militant Islam and Global Politics* (2009); *The Impossible Indian: Gandhi and the Temptation of Violence* (2012); and most recently, *Muslim Zion: Pakistan as a Political Idea* (2013).

**Arie M. Dubnov** is the Max Ticktin Chair of Israel Studies at the George Washington University and is a historian of twentieth-century Jewish and Israeli history, with emphasis on the history of political thought, the study of nationalism, and decolonization. He previously taught at Stanford University and the University of Haifa and was a Dorset

Fellow at the Oxford Centre for Hebrew and Jewish Studies as well as a Visiting Scholar at Wolfson College, Oxford. Among his publications are the intellectual biography *Isaiah Berlin: The Journey of a Jewish Liberal* (2012) and the edited volume *Zionism—A View from the Outside* (2010 [in Hebrew]), which seeks to put Zionist history in a larger comparative trajectory. He has also published numerous essays in, among others, *Nations & Nationalism*, *Modern Intellectual History*, and *The Journal of Israeli History*.

**Motti Golani** is an historian of the British Mandate and the state of Israel at Tel Aviv University and the former chair of the Israel Studies Department at the University of Haifa (2001–2005), as well as a former senior member at St. Antony's College, Oxford. Golani is the author of *"There Will Be a War Next Summer . . . ": Israel on the Road to Sinai Campaign* (1997); *Israel in Search of a War: The Sinai Campaign, 1955–1956* (1998); *Zion in Zionism: Zionist Policy and the Question of Jerusalem, 1937–1949* (2000); *"Wars Don't Just Happen": Israeli Memory, Power, and Free Will* (2002); *The End of the British Mandate in Palestine, 1948* (2009); *The Last Commissioner: Sir Alan Gordon Cunningham, 1945–1948* (2011); *Two Sides of the Coin: Independence and Nakba 1948, Two Narratives of the 1948 War and Its Outcome* (with Adel Manna, 2011); and *Palestine Between Politics and Terror, 1945–1947* (2013). Golani is currently working on a biography of Chaim Weizmann.

**Adi Gordon** is assistant professor of history at Amherst College. He is the author of *Toward Nationalism's End: An Intellectual Biography of Hans Kohn* (2017) and *"In Palestine. In a Foreign Land": The Orient. A German-Language Weekly Between German Exile and Aliyah* (2004) and the editor of *Brith Shalom and Bi-National Zionism: "The Arab Question" as a Jewish Question* (2008). His current research analyzes the conservative revolutionary movement in Weimar Germany.

**A. Dirk Moses** is professor of modern history at the University of Sydney. He is the author and editor of publications on genocide, memory, and colonialism, most recently, as coeditor, *Postcolonial Conflict and the Question of Genocide: The Nigeria-Biafra War, 1967–1970* and *The Holocaust in Greece*. He edits the *Journal of Genocide Research*.

**Kate O'Malley** is an editor of the Royal Irish Academy's Documents on Irish Foreign Policy (DIFP) series. She is a graduate of Trinity College, Dublin (BA, PhD). She has written extensively on Indo-Irish relations, and her book *Ireland, India and Empire* was published by Manchester University Press in 2008. Some recent publications include "Frank Aiken and Tibet" in *Frank Aiken: Nationalist and Internationalist* (2014); and "Metropolitan Resistance: Indo-Irish Connections in the Inter-War Period," in *South Asian Resistances in Britain 1858–1947: Interactions and Modes of Resistance* (2012). She is an occasional lecturer at Trinity College, Dublin, as well as a research associate of the Centre for Contemporary Irish History. She is secretary of the Royal Irish Academy's Standing Committee on International Affairs and a member of the Social Sciences Committee.

**Laura Robson** is a professor of modern Middle Eastern history at Portland State University. Her research interests encompass local, regional, and global iterations of internationalism and international governance, modern histories of mass violence, and the politics of ethnicity and religion in the twentieth-century Arab world. Her most recent book, *States of Separation: Transfer, Partition, and the Making of the Modern Middle East* (2017), explores the history of forced migration, population exchanges, and refugee resettlement in Iraq, Syria, and Palestine during the interwar period. She is also the author of *Colonialism and Christianity in Mandate Palestine* (2011) and editor of the collected volume *Minorities and the Modern Arab World: New Perspectives* (2016).

**Priya Satia** is a professor of modern British and British imperial history at Stanford University and author of the prize-winning book *Spies in Arabia: The Great War and the Cultural Foundations of Britain's Covert Empire in the Middle East* (2008). Her second book, *Empire of Guns: The Violent Making of the Industrial Revolution*, was published in 2018. Her work has also appeared in *Past & Present, American Historical Review, Technology and Culture, Humanity, Annales, History Workshop Journal,* and several edited volumes as well as in popular media such as the *Financial Times,* the *Times Literary Supplement, The Nation,* Slate.com, the *New Republic, Time Magazine,* and elsewhere.

**Penny Sinanoglou** is assistant professor of history at Wake Forest University. She received her PhD in history from Harvard University and her BA in history and Middle Eastern and Asian languages and cultures from Columbia University. She has published on twentieth-century British policy-making in the Middle East and works more broadly on questions of empire, nationalism, ethnic identity, and decolonization.

# INDEX